YOUR GOLDEN RETRIEVER PUPPY

MONTH by MONTH

TERRY ALBERT, DEB ELDREDGE, DVM, and ALAN GUNTHER

ALPHA

A member of Penguin Random House LLC

Publisher: *Mike Sanders*

Associate Publisher: *Billy Fields*

Managing Editor: *Lori Cates Hand*

Designer: *William Thomas*

Proofreader: *Monica Stone*

Indexer: *Brad Herriman*

First American Edition, 2015
Published in the United States by DK Publishing
6081 E. 82nd Street, Indianapolis, Indiana 46250

Copyright © 2015 Dorling Kindersley Limited
A Penguin Random House Company
17   18   10   9   8   7   6   5   4   3   2
001-289045-January2016

Published in the United States by Dorling Kindersley Limited.

ISBN: 978-1-61564-885-6
Library of Congress Catalog Card Number: 2015941380

DK books are available at special discounts when purchased in bulk for sales promotions, premiums,
fund-raising, or educational use. For details, contact: DK Publishing Special Markets, 345 Hudson Street,
New York, New York 10014 or SpecialSales@dk.com.

Printed and bound in the United States

This book is dedicated to my friend Howard Falberg, and in memory of his wife, Carol, in honor of their lifelong devotion to their beloved breed, the Golden Retriever. —Terry

CONTENTS AT A GLANCE

Adolescence 190

Teenagers are a challenge, as you'll learn this month. Watch for and treat coat problems if they develop, and help her learn concentration and self-control.

In Search of a Leader 218

Your pup begins to develop mature male or female physical characteristics this month. Expect him to test your authority; be sure to react kindly and fairly.

In Transition 250

You can begin comparing your puppy to the breed standard this month. You'll see some teenage behavior regression as you prepare for off-leash control.

Putting Your Golden to Work 280

At 11 months, he's almost an adult. You can more easily travel with him now and get him involved with dog sports. You also can work on obedience and tricks.

Your Golden Grows Up 314

More physical changes occur this month, and she goes in for her annual checkup. Continue training and exercise, and from here out, enjoy your best friend!

INTRODUCTION

One of the top 10 breeds in America for the last two decades, Golden Retrievers are loved for their outstanding temperaments and stunning beauty. The superlatives about these dogs you'll hear from owners are endless: *good-natured, great family dogs, eager to please, easy to train, superb athletes, friendly toward all varieties of animals and people.* These same traits have made them ideal dogs for helping people in many different roles: assistance for the physically handicapped, search and rescue, therapy visits, and more.

A Golden Retriever's devotion to his family is deep and endless. Wanting nothing more than to be by your side, this happy-go-lucky dog is always ready to play hard or just sit with you by the fire. But like any dog, Golden Retrievers need loving care, guidance, and discipline to grow into a well-behaved member of society. That's where this book comes in. Whether you're just beginning to research breeders near you for available puppies or you've adopted a rescue Golden Retriever, you're in for quite an adventure.

In This Book

Each chapter in this book covers a month of your Golden Retriever puppy's development. You learn what you can expect from your pup and how to deal with each stage of growth. It's easy to be overwhelmed by the challenges of raising a puppy, and we hope this book helps you through the first 12 months of this big adventure!

You learn what goes on at the breeder's during your puppy's first two months and how the care she provides affects your pup's future. You also discover how to choose the right breeder and pick the perfect puppy for your family. Then, you read about how to prepare for his arrival and, once you bring him home, make him comfortable with his new family.

Further chapters explain the various aspects, month by month, of your puppy's physical development, health care, nutritional needs, grooming, socialization, behavior, and training. Each chapter ends with a special section dedicated to building your friendship with your new Golden Retriever puppy—because after all, isn't that one of the most important things?

Although no two Golden Retriever puppies mature at exactly the same rate, the process is the same. If your pup grows faster or slower, it doesn't necessarily mean something is wrong. He'll catch up or slow down and turn out wonderfully normal!

The Extras

Throughout the book, we share additional information to help you raise your Golden Retriever puppy. Here's what to look for:

DOG TALK
These sidebars offer definitions of words you might not know.

HAPPY PUPPY
Look here for ideas on raising a happy and contented puppy.

TIPS AND TAILS
These sidebars share hints and helpful advice on dealing with the challenges of puppy raising.

Acknowledgments

I couldn't raise a dog or write a book without assistance from countless helpers. Special thanks to my advisers, Alan Gunther and Deb Eldredge, DVM, who offered valuable input and carefully reviewed every word. Also thank you to the many breeders, trainers, Golden Retriever owners, and other experts who shared their knowledge and experience: Tonya Struble, Michael Schooley, Robin Bowen, Jane Jensen, Jennifer Masterson, Laura Franci, Susan Maloch, Pat Schaap, Rebecca Barney, Dave and Catherine Geiser, Linda Barlow, Michael and Kathy Bogner, Judy Maraventano, and Lianne Morrison. —Terry

	SOCIAL	BEHAVIOR	TRAINING	PHYSICAL	HEALTH
MONTH 1			Littermates and mother teach appropriate canine behavior	Rapid growth	
MONTH 2	Breeder starts socialization				
MONTH 3	Socialization at home with new owner and other pets	Fear-imprint period	Begin house- and crate training		1st DHPP vaccine
MONTH 4			Enroll in puppy class		2nd DHPP vaccine
MONTH 5		Teething begins—heavy chewing period	Ready for basic commands	Switch to adult food	3rd DHPP and rabies vaccines
MONTH 6			Enroll in basic obedience class		
MONTH 7					
MONTH 8	Socialization in public			Moderate growth	Sexual maturity
MONTH 9		Adult teeth are in—chewing continues			
MONTH 10			Ready for more advanced training		
MONTH 11				Slow growth—reaches adult size	
MONTH 12 AND BEYOND					Annual vaccinations and checkup

The Littermate

Congratulations on selecting a Golden Retriever to join your family! Even before your puppy is born, hundreds of outside factors influence her future health and happiness.

In this chapter, we follow a litter's physical and mental development from birth through the first 8 weeks. You learn how the mother dog's health care, nutrition, and temperament affect her puppies, and you discover the crucial role the breeder plays before, during, and after the puppies are born. We also look at how the breeder starts socializing the puppies before they go to their new homes.

PHYSICAL DEVELOPMENT

A Golden pup is totally dependent on her mother during the first 2 weeks of her life, when she's unaware of anything in her world except food and the warmth of her mom and littermates. But by the time she's 8 weeks old, she'll have gone through several important developmental stages and be independent enough to leave the litter and come home with you.

Birth

In general, Golden puppies weigh about 1 pound at birth. Their weight can vary, however, depending on how many puppies are in the litter, with bigger litters producing smaller puppies. Weight can also differ among puppies in a litter.

The average litter size is 8 to 10 puppies, although it can range from a single puppy to as many as 16. With a large litter, the breeder spends more time ensuring each puppy gets a turn to nurse and also may have to supplement the mother's milk with hand-feeding.

As her puppies are born, the mother Golden Retriever severs the umbilical cord and removes the amniotic sac that surrounds each puppy. At birth, puppies have an incomplete nervous system and don't move spontaneously on their own, so it's up to Mom to get them started. She licks them to make them breathe, stimulate blood circulation, and prompt them to eliminate.

The breeder supervises the birthing process and removes the amniotic sac if Mom is busy with other puppies. She also cleans and ties off the stump where the umbilical cord was attached. She then puts an ID collar of sorts on each pup, usually rickrack or ribbon. Each collar is a different color so the breeder can keep track of each puppy and his or her development.

For at least the first 2 weeks, the *whelping box* is kept in a quiet, private place. Mom doesn't want other dogs around and won't welcome canine intruders. Too much commotion is stressful for her and her puppies, and she'll burn precious calories fussing and protecting her babies. She'll eventually calm down as she gets used to her duties, though. After the puppies' eyes open, the breeder often moves the whelping box to a more stimulating environment so the pups can begin getting used to household sights and sounds.

When the puppies are 3 or 4 days old, their blood is capable of clotting, so some breeders will have their veterinarian remove the front *dewclaws*. This used to be standard procedure for many breeds, but it's not necessary and is seldom practiced these days. Some people feel removing the dewclaws is important for hunting dogs because the dewclaws get snagged and torn in the brush while the dogs are working. Others feel that dogs use their dewclaws to help hold on to things, such as when they're chewing on something, and for climbing.

DOG TALK

The **whelping box** is a large nesting area where the mother gives birth to her puppies. It often has a ledge around the sides so Mom won't accidentally crush a puppy against the wall. The **dewclaw** is a vestigial toe and toenail dogs have partway up each front leg.

The period between birth and 2 weeks is called the neonatal period. Puppies sleep 90 percent of this time and eat the other 10 percent. They're born with a sucking/rooting reflex so they can nurse—this is more pronounced when they're 24 to 48 hours old. By 4 days old, this reflex disappears, and the puppies can nurse on their own.

At birth, Golden puppies have an underdeveloped, primitive sense of touch, smell, and orientation to objects. They can't see, hear, or move away from stimuli yet, so if something hurts, they'll squeal and wiggle in distress. By as soon as 2 days old, the puppies are able to move on their own toward Mom and compete for a place to nurse. To help them get around, the breeder usually places a surface such as fleece in the whelping box so the pups can dig in their feet.

A newborn's eyes and ears are closed. Her eyes might blink as a reflex, but she can't see yet because her retina isn't fully developed. She sleeps with her head tucked to her chest.

During their first week, the puppies whimper and move a lot in their sleep— kicking and jerking as they start to exercise their muscles. By 6 to 10 days of age, their sleep is quieter and their waking time is more active.

At 8 to 10 days, the puppies should be double their birth weight. By 7 or 8 days, a Golden's front legs can support her weight. Within another day or two, her rear limbs are able to support her pelvis, and she'll start to stand. By 10 to 12 days old, she'll be walking.

Her eyes and ears open at about the same time as she begins walking. At 10 to 14 days, her eyelids open. She can't see anything but shadows at this point, and blinking is still a reflex rather than a voluntary reaction. At the same time, her ear canals open, she starts to hear, and she'll startle at noise.

Weeks 2 and 3

Days 14 to 21 mark what's called the transitional period. During this time, the puppies' senses and motor skills are still poorly developed, but the pups are able to explore more of their surroundings. A sure sign of good neurological development at this time is, when she's set down, the puppy will extend her back legs in anticipation of reaching the ground.

During this time, the mother Golden is now producing peak amounts of milk. The pups are growing fast in these last days prior to *weaning,* and their suckling is strong and well developed. The puppies weigh approximately 3 or 4 pounds and gain about 1 pound during this week.

DOG TALK

Weaning is the process of gradually changing a puppy's diet from mother's milk to solid food.

Mom continues to clean up after her puppies until they're 3 or 4 weeks old and then the breeder takes over. By keeping their potty area clean, the breeder starts the housetraining process. At about 18 days, the pups move to a corner of the whelping box to relieve themselves. By 21 days, they have established a group elimination area.

The breeder enlarges their living area to take advantage of the fact that the puppies do not want to sleep and play in their own waste. She might add a wire pen so the pups can leave the whelping box to play, but they're still too young to have the run of a large room.

Around 19 to 21 days, a pup responds to light by moving her head away or blinking. Her hearing also continues to develop, and she'll startle to loud noises. Her sight improves as well, and she becomes more mobile.

When the puppies are 3 weeks old, the socialization period begins and continues until approximately 12 weeks of age. During this time, positive and negative experiences will affect a puppy's behavior for the rest of her life. To give her the best start possible, the breeder introduces a variety of household sights and sounds like the television, dishwasher, vacuum cleaner, and radio. She also handles each puppy more so they're used to human contact.

The puppies start interacting with each other, too, and they experience a dramatic increase in motor development as they start to chew and explore their surroundings.

Weeks 4 to 6

Goldens grow dramatically during this period, and the puppies' central nervous system continues to mature. Even that cute little wagging tail indicates neuromuscular development.

The puppies start to look more like dogs during this time, too. At 4 weeks, a Golden pup is a pudgy little lump that doesn't appear to even have legs and weighs roughly 5 or 6 pounds. By 6 weeks, she's found those legs and is making good use of them.

The pups can now orient to sounds and sights around them. The optic nerves mature by 28 days, so the puppies can see more than just shadows, and shapes begin to have meaning. By 30 days, they start to recognize familiar sounds. Their ears are fully open at 35 days (5 weeks), and the pups are more used to sounds and no longer startle to noise as they did when their ears first opened.

At 3½ to 4 weeks, their teeth start to come in, and the pups are able to chew semisolid food for first time. Mom starts to wean her litter around this time, and the breeder introduces puppy food. Often the breeder starts feeding the litter outside. The pups naturally wander away from the eating area after the meal to relieve themselves, which helps them learn a routine of eating, eliminating outside, and coming back inside after. At this time, many litters are well on their way to being housetrained before they go to their new homes.

By 4 weeks, puppies need to start eliminating on different surfaces. If a puppy is encouraged to potty on grass, dirt, concrete, and gravel now, she'll be willing to go on various surfaces throughout her life (for example, if she is boarded in a concrete kennel run). Both males and females now squat when they relieve themselves.

A host of new behaviors start when a Golden puppy discovers she has teeth. She now has the tools she'll use to explore her world, and everything that fits in her mouth is fair game. She'll chew dog beds, towels, chair legs, anything that moves … and anything that doesn't. She'll carry things around, and she'll tug on your pants leg.

Her interactions with her littermates change dramatically during this time, too. Puppies follow each other around play-fighting, guarding their toys, and growling. She'll compete for food and guard it from the others, and she'll shake her head while holding a toy. She'll start to understand how her jaw pressure affects others, learning the critical skill of bite inhibition. Play-biting leads to discipline from her littermates as well as from her mother, but it also teaches her to communicate without injuring. The mother Golden disciplines her puppies if they bite her too hard while nursing, which speeds up the weaning process.

At this age, individual puppies can be taken away from their mom and littermates for short breaks so they get used to being separated. This helps a puppy feel less frightened when she leaves her family to go to her new home.

Weeks 6 to 8

By this time, a litter of Goldens is a lot of fun. They start to gang up on each other, wrestle, sniff each other's faces and butts, and learn to recognize each other. Puppies begin actively hunting and playing—pouncing on bugs and butterflies—and they also begin play-mounting each other.

At 6 weeks, a Golden puppy weighs 8 to 10 pounds, with males being heavier.

The puppy's vision is not yet completely developed, but as the retina matures, she can follow objects with her eyes and respond to light. She can recognize shapes, so around this time, the breeder begins exposing her to other animals like cats, rabbits, and birds. At this point, it's enough for the pup to get acquainted with the sight, sounds, and smells of another animal. Too much interaction isn't safe for either species.

It's also an excellent time to introduce people of various sizes and shapes—a hat or umbrella dramatically changes what the puppy sees, even on the same person she just met. Research has shown that a puppy who has met a large variety of people, places, and things when very young accepts new and unusual things much more easily throughout her life.

By 8 weeks, a puppy is mature enough to learn and remember new things, and this is an excellent time to start training, especially housetraining. She's also getting a bit hefty to carry around, but until she's had all her inoculations, the breeder carries her whenever she leaves home. You should continue this practice when she arrives at your home. When she's inside, she should happily follow her new friends, but until she is able to walk nicely on a leash, let Mom and Dad carry the pup when you go out. Golden puppies are too heavy for small children to carry, so don't let kids drag Puppy around by her armpits or collar.

TIPS AND TAILS

Here's an easy way to carry your Golden puppy: with her facing sideways, scoop under her front legs from the side with one arm and over her rear with the other. Steady her hind end as you lift by holding up her legs while you hold the front of her body slightly higher. Hold her against your body so she feels secure and isn't likely to wiggle free.

HEALTH

A diligent breeder does her best to produce healthy Goldens. Even before the mother is bred, the breeder takes steps to prevent health problems in future puppies. When the puppies arrive, she monitors both the mother and the litter to ensure they all thrive and remain healthy.

Parental Health Clearances

Careful pretesting for inheritable defects helps ensure your puppy lives a long and healthy life. In some cases, an affected dog never shows symptoms but is still a carrier of the genes that can pass along the defect. If two carriers are bred to each other, a percentage of the puppies will develop the disorder.

The breeder should have her veterinarian conduct the following tests before the dogs are bred:

Brucellosis: This is a bacterial disease causing reproductive problems in both male and female dogs. Therefore, both parents should be tested before breeding. Brucellosis causes stillborn puppies, or pups who die within a few days of birth. Affected dogs should be spayed or neutered.

Hip dysplasia: Hip dysplasia is a crippling disease that affects some Goldens. Symptoms often don't appear until a dog is older, when arthritis begins to affect her movement. At 2 years old, a Golden's hips are mature enough to be x-rayed to identify the condition. The x-rays are sent to the Orthopedic Foundation for Animals (OFA) or PennHIP for grading. Based on the x-rays, the dog's hips are rated from excellent to severely dysplastic. The OFA's hip grades of "Excellent," "Good," and "Fair" are within normal limits.

Elbow dysplasia: Elbow dysplasia affects about 10 percent of Goldens and can also be identified through x-rays when a dog reaches 2 years old. OFA only grades affected dogs, designating grade I through III, to explain the level of degenerative joint disease associated with elbow dysplasia. Dogs with no elbow dysplasia are listed as normal.

Ichthyosis: Ichthyosis is an inherited skin condition that causes excessive dandruff and darkened, scaly skin in Golden Retrievers. Affected dogs are more susceptible to bacterial and yeast infections that cause itching. Recently a genetic test has been developed that can identify a dog as a carrier, affected, or clear.

Eye disease: Goldens are at risk for several eye conditions. Some are obvious at birth; others might not show up until late in life. With this in mind, conscientious breeders have their dogs examined every year by a board-certified veterinary ophthalmologist and certified clear of disease by the OFA Companion Animal Eye Registry (CAER) before breeding. These eye conditions include cataracts, entropion, ectropion, and distichiasis:

Cataracts are opaque spots in the lens of the eye that interfere with the dog's sight. Hereditary juvenile cataracts can cause mild vision problems. As the dog grows, the spots stay the same size, so the vision may actually improve. Nonhereditary cataracts often appear in older dogs and can lead to blindness.

Entropion and *ectropion* are inherited defects of the eyelid. In entropion, the edge of the eyelid turns inward, causing the eyelashes to irritate the cornea. In ectropion, the eyelid rolls outward, exposing the eye surfaces to irritation.

Distichiasis is a condition in which eyelashes grow in unusual directions, causing tearing and inflammation.

DNA tests are available to identify two additional eye diseases: pigmentary uveitis and progressive retinal atrophy:

Pigmentary uveitis: This eye disease, which almost exclusively affects Golden Retrievers, can cause cataracts, glaucoma, and even blindness. Often, the disease first shows symptoms in older dogs, so breeders check the OFA's CAER records for their dogs' direct ancestors and siblings.

Progressive retinal atrophy (PRA): PRA is an incurable disease that causes blindness. It's not widespread in Goldens, but in recent years, a genetic test has been developed to identify affected dogs, which helps breeders decide which dogs should be bred. The test can be done at any age. Some breeders state that their puppies are "clear (normal) by parentage." This means two clear parents were bred to each other so the puppies couldn't have inherited the gene and, therefore, don't need to be tested.

TIPS AND TAILS

Many Goldens don't show symptoms of a genetically inherited problem until they're adults. In Month 7, we go into further detail about these conditions and their effect on an adult dog's long-term health.

Subvalvular aortic stenosis (SAS): SAS is an inherited narrowing below the aortic valve that causes the heart to work harder than normal to pump oxygenated blood. The disease varies in severity, and in some dogs, it never progresses beyond puppyhood. But in severe cases, the condition can cause fainting or even sudden death. Breeding dogs are tested by a board-certified cardiologist and are declared clear if they're not affected by 12 months of age. The results are certified by OFA.

The Mother Dog's Care

Well before the puppies are born, the mother dog needs extra food and care. Because her health directly affects that of her brood, she needs to be in optimum physical condition when her litter is born.

Mom won't want to leave the nest when she's getting ready to whelp and for the first day after giving birth, but she needs to eat because the puppies need nutrition—and producing milk for a large litter of puppies uses a tremendous amount of her energy. The breeder feeds her in the whelping box every 4 or 5 hours so she can produce enough milk for her litter. The breeder also takes the mother out for a short walk several times a day so she can relieve herself and have a break.

The mother gets most of the breeder's attention during the first few days. A vet examines the *bitch* within 24 hours after whelping to be sure there are no retained placentas or unborn puppies. He also examines her milk to be sure it looks healthy and is safe for the pups.

The breeder cleans the bitch's nipples and mammary glands after each nursing session. This keeps bacteria from causing her pups to get sick and also protects Mom from mastitis (an infection of the mammary glands) and other problems.

The breeder takes Mom's temperature daily to be sure she isn't developing any delivery-related complications. One problem that can arise is pyometra, a uterine infection. If it's a small litter, Mom can have too much milk, which is very painful and can cause mastitis. The breeder also watches for signs of metritis, a bacterial uterine infection that can develop immediately after giving birth. Eclampsia, another postwhelping ailment, is caused by a calcium deficiency.

An unhealthy mother can pass an infection to her litter, yet the veterinarian can't give the mother most antibiotics for fear of her passing a toxic dose to her puppies through her milk. If an antibiotic is necessary, the puppies have to be removed from their mother and hand-fed.

TIPS AND TAILS

When you visit the litter to see your puppy, the mother might not appear as pretty as you expected. After her puppies are weaned, the mother dog *blows coat* and for several weeks, sheds so much of both her undercoat and outer coat that patches of skin might even show—even her tail thins out. Even if she was in excellent shape when the pups were born, she's undergone extreme physical and hormonal changes during pregnancy, delivery, and nursing. As she finishes nursing, her coat returns to normal, her mammary glands shrink back to normal size, her hormones stabilize, and her body gradually returns to its original condition.

Breeder Vigilance

Individual breeders might handle some of the details differently, but the breeder plays a significant role in the care of the mother Golden and her litter. The breeder's first priority during whelping is to assist with delivery. She cleans and stimulates a puppy if Mom is busy with the others, and she ensures the pups start nursing. If there's a lengthy delay between puppies, she may have to transport Mom to the vet for a caesarean (surgical) delivery.

After whelping, the breeder cleans the whelping box and continues to clean it daily while the pups grow. If bacteria and waste are allowed to accumulate, the health of the puppies and the mother is jeopardized.

The bitch goes through tremendous emotional and physical stress during the early weeks, and even the nicest female can get a little testy. To avoid upsetting her, the breeder keeps visitors and commotion to a minimum. Overhandling the puppies also upsets the dam, and an upset mother could kill or injure her brood.

The breeder also observes the mother and her litter, watching to be sure Mom bonds with her puppies and is caring for them. She checks daily to ensure everyone— Mom as well as puppies—has bright, clear eyes; doesn't have a runny noses; and shows no other signs of disease.

The breeder weighs each puppy daily so she can verify they're all gaining weight and getting enough food. They should double their weight in the first week; if they aren't, the breeder must figure out whether the mother doesn't have enough milk, if she has an infection, or if something else is going on.

One of the biggest health risks for newborns is exposure to parvovirus. The virus lasts in the environment for a year or more, and a person or an animal can pick it up on their feet simply by walking in the grass. To protect the litter, the breeder takes precautions when anyone enters the house. Family and guests are asked to take off their shoes before coming indoors, and visitors are asked to wear clean clothes and wash their hands when they arrive. These measures are continued until the pups have all left for their new homes.

When Puppy Problems Occur

If a puppy is fussy, she's usually cold, hungry, or in pain. The breeder needs to figure out what might be the problem quickly because it could be a life-threatening situation.

Too cold: Newborn puppies have very little fat, and their blood vessels aren't developed enough to retain heat on their own. Therefore, keeping the litter warm is the breeder's highest priority during the first weeks. Nestling with Mother and their littermates keeps the pups warm, and the breeder often provides a heat lamp for additional warmth. If Mom leaves the nest for even a few minutes, the temperature starts to drop and the puppy's metabolism slows. If this goes on too long, the pup becomes weak and can't nurse or digest her food. By 2 weeks old, the puppies can better regulate their temperature and don't have to sleep in a pile to keep warm.

Navel infection: The mother severs the umbilical cord with her teeth, but if she cuts too close, the pup's navel area can get infected. To prevent this, the breeder cleans and disinfects each pup's navel and applies an antibiotic ointment.

Fading puppy syndrome: A seemingly healthy puppy may fail to gain weight and gradually fade, acting listless and losing interest in nursing. If the breeder can identify the cause, she can take steps to save the puppy. Some causes are cold temperatures, not getting enough milk, or birth defects. If the mother was in poor health when the pups were born, she may not be able to produce enough healthy milk, which often contributes to this problem.

Swimmer puppy: A puppy who doesn't stand up by 10 days old and start walking soon after is called a *swimmer*. Her legs will splay out sideways, and she'll use a pedaling motion to propel herself around on her tummy. The condition is more likely to affect large or overweight puppies and may be caused by delayed development or muscle weakness. If allowed to continue, the puppy's rib cage flattens out and the condition becomes permanent. The breeder must step in and get the puppy up on her feet several times a day, putting her on carpet or other rough surface to give her some traction. With help, most puppies make a complete recovery.

Hernia: A small bump in the navel or groin area indicates a hernia. A veterinarian will identify the cause and decide whether it needs attention. Many hernias close on their own in a few weeks or months. If not, it can be repaired when the dog is spayed or neutered.

NUTRITION

Before she gives birth and while nursing, the mother dog needs extra food and water to produce adequate milk. As her pups grow, she needs still more calories and fat—up to three times her usual amount by the third week—to provide for them. Some breeders feed the mothers high-performance or puppy food for extra nutrition. If the mother's diet is still inadequate, her coat will look poor and she'll lose weight. She also might get uncontrollable diarrhea and become dehydrated.

The mother also needs a constant supply of fresh water. The moisture supplied in her milk is just as important to her puppies as its nutritional content. Both the mother and her pups can get dehydrated quickly; if she doesn't get enough water, she can't produce enough milk for the puppies. Young puppies process a lot of water through their systems because they need to maintain blood volume and stay hydrated.

By the fourth week, the puppies are ready to wean. At this time, the mother gradually reduces her food intake and her milk starts to dry up.

Mother's Milk

The mother's milk, especially during the first 24 hours after birth, is critical to protecting her puppies from disease. When born, the puppies' immune systems are not yet fully developed. If the mother has been vaccinated regularly, her first milk, called colostrum, contains *antibodies* that provide her puppies' *passive immunity* from diseases like parvovirus and distemper.

DOG TALK

Antibodies are large proteins the immune system uses to fight disease-causing bacteria and viruses. Through **passive immunity,** the mother shares protective antibodies with her puppies via her milk, which protects them from disease even though they haven't been vaccinated.

Breeders sometimes have their females tested to determine the amount of antibodies in her system before she's bred. The more she has, the more she can pass on to her pups. A healthy mother with a strong immune system can pass enough antibodies to her puppies during those first 18 hours to protect them until they can develop their own.

Puppies are only able to absorb maternal antibodies during the first 12 to 18 hours of life, so it's essential that they nurse as soon as possible after birth. After that, the mother's milk cannot provide any further protection.

The mother's milk changes as the puppies grow. It supplies all their nutritional needs until they're 4 weeks old, and its energy content increases steadily as the puppies become more active. The fat level in the milk also increases dramatically and then gradually decreases by weaning time. Calcium content increases as well until the puppies are 4 weeks old.

Supplementation

Supplements like vitamins and minerals aren't necessary if the mother is fed a complete food. In fact, excess nutrients can throw off the balance and cause problems. The veterinarian helps the breeder decide what, if any, supplements are needed for the mother. Some breeders feed their dogs yogurt or cottage cheese to boost her calcium levels when she's nursing, especially if she has a large litter.

If she's not producing enough milk, the pups must be supplemented with a homemade or commercially made milk replacer. The breeder feeds this to the puppies every 3 hours with an eyedropper or feeding tube or uses a baby bottle if they're older than 2 weeks old.

Weaning

Weaning starts naturally, initiated by the mother when the puppies are 3½ to 4 weeks old. If the mother doesn't have enough milk, weaning can start earlier. When the puppies' teeth start coming in, they hurt the mother when they nurse, so she doesn't let them nurse as often. She'll begin to spend less time in the nest, stand while they nurse, and leave when she's tired.

Weaning takes 1½ to 2 weeks. The process starts gradually, and the puppies continue to nurse during the transition. For the first week, they get one meal a day made of puppy food and water, blended until it's almost liquid. The breeder may have them lick the food off the end of her finger to help them understand what to do. The puppies make a terrific mess, lapping it up and stepping in their food. A few days later, the breeder increases to two meals a day. By 5½ weeks, the pups are fully weaned, although some moms let the pups nurse occasionally until they leave for their new homes.

By 6 weeks, the puppy teeth have fully erupted, and the litter is able to chew dry food for first time. Their food no longer needs to be soft and wet.

GROOMING

Even the tiniest puppies need some grooming to keep them clean and healthy. Their mother starts the process, and the breeder helps out when the puppies are a few weeks old.

Initial Grooming

Mom grooms the litter during the first weeks. Besides keeping them clean, her licking stimulates them so they'll eliminate. (By the time the pups are 4 weeks old, they can eliminate on their own.) Mom also keeps the whelping box clean.

During weaning (4 to 6 weeks), the breeder cleans the puppies' faces with a wet rag as they finish each meal because the watery gruel tends to get everywhere and can cause puppy acne. Acne in puppies is a surface skin infection, which, if not treated, can spread to the mother when the pup nurses.

Clipping Toenails

Sharp puppy toenails hurt Mom, and scratches can cause her teats to get infected. To avoid this, the breeder starts clipping the puppies' toenails at 4 or 5 weeks. She only needs to trim the front toenails to protect the mother. The rear nails give the puppies traction for walking.

Fortunately, thanks to the breeder starting the process early, by the time your puppy comes to you, she's already used to having her nails clipped.

SOCIAL SKILLS

It's never too early to start a Golden puppy's social education. These early experiences prepare your puppy for the many new people and things she'll encounter when she leaves the comfort of the whelping box.

Socialization Starts at 3 Weeks

At about 3 weeks, when a pup's eyes and ears are open and she's able to stand and walk, she's a sponge ready to soak up anything and everything she can in her exciting new world. Her experiences—both positive and negative—for the next 9 or 10 weeks will permanently shape her social and psychological development. Breeders and new owners take advantage of this limited window of opportunity to introduce their puppies to hundreds of people, places, and things—a process called socialization.

Socialization will be well under way by the time you bring home your puppy, but continue to invest time during these pivotal weeks of your Golden's development, and you'll reap the rewards for the rest of your dog's life. Well-socialized puppies grow up to be dogs who learn faster, can adapt to new situations with less stress, are confident, and are less likely to develop behavior problems.

HAPPY PUPPY

Researchers have tried to measure how much of a puppy's personality depends on inherited traits and how much is due to her environment. Her environment refers to her early socialization and training—things you can control to a great extent. The conclusion? About 35 percent of a pup's personality traits, such as shyness, dominance, and other factors, are inherited. This leaves 65 percent of her adult personality to be shaped by her environment—including you, the breeder, and her experiences.

Inadequate socialization during this period results in an adult dog who is fearful, possibly aggressive, and avoids contact with animals and people. An unsocialized dog will likely be turned out in the backyard to live alone, where she will become increasingly wild and poorly behaved. It's a sad scenario that happens all too often but can so easily be prevented.

Puppies Discover Their World

Before 8 weeks of age, a Golden puppy has no fear and approaches anything and anyone. Next month, she'll be less confident and feel much more vulnerable and hesitant. But for now, mildly frightening experiences are unlikely to permanently affect her personality.

In the 1980s, Pat Schaap, an expert dog trainer, developed "The Rule of Sevens" for socializing a puppy. With her permission, we offer them here:

By the time a puppy is 7 weeks old, he/she should have …

○ Been on 7 different types of surfaces: carpet, concrete, wood, vinyl, gravel, dirt, wood chips, etc.

○ Played with 7 different types of objects: big balls, small balls, soft fabric toys, fuzzy toys, squeaky toys, paper or cardboard items, metal item, sticks, hose pieces, etc.

○ Been in 7 different locations: front yard, back yard, basement, kitchen, car, garage, laundry room, bathroom, crate, etc.

○ Met and played with 7 new people: children, older adults, someone with a cane or walking stick, someone in a wheelchair, or walker, etc.

○ Been exposed to 7 challenges: climb on a box, climb off a box, go through a tunnel, climb steps, go down steps, climb over obstacles, play hide and seek, go in and out of a doorway, run around a fence, etc.

○ Eaten from 7 different containers: metal, plastic, cardboard, glass, china, pie plate, frying pan, etc.

○ Eaten in 7 different locations: crate, yard, kitchen, basement, laundry room, living room, bathroom, etc.

It's essential that you and the breeder repeat and build upon these early experiences constantly throughout the socialization period and throughout your Golden's life.

HAPPY PUPPY

The socialization period from 3 to 12 weeks of age is the most critical period in a puppy's life. What your puppy learns during this time largely determines if she is outgoing, happy, and confident, or shy, aggressive, and wild when she's an adult. Although later training and socialization might improve her behavior, it can't completely erase the effects of this early learning period.

Puppy Testing

By the time the puppies are 7 weeks old, you may have met the litter several times and are wondering how to choose which pup is right for you. Many breeders use puppy testing to help evaluate a litter. The breeder knows the pups well, and testing is a structured way she can evaluate the differences among puppies. It's not a pass-fail test; she simply observes the puppies' reactions to different situations while getting an idea of how each pup will react as he or she grows. Puppy testing is usually done at 7 or 8 weeks, before the pups leave for their new homes, before they've been influenced by training, and before the first fear period.

Many scientists and behaviorists have developed a variety of different puppy tests over the past several decades. Clarice Rutherford, a scientist and long-time dog owner, and Dr. David Neal, a veterinarian, first published a puppy test in 1981. As far back as the 1950s, scientists Scott and Fuller were evaluating how the early weeks of a puppy's life affect her lifelong personality.

You could ask the breeder if she does puppy testing and if so, if you could watch a session. She knows her bloodlines, has tested other litters, and can compare them to how previous puppies matured. One test doesn't deliver an ironclad verdict on a puppy's temperament; the troublemaker might be tired today and the shy one could have just woken up from a nap. The breeder knows this.

The tester looks at three major areas of interest:

○ How the pup interacts with the tester

○ If the pup seems willing to please

○ How quickly she forgives when the tester does something she doesn't like

By looking at the total picture of her responses, an experienced tester can come to some conclusions about the pup's personality at this point in her life. But don't expect a one-word description of a pup. She's not always pushy, submissive, or frightened.

The tester puts each puppy through a series of short manipulations. To test her willingness to be handled, she restrains her, holds her up off the ground, and gently pinches between her toes. Other tests check the pup's social attraction to people. The breeder asks her to come from a few feet away and then follow. Sensitivity tests explore how the pup reacts to loud noises, moving objects, and petting.

After observing the test, talk to the breeder about the puppy's overall reactions. Is she over the top, jumping on the tester, always active and hyper? Does she resist handling? Is she enthusiastic, outgoing, and eager to please? Is she quiet and thoughtful but willing to participate? Is she shy and fearful? Is she independent and aloof?

What do each of these personality traits mean for you? The breeder will help you look at each puppy's behavior to help you select the puppy who will best fit with your expectations, experience, and lifestyle.

BEHAVIOR

A puppy's mother and littermates begin teaching her how to successfully interact with others in her world. What she learns in the first 8 weeks of her life establishes a foundation you can build on when she comes to live with you.

Mom Is the First Teacher

A well-behaved, calm mother raises well-behaved, calm puppies. If she is fearful, stressed, or aggressive, she teaches her puppies to be the same way. She may be somewhat agitated and protective when her puppies are first born, but her instincts soon settle down and her temperament returns to normal.

As soon as weaning starts, Mom also starts to wean them from her constant attention. She spends less time with them, and they no longer depend solely on her for food. When out in the yard, she watches over them as they start to explore, and they discover they don't need her nearby every second.

She gently but firmly disciplines them when they jump on her or bite her ears—this is their first lesson in dog manners from Mom as she teaches them the doggie version of "No." Her growl and bark when she "yells" at her puppies sounds ferocious but is all for show. Often another "auntie" dog goes along with the pups, and they learn that another dog besides Mom will also discipline them if they get out of line.

A puppy learns to appease Mom if she senses Mother is getting annoyed. The pup rolls on her back and shows her belly in submission. She may even release a little urine. The scent reminds her mother, "See, I'm just a baby. I'm sorry." This skill comes in handy as the puppy grows and tries her antics on older or unknown dogs.

Learning from Littermates

As they play with their littermates, puppies practice the skills they'll use as adults. They learn to hunt, pounce, chase, and get along peacefully with each other as puppies, and the siblings teach one other how rough they can play and how hard they're allowed to bite. Bite inhibition is one of the most critical skills a puppy needs to learn, and she needs to learn it from her littermates.

A puppy who is in a single-puppy litter or removed from the litter too soon may never learn her dog manners. Her mother and her human family can help make up the difference, but it's no substitute for learning from her siblings.

	SOCIAL	BEHAVIOR	TRAINING	PHYSICAL	HEALTH
MONTH 1			Littermates and mother teach appropriate canine behavior		
MONTH 2	Breeder starts socialization			Rapid growth	
MONTH 3	Socialization at home with new owner and other pets	Fear-imprint period	Begin house- and crate training		1st DHPP vaccine
MONTH 4			Enroll in puppy class		2nd DHPP vaccine
MONTH 5		Teething begins—heavy chewing period	Ready for basic commands	Switch to adult food	3rd DHPP and rabies vaccines
MONTH 6			Enroll in basic obedience class		
MONTH 7					
MONTH 8	Socialization in public	Adult teeth are in—chewing continues		Moderate growth	Sexual maturity
MONTH 9			Ready for more advanced training		
MONTH 10					
MONTH 11				Slow growth—reaches adult size	
MONTH 12 AND BEYOND					Annual vaccinations and checkup

MONTH

3

Your Puppy Comes Home

Your Golden Retriever puppy is ready to meet his new family. He's gotten a good start in life from his mother, the breeder, and his littermates, and now it's your turn to take over his care and education. In his third month, from 8 to 12 weeks old, he'll grow and change dramatically. This is also the first critical period for socialization, so make that a priority this month.

In this chapter, we share the information you need to select the best puppy for your family, prepare for his arrival, and navigate his first few weeks with you. You learn the ins and outs of puppy-proofing, vaccines, health care, feeding, grooming, socializing, and the first steps of training.

CHOOSING YOUR PUPPY

You may have already given some thought to the type of Golden you want. If you haven't, before you decide on a breeder or visit a litter of pups, make some choices about the dog who will be part of your family for the next 10 to 14 years. This section offers information that will help you make educated decisions when you visit breeders.

Golden Retriever Characteristics

Golden Retrievers can vary in color from almost white to a deep fox-red color. A puppy's coat is usually lighter than his adult color will be. A pale gold pup, for example, will usually grow up to match the color of his ears. Each time he sheds, his coat will darken some, up until about 2 years of age. The exception is a deep red puppy; he'll be dark even when he's very young. The breeder will mark the puppy's registration form as "light golden," "gold," or "dark golden."

You might hear people describe their Golden as "English cream." In Europe, many Goldens are so light they appear white, possibly with some darker biscuit coloring on their ears. (This coloration isn't as popular in the United States.) There are no pure white Goldens, and extremely light or dark coloring is considered a fault in the breed.

Most Goldens have black pigment around their eyes and mouths and on their noses, although some have brown pigment and others have pink. The lighter pigment is sometimes related to coat color, with darker Goldens having lighter pigment. The coloring has no effect on a pup's health. As your Golden grows up, his black nose may become what's called a *snow nose,* where small patches fade to pink. Again, this has no health consequences.

Although very rare, occasionally a genetic mutation produces a pup with a black spot or patch on his head or body. Another "mismark," as it's called, is a pup born with white feet, a white patch on the chest, or a white blaze on his face. This is different from a normal Golden with lighter hair on his legs, belly, and tail feathering. These mismarks don't affect the dog's health, but a dog who has them would not be eligible to compete in a conformation show.

TIPS AND TAILS
There's no such thing as a purebred "Golden Lab." Golden Retrievers and Labrador Retrievers are two separate, unrelated breeds. Some service dog breeders purposely breed the two together, resulting in a mixed-breed dog.

Some differences in body type exist within the Golden Retriever breed. Some lines are bred for obedience competition or hunting, and these dogs have much lighter bones, less dense coat and higher energy than show dogs. Most Goldens fall somewhere in between the two extremes, and all Goldens are energetic and active.

There's minimal difference between the sexes. Dogs are individuals, and sex has little impact on their personalities. That said, females usually mature faster and tend to be easier to train when young.

If you're looking to get more than one Golden Retriever, it's generally *not* a good idea to get two puppies from the same litter. They're more likely to bond with each other more than their human family, and one will usually be more shy and reserved, relying on his sibling for cues. Two dogs from the same litter—especially females— might not get along because their personalities are too similar. Get your second dog from a litter with different parents, and wait at least 6 months before doing so. Then both of your puppies will bond to you, not their playmate.

What's Important to You?

When you've decided if you want a boy or a girl puppy, your next decision is whether you want show or field type. If you plan to hunt with your Golden Retriever, find breeders whose dogs have proven hunting ability. Ask if they hunt with their dogs, if they've obtained hunting titles, and if they've sold puppies to hunting homes. You also can ask for references. Many show dogs also hunt, and their breeders compete in hunting tests to ensure their dogs are still able to do what they were bred to do.

If you plan to compete in obedience, agility, or other dog sports, take this into consideration. Field, agility, and obedience dogs often have an intense drive to work and make excellent competitors, but they might have too much energy for some families. Again, if you're looking for a competition dog, ask breeders if their dogs have competed successfully in these venues.

Registration Papers and Contracts

When you purchase a puppy, you'll likely hear or read some unfamiliar terms and receive some confusing paperwork. Don't feel overwhelmed; this is typical of what all breeders provide. Let's look at what some of the items you'll be dealing with mean:

Contract: The contract between the breeder and a puppy buyer states the conditions of purchase. For example, some conditions might state the dog may not be bred, the breeder retains co-ownership, or the dog must be returned to the breeder if at a later time the owner can no longer keep him. The contract might also specify certain health guarantees, meaning the breeder will pay for treatment if the dog develops certain hereditary abnormalities.

AKC: This is the American Kennel Club, the main registry in the United States for purebred dogs. The AKC is a nonprofit organization.

Registration papers: Your puppy's breeder will provide AKC papers naming the puppy's sire and dam, his date of birth, his color, and other information. To register your puppy, you fill in the name you choose for your dog and submit the papers to the AKC.

Limited registration: Most pet puppies are sold on a limited registration, which means if the dog eventually produces puppies, they cannot be registered. The dog isn't eligible to be shown in conformation, but he is still eligible to compete in most performance events. Some breeders convert the registration to full status when the dog reaches 2 years old and the owner provides records of favorable health checks for hips, elbows, eyes, and heart. The only reason to change the registration status is if the puppy shows promise as a good representation of the breed in the show ring and ultimately a good breeding prospect.

TIPS AND TAILS

Are registration papers important? Papers are no guarantee your puppy is a certain quality or the parents were health-tested. But papers do give you the sire's and dam's names, and you can research their pedigree with the AKC and health clearances with OFA. Without papers, you have no guarantee your dog is a purebred Golden Retriever. The breeder might not have taken care to breed healthy, correct-looking dogs; follow any code of ethics; or offer any kind of guarantees.

Letting the Breeder Help

If you're not sure how to choose a puppy, your breeder can help you pick the right puppy for your family. She has lived with the litter for 2 months, and she has had time to get to know the personality of each pup. By the time the puppies are 10 days old, for example, individual puppies are more active as they try to be the first to nurse, while others hang back and need some help—she'll know this. The pups have been interacting since they were just a few weeks old, and the breeder knows who's the bossiest, who loves everyone, and who is the quietest. She's been watching their activity level, their dominance during play, and who makes the most eye contact with people.

When you interview breeders, tell them what activities you plan to do with your Golden Retriever. When the breeder knows what you have in mind, she can pick out the best pup for your family. She'll give the more active puppies to owners who want to hunt or compete in agility, for example. If you plan to do therapy visits with your Golden, she'll pick a more laid-back, people-oriented pup.

When you first talk to a breeder about buying a Golden puppy, know that a responsible breeder might ask you to complete a questionnaire and interview to be sure you would be a good fit for one of her puppies. After all, you both want the same thing: the right puppy in a home he will stay in for his entire life and grow up happy and loved.

At the same time, you want to ask some questions and make some observations of your own:

- Are the puppies raised in a clean environment?
- Are they well socialized?
- Are the other dogs in the breeder's house clean and well cared for?
- Do the other dogs seem to have good temperaments?

○ Does the breeder offer copies of all health clearances for the sire and dam?

○ Does the breeder offer a written contract and/or guarantee?

○ What does the breeder do with her dogs besides breed them? Are they performance dogs, show dogs, hunting dogs, etc., or is the breeder just breeding to make money?

The breeder should be happy to answer your questions. If she's not, look for another breeder.

Golden Puppy Personalities

Golden Retriever puppies, even those in the same litter, exhibit entirely different personalities. You can't label a pup with absolute certainty, but here are some characteristics you might see:

The **tank** bowls over his littermates, eats first, grabs the toy first, and hogs all the attention. His intense drive makes him a good prospect for hunting, drug detection, or performance sports. This same dog can be bull-headed and hard to train for a first-time owner. Teaching self-control from the time he is young helps channel his over-the-top personality.

The **social butterfly** is the life of the party and will keep you laughing. He's happy, enthusiastic, confident, and ready for anything, although he might be a little rambunctious and easily distracted. He's still a really fun dog and perfect for an active family with older children.

Mr. Sensible is also happy and enthusiastic, but he's a little more low-key. Whatever you want to do, he's fine with that. He's affectionate, willing, and eager to please you, but he has a calmer disposition than his "butterfly" littermate.

The **aristocrat,** often a female, is also affectionate but can be aloof and independent when she chooses. She might seem to learn slower, but don't let her fool you. She is thoughtful and methodical about everything she does.

The **quiet one** might have been raised outside in a kennel, and he might not have had much socialization. Very few Golden Retriever puppies are shy or fearful, but when one is hesitant to join playtime or seems a little skittish, a conscientious breeder steps in and helps the puppy catch up to his littermates. Patience and confidence-building exercises can make this dog a loving and devoted pet. He might not be a good choice for a family with small children who might overwhelm him, however, or for a first-time dog owner.

TIPS AND TAILS

A singleton puppy who has no littermates will be behind on his social skills. He hasn't learned how to play with other puppies, hasn't been corrected for biting too hard, and might be afraid of other puppies. Especially if you're a first-time dog owner, get a puppy who has had plenty of contact with other puppies.

PREPARING FOR YOUR GOLDEN PUPPY

It's fun to shop for your new puppy while you're waiting for him to arrive. In this section, we share a shopping list of the supplies you need to keep your pup healthy and safe:

Bowls: Stainless-steel bowls with nonslip rubber bottoms are easier to sterilize and last longer than other types of bowls. Your puppy will push the bowl around the floor as he eats, so the nonslip bottom helps keep the bowl in place. Plastic bowls get teeth marks that make them harder to clean, and ceramic bowls are pretty, but a bouncing Golden puppy can break even the heaviest crockery.

Collar and leash: Pick a collar that fits around his neck but has enough holes so you can loosen it as he grows. A flat nylon or leather collar is the only type of collar you need. When you put it on him, you should be able to fit two fingers between the collar and his neck. Be sure it isn't so loose he can pull out of it, though. Tighten the collar just so it rides close to his ears, not down by his shoulders.

One option is an adjustable martingale collar that slips over his head and tightens only when he pulls on the leash—there is no buckle. If he decides he doesn't want to go where you're going, he can't back out of a martingale collar. Don't leave a martingale collar on an unattended puppy, however; he could get caught in something and strangle.

Select a matching nylon leash, or get something made of leather or cotton rope that's easier on your hands. A 6-foot leash is helpful while your pup is learning how to walk nicely at your side. When he's older and taller, a 4-foot leash is long enough, and you won't get tangled up in the extra length. Stay away from adjustable-length leads for now. That'll just teach your puppy to pull, and you don't want that.

When taking your puppy on a walk, you might want to use a head halter in addition to a traditional collar. This style goes over his nose and behind his ears like a horse's halter, which makes it easier to control a pup who pulls. Some also have a clip that attaches to the pup's regular collar so if the puppy slips out of the halter, he's still attached to the leash. Your puppy will still be able to open his mouth to eat and drink while wearing a head halter.

HAPPY PUPPY

Golden Retriever puppies can be destructive. They see leashes, collars, bowls, crates, and beds as toys, and they can quickly demolish everything in their path. Choose sturdy, relatively chew-proof supplies, and be diligent about keeping them out of your inquisitive pup's reach. And be sure to provide him with plenty of things he's allowed to play with and chew instead.

Crate: From the very beginning, your puppy should spend some time in his crate. It's his safe haven from the world, a place he'll return to and enjoy throughout his life. The crate is also an essential housetraining tool. Choose a crate that's bigger than your pup, but not so big he can soil in it and sleep at the other end. Some crates come with a divider you can remove as your puppy grows.

Crates come in a variety of styles. Your puppy will feel safe and secure in a plastic crate that simulates a den. Some of the flimsy plastic crates aren't strong enough to hold a rambunctious Golden Retriever puppy, so choose a heavy-duty one. Many plastic crates are airline approved, so if you're going to travel, this is the one you need. Check with various airlines to confirm the crate you choose is acceptable.

Then there are wire crates, which have unique advantages. Your puppy can see out of all sides and feel like he's part of the action, even when he's confined. A wire crate often has a side door and an end door, so you can rearrange it to suit your room. If the pup won't settle down, you can spread a towel or blanket over the crate to block his view. Wire crates also allow air to circulate, which is important in hot weather. In addition, they fold down flat and are easier to store than plastic crates. If you opt for a wire crate, we recommend you get one made of heavy-gauge wire that will resist the efforts of a strong Golden Retriever puppy.

Mesh or fabric crates are best for adult dogs who are already crate trained, not puppies.

HAPPY PUPPY

If you can, consider buying two crates: a plastic one to keep in the bedroom for sleeping in and a wire one for the family room where he can spend time with you without getting underfoot.

Slicker brush: A slicker brush has short metal pins on a rectangular rubber backing. This is the brush you'll use the most because it gets out all that loose undercoat when your Golden Retriever starts shedding. You'll also use it for quick touch-ups when he rolls in dirt or leaves.

Wide-toothed metal comb: Use this comb to remove tangles and mats. It's especially handy for combing behind the ears and other tender spots where a wire brush is too rough. Many combs come with both coarse and fine teeth.

Toenail clippers: The breeder started the toenail-clipping process for you, and 8 weeks old is not too young to trim a puppy's toenails. The best clippers are guillotine style that squeeze and cut off the end of the nail. Be sure to get extra blades, because dull blades tear the nails. An alternative tool is a rotary grinder, similar to a Dremel tool. The grinder has a sandpaper-covered tip that grinds down the nail instead of cutting it.

Clippers: As your puppy develops his long coat, clippers come in handy for shaving mats, trimming long foot hair, and removing hair around his rear end to keep it clean.

Toothbrush and toothpaste: There's no time like the present to teach your pup to enjoy—or at least tolerate—having his teeth brushed. Get either a toothbrush or a fingertip brush and toothpaste formulated especially for dogs. Do not use human toothpaste on your dog or puppy; it will make him sick.

Pet gates: When he's not in his crate, you'll still want to confine your puppy so you can prevent housetraining accidents and discourage chewing. Pet gates come in sizes that block doorways or even large spaces between rooms. You can buy inexpensive plastic, fancy metal, or furniture-quality wood gates. Some styles mount permanently with screws, while others are pressure-mounted so you can remove them when your puppy grows up. Deluxe models have a pass-through gate so you don't have to take them down every time you want to walk through the doorway.

Exercise pen/playpen: A folding wire exercise pen (or ex pen) gives your puppy room to move around but keeps him confined. If he's acclimated to his ex pen when he's little, he'll respect the pen when he's bigger. Use the pen when you leave him alone and while you're at work. The pens are available in heights from 24 to 48 inches tall; get a tall one so he's not tempted to climb out.

Puppy toys: Anything that comes apart is not a good toy for a Golden Retriever because he can swallow small pieces that could cause a bowel obstruction. Most toys made especially for puppies just aren't strong enough for Golden Retrievers. Get larger, sturdier toys, even for the youngest pup. Heavy-duty rubber bones or knuckle bones are best.

Toys that dispense food entertain your pup while you're away. The heavy-duty KONG toy is good for Goldens. Stuff it with kibble and peanut butter, and freeze it before presenting it to your pup. Or get various kinds and leave a different one in his ex pen each day.

HAPPY PUPPY

If your puppy doesn't show an interest in his chew toys at first, coat a toy in chicken broth or smear on a few dabs of peanut butter. That'll get his attention!

Born to retrieve, Goldens always have something in their mouths. Yours will constantly bring his toys to you, and his favorites are probably stuffed animals. If you get stuffed toys, pick them up when you aren't able to supervise your pup. A toy made especially for dogs shouldn't have buttons or pieces that could easily come off, but he'll still do his best to pull out the stuffing or squeaky and eat it.

Balls awaken your puppy's retrieving instinct, so they're always a favorite. But be sure to get sturdy ones that are too big to get stuck in his mouth or swallowed.

Other fun toys include 1-gallon or 1-liter plastic water bottles, which are noisy, fun, and inexpensive. Take away and dispose of the bottles when your pup starts to chew pieces off of them. Knotted rope toys are fine until they start to fall apart, so replace them as needed. Rawhide chews soften as the puppy chews and can break apart. They also can cause an obstruction or upset tummy, so monitor your pup's activity with them.

TIPS AND TAILS

Test all toys you give your pup while you're home with him before you give him a potentially unsafe toy and then leave for work. Something you think is puppy-proof could be destroyed in minutes by his sharp, strong teeth.

If your puppy has the house strewn with toys, he'll have a hard time learning what's okay to chew and what's off-limits. Set up a toy box where you keep his toys, and let him pick out his favorite of the moment. Switch out toys regularly so they're more exciting to him when he gets the "new" toys.

Bed: Finally, be sure to provide your new addition with a bed. An inexpensive bed is fine until your pup grows up a bit. An old throw rug or beach towel keeps him just as cozy as a $100 plush bed. And just a heads-up: he'll probably destroy several beds between now and the time he's an adult, so don't feel like you have to invest in the higher-priced models at this point.

Puppy-Proofing Your House

Anything that can hurt a human baby can hurt your puppy. And because puppies don't have hands, he's going to explore his new world using his mouth. Anything he can sink his teeth into is fair game, and it's your job to be sure he stays safe. That means puppy-proofing your home.

Start by getting down on the floor for a puppy's-eye view of your home—you might be surprised what you find under the couch or in other puppy-reachable areas. Do the same in your garage and your yard, if there's a chance your pup can get out there. Puppy-proofing is an ongoing project, so remember that within a month, he'll be able to get to things that are out of reach right now.

TIPS AND TAILS
Have your children help you puppy-proof the house and yard. The kids will enjoy the challenge of finding things that might hurt the new puppy and helping you put them away.

Remove all dangling objects, too. While you're on the floor checking for stray objects, remove or reposition any hanging drapery or window blind cords, tablecloths, and houseplants that might be in your puppy's reach. It's tragic but not unheard of for a pup to strangle on a drapery cord.

Also, cover electrical outlets and tie up electrical cords out of Puppy's reach, or encase them in a cord-keeper or something as simple as a PVC pipe. A puppy who chews through a cord can be electrocuted and even killed.

Because you handle them so much, your scent is concentrated on remote controls and telephones, and your pup will gravitate toward these toy-size items that smell like you. Don't leave them out on the coffee table for him to find. In fact, take everything off the coffee table for the next year.

Move breakable knickknacks out of reach of puppy teeth, and later, adult Golden Retriever tails. A Golden's tail can wipe out an entire shelf of figurines with one swipe.

Paperclips, thumbtacks, pens, buttons, jewelry, coins, and other tiny bits that fall out of your pockets and off a table or dresser are very attractive to puppies—and very dangerous. Be vigilant about picking up anything your pup might find interesting. Look under the bed and dresser, under the coffee table, and under any other place that's convenient to your puppy's eye level.

Now is also the time to teach your kids to pick up their clothes. If they don't, they'll learn this lesson the hard way the first time Puppy carries underwear into the living room in front of company. Shoes and socks are heavy with your scent and, therefore, most appealing. Many a puppy has needed emergency surgery after swallowing a sock.

Wastebaskets provide an open invitation to a curious Golden. Purchase cans with hard-to-remove lids, or put the trash bin in a latched cabinet.

Relocate chemicals and cleaners from bottom cupboards in the kitchen, bathroom, and garage to higher, puppy-proof locations. Put medications and cosmetics out of reach, and use childproof latches to help keep Pup out of mischief.

Foods such as chocolate, onions, yeast dough, and coffee are dangerous for dogs, so keep these far out of his reach. (See Appendix C for a complete list of foods and other household hazards to keep away from your dog.)

In the bathroom, close the toilet lid so your puppy doesn't fall in and drown or drink toxic cleaners.

Screen off fireplaces or wood-burning stoves, too. An exercise pen works well for this purpose. Also put the wood somewhere he can't get to it.

TIPS AND TAILS

During the holidays, block your puppy's access to the Christmas tree with an ex pen or other fence. Ingested tinsel or ornaments can cut his insides or cause a fatal blockage.

Identify any poisonous houseplants you might have in your home (or yard), and remove them. It only takes a leaf or two of some plants to kill your beloved Golden. (See Appendix C for a list of poisonous plants to keep out of your pup's reach.)

Puppy-Proofing Your Yard

Even if your puppy won't be spending a lot of time out in the yard, you still need to puppy-proof it in case you ever need to let him out. As with the inside of your house, you need to be sure the outside of your house and yard are safe for your Golden Retriever.

If your yard is fenced in—and it should be now that you have a dog—check your fence for loose boards, holes, or anyplace you can see daylight through or under it. The slightest hint of an escape route will tempt your puppy to dig. Also be sure the tension wires at the bottom of chain-link fencing are securely fastened. Don't forget to look behind bushes and sheds, and block small spaces where your pup might get stuck, like between the garage and a fence or shed. And be sure to recheck your fence and all these areas regularly. You never know what he might do out there.

Your barbecue grill, drip pan, and the accompanying cooking tools are full of wonderful food smells. Store them out of your puppy's reach after use. Also stow away patio chair cushions when you're not using them.

Build a temporary fence around the pool, hot tub, or pond, if you have these water areas. Also block access to decks and balconies to prevent your puppy from falling off.

Bulbs and some outdoor plants, like oleander, are poisonous to your pooch. (See Appendix C for a complete list of plants toxic to your dog.) Cocoa mulch contains the same deadly ingredient as chocolate—theobromine—and a small amount can quickly kill a puppy. Keep compost bins off-limits from your puppy as well. Fermenting materials produce molds and bacteria that are toxic when eaten.

Just as you did indoors, keep chemicals out of your puppy's reach outside. Store garden and pool chemicals in a puppy-proof cabinet. Don't use snail or rodent bait in your yard because both are especially attractive to dogs. Likewise, keep fertilizers, pesticides, and herbicides out of his reach and consider limiting their use on your yard. These might not seem especially toxic to you or your children, but your puppy is low to the ground and his entire body is exposed to concentrated doses. And if you do treat your yard, keep your pup out of it for at least 48 hours afterward.

Puppy-Proofing Your Garage

You have to be just as vigilant in the garage. Antifreeze can kill your puppy quickly. Dogs are attracted to its sweet taste, and your Golden puppy will have no trouble getting under the car to lap it up. Motor oil and radiator fluid are also hazards. Check under the car often, and wipe up drips immediately.

Ice-melting products contain assorted chloride compounds, and even a small amount can be lethal for dogs. Your puppy might ingest it if he licks his paws after playing outside. To help protect him, check labels and buy pet-safe products.

HAPPY PUPPY
Watch your Golden Retriever puppy extra carefully the first few weeks when he's outside your home. He'll surely show you something you missed picking up or putting away.

Building Your Puppy's Professional Staff

It's easy to feel overwhelmed when you have a new puppy, especially if you're a first-time dog owner. But you're not alone. You have a staff of helpful professionals available to help you.

Your first and most important adviser is your veterinarian. If you don't already have one, ask your friends, especially fellow Golden Retriever owners, if they have a vet they like. If your breeder lives close, she can suggest someone nearby. Local trainers or kennel staff may also be able to recommend a clinic. You can also check with your state's veterinary medical association for a listing of local vets. The American Animal Hospital Association (AAHA) also maintains a list of members at healthypet.com.

After you've received some recommendations and chosen a potential vet, schedule a clinic visit to meet the veterinarians and staff. Make some observations while you're there:

- Is the clinic clean and neat?
- Does the staff seem friendly and willing to answer your questions?
- Do you like the vet's bedside manner?
- What are the doctors' specialties and education?
- Do they treat many Golden Retrievers?
- What kinds of Golden Retriever health problems have they treated?
- Are the hours convenient?
- Where are you referred to if there's an emergency during off-hours?

Also look for a dog trainer. Although your Golden won't start puppy kindergarten for a few weeks, start asking around now for a good trainer who offers puppy classes. Try to find an instructor who has experience training Golden Retrievers. Different breeds learn at different rates, and methods that work on a Sheltie, for example, might not work well for Goldens.

Ask if you can watch a class, and look for the following:

- Do the puppies seem happy and safe?
- Do students get enough individual attention?
- Are they having fun?
- Are their questions answered?
- Does the trainer offer more advanced classes for older puppies?
- Does the trainer use positive training methods?

TIPS AND TAILS

Puppies should *not* be wearing chain collars or be trained with any kind of force. If you see this while observing the class, find another trainer.

Ask the trainer what clubs or professional associations, like the Association of Pet Dog Trainers (APDT), she belongs to. Although obedience instructors aren't legally required to be certified in any way, you want to know yours is keeping up with knowledge and advances in the field.

You also could have a pet sitter come to your home in the middle of the day while you're at work so your puppy can get his lunch and a potty break. This helps him housetrain much faster. When you interview pet sitters, ask for references and proof of liability and property damage insurance. Ask about her experience with puppies and if she's a member of any professional organizations.

Many Golden Retriever owners have their dogs professionally groomed. Although he doesn't have much of a coat right now, find a groomer sooner rather than later so your puppy can used to the sights, sounds, and smells at the groomer's. Ask your friends with Goldens who they use. Most groomers have plenty of experience with Goldens, but ask her some questions anyway:

- How often does she think a Golden should come in for grooming?
- Does she do any trimming in addition to a bath and blow dry?
- Does she offer any puppy-intro packages where you can bring in your puppy to get used to the salon after he's had all of his shots?
- Is she certified by any professional associations?
- Is she licensed according to your state's laws?

A little due diligence now saves you time and angst later. You'll be glad you have your resources lined up before you actually need them.

DEVELOPMENT

A Golden Retriever puppy goes through dramatic physical and mental changes during the first few months of life. As he grows into his feet and adds pounds to his frame, his brain also develops, so his ability to concentrate and learn improves at the same time.

Physical Development

At 8 weeks old, your Golden Retriever puppy is starting a growth spurt that will continue until he's about 6 months old, when it slows down dramatically.

That roly-poly little butterball you brought home probably weighs 10 to 12 pounds. By the time he reaches 12 weeks, he'll weigh 20 to 25 pounds. He'll alternate being clumsy and sure-footed as his legs start to grow, and the little squirt who can barely keep up with you now will soon be galloping ahead and running circles around you. His muzzle will start to take on an adult appearance and look heavier, while his growing ears may look too big for his head. His sight and hearing ability are now fully functioning, as is his brain.

His coat also changes dramatically this month. His face becomes smoother and darker while the top of his head remains bushy. The fluff on his body gradually disappears, and his coat gets shorter and darker with less undercoat.

At this stage, different Goldens can vary by a week or more in their growth level, so if yours lags behind, don't worry too much about it.

Mental Development

Although your puppy is physically advancing, he's still emotionally immature. He's capable of learning, but his attention span is very short. He'll need his training lessons broken into tiny steps and reinforced with plenty of praise.

Remember, he'll retain anything he learns during this period—good or bad—for the rest of his life.

HEALTH

Start your Golden Retriever pup out right with proper health care. Like human babies, puppies need extra attention during their first year.

Your Puppy's Health Records

The initial health records from the breeder will help you set up a schedule with your veterinarian for future exams, vaccines, and parasite prevention. In your puppy's going-home packet, the breeder should provide a complete health history, including the dates the pup was wormed, the brand name of the wormer used, the dates of the first vaccines, and which specific vaccines were administered. If your puppy was treated for giardia or other parasites, that should be noted as well.

A copy of the sire and dam's health clearances, explained in the previous chapter, should also be included. You might also receive photos of the parents and a three- or four-generation pedigree chart.

HAPPY PUPPY

Your breeder also might give you a bag of the food your puppy has been eating, a familiar toy, and a piece of the blanket or T-shirt the puppies have been sleeping on. Put the latter in with your puppy the first few nights so he's comforted by the scent of his mother and littermates.

Along with your sales contract, receipt, and AKC registration form, the breeder might also give you articles and information on Golden Retrievers and puppy-raising in general. Go over each item with the breeder before you leave so you're comfortable you understand what you're signing and how to best use the information she provides.

Diseases, Vaccinations, and Schedule

The breeder will have given your puppy his first in a series of immunizations that covers distemper, hepatitis, parvovirus, and parainfluenza (DHPP)—the basic core vaccines every dog should have. Right now he's still too young for the rabies vaccine.

You might not hear about these ailments very often, but that's because most dog owners vaccinate their dogs so the diseases aren't overly rampant. But ask any shelter worker, and they'll tell you disease occasionally does break out in the shelter. Unfortunately, the only solution is to euthanize the entire population of shelter dogs to contain an outbreak. Needless to say, these diseases are pretty serious.

Distemper, a viral infection, causes upper-respiratory symptoms such as runny nose and fever. As it progresses, the puppy suffers from vomiting, diarrhea, pneumonia, and neurological problems. After the infection causes bleeding in the dog's intestinal tract, it's quickly fatal. Distemper is transmitted through saliva, urine, feces, and airborne droplets such as a sneeze, and your puppy can get it from another dog or a wild animal like a fox, ferret, raccoon, or skunk. The infection most commonly occurs in puppies 9 to 12 weeks old. Regular cleaning with detergents and disinfectants destroys the virus.

Canine hepatitis, caused by an adenovirus, was originally transmitted to dogs from foxes, and today it's common wherever dogs, foxes, or coyotes live, spread by direct contact with an infected animal. The affected puppy will have a fever and enlarged lymph nodes on his head and neck and may die within a day or two from internal hemorrhaging, liver disease, and swelling in the brain. Hepatitis comes on very quickly in puppies 6 to 10 weeks old, and there is no cure. Canine hepatitis is harder to eradicate from the environment because it's resistant to detergents and disinfectants.

TIPS AND TAILS

You might be confused when you see your puppy's vaccine records. DHPP is sometimes designated *DAPP*. If the *H* stands for hepatitis and the *A* stands for adenovirus, what disease was your puppy vaccinated for? Hepatitis is caused by the canine adenovirus type 1 (CAV-1), so the two terms are sometimes used interchangeably. To confuse matters more, there's an adenovirus type 2, which is part of the kennel cough (bordetella), group of diseases, which are much less serious.

Part of the kennel cough syndrome, the main symptoms of the parainfluenza virus are a dry cough and runny nose. If not treated, it can lead to secondary pneumonia and death.

Parvovirus is a relatively recent canine disease (that also affects coyotes), first striking in the late 1970s and now found throughout the world. It's one of the most highly resistant viruses and can survive in the environment for 5 months or longer. The symptoms include bloody, foul-smelling diarrhea; fever; and depression, and your veterinarian will test a stool sample to confirm the diagnosis. Parvo is treated with intravenous fluids and medications to control the vomiting and diarrhea. The disease is most severe in puppies 6 to 14 weeks old, and many die even with veterinary care. Chlorine bleach is the only effective disinfectant.

Many other noncore vaccines are available for dogs. You want to protect your puppy, but rather than overload his immune system all at once right now, discuss the various other vaccines with your vet and decide together if and when your puppy should receive them. Some optional vaccines include kennel cough (bordetella), Lyme disease, coronavirus, leptospirosis, and rattlesnake vaccine. We go into more detail about these in later chapters.

Your puppy won't be fully protected until he's had several booster shots. The vaccine he received at 6 to 8 weeks old primed his system to develop antibodies now that the ones he received from his mother's milk no longer protect him. Boosters are given at 3- or 4-week intervals up to a total of 3 times—for example 6, 10, and 14 weeks, or 8, 12, and 16 weeks. The last one is administered at about 14 to 16 weeks of age and then a booster is given 1 year later. After his 16-week vaccine, it's safe for your puppy to venture out in public with you.

Whenever your puppy gets a vaccine, wait in the vet's office for about 30 minutes before heading home. If he's going to have a reaction, it usually begins within a half hour. If you're still in the office when something happens, you can have the vet check him.

HAPPY PUPPY
Protect your puppy from infection by limiting his contact with the outside world until he is fully immunized.

Your Puppy's First Vet Appointment

Within a week of bringing home your Golden Retriever puppy, take him for his first vet visit. Bring along some treats, and make it a fun experience for him. Remember, what he learns now about the vet's office determines how he views it for the rest of his life, so do what you can to make it pleasant for him.

Carry him into the vet's office, and don't let him explore on his own on the floor. Although the office looks clean, your puppy is especially susceptible to illness at this age and could pick up something.

Bring the breeder-supplied health records to your first appointment. The veterinarian will recommend a schedule for future deworming and vaccines based on those records.

The doctor will do a complete physical exam. She'll listen to your puppy's heart and lungs, look in his ears, examine his mouth for abnormalities, check for a hernia on his belly, and make note of his weight and overall physical condition.

Dealing with Parasites

When a puppy moves to his new home, the stress of being in a new and different environment away from his mother and littermates may depress his immune system, allowing parasites like worms, giardia, or coccidia to take hold.

Roundworm, hookworm, and whipworm are intestinal parasites that grow and reproduce in a puppy's body. He might show no outward symptoms, or you could see the worms in his stool. Weight loss, a dry or wiry textured coat, diarrhea, or a potbelly are also indicators he could have worms. All three types of worms can be transmitted when the puppy accidentally eats, licks, or walks on contaminated soil and then licks his feet. Roundworms especially can be passed from the mother to her puppies.

If your puppy has worms, it doesn't mean the breeder did something wrong. Most vets assume all young pups have worms and advise a deworming now and again in 2 weeks. Even though the breeder wormed the pups, it doesn't kill all the worms. The first worming kills the adult worms, but it doesn't kill the larvae; the second worming kills the worms that have developed since the last worming. It could take several treatments over a period of weeks to eliminate all of them from your puppy's system.

If your puppy is having diarrhea, the vet might opt to test a stool sample to check for giardia and coccidia, two other parasites that sometimes affect puppies (and adult dogs as well). Your pup can ingest these single-celled parasites from infected water or soil or from contact with an infected puppy's feces. Both can also be transmitted to humans. Medication quickly kills the parasites.

Some topical flea-control products are made specifically for puppies. Ask your veterinarian what and how much to use so your pup doesn't get a toxic dose. Some orally administered flea-control products also prevent heartworm and other types of worm infestations and are available by prescription. Your vet should discuss these options with you, but feel free to ask.

NUTRITION

Feeding your new Golden Retriever is more involved than just setting down a bowl of kibble once or twice a day. Choose a food with the nutrients a puppy needs to develop strong muscles, healthy organs, and sturdy bones.

By feeding him quality food and establishing good feeding habits when he's a puppy, you'll help ensure his future good health.

Your Puppy's Nutritional Needs

Dog-food manufacturers want you to feed your pup puppy food for a year or more, but Golden Retriever puppies don't need excess nutrients to grow and thrive. In fact, many breeders recommend you buy one bag of puppy food and switch to adult food as soon as that's gone.

Puppy foods encourage overly fast growth, which can cause orthopedic problems later in life. They contain the same basic nutrients as adult food, but in slightly different amounts. A healthy, balanced diet includes protein, carbohydrates, fat, minerals, vitamins, and water. For puppies, manufacturers sometimes include additional protein, fat, vitamins, and minerals.

Dog-food ingredients are subject to regulation by the Association of American Feed Control Officials (AAFCO). AAFCO establishes the minimum and maximum percentages of each nutrient that must be present in a food to declare it "healthy and balanced." AAFCO also approves labeling "for puppies" or "for all life stages." They don't regulate what exact ingredients should make up the foods, however, and that's where it gets tricky to select a food for your Golden.

The quality of the ingredients is the most important factor when selecting a brand. Low-quality ingredients can affect your dog's digestion and behavior. Read the dog-food label, and choose a food that's higher in meat protein and fat and lower in grain carbohydrates. (Ingredients are listed in descending order according to volume.) Dogs are meat eaters and don't do well on a vegetarian diet.

TIPS AND TAILS

You might be interested in feeding your puppy a raw diet. Because cancer is common in Goldens, some breeders feel raw food eliminates cancer-causing chemicals and is, therefore, healthier for your puppy. A puppy's immune system needs time to grow and mature, and he'll be more susceptible to salmonella and E. coli when he's little. We cover the pros and cons of a raw diet in Month 12, but in general, we don't recommend it for dogs under 1 year old. You can discuss the issue with your veterinarian.

Your pup needs protein because protein contains the amino acids that help build his healthy bones, muscles, skin, and coat. The best protein sources are meat, fish, and poultry. Less-expensive protein sources come from plants, like wheat or corn gluten, and are harder for your puppy to digest.

Puppy and dog food labels should name the meat source (beef, lamb, or chicken) they contain. If you see *meat meal,* that's a good, concentrated source of protein. *Meat by-products* are made up of the less-desirable parts of the animal, such as the feathers or feet. Choose a food that has a specific meat source as the first ingredient, such as lamb or lamb meal.

Also important, carbohydrates provide sugars (glucose), starches, and dietary fiber. Simple carbohydrates, such as fruit, are easy for your puppy's body to absorb. Complex carbs like whole grains, potatoes, peas, and beans also provide fiber and starches to help his digestion. Additional starches are sometimes added to dry food during manufacturing to help the kibble retain its shape and texture.

Whole grains are a healthy source of carbohydrates. Refined grains such as white rice and white flour, on the other hand, are stripped of their most important nutrients—B vitamins, dietary fiber, and iron. These fillers add calories to a dog food but not much nutrition. Some "empty" carbohydrates, such as cellulose or peanut hulls, are used as fillers and help form a solid stool, but they have no nutritional benefit. They're also harder for your dog to digest and sometimes cause excess gas. Recent scientific studies have suggested that excess cereal carbohydrates—such as those found in grains, refined or whole oats, wheat, corn, etc.—cause hyperactivity in dogs, and that's the *last* thing a Golden Retriever needs.

Fat provides your pup energy and essential fatty acids and helps his body absorb the fat-soluble vitamins A, D, E, and K. Fats also add flavor and texture to dry food and are sprayed onto the food after cooking. The essential fatty acids help lubricate your puppy's joints and keep his coat shiny and healthy, while the calories in fat give him energy to grow.

Your pup needs certain vitamins and minerals in his diet. Vitamins are crucial to cell functioning. The fat-soluble vitamins A, D, E, and K are stored in his liver, and excess cannot be eliminated. Excess water-soluble vitamins C and assorted B vitamins are eliminated via the urine. If his dog food becomes rancid, the vitamins are destroyed, so manufacturers add antioxidants to extend the shelf life and prevent spoilage.

Minerals help your pup build healthy bones and teeth. Dog-food companies used to add a lot of calcium to their puppy formulas to aid growing bones, but this practice has changed because excess calcium can cause your Golden to grow too fast and develop overly large bones with less density, making them brittle and easily broken. Large-breed puppy formulas contain less calcium than small-breed foods for this reason. Calcium is necessary in the right amount because it works with phosphorus to aid functions such as muscle contraction. Additional minerals important to your puppy's overall body functioning include zinc, iodine, selenium, and copper.

TIPS AND TAILS
The quality of any dog food can be affected by heat, storage conditions, and age. Be sure to check the expiration date on the bag to ensure the food is fresh, and use food within 6 months of purchase.

If you're feeding a "complete and balanced" puppy food made with meat and other high-quality ingredients, you shouldn't have to add any vitamins, minerals, or other supplements to your puppy's diet. In fact, doing so can do more harm than good. So opt for a good-quality food, and discuss any nutrition concerns you may have with your veterinarian before supplementing your puppy's diet.

Making Diet Changes Slowly

The breeder will probably send home a small bag of the brand of kibble your puppy has been eating. If you're going to continue with this brand, that's fine. If you decide to change brands, make the change *gradually* to avoid upsetting your puppy's tummy.

Start by mixing 25 percent of the new food with 75 percent of the old food for several days. If your pup seems to tolerate it well with no diarrhea, you can increase the amount of the new food to 50 percent new and 50 percent old for a week. During the next week, mix 75 percent of the new food with 25 percent of the old. Eventually, you should be able to eliminate the old food completely with no problems.

How Much to Feed?

Golden Retriever puppies can easily become overweight, and fat puppies grow up to be fat adult dogs. You should be able to feel your puppy's ribs, even when he's only 8 weeks old. If you can't feel them, he's probably too fat.

There's no hard-and-fast rule about how much to feed your pup this month. Most breeders recommend about 2 cups per day. Whatever you do, don't blindly follow the recommendations on the bag of puppy food, which are usually far too high.

Proper Feeding Practices

During this month, feed your puppy three meals a day if possible. He'll survive on two meals a day if you work during the day and can't get home to feed him lunch, but he'll get pretty hungry. It helps to leave him with toys stuffed with food to supplement his other two regular meals.

When feeding, select a spot where your puppy can eat undisturbed, perhaps in his crate; you want to feed him in the same place every meal. Put his food down and leave it for 10 to 15 minutes. If he hasn't eaten after that time, pick up his bowl until the next mealtime. Because you know when he has eaten, you also know when he needs to go out, which helps with housetraining. By picking up his food, he'll also learn to look to you as the provider of his food—an important motivator when you start training.

Your pup doesn't need any table scraps or other goodies to make his food tasty. In fact, giving him scraps only teaches him to turn up his nose at plain kibble. Practice good feeding habits now to avoid a beggar later on.

Keeping Your Puppy Hydrated

Last but certainly not least is water. Water is the most essential nutrient your puppy needs. The lack of other nutrients causes illness, but your puppy cannot survive without water.

It's especially easy for puppies to get dehydrated, so keep plenty of water available to your puppy. Be sure to change it every day because fresh water encourages him to drink.

TIPS AND TAILS

The breeder adds water to your pup's food as she's weaning him, but after he's completely weaned, you don't need to add water to his food.

GROOMING

It might seem unnecessary to groom your puppy when he's only 8 weeks old, but you already have a reason to groom him: a Golden Retriever begins to shed his fluffy puppy coat by about 10 weeks, beginning on the middle of his back and working down the sides of his body. He usually finishes shedding his baby fluff by the time he's 12 weeks old. His new coat will be fairly short and wavy.

Plus, if he learns to tolerate grooming now, he'll be easier to groom throughout his life. He'll have a lot of coat when he's an adult, and it will need regular brushing. And once you see how much an adult Golden Retriever sheds, you'll be glad you took the time now to make him comfortable with brushing. Instead of looking at grooming as a chore, make it fun. It can be a wonderful opportunity for you to build your bond with your puppy.

Treating Him Kindly

Puppies need to feel secure. They've had close contact with their littermates and mom, and now they're all alone in the world except for you. Take advantage of his need to cuddle and teach him to enjoy handling at the same time. You'll need to clean his ears, trim his toenails, brush his teeth, and investigate injuries throughout his life, so you want him to be comfortable being touched anywhere on his body.

Remember, your pup is learning good and bad things during this time, so be sure your grooming and touching are always good. Never drag your puppy by the collar; if you want him to go somewhere, pick him up until you've taught him to walk on a leash. Never swat him with a newspaper or rub his nose in an accident; this doesn't teach him anything except to be afraid of you. You shouldn't ever use harsh discipline on your puppy. After all, he doesn't even know the rules yet. It's your job to teach him—and to teach him kindly.

HAPPY PUPPY

Every time you handle your puppy, show him that being touched is a good thing, and he'll look forward to your attention. Golden Retrievers are especially sensitive compared to other breeds. He'll read your mood quickly and respond well to a loving touch.

Massaging Your Puppy

Gentle massage is a loving way for your puppy to get used to handling and grooming. Massage him in short sessions when he's naturally tired and ready for his nap, and you'll soon have a happy, relaxed, sleeping pup.

Always keep the massage sessions fun and positive, with lots of treats along the way. He doesn't understand what you're saying yet, so your tone of voice is important. A soothing voice helps him calm down and relax in your hands.

To begin a puppy massage, sit on the floor with your legs out in front of you. Pick up your pup, and roll him on his back or side in your lap or on the floor between your legs. He'll struggle as you hold him, so reward him when he stops wiggling, even for a second, by giving him a treat and letting him get up. Let him move around a little between tries. If he's not happy to come back to you, you've pushed him too far. Remember, he doesn't have much of an attention span yet so keep things short and fun.

By the third time you put him on his back, he'll start to figure out what you want and calm down faster. After a few sessions, he'll relax quickly.

A firm touch is less likely to tickle, so keep that in mind as you slowly pet his body and legs and rub your fingers between his toes. Work with his paws until you can hold each one in your hand without your pup struggling to get free. Gently stroke his ears from base to tip, and turn each ear inside out. Stroke his tail from the base to the end, and pull your hand off the tip as if the tail was longer than it is. (Suddenly stopping at the end of his tail feels jarring to him.) Massage his mouth, and lift his lip and massage his gums with your fingertip. Let him fall asleep if he wants to.

Let him sleep on your lap or next to you for a bit if he wants to. If he's still awake, take him out for a potty break and then let him play.

Introducing the Brush

When he readily allows you to hold onto a paw without wriggling it away, introduce your puppy to the brush and other grooming tools. At this point, you aren't trying to do a complete grooming job; you just want him to see the tools, let him feel them on his body, and give him lots of praise for allowing you to touch him with them.

Let him investigate each tool for a minute or so while you praise him and hand out treats. Let him feel the sensation of each tool on his body for a second, and immediately praise him and take it away.

Gradually work up to brushing his tummy, chest, neck, and legs. Do this several times a week.

Trimming His Toenails

In another session, reintroduce the toenail clippers. Although the breeder probably trimmed his toenails, he was so young then he might not remember it anymore. He needs a refresher course now because he's in a new home with new people.

Hold him on your lap or put him on a table so he can't run away. Stroke his leg with the clippers while you hold his foot and let him investigate this strange object. Tap lightly on his toenail, and give him a treat when he doesn't pull back. Do this for all four feet and each toenail. Break it into several sessions, or take play breaks in between feet or toes, and stop when he's done something right. If you have to, back up a bit in the process. And remember, quitting is his reward for doing the right thing.

Once he accepts the tapping on his toenails, trim off a tiny piece of one toenail. Praise him while you cut, and immediately give him a treat and release him. The point is not to actually shorten his nails, but to get him used to the feeling of the pressure from the clippers. If he can't tolerate that, just close the clippers for a second on his nail and release without cutting.

Watch out for the quick. This is a blood-filled vein that runs down the middle of each nail. If you accidentally cut the quick, it will hurt and bleed, and your pup will *not* want you to do it again! Some Golden Retriever puppies have dark toenails, and you won't be able to see the quick through the nail. The more often you trim his toenails, the farther back the quick will recede and the less likely you are to nick it. Always err on the side of caution and cut back less than $\frac{1}{32}$ inch of each nail.

If you do accidentally cut the quick, hold your fingertip tightly over the end of the nail until the pressure stops any bleeding. Then apply a product called Kwik Stop or run a bar of soap across the tip of his nail to help the blood clot.

If you choose to use a nail grinder, you'll be less likely to cut into the quick. To get him used to the sound of the grinder, turn it on and run it about 1 foot away from him so he gets used to the noise, gradually moving it closer. You don't want him to investigate it with his mouth or nose while it's running; it might hurt him. And before you use the grinder on his nails, pull any long fur away from his toes so it doesn't get caught up. The grinder can get hot, so just touch it to his nail for a second or two at first. Gradually work up to several seconds, and check it often to be sure it's cool to the touch.

Whether you use clippers or a grinder, try to hold a grooming session every 3 days. That might seem like a lot, but it's much easier to trim off just a little every so often than to try to clip his nails way back in one session. Plus, it gives you that much more bonding time with your pup.

SOCIAL SKILLS

Golden Retrievers are naturally happy and outgoing dogs, but they still need proper socialization when they're young to ensure they mature into well-adjusted adults. Systematically introduce your puppy to the creatures and experiences he'll encounter throughout his lifetime. By starting when he's young and carefully controlling his interactions, you prevent future behavior and temperament problems.

The Golden Retriever Temperament

Originally, the Golden Retriever was developed as a hunting dog. The same characteristics that make a Golden a good hunting dog also make him an excellent family dog.

He has to cooperate with the hunter, for example, and be ready to obey and eager to please. Intense and focused on the job at hand, Goldens have a strong work ethic and great perseverance; at the same time, they're able to wait quietly for hours in a duck blind between retrieves.

For you and your family, he's ready to play at a moment's notice or happy to lie quietly at your feet for the evening. He'll work for you at whatever task you send his way for no more payment than the chance to be with you.

Not independent like a Bloodhound or a guarding breed, Golden Retrievers are all about their people. Lousy watchdogs, yours might tell you someone is at the front door, but he has no desire to scare anyone away. His sense of humor keeps you entertained, and his happy-go-lucky attitude lasts his lifetime.

The Fear-Imprint Period

Golden Retriever puppies are naturally curious and interested in everything around them. But between 8 and 12 weeks, most puppies go through a fear-imprint stage when they're more likely to be significantly affected by a scary experience. A traumatic encounter during this phase could spoil his attitude toward that thing for the rest of his life.

DOG TALK

The **fear-imprint stage** lasts for several weeks and usually starts soon after you bring home your puppy. Overwhelming or frightening incidents that occur during this time might stay with him for the rest of his life, and he'll always react to them with fear.

Most pups won't experience anything overly frightening at this age, but it's worth taking precautions to avoid unnecessary scares. This is a bad time to discipline him severely, yell at him, or force him to approach something he finds scary—if there's ever a good time for any of these things.

When something traumatic does happen, it's hard to know how your puppy looks at it. For example, if an 8-week-old pup, just entering the fear-imprint period, is badly startled when someone drops a bowl of apples behind him, it could cause a lifetime phobia. But what exactly the puppy becomes afraid of is difficult to predict. It could be objects hovering over his head, things coming up behind him, apples, bowls, or some other factor the pup focused on during the incident.

In spite of the potential risks, you still need to socialize your pup during this time. But don't force him to do anything he's not comfortable with. Allow your worried pup to approach a scary person or thing in his own time. Try not to overwhelm him or accidentally reward his fearful behavior. If you overreact, he might decide there really *is* something to be frightened about—or he could conclude he's being praised for acting scared, and he'll continue to act frightened to get attention from you. Sometimes Golden Retrievers are *too* smart.

If he barks or makes a big fuss when he sees something, try to ignore it and praise him when he calms down. Remember, praise desired behavior, ignore unwanted reactions or frightened behavior, and keep patiently working with him. Continue to present experiences he was familiar with before this period as well as introduce him to new things. In about 2 weeks, he'll regain his confidence.

There's a balance between overprotecting and overwhelming your puppy. With that in mind, it's time to start the socialization process in earnest.

Socialization Basics

The first critical period of socialization ends by the time your puppy is 12 weeks old. During this time, your puppy learns easily, and what he learns, he'll remember for his lifetime—good and bad. Your goal over the next few weeks is to introduce him to myriad positive experiences.

Socialization is not a one-time thing; you need to expose him to new things every day. If you bring home your Golden Retriever puppy at 8 weeks of age and he never sees another dog, person, or place until he's 16 weeks old or older, he won't develop into the outgoing, confident dog he has the potential to be. An unsocialized puppy can become excessively fearful or aggressive, not typical Golden Retriever traits at all.

Your puppy's breeder started his socialization when he was just a few weeks old (see "Social Skills" in Month 1). Now it's your turn to continue his efforts. Remember that because your pup hasn't yet completed his vaccines, this isn't the time to take him to the park or out in public. But there are still many things you can do to socialize your pup.

Invite a variety of people to your home one at a time or in small groups. Your pup needs to meet people who are tall, short, fat, thin, old, and very young. He should see hats, coats, uniforms, umbrellas, and wheelchairs. For example, ask a guest to sit on the floor, toss your puppy a treat, and speak to him in a happy voice to encourage him, and then ignore him while he works up his courage and decides to investigate. When your puppy approaches someone new, praise him for being brave.

If your puppy is fearful, start with the new person at a distance so your puppy can get used to her before getting too close. Act like the stranger is no big deal. Talk in a normal tone of voice, and shake hands or touch the person's shoulder so your puppy understands that you think the scary person is just fine. Always give your pup the opportunity to interact with new people while they give him treats and pet him. Do this several times a week until he's at least 16 weeks old.

TIPS AND TAILS

Include your mail carrier in the socialization process. After all, he or she will likely visit your home or doorstep every day for the rest of your dog's life. Provide a box of dog biscuits, and ask your mail carrier to offer one to your puppy every time he delivers the mail.

Although your puppy saw many things while at the breeder's home, those same things might seem new to him in at your house. Continue to expose your puppy to various surfaces, including asphalt, gravel, concrete, grass, snow, dirt, and puddles.

When he has a chance to interact with his environment, he's more likely to remember it, so feed or play with him on each material.

Accustom him to different locations, too, such as the bathroom, the living room, the garage, the patio, his crate, and your car. You can safely take him to homes that have no pets, or pets who are vaccinated and friendly if you carry him to and from the house. Or visit the vet's office or groomer's salon for a pet-and-treat session.

Introduce your Golden Retriever puppy to assorted sounds, like the lawnmower, televisions, the dishwasher, music, thunder, yelling, kids, sirens, motorcycles, gunshots (if you're going to hunt), and other loud noises. Start with the sounds far away and slowly move closer, or record loud sounds and play them back while gradually increasing the volume. Remember that at this age, you want him to have positive experiences, not terrify him to the point he'll be emotionally scarred for life. If your puppy seems worried, back up and adjust the exposure accordingly.

Set up some physical challenges for him, and let him figure out each item for himself. Construct an obstacle course in the backyard, for example, and have him climb steps, go through a tunnel, play in a cardboard box, climb over and under obstacles, and walk up a ramp or small teeter-totter. Or place a board across several bricks, and teach him to walk on it.

By allowing your puppy to figure out new things for himself, you're helping him build confidence and problem-solving skills. When he reacts in a calm and happy manner, praise him. You're there to provide a comfort zone for him, and he needs to know all is going well. You're also there to protect him from overwhelming situations and remove him when something is just too much for him.

Also remember that you're quite large in relationship to your puppy. If you greet your puppy by bending over him, you block his view of everything else in the world—a terrifying thing to a little puppy. Think of how uncomfortable you are when a large person gets in your personal space and hovers over you—you want to move away. No wonder a puppy is sometimes afraid of big, new people.

Make introductions easier on your puppy by inviting everyone to get down on the floor at his level. Pet him by scratching his chest rather than patting him on top of the head. A hand looming over him will cause him to shy away, but the palm of your hand, down low and reaching in his direction, isn't so scary.

Your Golden Retriever Puppy and Children

Goldens and children were made to be together. If you don't have kids, borrow some and have a puppy party. Puppies need to learn how to interact with children, and equally as important, children need to learn how to properly interact with puppies.

Start by inviting over one well-behaved child at a time. For the initial introductions, keep the sessions short, calm, and controlled so your puppy doesn't get overtired or overwhelmed.

Some children don't know how to play with a puppy. Avoid tug-of-war and teasing games. Teach the kids to give the puppy a treat for looking at them when they say his name. Help them teach the pup to sit or learn a trick like shake. Play "puppy-come" games, where everyone sits in a circle and each child calls the puppy in turn and rewards him with a treat when he comes. Have the child brush the puppy, hold his leash, pet him, hug him lightly, or toss a toy a few feet away for him to run after.

TIPS AND TAILS
Never leave your puppy alone with children. It's up to you to protect him while you supervise and direct the activities.

As more kids visit, there likely will be lots of yelling and running around. You want your pup to get used to the commotion, but all this activity encourages him to join in. Children often run and scream, waving their arms and batting at the puppy when he jumps on them. To him, this is an invitation to play.

Teach kids to "be a tree" when your puppy gets too excited and starts nipping or pulling on their clothes. Have the child fold her arms across her chest, stand perfectly still, and not look at the puppy. When your pup stops leaping, quietly praise him and have everyone stay settled for a few minutes. Distract him with a toy or chewy, and put him on a leash to prevent him from jumping and nipping again.

Watch your puppy's reactions as he plays with children, and remove him if he seems overwhelmed. And remember that puppies this age tire quickly. After a short play session, he can snuggle while he falls asleep in a child's lap.

Introducing Other Family Pets

If you have other dogs in the house and they're over 6 months old, choose a neutral territory, such as a friend's house, for them to meet your puppy for the first time, before you even bring him home, so they won't see him as an invader. Leash your older dogs, and introduce each one to your puppy, who can remain unleashed, one at a time. Keep a loose hold on the adult dog's leash; a tight leash could make the dog feel restrained and like he can't get away, which could make him more likely to lash out at the puppy.

If things get tense, pick up your puppy, remove him from the adult dog, and start with them farther away from each other next time. Praise the older dog and offer treats, so he'll think the puppy brings good things. Be sure the older dog gets plenty of attention so he doesn't get jealous and take it out on the pup.

Also, don't leave your pup alone with the older dogs. They need supervision for several weeks until everyone is comfortable and the puppy has figured out his place in the hierarchy (see "Socializing to Calm Adult Dogs" in Month 4). Use baby gates and ex pens to separate them when you can't supervise.

If you have a cat, know that the cat takes much longer to get used to your pup than the puppy to her. A cat's first instinct is to run, and a puppy's is to chase—what fun! It might take a few weeks for things to settle down. Be sure your cat has a place up high where she can get away from the puppy. Baby gates, for example, can block Puppy's access to the cat's territory.

Let them smell each other through a closed door, and take the puppy on a leashed tour of the cat's favorite room, letting the cat leave when she wants to. At night, when the pup is in his crate in your room, Kitty will have a chance to get used to his smell and learn the pup can't get to her while he's crated. Whenever the cat is around for the first week or two, leash the pup so he can't chase her. When he gets too close, Kitty will hiss and swat him. They may eventually become great friends, or they may just tolerate each other, but you need to introduce them slowly and help give Kitty a break or escape when she needs it, especially at first.

Small pocket pets like birds and hamsters and caged animals like snakes are safest in their cages when a young Golden Retriever puppy is on the scene. He can get used to their presence from his crate, so don't try to introduce them nose to nose—you're the one that's likely to come away with wounds. If you don't make a big deal of it, they won't either, and everyone can peacefully coexist without interacting. Keep the doors to the pet rooms shut when you're not able to supervise, so a curious puppy doesn't knock over a cage or aquarium.

TIPS AND TAILS

Prevent your puppy from leaping on or otherwise interacting too much with other animals. A bird can peck or bite, and a cat will scratch and hiss at an overactive puppy. You want meeting new animals to be a positive experience for your pup—and avoid injury to both parties. His first exposure to other species should be from a distance or otherwise controlled.

Introducing Other Puppies

Your puppy needs contact with other puppies, too. Puppies teach each other acceptable dog manners; if one plays too rough or bites, the other one disciplines him or simply quits playing with him. You might be able to set up play dates with your pup's littermates, or your veterinarian might have other puppies in his practice he can refer to you.

Limit your puppy's contact with other dogs, both puppies and adults, unless they're completely vaccinated and show no signs of illness. Wait until after the second set of vaccines at least before you set up a puppy playtime.

BEHAVIOR

Perfectly normal puppy activities might test your sanity if you're not used to having a puppy in your home. It's best to plan ahead for a few inconveniences and challenges during the first few weeks your Golden Retriever is home.

Sleeping Through the Night

At night, put your puppy in his crate by your bed, and expect to get up and take him out once or twice throughout the night. His little bladder can't hold it more than a couple hours at this age. By 10 to 12 weeks, he should be able to sleep through the night.

Pick up all water an hour or two before bedtime so he doesn't fill up right before he goes to bed. And give him one last break outside before you put him in his crate for the night.

Curiosity—Not Just for Cats

Without constant supervision, your Golden Retriever puppy will develop unwanted behaviors, which will turn into habits and be much harder to deal with later. As your Golden pup gains confidence, he'll start to explore his world more and more. If left to his own devices, he'll discover that digging is fun and chewing keeps him entertained. These are normal doggie behaviors, but they're not something you want to encourage. That same curiosity leads Puppy into every nook and cranny, searching for more exciting things to eat and play with, exposing him to things that could hurt him.

Always supervise your pup when he's out of his crate. You'll both be better off.

When Your Puppy Starts Biting

As your puppy starts exploring, he uses his mouth and especially his teeth to discover new things. He tastes *everything,* and because he doesn't know his own strength, he tests to see what happens when he bites hard or tugs.

It is *never* okay for him to use his mouth on a person. A puppy needs to have learned effective bite inhibition by the time he is 16 to 18 weeks old, when his adult teeth start to come in. His littermates started the job as they played and taught each other when a bite was too hard; you need to continue teaching your puppy bite inhibition, from the first day you bring him home, using the methods his littermates used.

When Puppy starts nipping at your arms or clothes, yelp loudly like another puppy would. This tells him you're displeased. Then fold your arms and turn away from him, ignore him, and abruptly leave the room. Game over. He'll get the message after a few tries.

When you see him consider biting but then think better of it, praise him. Redirect his attention to a toy or an acceptable chewy. If he's too wound up to quit, put him in his crate for a 3-minute time-out.

If family and friends are consistent in their reactions, he'll quickly learn to keep his teeth to himself.

TRAINING

At 8 weeks, your puppy is capable of learning specific lessons and connecting his actions with certain words. Teaching him good habits now prevents him from developing bad habits later. After all, it's much easier to stop problem behaviors before they become a habit than change them when he's a teenager.

Training Techniques

Positive training methods make learning fun. There's no need for harsh corrections with a puppy this young. Instead, interrupt him and redirect his energy to something else. The most effective correction is responding to an undesirable action with a growly tone of voice or a short time-out.

Your pup's attention span is limited right now, so keep your training sessions short—no more than 5 minutes at a time. Remember, he doesn't understand what you're saying to him right now, but your body language and tone of voice communicate your meaning. Always reward him for doing something right. Lure him with treats, or shape him into position and reward him. Add the command name when he understands what you're asking him to do.

A Family United

An 8-week-old puppy needs to feel safe and secure so he can grow up confident and well adjusted. He must be certain that he understands the rules of the house and know that everyone reacts the same to his behavior.

To make this happen, everyone in the household needs to agree on the rules when it comes to the dog. Golden Retriever puppies are cute and cuddly, but will you want him on the couch when he's an adult? Will he have access to every room? Where will his preferred elimination spot be? Where will he eat? Should he be prevented from jumping up on all people, or are there some exceptions? If you are inconsistent in enforcing the rules, your puppy will be confused—and you'll wonder why he isn't learning anything. Decide on the rules together, and enforce them equally.

Also agree on the words you'll use for different commands. Does "Down" mean "lie down" or "get off me"? Do you call him by saying "Come" or "Here"? Too many names for the same action only confuse your puppy.

Agree on discipline, too. Rather than drag the pup by his collar when you want him to go somewhere, hang a few leashes around the house so anyone, anywhere can easily hook him up to control his behavior. Agree that you all will ignore bad behavior or distract him rather than hit him or yell at him.

Prioritizing Housetraining

Start housetraining your Golden Retriever puppy the first day you bring him home. He'll need to go potty as soon as he wakes up, within 15 to 30 minutes after eating or drinking, and after a play session. For the first week he's home with you, he'll need to go almost hourly. By 12 weeks, he should be able to last an hour and a half during the day between potty breaks.

Keep him close and supervise him during this time, put him in his crate or ex pen, or leash him and tie the leash to your belt so he's always near you. Don't allow him to make a mistake.

When you take him out, go to the spot you want him to use and he'll probably pee immediately. Don't play or entertain him right now. Just stand there and wait. You could tell him to "go potty" while he's eliminating, and eventually he will associate it with the activity, but right now he has no idea what it means.

Be sure to praise him to the skies when he goes, and offer him a treat. He'll quickly learn that pottying outside produces treats. If he doesn't go immediately, put him back in his crate for 20 minutes and try again. When he performs, give him some supervised freedom indoors before confining him again.

It's worth repeating: you must go outdoors with your puppy and praise him when he eliminates so he'll know he's done the right thing. If you just put him outside, how will you know he's done his business? And how will he know what he's supposed to do?

Housetraining often takes longer in winter, when it's cold and snowy outside. You don't want to go out and stand in the cold, and your puppy doesn't want to get his feet and tummy wet. Dig out a snow-free area, or erect a small shelter over his potty spot so you both won't mind so much.

When you leave your pup at home alone or can't supervise him, set up his ex pen and include inside his crate (with the door open or removed), some water, and a spot where he can relieve himself. He'll select a corner of the pen to use. Encourage him with a piece of turf, a piddle pad, or even a doggie litter box in that spot. The best solution is to use the same surface he's expected to use outside. He'll quickly make the connection.

TIPS AND TAILS

Your pup will naturally want to jump up against his ex pen you've set up to confine him, and if he doesn't stop now, he'll learn to knock it over. Never pick him up when he's jumping; ignore him until he puts his feet on the floor. Don't pet him while he's on his hind legs, either. That's just rewarding him for pushing on the pen. Instead, rattle the pen until he backs down and only then praise him. This method also works when he's jumping against a pet gate.

If he has an accident in the house, you have to try to catch him in the act and interrupt him. Make a loud noise, scoop him up, and take him straight outdoors. Wait outside with him while he finishes going, and praise him.

If you don't see the indoor accident happen, clean it up and forget about it. If you scold him at that point, after the fact, he'll have no idea what you're mad about.

Crate Training

The crate is a training tool for you and a safe haven for your Golden Retriever puppy—and it needs to stay that way. Don't ever use the crate as a punishment, and don't ever confine your pup in it for more than a few hours at a time.

To introduce your puppy the crate, toss in a treat and let him go in, get it, and come back out when he's ready—don't close the door, and don't make him stay inside. Do this a few times throughout the day, always leaving the door open so he can explore it on his own. At mealtime, place his dinner inside the crate, again with the door open. After a few meals, however, begin closing the door behind him while he eats. (Many breeders will have already introduced your puppy to a crate, which speeds up the process, but you still might need to start slowly.)

He might whine and cry a little the first few times you close the door. If he does, wait until he settles down and then reward him by letting him out. If you let him out because he doesn't like it, he learns that making a fuss gets him what he wants.

At bedtime, place the crate next to your bed. Give him a chewy toy, place the blanket the breeder gave you (with his mother's smell on it) in the crate, put him in, and close the door. You might not get much sleep the first night!

Practice your putting puppy in his crate for a few minutes at a time while you read or watch TV nearby. Give him a chewy filled with treats, and let him see you leave the room and return a few times. He'll soon be comfortable and settle down for a good chew and a nap. Save the best chew toys for crate time, so he looks forward to it. And always wait until your puppy is quiet before you let him out.

Limiting His Freedom

For the next few months, your pup is still too young to have the responsibility of the entire house and yard. With no one there to instruct him, he can learn bad habits like digging in the wastebasket and chewing. He also can get hurt very easily.

Indoors, use pet gates to block his access to other rooms. If he's scolded for having an accident in the house, he'll just go to another room—in his mind, you can't see him and he doesn't get in trouble, so it must be okay. He's figured out that peeing in front of you is bad, but doing it out of your sight is fine. Housetraining will progress faster if you keep him in the same room with you.

If you have to leave him outside for a while, put him in his ex pen. He'll get to enjoy the great outdoors but remain safe.

Teaching "Come"

"Come" is an easy command to train—and lots of fun for you and your Golden Retriever puppy. The way to get a lifelong reliable recall is to start training early, and always call him for a positive reason. Take advantage of his willing nature; he'll probably race to you as soon as you call. If good things happen every time he responds, he'll always be happy to come to you. If you're going to do something he won't like, you should go get him.

To introduce come, first put your puppy on his leash. Get down on his eye level, a few feet away, and open your arms wide. In a high, happy voice, say, "Come!" or "Come here!" and cheer him on as soon as he looks your way so he won't go back to what he was doing. Praise him all the way to you, and give him a treat when he arrives. If he doesn't come, encourage him with a little tug on the leash and reel him in if necessary.

Practice from just a few feet away at first. Later, hook him to a longer lead, like clothesline rope, so you can enforce the recall. Start over in a new place from close up again, and gradually work back up to farther away.

Have family and friends call your pup, too. Play a game in which one person calls him and then another. Keep it short, and always stop before he gets tired.

TIPS AND TAILS

Here's a helpful training tool: put a few pieces of kibble in a small food storage container, and shake it when you call your puppy. He'll soon learn that the shaker means treats—you can even shake it from another room, and he'll come running. Make several shakers, and set them around the house so you can find and use them easily.

YOU AND YOUR PUPPY

During the first few weeks, you and your puppy are both learning about each other—and keep in mind that he's learning even if you aren't actively teaching. He's figuring out his name, who's who in his new family, what makes you happy, what he shouldn't do, and what his new routine is. You're starting to recognize when he needs to go out and when he's tired, hungry, frightened, or wants to play. You're all settling into your new life together.

Naming Your New Puppy

Your Golden Retriever puppy has two names, a call name and a registered name. His call name is the one you use every day. His registered name is the one listed on his AKC papers. The two don't have to be similar at all.

The best call names for your pup are short (one or two syllables) and snappy; have a happy, upbeat sound; and are easy for him to recognize among your other words. If you make his call name too long, you'll undoubtedly shorten it to a nickname—Frederico will soon become Freddy, Francesca will be Franny, etc. Also, don't choose a call name like Flo, which sounds too much like "no." And think about what the name will sound like when you call him from across the park. Will you be embarrassed? Will he recognize what you said?

His AKC registered name is limited to 36 characters, and that includes any spaces. (For an extra fee, you can have up to 50 characters.) With the breeder's permission, the kennel name can precede the puppy's name, as in, Windy Acres Coming Storm. In this example, Windy Acres is the kennel name, and Stormy is his *call name*. Remember, his call name could be anything, and it doesn't have to be related to his registered name. Sometimes the sire or dam's name is first on the registration, as in Samantha's Sunny Surprise. Here, the dam's name is Samantha and the dog's call name is Sunny. You also can make up a registered name that has nothing to do with the dog's kennel or parents. It's up to you.

DOG TALK

Your Golden Retriever's **call name** is the name you use for him every day. It may or may not have anything to do with his AKC registered name.

What to Expect During the First Week

Today is the big day! The breeder has done her job, and now that wonderful ball of fur is delivered into your arms—ready or not. Let's review what you should expect the first few days.

Your puppy might fall asleep in your arms on the way home. Take him outside as soon as you arrive so he can relieve himself in his designated spot. Once the smell is there, he'll know to go in that place again. Let him explore around outside for a few minutes—supervised, of course.

Once you're sure he's emptied his bladder and bowels, bring him inside and let him explore the main room where you spend most of your time. If he has an accident, clean it up, but otherwise ignore it. At this point, he'll be too confused to remember anything you try to teach him.

Let your Golden Retriever puppy tell you what he wants to do next. He might approach you for attention. If so, get down on the floor with him for quiet introductions, let him sniff you, and maybe give him a few treats. He might fall asleep immediately at this point. Remember, puppies need a lot of sleep and tire quickly. Don't overwhelm him with lots of noise or roughhousing, but do give him enough exercise so he'll sleep soundly that first night.

On the first day, let him get to know just your family. (Visitors can meet him later.) After a few days, he'll recognize individual family members. It's everyone's job to make him feel welcome and safe. As he starts to settle in, he'll watch what you're doing and start to follow you. He'll be excited to see you and begin to learn his name.

Be sure his basic needs for food, water, and sleep are met. Take him out hourly for potty breaks. Be patient with accidents and chewing.

HAPPY PUPPY
Golden Retriever puppies are naturally happy and outgoing. During this period of his life, playing is fun *and* instructive. This isn't the time to be serious about anything. Make training a game, and he'll learn fast and remember forever. Even a pup who makes a mistake can be corrected in a positive way by distracting and redirecting him to an acceptable behavior. A full tummy, a soft toy, and a warm bed all make for a *very* happy puppy.

Practicing Patience

A Golden puppy doesn't learn everything on the first try. It takes at least three repetitions for him to start getting the idea, and you might have to start all over tomorrow with the same lesson. He will make mistakes, have accidents, chew things, and whine in his crate—he's just a baby. Forgive him, and keep training. He's learning how to learn, and he wants desperately to please you. He just needs time to figure out right from wrong.

When you run out of patience, let another family member take over for a while, or put your pup in his ex pen or crate for a time-out. If you lose your temper, he'll be frightened and see you as unpredictable.

Also, diligently manage your puppy's environment. Even though you puppy-proofed your house and yard, he still requires direction, supervision, and confinement. Keep temptation out of his reach, and you prevent trouble before it occurs.

The Importance of a Routine

A puppy starts to feel safe and secure when he knows what's expected of him and also when he'll be fed, walked, put to bed, and left alone. Set up a daily schedule with fixed times for every activity, and stick to it as much as possible. Try to keep weekends the same as weekdays. If you get up at 6 A.M. on weekdays, he'll quickly learn to anticipate getting up at that same time on weekends.

Many people take a few days off from work when they get their new pup. Don't shower him with attention for several days in a row and then suddenly go off and leave him alone the next day. Introduce his schedule immediately. A young puppy sleeps as much as 16 to 18 hours out of every 24, so he needs a lot of rest and quiet time, even when you're home.

	SOCIAL	BEHAVIOR	TRAINING	PHYSICAL	HEALTH
MONTH 1			Littermates and mother teach appropriate canine behavior	Rapid growth	
MONTH 2	Breeder starts socialization				
MONTH 3	Socialization at home with new owner and other pets	Fear-imprint period	Begin house- and crate training		1st DHPP vaccine
MONTH 4		Teething begins—heavy chewing period	Enroll in puppy class		2nd DHPP vaccine
MONTH 5			Ready for basic commands		3rd DHPP and rabies vaccines
MONTH 6	Socialization in public		Enroll in basic obedience class	Switch to adult food	
MONTH 7		Adult teeth are in—chewing continues		Moderate growth	Sexual maturity
MONTH 8					
MONTH 9			Ready for more advanced training		
MONTH 10					
MONTH 11				Slow growth—reaches adult size	Annual vaccinations and checkup
MONTH 12 AND BEYOND					

Finding Her Way

This month, your Golden Retriever puppy's focus is more social than studious. She looks to you for everything, she follows you anywhere and everywhere, and she's eager and happy the majority of the time. The period between 12 and 16 weeks, or 3 to 4 months, is a lot of fun for your family and your puppy. You continue socialization, take her to puppy class, and begin to set the foundation for future learning and good behavior.

This month also is a challenge as your joyful toddler becomes more active. Overenthusiastic about everything, she acts first and thinks later. She starts teething, and her entire world changes as she gnaws on whatever might comfort her sore mouth.

Keep in touch with your breeder, and call her when you have questions about your puppy's development. You might be worrying about something entirely normal, but you won't know it's normal unless you can ask an expert. Plus, she'll enjoy hearing about your puppy's progress.

PHYSICAL DEVELOPMENT

Expect big changes in your Golden Retriever puppy this month. She loses her roly-poly physique as her legs get longer in proportion to her body and her puppy coat finishes shedding out. Her tail grows long and stringy. Her feet are growing, too, and they start to look more like they will when she's an adult. She might even look a bit out of proportion because all her parts are growing at different times. She also begins teething during this month, and that means chewing.

Size and Weight

A 12-week-old puppy weighs around 20 pounds—almost double what she weighed at 8 weeks. She'll almost double her weight again this month. And by 16 weeks, she'll be about half of her adult height and weight.

Because so many variations exist within the breed, it's hard to give one set of specific height and weight measurements for Golden Retrievers at this age. Assess your puppy's body condition (see Appendix B), and work with your vet to estimate what her healthy weight should be this month.

Teething

By 16 weeks, your puppy is teething—something females usually do earlier than males. She's losing her baby teeth and her adult teeth are pushing through her gums. Her incisors, the small front teeth on her upper and lower jaw, start to come in first.

As with human babies, the teething process is painful, but instead of fussing and crying like a baby would, your puppy chews to relieve the pain. Hide your most precious possessions, shoes, handbags, phones, and remotes, or they'll become her teething property. She doesn't target these items with evil intention—they smell like you, and that comforts her. When you catch her chewing on something you'd rather her not destroy, trade it for an approved chew toy. (You might see some blood on her toys; that's normal.) Provide your pup a variety of safe chew toys, and keep them handy because you'll be negotiating plenty of trades. Rotate the toys so she has just a few at a time. Then they'll seem new and exciting when you offer them.

TIPS AND TAILS
Don't yell and chase your pup when you catch her chewing. She'll think you've suddenly lost your mind, and she'll be afraid of you. And the next time, she'll hide with her prize, and you'll have trouble getting it away from her.

Frozen bones, cold carrots, ice cubes, or stuffed frozen KONG toys feel good on her sore gums and keep her occupied for longer periods. Keep in mind that frozen treats will make a mess, so confine her when you give her these gum soothers, or give them to her outside. You also can rub her gums with a teething product like Orajel or use a natural remedy like chamomile. And to make mealtime easier, soak her food in a few tablespoons of water so it won't be painful to chew.

Know that on occasion while she's teething, she might not feel like eating—that's normal. And she might not want her mouth touched. Remember, that area hurts right now.

Your puppy might get bad breath, have soft stools, or be a bit lethargic during teething. All this is normal, but if you're concerned, consult with your veterinarian to rule out an infection or other problems.

HEALTH

At this stage of your puppy's life, some new concerns are worthy of your attention. The most important things to watch for this month are signs that your puppy has eaten something she shouldn't. Because she's teething, revisit your puppy-proofing efforts (covered in Month 3) and supervise her carefully. When you can't watch her, confine her.

When to Take Your Puppy to the Vet

As you and your Golden puppy get acquainted, you might worry about her and what's normal for her. It can be difficult to know when a case of puppy diarrhea or vomiting means it's time to head to the vet. What might be a minor condition in an adult Golden Retriever can quickly become critical in a puppy, so watch her carefully. If signs of illness continue for more than a few hours, contact your veterinarian.

If you see any of the following, go to the veterinarian:

Diarrhea or vomiting: A puppy can get an upset tummy from eating too much or too fast. Maybe she swallowed a piece of stick in the yard or ate too much grass. Or she might have parasites. If her feces contain blood or mucus, it could be a sign of parvovirus. Vomiting is also a symptom of poisoning. If your puppy is staggering or shaking, *take her to the vet immediately.*

Refusing food or water: A puppy can get *dehydrated* quickly, so offer your Golden Retriever plenty of water wherever you are. If she doesn't want to drink, offer her ice cubes. They'll provide the moisture she needs but not make her queasy. Gnawing on the ice cubes also gives give her something else to think about other than how she feels.

DOG TALK

Dehydration is an excessive loss of body fluids, especially water, commonly caused by overheating or illnesses. To check your puppy for dehydration, lift the skin along her back. If she's well hydrated, it should make a tent shape and drop immediately back into place. If her skin remains standing in a ridge, she's dehydrated. Also check her gums; they should be moist, not dry.

Your puppy might sometimes skip a meal. If meal skipping is accompanied by lethargy or listlessness, it could indicate something is seriously wrong. When she feels like eating again, start off slowly, feeding her a bland food like cooked plain skinless chicken and steamed rice or cottage cheese. When she feels better, gradually switch her back to her regular food.

If she doesn't feel better within 12 hours, call your vet. Your puppy could have a blockage caused by something she ate, such as socks, gravel, sticks, or bones.

Sudden changes in activity level: Beyond being a tired puppy taking a nap, is your pup lethargic, dull-eyed, and uninterested in her surroundings? Or is she frantic and hyperactive? Sudden changes like this might be a sign of fever, disease, or something as minor as a thorn in her foot.

Signs of pain or injury: Is she limping, whining, or crying when you touch her? Does she bite or snap at you when you try to get close? If so, she might be trying to tell you where it hurts.

Breathing problems: If she's gagging, wheezing, or suddenly appears unable to breathe, this could be an emergency. She could have something stuck in her throat, or she might have been stung by a bee.

Fever: A puppy's temperature, taken rectally, is usually between 100°F and 102.5°F, and her nose is normally moist and wet. When she has a fever, however, it may be dry and warm. Feeling your puppy's nose isn't a foolproof way to detect a fever, though. Use a digital thermometer to get an accurate reading.

TIPS AND TAILS

To take your puppy's temperature, use a rectal thermometer lightly coated with petroleum jelly. Keep her occupied at the front end with treats as you hold up her tail and gently place the thermometer in her rectum about 1 inch. Hold it there for 2 minutes or until it beeps (if you have a digital model). Call your veterinarian if it reads over 103°F.

Urine or bladder problems: If an almost-housetrained pup is suddenly having frequent accidents, if you see blood in her urine or if it's a dark color, or if she's straining to go, she could have a urinary tract or kidney infection.

Constipation: Straining to eliminate could mean your pup isn't drinking enough water. Offer her canned food, which contains more moisture than dry food and helps get things moving. She also might have eaten something that caused a blockage. Sometimes, a puppy appears to be straining when she actually has diarrhea, so try to get an accurate read on what's happening.

Eye or nose discharge: If you see this, it could mean she inhaled a foxtail or has something in her eye. It could also be a sign of upper-respiratory illness.

Unusual odor from mouth or ears: This could indicate she has a broken tooth that's infected or some decayed food stuck in her teeth. She also could have an ear infection or ear mites.

The veterinarian will want to know when the symptoms began and how the puppy has been acting. For digestive issues, you might be asked to bring in a stool sample.

Getting Her Booster Vaccines

Three or four weeks after your puppy's first vaccines, you should visit the veterinarian for her second DHPP vaccine. Each booster continues to build her immunity by stimulating the production of antibodies that protect her from disease.

At 12 weeks, she's not completely protected yet. The final vaccine, at 14 to 16 weeks, completes the series, after which she can start visiting the outside world. At 16 weeks, or 4 months, your veterinarian gives your pup her first rabies vaccine, which is effective for 1 year. Your pup needs a booster for both DHPP and rabies 1 year later.

The core vaccines all dogs should have—distemper, hepatitis, parvovirus, and parainfluenza—all have a low risk of side effects. But you should be aware of the symptoms in case your dog has a reaction. They can occur minutes, hours, or days later and can last from a few minutes to hours.

At the site of the injection, bad reactions include pain, swelling, hair loss, inflammation, abscess, or intense itching. Reactions to nasal or oral vaccines could include ulceration in the nose or mouth, eye discharge, or coughing.

The most severe vaccine reaction in dogs is anaphylactic shock, which is an extreme allergic response, and tends to occur very quickly after the vaccine is administered. Symptoms include difficulty breathing, swelling at the injection site, low blood pressure, and weakness. A mild allergic reaction can be treated with an antihistamine, but consult with your vet before administering any over-the-counter drug so you don't overdose or give your puppy anything toxic.

Dealing with External Parasites

Gone are the days when you had to constantly spray, dip, and bathe your dog in toxic pesticides to get rid of fleas and ticks. For the most part, you can control or eliminate these pests with over-the-counter products. However, some situations do require a visit to the vet. Here's how to check your pup for these nasty critters:

Fleas: Roll your puppy on her back, and look for fleas scrambling across her tummy to hide. Often you'll just see flea "dirt." The black specks are flea droppings, and the white specks are their eggs.

Ticks: Ticks feed on your dog's blood (as do fleas). A tick embeds its head in your dog's skin and can remain attached for several days, filling up with blood. A full tick looks like a grape hanging off your puppy's body.

Both fleas and ticks can quickly get out of hand if you don't protect your puppy. Ticks can transmit serious diseases to your dog—and to you—such as Rocky Mountain spotted fever, ehrlichia, and Lyme disease. In addition, ticks have a toxin in their salivary glands that can cause a condition called tick paralysis, which causes a dog's hind legs and ultimately her entire body to become progressively weaker. Fleas can spread bubonic plague, a bacterial infection that although rare today, still exists.

A puppy who has been bitten by a flea or tick may become lethargic, have a nasal discharge, or exhibit joint pain and lameness. If these symptoms occur, take her to the vet to test for parasite-borne diseases. Your pup also might have an allergic reaction to flea saliva and develop a skin infection that requires treatment.

Most topical preventives, like Advantage II or FRONTLINE Plus, are approved for puppies. The necessary dose is usually in proportion to your dog's weight, but read the label carefully. These products are easy to apply between your puppy's shoulder blades and partway down her spine, where she can't lick or scratch off the medicine. The product distributes through your pup's coat and oil glands in the skin without being absorbed completely into the body, and many are even still effective after your pup swims or has a bath. Most are effective for 30 days, and fleas or ticks are usually killed with 12 to 48 hours. A bonus: the pests don't have to bite your puppy to be killed, as with some preventives.

Sometimes a dog has an allergic reaction to a topical product, with symptoms including itching, redness, or swelling. If your pup exhibits these symptoms, bathe her with a dish detergent such as Dawn that will remove the product without harming her.

TIPS AND TAILS

Oral flea and tick preventives are often combined with heartworm pills in a single dose, administered once a month, to offer continuous protection for your puppy. Some brands also kill lice and other types of worms like roundworm, hookworm, and whipworm. An additional advantage to oral products is that they don't leave a greasy residue on your dog's coat or cause skin irritation.

You'll find flea dirt not only on your pup, but also in her bed, in her crate, and anywhere else she's been. Fleas jump off your dog and hide in the carpet until another warm host walks by they can latch on to. You haven't eliminated all the fleas around you just by treating your puppy; you'll have to treat other dogs, the cat, your yard, and your house to completely get rid of fleas. Nontoxic borax-based products and services like Fleabusters that dehydrate and kill fleas are available to treat your house and yard.

Ticks are common in the woods and in fields of tall grass. They like to hide several feet off the ground along hiking paths, waiting for an unsuspecting victim— you or your puppy—to latch on to. The more remote and overgrown an area, the more likely you and your Golden Retriever are to come home with a few hitchhikers, so stick to open trails as much as possible.

When you get back to your car, go over your dog thoroughly so you can remove any ticks before they attach to your puppy and start to feed. Rub her hair against the direction it grows so you can see down to her skin. A black speck no bigger than a pencil point can be a tick. Ticks look for warm spots, so pay special attention to your dog's armpits, in the folds of her neck, her groin, and her ears.

At home, go over your puppy with a flea comb to remove any hangers-on. Just because you remove a tick doesn't mean it won't hop right back on. Ticks have a hard shell that's hard to crush, so to be sure any you find and remove from your pup are gone for good, douse the tick in alcohol or insecticide.

After a tick is attached and feeding, it's much harder to remove. Using tweezers or a specially made tick-puller, grasp the tick as close to your pup's skin as possible. Slowly pull the tick away from your dog's body. The head breaks off easily, and you don't want to leave it embedded where it can cause an infection, so if it breaks off, be sure to make a second pass to remove it. Resist the temptation to crush an engorged tick; it's filled with blood that will explode everywhere. After you've removed and killed the tick, clean your puppy's skin and dab some antibiotic ointment on the spot where the tick was attached.

Fleas and ticks are common on rats, mice, rabbits, deer, and coyotes, so plenty of opportunities exist for your puppy to be reinfested. Even if your Golden Retriever doesn't currently have fleas or ticks, consistent use of flea and tick control products will protect her.

NUTRITION

A growing puppy needs plenty of food, but what she eats is also important. In addition to you ensure she's getting enough food, be careful that she's eating the right kind—and also not learning any bad habits like begging.

Appetite and Growth Spurts

Your puppy needs more food this month to keep up with her growth—up to about 4 cups a day. She'll probably eat as much as you give her, so don't think she's still hungry just because she's wolfing down her food. Increase her food in small amounts—about ¼ cup at a time—to match her growth, not her appetite.

Don't forget, you're also using a lot of treats for training, and those adds to her total calorie count. Use part of her daily kibble ration as training treats to help avoid caloric excess.

Feeding Your Puppy

The eating habits you teach your Golden Retriever puppy now are established for life. If she has to compete with other dogs for her food, she'll learn to gulp down her meals. If you feed her from the table while you eat dinner, you're creating a lifelong beggar. Set up a proper feeding routine now, and stick to it.

Feed your dog at the same times every day. If she knows when mealtime is, she won't pester you throughout the day. If you feed her just before you sit down for your dinner, she'll be full and not so anxious to join you. After she's eaten, that's it—no seconds. Don't let those big, sad, "Oh please, I'm starving!" puppy eyes fool you.

If you absolutely have to give her something from the table, wait until you're done eating, get up from the table, and put the food in her food dish. If you toss a couple scraps on the floor while you're scraping dishes, you'll have a pest for life.

If it's too late and you already have a beggar on your hands, put her in another room, put her in her crate, or tie her across the room until you're finished eating.

Feeding tables scraps can be dangerous to your dog. "Give the poor dog a bone" is one of the worst things you can do, especially if it's a cooked bone. Cooked bones are dry and brittle and can break apart easily and puncture your puppy's esophagus, stomach, or intestines. Poultry bones are smaller and more dangerous than beef, but even large pieces can cause intestinal blockages. Raw bones are safer, but raw poultry bones are still risky.

TIPS AND TAILS

People who feed their dog a raw diet often grind the raw bones to minimize danger.

Holiday leftovers are especially hazardous for dogs. Greasy turkey (and the bones) tossed in the trash is just too tempting for a curious puppy or even an adult Golden Retriever to resist. Besides the danger bones present, fatty foods can cause pancreatitis, a potentially fatal inflammation. Severe vomiting, diarrhea, dehydration, and lethargy are symptoms of pancreatitis, and your puppy will require several days of hospitalization—if she survives.

GROOMING

Your Golden Retriever puppy needs regular grooming to keep her in good condition and ensure she's in good health. With routine grooming, your puppy will look and feel better, and you'll catch small health problems before they become big issues. Best of all, you'll enjoy time together.

Grooming Your Puppy

A Golden Retriever's thick double coat is both water- and dirt-repellant. She'll shed this coat heavily twice a year, in the fall and spring, and she'll need more of your attention during this time for grooming.

A weekly grooming routine should include the following:

- Brush her coat
- Clip her toenails
- Check her ears and clean if necessary
- Brush her teeth

In Month 3, you introduced your pup to some grooming tools and started teaching her to enjoy being groomed. This month, you continue grooming … in spite of her protests. An active Golden Retriever puppy is in no mood to sit still, and she'll wiggle, bite, and play puppy games to get out of being groomed. Take her for a long walk or vigorous play session just before it's time to groom so she'll be tired and sit still for you while you work. Give her a toy stuffed with peanut butter or biscuits, and let her gnaw on that as you groom her.

Break grooming into small sessions, and reward her for sitting still. For example, trim one toenail, give her a treat, and brush her for a minute. Then trim another toenail and give her a treat. Stop after a few minutes, and do some more a half hour later.

Include a health check as part of your routine. Here's what to look for:

Skin: Check for lumps and bumps, cuts, and scratches. Carefully examine under her legs against her body where ticks and grass seedlings might stick to her.

Coat: Her coat should be soft, not wiry, dry, or frizzy. If it is, take a stool sample to the vet to be checked for parasites or worms.

Feet: Examine her paw pads to be sure they're not raw or cracked. Look for thorns or other foreign objects embedded between her toes or in her pads. Check her toenails to look for any broken or infected nails that need attention.

Mouth: Check to see if her gums are red or sore, especially while she's teething. Look for broken teeth or objects stuck between her teeth, and check for lumps or cuts on the roof of her mouth and under her tongue. Be sure her gums are bright and pink.

Eyes: Her eyes should be clear and bright, not cloudy or with mucus in the corners. Be sure no grass or other irritants are in her eyes.

Ears: Wipe out her outer ear with a damp cloth or cotton ball, and look to see if there's discoloration or debris down in her ear. Smell her ears; a bad smell means an ear infection.

If you look your puppy over carefully on a regular basis, you'll recognize immediately when she's injured or ill. When she's used to being checked over, she'll also be more likely to let you examine her when she's not feeling well.

Setting Up a Grooming Schedule

Pick one afternoon or evening once a week, and spend some quality time cuddling and grooming your Golden Retriever puppy. Place a beach towel or old sheet in front of the TV, and combine grooming time with your favorite sitcom. Set out your tools: brush, flea comb, toothbrush and toothpaste, toenail clippers, Kwik Stop, and treats. By the time you're ready, Puppy will be ready, too, because she knows what's up.

Once a week might not be enough. If you're an especially tidy housekeeper, you'll soon realize that Goldens shed a lot, and the more often you brush her, the less often you'll have to vacuum. Two or even three short brushings a week might be necessary.

Regular brushing helps stimulate oil production in her skin and brings out the luster in her coat. During shedding season, you might want to take the grooming party outside because you'll have lots more hair to deal with.

Other grooming chores, like teeth and toenails, might only need to be done once a week or every two weeks. And you might want to skip tooth-brushing while she's teething if her mouth is too painful. If so, rub a little pet toothpaste on your finger and let her lick it off to keep her in the habit.

SOCIAL SKILLS

Your last opportunity to have a significant impact on your puppy's personality is between 12 to 16 weeks. This month ends the first critical period of socialization, so continue the lessons you started last month by exposing her to more people, sounds, smells, and textures.

Socializing to Calm Adult Dogs

If you have another dog in your household, you've seen him interact with your puppy. But one canine friend does not make a socialized puppy. Your puppy needs to meet dogs of different breeds and sizes while she's young. One-on-one encounters are safer.

Choose your puppy's companions carefully. The only adult dogs your puppy should meet now are well-socialized and tolerant dogs of both sexes. A puppy needs older dogs to teach her lessons you and other puppies can't teach. Adult dogs generally forgive a pup or discipline her lightly for her transgressions while she's still so young. It's better that your puppy learn her doggie manners now, when no one is likely to hurt her.

When she meets an adult dog, your puppy will use the same appeasement behaviors she offered her mother back in the litter. She'll approach the adult with a low-slung "I'm a little puppy" wiggle and her tail tucked between her legs. Then she'll roll over and offer her tummy for a sniff. She might even release a little urine so the adult dog can tell how old the puppy is. By doing this, your puppy is communicating that she's not challenging the older dog and that she's not sexually mature yet. She might also lick the adult's muzzle or lift one paw toward him, both submissive behaviors she learned when just a few weeks old.

A pup who doesn't offer submission when she approaches an adult may be chastised. Most dogs will tolerate a baby until she steps out of bounds. Leaping on the adult, walking over him, yanking on his tail or ears, chasing, pouncing—all play behaviors—are fine until the grownup has had enough.

Another favorite puppy ploy is to try to steal a bone or toy from the adult dog. You'll see the grownup purposely put the bone just out of reach and watch the puppy approach it. When the puppy attempts to take the item, the adult will come to his feet with a bark and reclaim his rightful ownership.

An adult dog uses varying degrees of discipline. He might growl, give a severe look, air snap, or even give a short, sharp bark—all low-level corrections. After one or two incidents, most puppies understand. Some pups, however, are oblivious to the message, and the adult will ramp up his response. He'll roar like a lion, chase away the pup, or stand over the puppy and plant a paw on her body. All this sounds very ferocious, but no one gets hurt.

TIPS AND TAILS
When introducing your puppy to an adult dog, try to stay out of the action and let nature take its course as long as possible. Don't discipline the older dog; he's just establishing the dog rules, and your puppy needs to learn this valuable lesson.

Monitor the behavior of both dogs to ensure a safe encounter. If your puppy is persistently obnoxious, step in and stop her, and give the older dog a break before he loses all patience. If the older dog is standing over the puppy with his hackles up, stiff tail, and ears forward, or if he's chasing the puppy, this might be a sign of an overactive prey drive. Stop it before instinct takes over and your pup gets hurt.

Meanwhile, don't make excuses for your puppy. "She's just a baby. She doesn't know any better," isn't going to teach her a thing. And if you step in and rescue her, she'll learn she can be a brat with no consequences.

Socializing to Many People and Things

Get creative this month when it comes to socializing. The fear-imprint period is over, and your Golden Retriever pup is more responsive and outgoing. Invite the cheerleading team to come over, a football player in uniform, kids wearing backpacks, and other people in unusual clothes.

Let her investigate your wet umbrella when you come in. Then pick it up and hold it over your head and shake the water off onto her. Let her walk over a metal grate or figure out a pile of rocks. Although her vaccines are almost done, she doesn't have full immunity yet, so still limit her exposure to public places.

TIPS AND TAILS

Have a family contest to see who can come up with the most interesting new thing to introduce to your puppy.

It might seem obvious, but if you pet a puppy in different ways, you get different reactions—the way you pet her can even cause her to mouth or bite at you. Here are some tips for petting your pup:

- ○ Stroke her in the same direction her hair grows. Rubbing against the growth might be uncomfortable and make her move away from you.

- ○ Scratch her chest rather than reach for her head. An incoming hand is the perfect target for an excited, mouthy Golden Retriever puppy, and a shy pup will cower at a hand looming over her.

- ○ Pet fast if you want her to get excited (keep in mind she'll probably start to mouth you), and stroke slowly if you want her to calm down.

- ○ Stop before your puppy decides she's had enough. Always leave her wanting more.

When your puppy meets new people, she might offer her belly and release some urine, just as she did when meeting adult dogs. This is normal canine behavior, and Golden Retrievers almost always outgrow it.

An especially submissive Golden, however, might continue to urinate even when she no longer rolls over on her back to greet someone. To prevent submissive urination from becoming a habit, avoid situations that cause her to urinate. Let her approach people rather than allowing them to loom over her or corner her. It might seem like no big deal to you, but from your puppy's viewpoint, this new person might as well be King Kong.

Also, don't punish your puppy for the submissive urination. That will just frighten her more. You want to build her confidence, not punish her for what's a purely physical reaction. Golden Retrievers are especially sensitive, and what seems like a minor correction to you can be terrifying to her.

That said, don't comfort her, either. Your sympathy and worried voice might have the opposite effect of what you intended and convince her there was good reason to be afraid.

BEHAVIOR

Your Golden Retriever's personality really starts to shine this month. She'll gain confidence as she has successful experiences, and she'll enthusiastically tackle new challenges. While she wants to stick close to you, she also wants to check out the world. She takes her cues from you when she's unsure, and she fearlessly follows you everywhere.

Enjoy it now and take advantage of her devotion because next month she'll be a preteen and ready to take over the world on her own.

Preventing Separation Anxiety

We all wish our dogs could be with us all day every day, but it's not always possible, and our puppies need to learn to spend time alone. A dog who can never be left at home without destroying the house might suffer from separation anxiety. Teach your Golden to feel safe and comfortable alone while she's still a puppy, even if you're home all day. Your life or job situation might change someday, and you're heading off future trauma now by teaching this lesson when she's young.

She's not yet mature enough to have the run of an entire house or yard, so confine your puppy in her crate or pen when you're gone. What you might think is separation anxiety might really be simple puppy mischief. When you're not there to supervise, she's free to indulge her curiosity and entertain herself in doggie ways. She knows she can't dump the trash and eat the kitty litter in front of you, but when you're gone, she makes her own rules.

Teach your puppy not to rely on your constant attention every minute you're at home. Set up her crate, pen, or wherever she can stay when you're gone, and practice leaving her there for short rests during the day. She'll learn to feel safe there, chewing on her toy and listening to household noises. She'll also realize that being in her pen doesn't always mean she's going to be left for long periods.

Deafening quiet could unnerve your puppy, so when you leave, turn on the radio or television so the house still has some signs of activities she'd hear when you're home. Background noise also blocks out scary sounds from outdoors, so she won't react to unknown terrors.

HAPPY PUPPY

Exercise your puppy before you leave her alone at home. Take her for a walk, practice obedience, or a play a game. Then give her a chance to settle down and relax so she won't still be excited when you put her in her pen.

She'll quickly learn that the rustle of keys followed by you picking up your briefcase or purse, getting your jacket out of the closet, or picking up your books all mean one awful thing: you're going and she's staying. While you're teaching her to spend time alone, occasionally go through your leaving routine without actually leaving. Pick everything up, fiddle with it, put it back down, and go back to what you were doing.

Don't make a fuss over your puppy when you come and go. Put her in her pen and do something else for a few minutes before you leave. Then just leave. Big good-byes and petting just rev her up and upset her. When you come home, ignore her while you put down your things and get settled. Then greet her calmly and take her outside for a break.

Minimizing Mouthing and Overexcitement

Puppies learn by playing, and her over-the-top behavior this month includes plenty of chasing, pouncing, biting, and mounting. We talked about puppy biting in Month 3, but now your Golden Retriever is constantly grabbing and biting everything she sees. As you walk through the house with a puppy attached to your ankle, you'll be wondering what on earth you can do to get her to stop this.

Goldens are an oral breed, and they're genetically wired to use their mouths. The behavior goes back to what they were bred for—carrying a bird back to the hunter. A good hunting dog has a soft mouth, but a Golden Retriever should never put her teeth on her people. Don't allow puppy-biting to continue—a 70-pound piranha is not what you signed up for when you got a Golden.

Mouthing and overexcited behavior go hand in hand. Here are some tips to minimize both:

- Stop the game if she won't quit mouthing. Step in and halt the action when she plays too rough with children or other puppies.
- Pet her body first, not her head. Your hand reaching toward her face is an easy target. Also pet slowly using long strokes on her body and head.
- Don't roughhouse. Your hands darting at her encourage mouthing. Rough handling of her head, even in fun, also invites her to play-bite.
- Be sure she's getting enough exercise and sleep. A wound-up or tired puppy is more likely to jump and bite.
- Schedule play dates with other vaccinated puppies. They'll discipline her if she bites too hard or plays too rough.

○ When she's really excited, use muted body language and a quiet voice. Calm her with some quiet massage and petting, and offer her a chew toy *after* she calms down, not *before*, so she doesn't think it's a reward for all her frenzied activity.

○ If she's too wound up to accept handling, attach a leash and let her drag it after her so you can lead her away from an overactive situation to a place where she will calm down.

○ Teach her to bring you a toy when she's overexcited or mouthing you. Make a big deal out of it, and she'll quickly learn to go get her toy whenever she's excited.

○ Give her a short time-out in her crate or pen.

Dealing with Vocal Discovery

You'll wake up one morning this month and realize your puppy has discovered she can do things with her voice. Barking at the cat makes the cat run, barking at other puppies makes them play, and barking at the mailman makes him go away. This is about the time many Golden Retriever owners throw up their hands and enroll in puppy classes.

It starts when she barks excitedly and you respond. Next thing you know, she's standing in front of you barking for attention. And it works, doesn't it? You immediately take action, if only to shut her up. This rewards the behavior in her mind, and before long, you have a chronic barker.

When she's barking for attention or is just getting too wound up, put her in her crate for a time-out. Don't let her out until she's quiet, and don't talk to her while she's calming down. It could take 5 minutes or as long as a half hour.

If you give in and release her, she decides that if she barks long enough, there's a chance you'll let her out, so she'll keep trying until she hits the jackpot. Don't accidentally reward her for barking, and she'll eventually grow out of this stage.

TRAINING

Between 12 and 16 weeks, start teaching your puppy specific behaviors. She needs to learn vital skills by the time she's 5 months old, but if you don't start until then, she'll be too distracted by adolescence to learn much. The commands you teach her now build a framework for later training and communication.

Right now, your Golden Retriever puppy is focused on you and is an eager student. She's realized that watching and listening to you produces good things. She's able to connect your words to her actions and remember what worked for her yesterday. And whether or not you're teaching, she's certainly learning.

When teaching your puppy something new, work with her in a quiet place with no outside interference—no TV, video games, or other household activities. You want her to focus on you and only you. After she learns a behavior, you can teach her to respond in spite of surrounding distractions.

Enrolling in Puppy Class

You're doing everything right for your Golden Retriever puppy. She's meeting new people every week, you've started training, and her housetraining is going well. Even so, puppy class, often called puppy kindergarten, is an essential part of her education and social development.

The window of time during which this benefits her the most is closing fast, however. You started searching for a trainer when you first got your puppy. (See Month 1 for tips on selecting a puppy trainer.) Now it's time to finalize your decision and enroll in class.

HAPPY PUPPY

Approach training as a game. Your puppy's attention span is still short, and she'll learn faster if she's having fun. If she's really active, train after she's had a short play session, when the edge is off and she can concentrate better. Adjust your methods to her personality and mood for best results.

You might be worried about enrolling in a training class, knowing your puppy isn't yet fully immunized. But at some point, the risk of inadequate socialization is greater than the risk of disease. If you select the school carefully, her chances of getting sick are less likely.

Choose a facility that's clean and well maintained. Check out the health requirements for all dogs entering the premises, including those for other classes beyond the puppy class. All dogs should be vaccinated, and no unknown dogs should be allowed. Some facilities rent their space on weekends for dog clubs and competitions; does this one? What are the health requirements for dogs who attend these events? Do they thoroughly clean and disinfect the space afterward?

Most classes accept puppies from 10 weeks up to 4 months old, so expect to see a mix of old and young, big and small. Unless your puppy is very young, Golden Retrievers are usually at the larger end of the scale. The instructor should separate the pups if the big ones are overwhelming the little/younger ones. No one wants a sensitive puppy to be overwhelmed and frightened nor a bully rewarded for pushing other puppies around. Puppy class is for developing social skills and confidence, not destroying them.

Don't be offended if your bundle of joy is singled out during class. Any pup who plays too roughly should be removed and introduced slowly to just one or two puppies at a time. That's a lesson she needs to learn, and that's why you're at class.

Classes are a combination of playtime and lessons because all play, all the time gets the puppies too fired up. Your puppy learns the difference between active playtime and when she has to settle down or pay attention, and her reward for calming down is to go back and play some more. She's also handled, trained, and corrected by new people during class. Equally important is the opportunity to play and learn her dog manners and bite inhibition with other puppies.

The instructor will set up play equipment that presents new and fun challenges you don't have at home, such as agility equipment. While observing you with your pup in class, the instructor will be able to identify potential problems and help you explore solutions.

Bring the entire family to puppy class. Puppy classes are as much about training you as they are training your Golden Retriever, and everyone in the household needs to be consistent. You learn how to teach your puppy, properly reward her, and introduce her to basic obedience exercises like sit, down, and come, while you learn how to shape her behavior to manage play-biting, jumping up, and chewing. You also practice social skills like meeting new people and animals, and you learn how to handle situations when she's afraid. In addition, you play new games with your puppy that both teach and build your bond with her. And you can ask your instructor questions when you get stuck on a problem.

Many puppy class instructors follow the American Kennel Club S.T.A.R. (Socialization, Training, Activity, and Responsibility) Puppy Program. This is a 6-week course that ends with a quiz for both owners and puppies. Owners also make a Responsible Dog Owner's Pledge to accept responsibility for the care and training of their puppy. For more information, visit akc.org/starpuppy.

Teaching "Sit"

"Sit" is an instruction you'll use over and over again, and it's easy to teach. For example, you'll tell your pup to sit in many situations throughout her life: before you put her food down, so you can attach her leash, to greet people, for a vet exam, or before you go through a door. The first thing she'll learn is to sit for a treat. Many people teach their puppy to sit for her dinner as early as at 8 weeks.

Let's review the steps for sit. (Your pup doesn't need to be on a leash unless you have trouble keeping her attention.) With your puppy standing, facing you, hold a treat just above and in front of her head—don't hold it so high she tries to jump up and take it. She'll look up to reach for the treat, and as she does, slowly move your hand backward toward her tail, keeping the treat just above or in front of her nose. She'll naturally rock back and sit as she looks up and as you lean into her. Immediately feed her the treat and praise her while her rear is still touching the ground. Then say "Okay!" and let her get up. She'll soon learn that "Okay!" means she's finished and can move.

TIPS AND TAILS

If you have trouble getting your puppy to sit, have her stand with her back near a wall or a piece of furniture. Then she can't back up because she has nowhere to go.

Repeat this three or four times, and you'll find she starts to sit as soon as you lift your hand. As a bonus, you're teaching her the hand signal for sit before she's even learned the word! When she reliably sits for you, add the word "Sit" just before she actually sits. (Don't say "Sit down." You want to save "Down" for another behavior.) Pretty soon she'll associate the word with the action.

When she understands the word "Sit," ask her to sit without the hand signal or lure. Produce the treat and praise as soon as she responds. If it doesn't work, that means she doesn't understand yet, so back up and work some more on the first steps.

At first, let her up as soon as she gets her treat. Once she's responding well, wait for a second or two before you release her with "Okay." Don't stare at her during this time; that will make her uncertain and she'll stand up. Work up to a few seconds before you release her and then alternate with some immediate releases and letting her sit for a few seconds sometimes. You'll see her fidget and think about getting up. Try to release her while it's still *your* idea, not hers.

When her sit is consistent, ask for it in other rooms and outside, with you facing her, and with you at her side. Always praise her warmly, even if you don't have a treat. Pretty soon she'll sit whenever you look at her!

Be sure to invite everyone in your household to tell her to sit. Hand out treats, and have your guests tell her to sit before she greets them.

Teaching "Down"

"Down" is an easier position for a puppy to hold when she has to stay in one place for more than a few seconds. Down also is useful when you're out in public, standing and talking to someone, waiting in the vet's waiting room, when you groom her, and when you need her to settle for a period of time. A dog can hold a sit for a minute or two, but she can be trained to stay in the down position for 30 minutes or more.

Down is a little harder to teach, for several reasons. Your little wigglewort will want to play instead of letting you manipulate her into a down. Down is a submissive position, and she might not want to accept your control. If you've been practicing handling her, she'll learn the down much more quickly.

Let's review the steps for down. With your puppy sitting (try this on a slippery floor to make the process easier), hold a treat in front of her nose and slowly lower it to the floor. When your hand gets to the floor, pull the treat slowly away from her while pressing down gently between her shoulder blades. She'll likely lower her body to the ground. If she does, watch her elbows. As soon as they touch the ground, feed her the treat, praise her, say "Okay," and let her up.

Some dogs will feel the pressure of your hand and immediately push back—a natural opposition reflex. If your puppy does that, you'll need to try a different approach. Instead of pressing between her shoulder blades, scoop your arm under her front legs and pull them forward, lowering her body to the ground.

TIPS AND TAILS

Training your Golden isn't a one-person job. Take advantage of your family's interest in your new puppy to involve everyone in training and socialization. When you play and train together, you all learn how to work with her, get the results you want, and be consistent in what you teach her. As an added bonus, your pup will respond and bond with all of you.

Another method to teach down is to sit on the floor and bend one knee with your foot on the floor. Lure your pup under your bent leg with a treat. She'll have put her front end down to reach under and get the treat. As soon as her elbows touch the floor, give her a treat, praise her, and release her. Lure her farther each time until her entire body is down before you give her the treat.

Whatever method you use, you might have to scoop under her rear legs to settle her back end. Sometimes she'll get stuck with her rear up in the air. Help her understand that *all* of her needs to be on the floor.

As you did with the sit, practice numerous times over several sessions. Then start practicing in different places and on different surfaces. Your puppy will test you and try to get out of getting down by rolling over, wiggling, and biting at your hands, but have patience! Don't give her a treat until her elbows and back legs are on the floor.

When she anticipates what you're asking, she'll get down as soon as you start to shape her into position, and eventually, you'll be able to touch her less and less. Pretty soon, the motion you use—luring her nose down with a treat and pulling it out in front of her—turns into a hand signal, and you can add the command "Down" as she starts to comply. Always follow through and be sure she goes all the way down.

Up until now, you've been on the floor with your puppy, and that's the picture she has in her mind of the exercise. She won't understand what you're asking if you stand up and tell her "Down." Gradually work with her until you can be up on your knees and then stand up completely and she'll still comply. Don't bend down toward her when you give the command; stay upright. Bending over her is an invitation to get up and come to you.

HAPPY PUPPY

Once she can do both a sit and a down in response to a verbal command, play a game of push-ups with her. Ask for a sit, a down, a sit, and a down, alternating several times. When she understands it's a game, she'll pop up into a sit and throw herself into a down. She'll also begin to anticipate the next command, and you can make her wait until you tell her. She's learning to listen and respond quickly—and you're both having a lot of fun.

Your Golden Retriever responds to your body language and tone of voice more than she hears the words you say, so talk to your puppy as you train her.

Some people, oftentimes women, politely ask their dog to comply—"Puppy, sit?" If you do this, your puppy hears that you're not sure about what you're saying and worries. Another approach is baby talk, which tells her it's playtime rather than training time. Either way, she gets confused.

Others, including many men, take the words *obedience command* seriously. They stand up stiff and straight in an authoritative pose, and bark out a gruff "Sit!" Their harsh tone and overpowering body language make the puppy think she's done something wrong. About this time, the owner thinks his dog is a sissy, and the puppy decides her owner is a tyrant.

Rather than go to either extreme, give your pup a command once, say it firmly, expect her to comply, and reward her with happy body language and warm and loving praise. You're not just teaching an obedience command here; you're building a relationship of mutual respect and trust.

Introducing Leash Walking

Until now, you've been carrying your puppy out in public, and she happily follows you around at home. But she's getting heavy, and it's time for her to learn to walk nicely at your side. In this section, we learn leash walking.

Break this training into short sessions. At the beginning of each session, start with something she knows well to boost her confidence before you move on to new things.

To begin, take your hungry puppy to a confined area with no distractions. Hook the leash to her flat collar (no chain collars, no harnesses), and let her drag the leash around, get tangled, and figure out how to untangle herself. Let her step on it and get stuck. She'll soon figure out to move her feet or give to the pressure of the leash to relieve the pull on her neck.

You can stand, kneel, or sit on the ground. Hold one end of the leash steady, and put just enough pressure on it that she feels it. Every action provokes a reaction, and her first instinct when she feels the pressure is to pull away from it. She might struggle, flip over, bite at the leash, and throw a full-fledged tantrum. Be a statue, don't say anything to her, and let her figure it out.

Continue to hold firmly, but don't pull her. The instant she gives the tiniest bit to the pressure and the leash slackens, release the leash, praise her, and give her a treat. If you loosen the pressure before she gives to it, she learns that struggling makes it go away. You want her to learn that calmly moving *toward you* makes the pressure stop. Pick up the leash again and repeat the lesson. After a few tries, she'll realize that if she yields to the pressure, you'll give her a treat.

TIPS AND TAILS
As much as you're teaching her, she's also teaching herself what leash pressure is and how to make it stop, so set her up for success. Make it easy for her, and don't move on to the next step too quickly.

Stand up and step backward, keeping light, steady pressure on the leash. Wait quietly until she leans toward you or takes a step in your direction. Don't look directly at her while you're waiting because she might be intimidated by your gaze and afraid to move forward. And don't go to her; remember, she is learning to come to you.

Encourage her with praise when you see her even think about moving forward. If she comes all the way to you, great! That's where you want her, so give her some extra loving every time she comes to you. If she balks, just keep the steady pressure on until she gives in and complies. She's likely to be confused, and you might have moved on before she really understood what you wanted. Practice backward steps until you both can move two or three steps without pressure.

Now turn so you're sideways and a step ahead of her. Because you're no longer facing her, it presents a different picture, and she'll be confused at first. Repeat the previous steps in this new position. Pay careful attention to the feel of the pressure on the leash. Without looking, you should be able to tell if she's giving in to the slight pull.

Stand with your puppy at your left side with the leash in your hands and the clip hanging loosely from her neck. Take one step forward with your left foot, and tighten the leash slightly as you do so. If your puppy moves with you, give her a treat, praise her, and have a party! She did just what she was supposed to do! If she balks, stop and wait until she gives in to the pressure and then quietly treat, praise, and take another step.

TIPS AND TAILS

When you want your dog to walk with you, always start out with your left foot. That's a visual signal down at her eye level that it's time to move. When you want her to stay in place, step off with your right foot.

Work up to taking several steps before you stop and praise her. If she pulls against the leash, stop briefly and try again. This trial-and-error method keeps her thinking. She'll catch on as she understands what works and what doesn't.

At this point, just before you take your first step, add your command word: "Let's go," "Walk," or whatever you decide to use. Don't use "Heel"; that's a precise position used in obedience competition where a dog is at your left side, her ear lines up with the seam of your pants, and she's looking at you. You might want to teach a variation of heel later for when you take her out in public or if you plan to compete with your dog. For now, you're just teaching her to walk nicely at your side with no pressure on the leash, a much looser position.

Don't add steps too quickly. Remember, you want her to be successful, so you'll have to take small steps with her training. When she starts getting pretty good at leash walking, you can add variations to make it fun for both of you. For example, take several steps, turn in the opposite direction, and invite her to catch up. Go fast, go slow, turn left, turn right, and walk in a circle. Always encourage her, praise her, and give her treats when she's by your side or catches up. She needs lots of feedback.

By now, she's walking well in the living room, but that's not the real world. Practice in the backyard, on the driveway, and in other places so she *generalizes* the concept of walking on a leash.

DOG TALK

A puppy **generalizes** a lesson when she learns that a particular command means the same thing in many different places and situations. For example, "Sit" means "rear end on the floor" in the living room, on the driveway, in the garage, in the yard, and at puppy class. She also learns "Sit" means sit when someone else uses the word, even when the person is standing, sitting, or across the room.

When she's walking nicely in a few places, add a mild distraction, like a family member walking at a distance. Remember to keep this practice short—just a few minutes.

If you begin to lose the puppy's attention, try to get it back quickly. As soon as her attention to you wanders, make noise, change directions, skip, or pull a squeaky toy from your pocket. She'll hurry to catch up and find out what she missed. Be more interesting than that distraction could ever be, and always praise and reward her when her attention is back on you. Gradually add other distractions as she gets the hang of the game, such as a ball, a cat, a child on a bike, or a car going by.

Natural distractions, like a good smell or a leaf, will always tempt your canine buddy. If you stop and wait while she sniffs, *she's* teaching *you* the rules of the walk. If you decide to let her sniff, give her permission before she gets to the item. Give this permission a name, like "Go sniff." Practice calling her back to continue walking, and praise her when she responds. She'll soon learn.

Housetraining Progress

Golden Retrievers are relatively easy to housetrain compared to other breeds, and by the end of this month, yours should be almost, if not completely, housetrained. She should easily sleep through the night in her crate without needing to go out.

If this isn't happening, first be sure she doesn't have a urinary tract infection by having your vet check a urine sample. If she's healthy and still having accidents, review the housetraining process outlined in Month 3, and tighten your supervision.

The main cause of delayed housetraining is that owners stop going outside with their puppy each time she needs a break and, therefore, she hasn't really learned why she's out there. They let her out, and give her a treat when she comes back in. They don't know if she's eliminated or not, and the puppy thinks she's being rewarded for coming in, so she doesn't take her time and get the job done.

If she's having accidents in the house, keep her in the same room, next to you, on a leash. Do you recognize the signals that she needs to go out? If you're busy and can't watch her, put her in her crate. Every time she pees in the house, she's essentially being rewarded for her behavior. The smell remains, too, and it becomes harder for her to understand why she can't go there again.

So plan ahead. Keep track of when she eliminates, and you'll begin to see a pattern emerge. Anticipate those times, and take her out before she asks. If she doesn't go, confine her in her crate for 30 minutes and try again. These methods should help you catch up on her housetraining and quickly make a difference.

Handling Your Golden Puppy's Collar

When your Golden Retriever gets too heavy to pick up, you might be tempted—especially when she's been in some especially aggravating mischief—to take her by the collar and drag her outside or to her crate. Think again. It only takes once or twice for this action to create a hand-shy dog who avoids being caught—or worse, who might snap at you to get away from punishment.

Instead, keep leashes hanging on every doorknob so you can hook her up and escort her on leash. A puppy who hangs back and resists being dragged will usually happily follow you on a leash.

Or grab a few treats, show them to your pup, and she'll quickly stop and follow you. If she doesn't want to go out, for example, let her see you put the treats just outside the door and close it. The same method works with her crate. Put the treat in her crate, and shut the door with her outside. Pretty soon she'll want to go where the treats are, she'll happily comply with your wishes, and you'll have successfully distracted her from her misbehavior and turned it into a learning opportunity.

Still, your puppy needs to allow you to take her by the collar without protesting. Someday, your 60- to 80-pound Golden Retriever will crash out the gate or front door, and you need to know you can grab her in an emergency without getting into a wrestling match. By that time, she'll be much stronger than you so you might not win.

You've been working on handling your pup. Now it's time to focus on this specific lesson. Take hold of her collar, and offer her a piece of kibble while you maintain a hold.

If she shies away, start by reaching for other parts of her body where she enjoys being touched. Do this many times, and when she's comfortable with you touching her collar, wrap your hand around it for a few seconds and release. Every once in a while, grab the collar quickly. Don't do this often and never more than once per session—you don't want this to turn into a hand-biting game. She'll soon learn you aren't coming at her to hit her.

Everyone in the family should practice this skill with your puppy so she trusts all of you.

YOU AND YOUR PUPPY

You love your new puppy and want to keep her safe, so select puppy-appropriate toys and supervise while she plays with them. Even though she's still just a baby, try not to overprotect her. As you play and get to know each other, you'll learn to read her canine body language and communicate better with her.

Choosing Safe Toys

Your Golden will destroy toys no other puppy on earth could dismantle. Remember, Golden Retrievers are mouth-oriented, and chewing is an important part of their play. If you don't provide chew toys for her, she'll make her own—usually your designer shoes, the coffee table leg, or your pricey new phone.

There's no magical list of safe toys. The best way to know for sure is to test them on your pup. Look to these categories:

Toys she can tear apart: Many toys are fine as long as you're there to take them away when they start to fall apart.

Toys she can have when you leave her alone: Super-tough indestructible toys (you'll soon learn which ones these are) will last several months before they break.

Real bones and chewies: These are made of natural substances, and you can offer them to her while she's young if you supervise her carefully.

Stuffed animals with squeakers inside can be shredded in minutes, or they could last for days. Knotted ropes, tough fabric toys, Planet Dog Orbee-Tuff toys, tennis balls, and other items might be safe now, but as she grows and her mouth gets stronger and bigger, she'll easily shred or swallow them.

A Galileo Bone is a super-tough version of the Nylabone and is almost indestructible. These are usually safe to leave with your pup when you're not home. Hard rubber toys like a KONG—that you can stuff with treats and freeze—last for several months. A frozen, stuffed KONG also eases her teething pain. As with other toys, check her KONG for cracks or missing chips of rubber, and throw it away when she's started to break it up.

Real bones and chewies, as opposed to rubber or nylon versions, are made from real animal parts, which are fine for a puppy, but most of these products are unsafe for an adult Golden Retriever. Many varieties are available, including marrowbones, stuffed bones, smoked or filet mignon–flavored bones.

Check to be sure they don't cause diarrhea and that no bits and pieces have broken off and are in her stool. A Golden Retriever puppy's strong jaws can break off sharp chunks that she'll then swallow. Pieces can lodge in her intestines and cause a life-threatening blockage that requires surgery; a small chunk could lodge in her windpipe; or a sharp sliver could perforate her intestine. Be vigilant if you give your puppy or adult Golden these toys.

Here are some examples of real chews:

Rawhide bones, made of cowhide (leather) are not digestible, which means a puppy's body cannot break down the material and pass it through her system and eliminate it. Rawhides soften as your puppy chews, and she can tear off a large piece and swallow it.

Bully sticks are made of beef muscle and are digestible. Your puppy will get hours of entertainment from a bully stick, but take it away when it gets small enough to lodge in her mouth or swallow.

Stuffed bones and **knuckle bones** are made from femur bones and are cut, cleaned, and sterilized. The long parts of the bone are filled with peanut butter or meat-flavored mixture, not necessarily real meat, and could contain additives and chemicals. The outside will splinter after a certain amount of chewing, so take them away when they reach this point.

Cooked bones, as mentioned earlier, are never safe for any dog. Cooking dries out the bones, making them splinter easily. Your puppy could swallow chips or sharp pieces, which could then hurt her insides.

Pig snouts are made of flesh, not bone, which your puppy can more easily digest.

TIPS AND TAILS

Choose products made in America wherever possible. Many imported chew bones are processed with chemicals that are dangerous to your puppy.

Overprotecting Your Puppy

There's a fine line between protecting your puppy and *overprotecting* her. Allow your pup to figure out new things for herself as much as possible. She doesn't have much experience yet, so she'll try things and inevitably get stuck sometimes. If she's cautious, let her take her time.

For example, if she climbs into a cardboard box tipped on its side and it falls over, there's no longer a door to escape out of. Resist the temptation to rescue her. Let her poke around and try different things. Unless she collapses in a blind panic, she'll eventually climb out or knock the box over. Then you can throw toys in the box to encourage her to continue exploring what the box will do. Will the flaps hit her as she crawls out? Does the bottom break out if she paws at it?

A puppy who is allowed to experiment grows up self-confident and eager to try new things. She develops problem-solving abilities and learns to think for herself. If you're overprotective, she grows up shy and fearful, expecting you to step in and save her from every situation. This learned helplessness is hard to undo once she grows up. Her dependence on you will lead to separation anxiety and other unwanted behaviors.

Of course, you'll want to protect her from a charging dog or a horde of unruly children. But whenever possible, when it's safe, let her learn about her world in her own way.

Understanding Canine Communication

Dogs have three primary ways of communicating with each other:

- Body language
- Voice
- Smell

They'll try to communicate with you the same way, so learn how to read your puppy and what she's telling you. Look at the total dog, her posture, her arousal level, and what might be triggering her response.

Some behaviors are obvious, and it won't take you long to recognize them. A play bow and bouncing around, for example, are signs of a happy puppy who is ready to interact with you.

A wagging tail is pretty obvious, too … or is it? It can mean many things. If she holds her tail high and stiff, she's excited or curious. She might wag her tail furiously while she barks at a stranger. A slowly wagging tail could mean she's uncertain. A tucked tail indicates fear or submission.

Her ears also tell a story. If they're forward and alert, she's interested, happy, or paying attention. If she folds her ears back and down, she might be worried, frightened, or submissive.

Even her mouth helps show her state of mind. A drooling puppy or one licking her lips might be stressed. If she's trying to lick your face, that's a submissive gesture she used with her mother. What might sometimes look like a snarl could actually be a smile.

In addition, look at her fur. The hair along her spine could stand up (known as *piloerection*) when she's overly excited or meeting a new dog.

You'll quickly learn the different tones of your Golden Retriever's bark, from the "someone's here and I'm upset" bark to the "I'm happy you're home" bark. Other variations include "I want something," "I need to go out," and "Ouch."

A whimpering puppy could mean she wants something. She might also yelp in pain or because she wants your attention.

A growling pup might be playing with a buddy or threatening a tennis ball. Most growly Golden puppies are just trying out their vocabulary during play. Golden Retrievers—both puppies and adults—like to talk to you, especially when they're playing with a toy.

TIPS AND TAILS

If you have a truly aggressive puppy who growls as a threat and follows it up with a warning snap or bite, get help from a qualified behaviorist *now*.

Our noses don't give us even a fraction of the information a puppy picks up when she smells something. Puppies smell another dog's urine, feces, anal glands, tail glands, and more, all of which gives them information about the other's identity, age, and sexual status. They can tell if their friend Rover peed on this bush yesterday or if a rabbit was in the backyard overnight. Smells tell your pup vital information about what's going on around her.

The Importance of Play

When you brought home your puppy, you removed her from her entire social group—her mom and her littermates. She needs you to be her playmate now. She needs to run, chase, wrestle, bark, and explore. Because she spent hours alone while you're at work, she'll be raring to go when you walk through the door at night. Fifteen minutes of play here and there is hardly adequate in her eyes.

Now you know why she endlessly drops a toy at your feet, chases and nips at your pant legs, pesters your other pets, and just generally gets into mischief. She needs to play!

Toys and chewies help occupy her time, but she needs time with people and other animals, too, not just to teach her social skills, but also because she gets lonely, like any living being.

HAPPY PUPPY

If you work full-time, consider hiring a pet sitter to come in for a midday play session to keep your puppy company.

Balancing Teaching, Guidance, and Play

Right about now, you might be thinking that owning a Golden Retriever puppy is a lot of work. In some ways it is because you're adding another family member who needs education, discipline, and love to grow into a socially acceptable adult.

But don't lose sight of why you got your puppy. While you teach her new things, play with her, and redirect her misbehavior, remember she's just a baby and she's not purposely trying to get into trouble. She's trying to figure out the world around her, and she can only do that by trial and error. She'll learn faster through fun and play than via punishment and isolation. And you'll both have a lot of fun while you navigate these first memorable months together.

	SOCIAL	BEHAVIOR	TRAINING	PHYSICAL	HEALTH
MONTH 1	Breeder starts socialization		Littermates and mother teach appropriate canine behavior	Rapid growth	
MONTH 2	Breeder starts socialization				
MONTH 3	Socialization at home with new owner and other pets	Fear-imprint period	Begin house- and crate training		1st DHPP vaccine
MONTH 4		Teething begins—heavy chewing period	Enroll in puppy class		2nd DHPP vaccine
MONTH 5	Socialization in public		Ready for basic commands	Switch to adult food	3rd DHPP and rabies vaccines
MONTH 6					
MONTH 7		Adult teeth are in—chewing continues	Enroll in basic obedience class	Moderate growth	Sexual maturity
MONTH 8					
MONTH 9					
MONTH 10			Ready for more advanced training		
MONTH 11				Slow growth—reaches adult size	Annual vaccinations and checkup
MONTH 12 AND BEYOND					

The Rebel

This month your Golden Retriever puppy isn't quite a teenager but he's not a baby either, and he grows dramatically between months 4 and 5 (weeks 16 through 20). In this month, we talk about physical changes like teething and growth. We also look at how you can monitor his health through all the changes he's going through. Also, by now he's completed his vaccines so you can take him out in public to continue and expand his socialization.

In addition to his physical changes, his behavior is rapidly changing, too, as he grows and gains confidence. You'll see him exert his independence, and he'll test your limits to see what the rules are and what he can get away with. You have a good foundation in place to guide you both through this headstrong month, and your consistent training and guidance will prevent behavioral problems before they become entrenched habits. Your priorities right now are exercise, teaching, and plenty of chew toys.

Your Golden Retriever is ready for a license, microchip, and ID tags. And of course, your active puppy will give your entire family hours of laughs and fun.

PHYSICAL DEVELOPMENT

Think of your puppy as a preteen right now. Some physical characteristics are permanent, but his awkward proportions and teething pain are, thankfully, temporary.

Males and females often look a lot alike at this age. At the same time, puppies from the same litter might look very different from each other because they develop at different rates. His coat is still short and not very thick, and his head might look out of proportion this month as his muzzle elongates and his head develops. Don't worry—he'll look like a Golden Retriever again soon!

His housetraining should be almost complete by now. He should be able to hold it for 2 hours during the day and sleep through the night.

All Paws and Legs

During this month, your pup's body grows rapidly and at different rates. He'll reach approximately 60 percent of his adult height this month and about half of his adult weight.

For a while, he'll look out of proportion and clumsy because he's growing from the outside in. His paws, nose, ears, and tail will be too big for his body—almost adult size. Eventually his torso will start to lengthen, and his legs will gradually catch up.

A male who will eventually weigh 65 to 75 pounds weighs about 30 to 35 pounds at 4 months. An adult male who is 24 inches tall is about 14 inches at the shoulders during Month 5. A female who will weigh 55 to 65 pounds at adulthood weighs roughly 26 to 32 pounds and is about 11 or 12 inches tall at the shoulders this month. Note these are estimates based on a dog who falls within the *breed standard* when mature. Your dog might be larger, but most Golden Retrievers aren't smaller than the breed standard.

DOG TALK

The **breed standard** is a description of the ideal Golden Retriever as developed by the Golden Retriever Club of America, the parent club of the breed in the American Kennel Club (AKC). The standard specifies guidelines for size, color, structure, and temperament.

His brain is developing, too, and by 5 months old, he'll have a maturity level similar to what you'd expect in a 10-year-old child. He's still very much a puppy, and he's approaching puberty. He'll be very active and always a step ahead of you this month, much to his delight.

TIPS AND TAILS

You might think all Golden Retrievers look alike, but some have identifying characteristics that set them apart from their fellow pups. Does your puppy have a "zipper" or cowlick on his nose? This is a little ridge of standing-up hair that runs down his forehead between his eyes. There's nothing wrong with this little quirk, and many owners point to their dog's zipper with pride.

Teething Continues

This month, his adult molars along the sides of his mouth start to come in, followed by his canine teeth—the two upper and two lower fangs in the front. His teeth won't finish emerging to their maximum height until he's 10 to 12 months old, so that means he'll continue to chew voraciously during the next few months to ease his teething pain.

Except for his canines, his adult teeth come in behind his puppy teeth. If his puppy teeth aren't loose and falling out by 6 months, have your vet examine his mouth. If his puppy teeth don't fall out soon enough, his emerging adult teeth can come in crooked and cause bite problems.

HEALTH

Vaccines and heartworm prevention are priorities for your puppy during his fifth month because once his vaccines are completed, he can safely venture out in public with you.

As you travel with your pup, you might find he gets carsick, so spend some time acclimating him to the car to prevent tummy upsets.

Finishing Puppy Vaccines

If you didn't finish your Golden Retriever's vaccines last month, be sure to schedule a vet visit this month to get his last DHPP booster. The series should be complete by 16 weeks of age.

He also gets his first rabies vaccine this month.

Considering Additional Vaccines

After your pup has completed his core vaccines, discuss additional vaccines with your veterinarian so you can decide together when and if your puppy needs them.

Noncore vaccines should be administered based on your geographic location, lifestyle, and risk of the disease. Consider the environment your Golden Retriever will be exposed to—outdoors, hunting, contact with other animals, tick-infested areas, etc. Regional considerations also come into play—for example, if you live in an area with rattlesnakes.

Here are some other vaccines to discuss with your vet:

Bordetella: Commonly called kennel cough, bordetella is a group of upper-respiratory bacteria that causes coughing, sneezing, and other symptoms similar to the common cold in humans. Kennel cough is highly contagious and spreads from dog to dog rapidly. Healthy adult dogs recover quickly, but in puppies, it can progress to pneumonia. There are several strains of kennel cough, and the vaccine doesn't protect against all of them.

The vaccine is given either intranasally, orally, or by injection and is required by boarding kennels and dog daycares. To be effective, a booster should be administered a week before exposure to other dogs. So if you're going to board your puppy, he should receive the vaccine at least 1 week before going to the kennel followed by a booster every 6 to 12 months.

Coronavirus: This disease can be quite severe in puppies, especially if he also has other infections. The virus is transmitted by contact with infected oral and fecal secretions. Once a dog is infected, the disease is shed in his stool for several months. The puppy might have no symptoms at all, or he might have diarrhea, which can cause dehydration. Coronavirus is rarely fatal and responds well to treatment, so vaccination is not usually recommended.

Giardia: If you camp, hike, or hunt with your Golden Retriever, you might consider this vaccine. Along with coccidia, giardia is a single-celled protozoa the dog ingests through infected water or soil. Puppies kept in dirty living situations often get giardia or coccidia. Adult dogs who hunt or spend a lot of time outdoors in the woods or near water may be reinfected over and over. The main symptom is watery or mucousy diarrhea. The vaccine doesn't protect against infection, but it does prevent the dog from shedding the protozoa. Giardia is a *zoonotic disease,* which means humans can also be affected by it. It's inexpensive and easy to treat, so most people don't choose to vaccinate for giardia.

DOG TALK
A **zoonotic disease** is transmissible from one species to another—for example, from dogs to humans.

Lyme disease: Transmitted by a bite from a tick, Lyme disease is one of several tick-borne diseases. If your dog spends time in the woods, or if ticks are common in your area, discuss this vaccine with your veterinarian. (Note it doesn't protect against other tick-borne diseases, though.) The initial vaccine is two doses, 2 to 4 weeks apart, followed by annual booster at the start of tick season, which could vary depending on where you live.

Leptospirosis: Leptospirosis is a bacterial disease transmitted by skin contact with the urine of infected animals, primarily rats and mice. It can also contaminate streams, rivers, and lakes, where a dog might ingest it. Dogs should receive this vaccine only if you live in an area where there have been known cases of the disease. Two doses are recommended, 2 to 4 weeks apart, along with an annual booster. Leptospirosis is another zoonotic disease and is, therefore, transmissible to humans.

Rattlesnake venom: This vaccine protects against western diamondback rattlesnake venom; it also provides some protection against the eastern diamondback rattlesnake. If you live in an area where these snakes are common, the recommendation is two doses, 1 month apart, and a yearly booster.

Tetanus: Tetanus is commonly found in soil contaminated by horse and cow manure, and it enters the body through an open wound. This vaccine isn't often recommended because dogs have a natural resistance to infection from the bacteria.

Heartworms and Preventatives

Heartworm is caused by a parasitic worm and is transmitted to your dog by mosquitoes. Formerly confined to the Southeast, today it affects dogs throughout the United States.

The mosquito bites an infected dog and ingests the heartworm larvae in that dog's blood. Then the mosquito moves on to your dog, bites, and injects the larvae into your dog, where they migrate to the bloodstream. There they grow into mature heartworms that attack the pulmonary arteries that lead from the lungs to the heart. As the worms reproduce, your dog's body tries to fight them off and sometimes has an allergic reaction to the worms.

You can prevent heartworm infestation in your puppy by administering a monthly prescription preventive that kills the immature larvae before they have a chance to grow or reproduce. The preventative medication can be started any time after your puppy reaches 8 weeks of age and well before mosquito season begins in your region.

Once a puppy reaches 6 months old, your veterinarian will need to do a heartworm blood test before beginning the medication. Then, your Golden Retriever will require an annual retest. Some people discontinue the preventative during the winter months, so a retest is required before you restart in the spring.

Symptoms of heartworm include coughing, weight loss, vomiting blood, and ultimately heart failure and death. Treatment of heartworm is long and hard on your dog. Arsenic is used to kill the worms, and the dog must be strictly confined. Too much exercise can cause a large mass of worms to go into the lungs and cause serious complications.

During treatment, the worms die slowly over a period of 4 to 6 weeks and their bodies are passed into the lungs, where your pup's immune system destroys them. When that step is complete, your dog is treated with another medication to kill the surviving larvae. A heartworm test at the end of treatment confirms that the parasites are completely gone.

As you can see, although treatment is an option, prevention is by far the best choice for dealing with the threat of heartworm.

Giving Your Puppy a Pill

Golden Retriever puppies will eat anything, so you might never have a problem giving yours a pill. Hide it in a dab of peanut butter, liver sausage, cheese, or canned food, and you're done … you hope.

However, some Goldens are masters at eating *around* the pill and then spitting it out. In this case, you'll need to be more assertive. If you've been doing handling exercises with your puppy, he's used to you looking at his teeth and touching his face, so you're halfway there.

Standing behind your pup, put one hand over his muzzle and your thumb and middle fingers behind his large canine teeth on either side. Squeeze in his lips. Then pry open his mouth with your other hand, push the pill to the back of his tongue and down his throat, and close his mouth. Hold his mouth closed, and stroke his throat with your finger until he swallows. Give him a spoonful of canned food, cheese, or other special treat so he'll keep swallowing and you can be sure the pill is down.

If that method doesn't work for you and your pup, you can purchase an inexpensive pill gun from your vet. This is basically a long syringe that holds a pill on the end. Coat the pill with butter so it goes down easily, stick the plunger in the back of your pup's mouth, and inject the pill. Hold his mouth closed and stroke his throat until you feel him swallow the pill.

Dealing with Tear Stains

Your Golden Retriever puppy might get runny eyes from occasional eye irritations like dust or clogged tear ducts. Puppies sometimes have temporary tearing as their eyes grow, but the condition eventually disappears. Chronic runny eyes can cause tear stains, reddish brown streaks running down his face from the inside corner of his eyes.

For constant tear stains, your vet might refer you to a canine ophthalmologist who can determine if flushing out your pup's clogged tear ducts would be beneficial, thus minimizing tear stains. The ophthalmologist will conduct in-depth examination of your puppy's eyes, checking for entropion, juvenile cataracts, or other possible causes.

If your puppy has tear stains, clean the area daily with a damp cloth and keep it dry to prevent infection. If your vet agrees, eye drops or saline solution might help prevent further irritation. Pet supply stores carry products that will fade the tear stains, but most stains don't go away completely until the hair is replaced by new growth.

Coping with Carsickness

Now that his vaccines are finished, your puppy can go out in public with you. Golden Retrievers love nothing better than a car ride, but all that excitement can be too much, and suddenly … he's carsick. A puppy's ears and sense of balance aren't mature yet, so he's more likely to get sick than an adult dog. And once he's gotten carsick, he dreads riding in the car, making it very likely to happen again. Typical signs he's getting sick include yawning, panting, whining, drooling, and eventually retching and vomiting.

To help prevent carsickness, confine him in a crate so he can't wander around the car or look out the windows, which contributes to nausea. Cover the crate so he can't see out, and be sure to anchor it so it doesn't fall over when you go around a corner. Or put him on a harness and attach it to a seatbelt so he faces forward. Lower a couple of windows about 1 inch to equalize the air pressure in the car and keep it cooler inside. Give your pup a toy he loves when you put him in the car—call it his special car toy, so he makes positive associations with car rides.

TIPS AND TAILS

An airbag is dangerous to puppies, so disable it or put him in the backseat (like you would a human baby).

Ginger is a natural treatment for nausea, so a gingersnap cookie might help settle his stomach. Or open a capsule of ginger and pour the granules onto some food or a bit of yogurt. Also limit his food and water an hour before travel.

If nothing seems to work, talk to your veterinarian about motion sickness medication for your dog.

If your puppy has developed a phobia against riding in the car, retrain him to think of it as a fun experience. Stop taking him on long car rides for a couple weeks. Instead, take him on short trips to fun places. If every car ride takes him to the vet or boarding kennel, no wonder he gets nervous about the trip!

You could also feed him treats or meals in the car. If he won't get in, start by feeding him next to the car and work up to a treat on the running board, a treat on the car floor, and one on the seat. Don't start the engine or go anywhere; just let him get used to the idea that the car isn't a bad thing.

Then start the car and turn it off immediately while he's in the crate or backseat. Sit in the car with the engine running for a minute or two while he eats and then shut it off and let him out.

Gradually progress to where you drive to the end of the driveway, down to the corner, and around the block. Your goal is a series of short, pleasant trips without your puppy getting sick.

NUTRITION

Your puppy's appetite might fluctuate this month because his growth is uneven—one day his legs are longer, the next his feet are growing, and then nothing might change for a week. Teething pain also contributes to his occasional lack of appetite. This is normal and nothing to worry about, unless you see symptoms of illness.

Monitoring Your Puppy's Weight

There's no hard-and-fast rule about how much a Golden Retriever should weigh at any given age because their size varies so much within the breed. A shorter, stocky Golden Retriever looks heavier even if he's the right weight. A taller, lanky Golden puppy has finer bones and looks lighter overall. A taller puppy doesn't necessarily need more food. If you hear or read that his weight should fall somewhere between 26 and 35 pounds, that's not very specific, so you really need to look at your dog's body and condition to assess his weight (see Appendix B).

Even though a young puppy gets a lot of exercise, he can still eat too much and get fat. An overweight puppy has a higher risk for injury because his bones aren't strong enough yet to carry the extra pounds. If you can't feel his ribs or see that his tummy has a little tuckup behind his rib cage (see Appendix B), cut back on his food a bit. Give him a little more in the morning and less at night so he'll have extra calories to get him through his active day.

If his coat is shiny, his eyes are clear, and his body feels and looks good, you're feeding him the right amount. If his coat is dingy, his eyes are runny, or his tummy looks bloated all the time (not just after he's eaten), he might have worms and need another round of deworming treatment.

Switching to Adult Food

If you haven't switched him to adult food yet, do it now. As you did when you brought him home and changed brands of food, make the switch gradually. Mix 25 percent of the adult food with his puppy food for several days. Then go to 50 percent of each for a few days. Complete the switch after a week or so.

Now is also the time to switch your Golden puppy to two meals a day. Start by gradually cutting back the amount of his midday meal and adding it to his other two meals so he's still eating the same amount but at fewer mealtimes. Right now he's consuming 3 to 5 cups a day—more than he will as an adult. (Usually the recommended amounts on the dog food bags are too much food for a Golden Retriever.)

Most dogs today don't do the work they were bred for, and a pet Golden doesn't necessarily need food designated specifically for Golden Retrievers. A quality adult dog food is perfectly adequate.

Paying Attention to the Feces

A puppy's bowel movements provide important clues about his health. Examine a fresh stool for an accurate assessment.

It should be formed and solid, not runny or extremely dry. Blood or mucus could be signs of illness, a sudden change of food, or a result of eating something he shouldn't. A very black stool could have digested blood in it. Also look for foreign objects such as grass, gravel, fabric, or bits of plastic from a toy or bone. Freshly deposited feces also could contain live worms if he's infested.

While you're changing your pup to adult food, check for loose stools or diarrhea. Cut back on the new food, or slow down the transition, if he has loose stools. You can also add 1 tablespoon yogurt to his meal to help his digestion.

Keep an eye on your puppy's stool volume, too. A large amount of stool could mean your puppy isn't absorbing his food well. Or you might be feeding him too much. Decrease his food a little, or change to a higher-quality food. Dogs who have a small stool volume are using their food to its maximum potential.

GROOMING

Although he doesn't have much of a coat yet, eventually he will grow the Golden Retriever's standard thick, double coat. As he grows up, he'll require regular weekly grooming sessions—and more often during shedding season. His ears also need regular attention so you can catch problems before they become chronic.

If you keep up with it, grooming shouldn't take more than 20 to 30 minutes a week to complete.

A Golden Retriever's Coat

A Golden Retriever's outer coat contains natural oils that repel dirt and water—perfect for a hunting retriever and an added bonus for the pet owner. (However, his coat should never feel oily or greasy to the touch. If it does, he might need a change in diet. Ask your breeder or have him checked by your vet.) The soft undercoat protects your puppy from extreme cold and heat. Dogs that spend a lot of time indoors or live in a hot climate won't develop such a heavy coat.

Goldens shed lightly year-round and heavily twice a year, usually in the spring and fall. Females also shed heavily about 12 to 16 weeks after their heat cycle—about the same time they would be blowing coat (shedding) if they were weaning a litter of puppies.

Even if a female isn't bred, she'll normally drop coat at this time. The undercoat starts to shed first, followed by the outer coat, so you might have to brush her daily during shedding season. Frequent brushing speeds up the shedding process, and the sooner the old coat comes out, the sooner the new coat grows in.

Spayed females don't shed like unaltered females do because they don't have the hormonal signal from a heat cycle. Their thick undercoat is cottony and mats easily, and sometimes it appears softer and curlier than a male's or unaltered female's, so it needs more grooming, with special attention paid to removing the excess undercoat.

TIPS AND TAILS
The age of your puppy's first shedding cycle depends on when he was born. A puppy born in September might not shed his puppy coat until the following May or June. A puppy born in the spring might not get a heavy coat his first winter. A lot depends on the climate where you live and the type of coat his parents have.

Frequent brushing speeds up the shedding process, and the sooner the old coat comes out, the sooner the new coat grows in. Frequent brushing also distributes the natural oils in your Golden's coat and keeps it healthy and shiny. Brushing removes a lot of dirt that gets down in the undercoat, too.

You've been teaching your puppy to tolerate and even enjoy grooming, so getting him used to brushing shouldn't be much of a problem. If the weather is nice, you'll save yourself a lot of cleanup later if you brush him outside. And in the spring, the birds will thank you for this because they'll use the excess fur for soft nesting material!

To begin, first brush lightly over his outer coat with a slicker brush to remove the loosest hair. Some people stop at this step, but don't, because you haven't really accomplished much yet. To continue, begin brushing again, this time at his rear end, and work your way forward, brushing in the same direction his coat grows, away from his head. Lift a section of hair with the back of one hand while you brush with the other so you can get close to his skin and remove more hair—a process called *line brushing*. Don't forget the feathers on his rear legs. Even his tail needs attention. His coat is heaviest under his throat and along his shoulders, so pay extra attention to these areas.

Be careful as you brush. A slicker can scratch his skin, so don't use too much pressure, especially near his skin.

TIPS AND TAILS

Use a spray-on conditioner on each section of his coat when you brush him—mane and tail detanglers made for horses work well for this. The brush will go through more easily and cause less breakage.

Next, use the slicker to brush *against* the direction his coat grows to loosen more undercoat. (This is the one time you brush against the grain.)

By now you're covered in dog hair, but you haven't gotten it all yet. Switch to a wide-toothed metal comb because you still have mountains of undercoat to remove, starting again at his rear end and working your way forward. Comb out his front armpits and around his ears, areas especially prone to mats. Clip out any mats that are too thick to be combed out. By taking this extra combing step, you might be able to brush less often.

Use a damp cloth on his face and outer ears rather than a brush or comb. When you're completely finished brushing, run the wet cloth over his entire body to pick up any stray hairs and remove static electricity or dandruff. A fabric softener sheet also removes static in dry weather.

Golden Retrievers shouldn't have doggy odor. If yours does, check his ears for a problem. If his coat is dry and he has dandruff, he could have a skin condition or allergies. If you've left soap in his coat after a bath, it could also cause irritation. (See Month 6 for more on bathing your pup.)

Cleaning His Ears

Goldens are susceptible to ear infections. Because your puppy's ears lie flat against his head, they limit airflow and trap moisture and debris inside. Goldens are also prone to allergies, which cause redness and inflammation in the ear area.

Wipe out his ears every week so he's used to the procedure and will be more tolerant if he needs treatment. And after he swims, hunts, or runs outdoors in tall grass, check his ears for dirt, grass seeds, ticks, and moisture, and dry and wipe out his ears thoroughly.

Using a barely damp soft cloth or paper towel wrapped around the end of your finger, hold up the ear leather (the flap) and away, and wipe his ear from the inside to the outer edge. Also clean out all the nooks and crannies with a cloth covering your little finger. This is all he should need on a regular basis. Cleaning too often removes the protective layer of wax that protects his inner ear so don't overdo it.

If his ears are especially dirty, use a cotton swab to gently clean his ear canal. If your puppy doesn't cooperate, this might take two people—one to keep him still and one to clean his ear. Again, hold up the ear leather. Turn the swab in one direction as you put it in, and hold it in the same direction as you reverse out of the ear so you won't redeposit the dirt. Don't go too deeply because you don't want to damage your puppy's eardrum. Also, if your puppy thrashes around, you don't want to accidentally poke into his inner ear.

If something gets down in his ear canal, it can cause an infection. If you see reddish-brown gunk in his ears or they smell bad, it could be a yeast infection caused by water, an infection caused by a foreign object, or even ear mites. A Golden with an ear problem will shake his head, hold his head at an odd angle, scratch at his ears, and even whimper as he tries to ease his discomfort. He might even be unwilling to let you touch his ears. Visit the vet for an accurate diagnosis and treatment plan.

TIPS AND TAILS

If your Golden develops chronic ear problems, your vet might recommend medication or regular cleaning with an ear wash product. Squirt the ointment into his ear, and massage the base of his ear where it meets his jaw line. This pushes the medication deeper into his ear canal. Your pup will immediately shake his head, which distributes the ointment in his outer ear. If you use an ear wash, thoroughly dry his ears after cleaning. A diet change might also help with chronic ear problems.

Trimming His Nails

Trim your dog's toenails weekly as part of your grooming routine; otherwise, they'll cause his feet to splay, which affects his balance and ability to stand and walk correctly. Overly long nails also contribute to the development of arthritis as his legs take on added stress. (We cover toenail trimming more in Month 3.)

And don't forget the dewclaws while you're trimming. If they get too long, they can easily snag when he's scratching or digging.

SOCIAL SKILLS

Finally your Golden Retriever puppy is able to go out with you and meet the world. He can accompany you on walks, to the park, to family activities, and on other outings.

As bold and confident as he is at home, he's now on unfamiliar turf, so he might be uncertain your first few times out. But that will soon change as he meets new friends. And do introduce him to new friends. That's part of his necessary socialization. By teaching him to like and respect people now, you're preventing future problems.

The Jolly Routine

Actions speak louder than words, so when your puppy is uncertain or frightened, show him by your behavior that there's nothing to be afraid of.

Select an item that makes your puppy wag his tail when he sees it—a ball, a squeaky toy, a stuffed animal, or another small toy. When you're out and about and you spot something you know will scare him, like a large truck driving by, pull out the toy. If possible, before he can even react to the scary thing, act happy, play with the toy, and pretend you're having a wonderful time. Expect your puppy to be confused, but keep going. After a minute or two, put away the toy and ignore him. Wait about 5 minutes, pull out the toy again, and repeat your excitement. You'll know your routine has started to ease his fears when he wags his tail as soon you produce the toy.

You might not have time to head off his fear, but this is a good starting point to distract him from what frightens him. It could take up to 6 weeks of repetition to change his attitude about whatever scares him, but those few weeks hardly compare to a lifetime of fearlessness.

Socializing to Strangers

When you're out in public with your puppy, you are his protector. Well-meaning strangers will charge up to him, hands outstretched, to say hello. Children will crash toward him with a toy and throw their arms around his neck.

As you try to keep people from overwhelming him, they'll respond, "Oh, it's okay! I *love* dogs!" That's good for them, but this isn't about them; it's about your puppy. And after a few of these bulldozer encounters, your pup will hide in fear or take off in the opposite direction when someone approaches him. Worse, he might feel cornered and snap.

Don't let that happen. Turn into a linebacker, and block all comers from your puppy. Don't be afraid of being rude. After all, you wouldn't let them charge at your children, would you? If you do your job, your puppy won't feel he has to defend himself from others.

TIPS AND TAILS

A dog who grows up fearful of strangers will think he has to take matters into his own jaws when danger approaches. He'll bark aggressively and even bite to protect himself—or you—when someone approaches.

Hold your hand up to stop the incoming person. If your puppy seems happy and ready to interact, let him approach the person first. Have the person stop, stand sideways to your puppy (which is less imposing), and even crouch down so he'll feel safe. Use your jolly routine so your puppy understands everything is safe.

Let him watch the person and decide for himself if he wants to say hi. If he still isn't comfortable, respect his wishes and don't force him. Put a serious look on your face and explain he's "in training." Hand the person a treat, invite them to toss it in your puppy's direction, and move on.

Socializing to Children

At home or in public, your Golden Retriever will meet children of all ages and, you hope, love each one immediately. Tell children you meet to "ask the puppy" if he would like to meet them. If your puppy says no, ask them to respect his feelings today because he may be tired.

How do you know if your puppy isn't in the mood to play? He'll hide behind you, crouch down, avoid looking at the kids, or move away.

If he's ready to say hi, put two fingers through his collar to keep him from jumping on the child. Have the child stand quietly and speak nicely to the puppy—not in a high, squeaky, excited voice—and let your pup choose to approach the child, not the other way around.

Have kids pet him on his chest or his back where he won't dive for their fingers, and let them put a treat on the ground for him to eat.

Socializing to the Groomer

Many Golden Retriever owners have their dogs professionally groomed every 6 to 8 weeks if they don't do it themselves on a regular basis. Your groomer will be eternally grateful if you bring in your pup for an introduction at a young age, before he has nasty mats and long toenails. Even the nicest Golden Retriever might panic and snap at a blow dryer or grooming noose.

Now that he's had all his shots, it's the perfect time for your puppy to meet the groomer. Expect to pay something for these introductory visits—you're taking up the groomer's time, after all. Your groomer will put your pup in the tub and spray some water around him. She'll stand him on the grooming table and let him explore the surface and the different tools she uses. She'll also handle him, run the brush over him, and give him a few treats that you provide. She might run the dryer nearby while barely letting the air reach him, and she might put him in a crate for a few minutes. She might let you stand nearby and watch, but don't interfere unless absolutely necessary for your pup's safety.

After a practice visit or two, leave your pup at the groomer's while she bathes him. Regular visits prepare your Golden Retriever to accept the groomer and the grooming process without a problem throughout his life.

Going for a Walk

Enjoy daily walks, when your pup can experience new sights, sounds, and smells. A walk is also the perfect time for your puppy to practice sit, down, walking politely, and paying attention to you.

Don't worry about how far you get on your walks. There's so much to experience, you might not get very far while he meets people, sniffs, and explores.

Right now, walk your puppy on a 4- or 6-foot leash. A long line or retractable leash won't give you enough control, and he could easily pull it out of your hands if he gets frightened and runs. Also, don't let him off leash in parks, on trails, or at the beach unless you're in a fully fenced enclosure.

TIPS AND TAILS

Remember that your Golden Retriever puppy is still a puppy and will tire easily. Plan to walk about 10 minutes per month of age. So if he's 4 months old, a 40-minute walk will tire him out.

While you walk, he might balk at new things he sees, like mailboxes, parking lot flags, or a motorcycle zooming by. He might bark at cars or kids on skateboards. If he sees a street vendor dressed like a pizza and tossing around an advertising sign, don't be surprised if he spooks. He'll think he's encountered an alien!

The world is full of exciting new smells and sounds he'll discover as you spend time together walking. He'll encounter trash in the gutter and gum on the sidewalk. He'll know where the nearest restaurant is and quickly recognize the scent of other dogs. Busy traffic will smell like burning rubber, and honking horns and police sirens will startle him. Let him investigate for himself without comforting him, and use the jolly routine to help him gain confidence when you see him faltering.

There are a few places you shouldn't take him yet. Street fairs and festivals have hundreds of people jammed together, loud music, food smells, and traffic. Remember, his eye level is around your knees, so all these unfamiliar things coming at him from above his head can be terrifying to him. Work up to crowded situations slowly. And don't take him to Fourth of July celebrations or anywhere fireworks are being used.

Visiting Dog Parks

Visits to the dog park can do more harm than good at this age. You have no way of knowing if all the dogs there are vaccinated or trained, and many owners chat with each other and ignore their dogs, allowing them to bully other dogs unmonitored, squabble over toys, and even fight. There's no "lifeguard" on duty enforcing rules or asking owners to remove rude or aggressive dogs at dog parks. Remember, you alone are your dog's protector. And you never know—your own puppy might play too rough at this age, too!

Puppies mimic other dogs' behavior. Any kind of aggression from others could teach your puppy that this type of behavior is appropriate. You don't want your Golden Retriever to grow up to be a bully, so if you see other dogs playing rough or acting aggressively at the dog park, leave.

At peak periods, usually early evenings and weekends, the dog park is crowded and play can easy get out of control as the dogs become overstimulated. A normal dog can quickly be overwhelmed, much less a shy or sensitive puppy. Most Goldens aren't ready for this kind of interaction.

If you must go, consider taking him on quiet weekday mornings when the park isn't so busy, especially when he's young and it's new to him.

TIPS AND TAILS

Wherever you are, be a responsible dog owner and clean up after your puppy. Carry pickup bags, and either deposit them in nearby trash cans or take them home with you. In some jurisdictions, you can be cited if you're caught leaving your dog's droppings.

BEHAVIOR

Your young Golden Retriever's behavior changes dramatically this month as he asserts his independence and explodes with endless preteen puppy energy. Prepare yourself with consistent puppy management techniques and a sense of humor, and you'll get through this fun and challenging period with your sanity intact.

Your Shadow Disappears

While your puppy is busy physically growing this month, his mind is equally busy absorbing everything it can. He'll have endless energy, and very little self-control; he's easily distracted, and he'll use any excuse to ignore you. During this period of creative obedience, he'll tease you by coming close to you and then quickly taking off again or grabbing toys and playing keep-away. Busy, busy, busy! How will you get him under control?

Be sure your puppy gets plenty of exercise, training, and mental stimulation this month. It might seem harder to get his attention, but keep working on handling and control exercises. And know you can demand more from him now because he's not an infant anymore.

If he's not listening to you, let him drag a leash when you're there to supervise. That way, you'll be able to pick up the leash and get his attention to enforce your instructions.

Keeping Your Golden on Leash

When you two are away from the house—whether you're taking a walk down the sidewalk in your neighborhood, hiking in the woods, or romping in open fields— *never* let your puppy off leash. At this age, he probably gets pretty fired up when it's time for a walk. He's impulsive, distracted, and prone to developing selective hearing. In other words, he ignores you.

In addition to the leash, make liberal use of the sit command to get his attention back on you while you're on walks.

HAPPY PUPPY

You'll know it when you see it—suddenly your calm, well-behaved Golden Retriever puppy will cut loose and take off around the yard or house (or both!) for no apparent reason, moving so fast his rear end looks like it's in front of his chest. This zooming is pure puppy exuberance, so let him run and burn off some steam. Zooming is a better activity for outdoors, where random items in his path—like furniture and children—won't interrupt his fun.

Dealing with Chewing

At 5 months, your Golden Retriever puppy is still teething so expect to see him chewing this month. Continue to provide him with sturdy chew toys. As he gets bigger, some of the old toys and bones may no longer be safe, so monitor what he's got around him and in his mouth, and remove the unsafe toys. When his adult teeth are in, he'll continue to chew to ease his gum and mouth discomfort.

With that in mind, monitor his behavior and redirect him to appropriate chewies. Don't give him household items like old shoes. He'll have trouble telling which ones are his to chew and which ones he should leave alone.

Also take steps to ensure he just can't chew certain things. Don't put a bed in his crate if he's a chewer. Keep your family's clothes picked up and all shoes put away. Close bedroom doors. And use a bitter spray product, available at pet-supply stores, on items you don't want him to chew. The bitter spray makes whatever it's sprayed on taste bad so your pup will avoid it. If you don't have bitter spray, you could use mouthwash or red pepper sauce mixed with water instead. Be careful not to spray your homemade mixture on surfaces that will stain or fade.

If you find he's chewed something, put him in another room so he doesn't see you clean up the mess. If he watches you, he'll be fascinated that you're paying so much attention to what he's done, and he'll do it again for you.

Working on Bite Inhibition

The last critical window for your puppy to learn proper bite inhibition is 16 to 20 weeks. His puppy classes are teaching him not to bite hard or bully other puppies. Friendly adult dogs are teaching him his dog manners. You are continuing to socialize him to many people of all sizes and ages, you've taught him not to play-bite, and you handle his body regularly so he'll let you touch him anywhere.

You can't guarantee your puppy won't ever be hurt or frightened enough that he would bite someone. But if he's been taught never to touch a person's clothing or body with his teeth, his reaction is likely to cause much less damage—hopefully just a growl or nip instead of a full-on bite. Your veterinarian and groomer, among others, will thank you.

If he touches you with his mouth, yell "Ouch!"—just like you did when he was little—and leave him abruptly. Give him a few seconds to ponder his crime and realize the fun stopped when he put his mouth on you. When you return, ask for a sit, a down, and a few minutes of calm. Then return to what you were doing together.

Help him learn that he can play hard and still respond to your commands. Get him excited and then ask him to settle by doing a sit or down. Be sure he'll stop and calm down for anyone who's going to play with him, too. He'll soon learn that roughhousing does not have to include biting of any kind.

Correcting Your Puppy

By now, your Golden Retriever puppy has an idea of right versus wrong in many situations, but during this rebellious phase, you'll have more trouble getting his attention.

Commonsense discipline has its place while you're raising your puppy. It's never necessary to yell at or hit him. Instead, use a sharp phrase like "Ack!" or "Psssst!" to interrupt what he's doing, immediately praise him for stopping, and redirect him to something else like a sit or walking away.

TIPS AND TAILS

Don't use his name when disciplining your puppy. If he hears "[Name], no!" he'll eventually think his name is a correction, and you don't want that.

You might wonder why we didn't suggest you use "No" to interrupt your pup. "No" too easily turns into "No, no, no, no, NO!" and when you get excited, your puppy just hears you making a bunch of noise. You don't sound calm or in charge, and your puppy will ignore you until you get to the last angry "NO!"

Outgrowing Bad Behavior—Not Gonna Happen

"He's just a puppy" is an excuse that isn't going to work for much longer. If he realizes there are no consequences when he misbehaves, he doesn't know his behavior is unacceptable. Any bad habits he's forming now will be much harder to deal with when adolescence is in full swing next month. Remember, a habit takes much longer to *break* than to *make*.

Sure, you're tempted to let him get away with unacceptable behavior like jumping on you once in a while because it's tiring to supervise him *constantly*. But by doing this, you're inadvertently rewarding his bad behavior. When he gets away with something sometimes, he'll try it again and again.

On the other hand, if he *never* gets rewarded for jumping, he'll eventually quit trying.

HAPPY PUPPY

Don't forget to praise your puppy when he's doing something right. Once he's learned a behavior, it's easy to take it for granted. But if you don't reinforce it, the behavior will begin to deteriorate, and suddenly you have a puppy who acts like he never learned it in the first place.

The entire family needs to be consistent with discipline and training. When one person in the family allows the puppy on the couch and someone else doesn't, he soon figures it out and will jump on the couch when the enforcer isn't around.

Stick to your guns, and enforce all the rules, all the time, and make liberal use of the crate for short time-outs when you can't watch him. Loving discipline, plenty of exercise, and readily available chew toys help you and your puppy negotiate this stage.

TRAINING

Scientists call this age the *avoidance period*. Your Golden Retriever puppy is no longer hanging on your every word, and because there's so much to see and do in the world, he wants to do all of it *right now!*

This month, break his lessons into small steps so you can keep his attention and improve his chances for success. Practice a lot this month, and train thoroughly, always being patient but firm.

Also be sure to keep training fun or he'll quickly lose interest. A few 1-minute training sessions throughout the day have a bigger impact on him than one 10-minute session, and he'll learn to look forward to these short lessons in his everyday life.

What's in a Name?

Your dog's name should be a wonderful word he happily responds to. Does your puppy know his name? Does he react to it? If he doesn't, it's time he learned.

Load up your pocket with treats, and take him out in the backyard or for a walk. Let him get distracted, sniffing at the grass or another mildly interesting scent. Say his name once, in a normal voice, without a loud or urgent tone. Does he turn and look at you? Or does he ignore you? If he looks at you, give him a treat and have a happy dance.

Usually, when you say a person's name, you expect him to look at you, and you then tell him what's on your mind. You wouldn't say his name and then ignore him. Often that's exactly what we do to our dogs. Or when he doesn't respond immediately, we say his name several times. He might think his name is Rover … Rover … *Rover!* The more we chatter, the less he listens. If your puppy isn't listening, practice getting his attention and rewarding him when he responds to his name.

TIPS AND TAILS

Your puppy's name is not a command. If you mean "Come," say, "Rover, come," not just "Rover." And never use his name as punishment. That's a surefire way to get him to ignore you when you call.

How many names does your puppy have? Is he Roverdoofusgoofus when he's being a darling little puppy, and Rover-roller-over when he's into mischief? Is he Rover-Johnson-come-here-right-now when he misbehaves? All these names could further confuse him.

Don't waste the power of your puppy's name. If you say his name, have a reason for doing so, and give him something to do when he responds to you. You need to be worth leaving that luscious scent behind.

Reinforcing Household Rules

As adolescence approaches, your preteen Golden Retriever will test the rules again and again, and you'll wonder where all his training went. The more consistent you are in enforcing household rules now, the more control you'll have in the coming months. In fact, if he hasn't mastered some basic obedience by the end of this month, he'll only get more difficult to train.

Sit, down, and walking on a leash should be your training priorities right now, and you should use them often. Have him sit before you feed him, or have him lie down by your chair when you're watching TV. Your puppy might be pushy now, poking you to be petted, but have him earn him attention by asking him to sit first.

If your pup is misbehaving, hook a 6-foot leash to his collar, and let him drag it around while he's in the house. When he's misbehaving, pick up the leash and lead him away from trouble, and don't reward him with playtime. If you grab him when he has something in his mouth, you've rewarded him by touching him and interacting. He'll think it's a great game, and even if you're stern with him, to him, negative attention is better than no attention at all.

If he's not allowed on the couch, he will try it this month. Rather than pull him off, pick up the leash and hold it with steady pressure to get him off the sofa, like you did when you were teaching him to walk on leash. He should respond to the pressure of the leash and get off the couch. Reward him with praise when he does.

Your puppy needs to learn "inside rules," and especially that he needs to settle down while he's in the house. You can use his ex pen to confine him temporarily, or if he's really rambunctious, he could benefit from a tie-down—a leash looped over a shut-door doorknob, affixed to a large or heavy piece of furniture, or attached to a large eye screw fastened to the wall. (A chain leash is excellent for this because he can't chew it. Otherwise, spray the leash with bitter spray or mouthwash to prevent chewing.) Either way, he can be within eyesight of his family while still enjoying some freedom. Give him a chew toy to occupy him, and with his limited mobility, he should settle down and relax.

HAPPY PUPPY

Children in your house need to follow inside rules, too. Don't let them play wild chase games or throw balls for the puppy indoors. He won't understand that he has to settle down unless everyone is consistent in his training.

Cutting Back on Treats

When you first teach your puppy a new command, you reward him with a treat every time he does the right thing. But you don't want to carry food in your pocket for the rest of your life. So how do you make your puppy comply without depending on treats forever?

Switch his reward from physical to praise. Every time he complies, praise him with a word, like "Good!" along with the treat. Gradually, he'll associate the word with the treat and recognize you are pleased. Always use an upbeat happy tone of voice when saying "Good!" Remember, he reads your tone and body language more than what you say.

As he gets used to being rewarded with "Good!" gradually cut back on treats. First, hide the treats in your pocket and don't pull one out until he sits or does whatever you're asking him to do. A treat is not a bribe; it's a reward. Continue to always praise him, but begin to occasionally skip the treat so he never knows when he'll get one. And don't use a pattern because he'll quickly figure it out. If you give a treat every third time, he'll pick up on that, and he won't respond nearly as enthusiastically the other two times. Mix it up so he doesn't know what to expect.

It might help to think of yourself as a slot machine. If you played the slots and got $1 back every time you played, the activity would get pretty boring. But if once in a while, just often enough to keep you playing, you won $50, and even once won $1,000, you'd play all night in hopes of getting another big win. It's the same with your puppy. Occasionally, give him a jackpot of a handful of extra tasty treats he doesn't usually get. This motivates him to keep playing the obedience game so he can get the jackpot again. Golden Retrievers *love* this.

If you fade the use of treats too fast, he could lose interest. Goldens are so food-motivated that he might hold out. If that happens, back up a little and give him treats more often.

HAPPY PUPPY

You don't always have to use treats as his reward. Interrupt a training session with a game of fetch, or pull a squeaky toy from your pocket. Releasing him from working might be enough reward. Mix up his rewards with tricks and fun time, and you'll always have a reward handy when you need it, even if you don't have a pocket full of cookies.

Remember that when you're a teaching a new skill, give your puppy a treat and praise every time he does something right. Don't reduce the frequency until you're sure he understands the exercise.

Teaching "Stay"

Before you teach him to stay, your Golden Retriever puppy should always sit promptly when you give the "Sit" command (which you taught him in Month 4).

Stay has two components: time and distance. However, you can't work on both at the same time because your pup will get confused. So begin by first lengthening the time he stays and then work on distance, cutting back the time as you do to almost nothing. Once he stays when you walk away from him, you can start building time back into the exercise.

Teaching "Sit-Stay"

As always with a puppy, your body language helps him stay. Have him sit at your left side on a loose leash. Step off with your right foot, and pivot in front of him, several inches away. (If you crowd him, he's more likely to stand up.) If he stays sitting, praise him, give him a treat, pivot back into position at his right side, and release him by touching him and saying "Okay." Practice pivoting into position and back without letting him stand. Do this a few times until he's used to it, and take a short break.

If he has trouble staying as you pivot, put your finger against his muzzle as you turn. It should be just enough to stop him from moving.

When teaching him to sit, you gave him a treat as soon as he sat. Now, as you teach him to stay, pivot in front of him and wait a few beats. He might look confused, and if he makes eye contact, smile at him and say nothing. (Too much eye contact will intimidate him and make him stand up.) Gradually increase the time he sits to about 15 seconds. This takes a lot of concentration, and he's probably sitting there worried he's supposed to be doing something, so intersperse a few instant releases to vary the length of time he's sitting.

If he stands up before you can release him, put him back in the original position and try another, shorter stay. Don't restart where he came to you; go back to the beginning. Don't say anything while you move him; just put him back in the sit. Keep practicing until you can get a 30-second stay. As you walk together and at other times of the day, ask him to do a short stay to reinforce his training.

Next, add the hand signal and command word. Before you pivot in front of him, put the palm of your hand in front of his nose and say "Stay."

When he's consistently holding a stay, you can throw in some variations. This time when you pivot, step farther away, about 1 foot. He might try to get up and move closer to you, and he'll be watching you intently, waiting for a signal that it's okay to move. As soon as you so much as twitch, he'll try to stand up. Before he's all the way up, lean into him and he should sit back down. He'll read your body language and know to go back into the sit.

Don't repeat the word "Stay" over and over, and don't stare into his eyes. Relax your posture, as if to tell him, "We aren't going anywhere," and quietly praise him during the stay.

TIPS AND TAILS

To release your pup from the stay, always go back to him and touch him. You want him to relax and wait patiently; otherwise, as soon as you step toward him, he'll think he's finished and stand up. Praise him quietly as he stays, walk back to him, praise him again, and touch him as you say "Okay" to release him. Don't ever call him to you from a stay, or he'll be anxiously watching for a command.

Practice variations on the stay—up close, farther away, and for various lengths of time. When he's working well at 1 foot away for 30 seconds, try standing farther back, about 18 inches. As you step backward, he might think you want him to come with you, so be sure to keep the leash slack. Say "Ack!" and lean toward him if he starts to get up. Go back to him, and release him immediately if he stays in the sit. If he doesn't, put him back in position and don't step as far next time. Mix it up with some stays where you're right in front of him again. Each time he's successful, touch and release him. Quit when you're ahead, and right when he does something correctly.

It'll probably take you a full month to get a steady 1-minute sit-stay from 4 feet away. Doing something, like sit or down, is an action concept. Not doing anything, like stay, is a little harder for him to understand.

Teaching "Down-Stay"

Once he grasps the idea of the sit-stay, down-stay is much easier for him to learn. Teach him the down-stay in small increments, as you did the sit-stay. As you work, first add time and then reduce the time as you add distance. When he stays better with you at a distance, rebuild the time.

Teach him to relax while he's down. If he's lying in a sphinx position, up on both haunches, he's ready to spring into action, so teach him to roll onto one hip instead. Watch him when he's resting, and figure out which hip he usually chooses.

Assume that as you face him, he usually rolls to his right hip. So as you put him in a down (which you taught him in Month 4), hold a treat in your right hand and push the treat back toward his *left* hip. As he follows your hand, he'll roll onto his right hip. If he doesn't get it, you can help him by putting pressure on his left hip with one hand. When he gets the idea, have him roll onto his hip every time he does the down. Making this an automatic part of the down helps you both be more successful with the stay.

The hand signal for down-stay is the same as for the sit-stay: put your open palm in front of his face as you give the command "Stay." Stand up straight, and pivot in front of him. (If you bend over him or look him in the eyes, he'll get right up.) Stand relaxed with your weight on one hip. He needs to see that nothing is going to happen so he can relax. If he fidgets, say "Ack!" but don't go back to him unless he gets up. When he's still, go back and release him. If he gets up before you let him up, put him back in place and start over a little closer to him.

Your puppy will try to creep toward you. When he moves forward, correct him with your voice. He'll stop, and a few seconds later, he'll creep forward again, inching his way to you. Golden Retrievers love this little game. When he creeps, go back to him without a word, stand him up, take him back to the starting point, and put him back in his down-stay. If you have to, put a piece of tape on the floor to remind yourself where you started.

When his stay is solid for about 30 seconds and you're 2 feet away, add a small variation. Fidget a little, and shift your weight slightly while you have him down-stay. This teaches him to stay even if you move. He's not to get up, no matter what you do, until you release him.

Going Up and Down Stairs

Your Golden Retriever puppy needs to learn to climb and descend stairs. If he doesn't learn this skill as a puppy, he'll probably be afraid to ever try stairs when he's an adult.

TIPS AND TAILS

Before you've taught him to be comfortable with stairs, use baby gates at the top and bottom of any stairways in your home to keep your puppy safe. And it'll be less stressful for you both if you start teaching him about stairs at home without outside distractions. If you don't have stairs, introduce him to them where he's already comfortable, like a friend's home or a quiet corner at the park.

One or two stairs aren't nearly as frightening as a full staircase, so start by teaching your pup to go up and down one or two steps, preferably carpeted stairs, which are easier for him to negotiate without slipping. Once he's mastered a few carpeted stairs, you can introduce him to a full-length staircase or take him out in public to try it.

Your goal is to keep your puppy from racing up and down the stairs uncontrollably. As a small puppy, he could be badly hurt or even killed if he tumbles head over heels down a stairwell. When he's an adult, you both could take a dangerous spill. Teach him that the stairs are a place of calmness and serenity, where he climbs and descends one step at a time at a leisurely pace.

Start with a hungry puppy on his leash and a pocket full of really tasty treats, like cheese or chicken. Or do this at mealtime and use his kibble. Kneel on the floor next to the foot of the stairs, and have him come over to you. Lift up both of his front paws, place them on the bottom stair, give him a treat, and let him go. After a few tries, he'll put his feet up on his own when you lure him with the treat.

After a few repetitions of this, place the treat farther up and back toward the second stair so he has to lift his rear feet onto the stair to get to the treat. When he gets one back foot up, praise him and feed him. When he gets all four feet completely on a stair, praise him quietly and have him stand or sit there for a second.

As you gradually add more stairs, have him stop on a stair and sit or lie down for a treat. This keeps it from becoming a race to the top (or bottom). To make it more fun, set a treat on each stair and let him sniff his way up. As he goes down, have him stop and sit often for a treat.

When he's familiar with one set of stairs, introduce him to new locations. You might have to start over the first few times until he discovers that most stairs are alike.

If you have open stairs with no vertical backs, like those going to the basement or to a second-floor apartment, have him practice climbing and descending those stairs, too, because they'll look entirely different to him and seem much scarier. They're also more dangerous for your pup. If he gets in a hurry, he could slip, his leg could slide through the opening, and he could break a leg or tear a muscle. Practice these stairs as if he's never seen a staircase before, so he understands how to go up and down safely.

Teaching a Flawless Recall

Calling your puppy to you should always result in a reward for him when he obliges. Up until this month, he probably came joyously when you called and followed you everywhere. Now you're seeing a suddenly independent puppy, who might ignore you completely or at least until it suits him.

Someday, you might encounter a situation when he needs to stop what he's doing immediately and come to you right now before he heads into danger, such as into traffic while darting after the neighbor's cat. To be ready for this, practice the recall. And to make it more effective, train when lots of distractions—other dogs, cars, people, rabbits, and good smells—are around to compete for his attention. He needs to learn that despite anything and everything around him, when you tell him to come to you, he must drop everything and come to you.

TIPS AND TAILS

In your Golden Retriever's mind, "Come" from 20 feet away is very different from "Come" from 6 feet away. Don't call him to you if you can't enforce the command; otherwise, he'll learn that he doesn't have to respond and you'll just be background noise.

Start teaching him the recall at home, and move to working outside when he understands the command. Keep a treat shaker with you to grab his attention if you need it.

Begin by attaching a long line to his collar. Try a 30-foot length of lightweight string or clothesline; these materials are light enough that he doesn't have the weight of a leash to remind him he's under your control. Take him to an enclosed area, and let him wander for a bit.

When he's 10 to 15 feet away, call him to you using your best happy voice. As soon as he looks at you, jump up and down excitedly and encourage him to come to you to see what you're going on about. Continue praising and encouraging him while he comes toward you. If he doesn't come immediately, reel him in with the line. Praise him (even if you pulled him to you), play with him, and give him treats, but then let him go back to what he was doing. He'll learn that coming to you doesn't necessarily end his fun. And don't be a pest; just call him once or twice each 5-minute session. If you have trouble getting his attention, rattle your treat shaker.

Add distractions as part of this training. This is where the kids can have some fun, playing catch or dancing around to get him interested. Be sure they understand that as soon as you call your pup, they are to freeze and not look at him. As he gets good at the game, they can continue distracting him while you call. Take turns holding the line so he'll come to everyone in the family.

Practice with the long line at parks and other places you regularly take him so he'll learn that the rules are the same no matter where you are. Have him check in occasionally, reward him, and let him return to play. Teaching him to come when called is not a one-day project, so practice often and in many places.

Catching Your Pup

There might come a day when your Golden Retriever gets away from you and refuses to come—he's just having too much fun to stop and come to you. Picture the recall as he may see it: you're at the park, and he's running and playing. He sees you take out the leash, a sure signal the party's over. Behind you, he sees the car, another sign it's time to go home. Forget it, he's not coming!

You're bound to be angry and frustrated, but don't let it show. Who wants to come to someone who is yelling and screaming at them? He'll tuck his tail and take off in the other direction.

Here are some methods to help you catch him—these also work while you're training him on the long line:

- As he approaches you, stand sideways to him. A full frontal greeting is intimidating and might cause him to back away from you.

- Crouch down to his eye level, open your arms wide, and happily call him. When your body language is happy, he's more likely to respond.

- Change the picture he sees. Don't get the leash out until you have your hands on him. Or never put it away, but keep it hanging around your neck or from your back pocket rather than in your hands.

- Don't call him with your car or the exit gate right behind you in his line of sight. Stand where it looks like this is just another checking-in recall.

- Carry a squeaky toy or ball, and let him see you playing with it. Toss it in the air, juggle it, and dance around like you're having a great time. All that fun is hard to resist.

- Fall down on the ground. Make a big drama of it, and he'll wonder what's up and come running. He'll be licking your ears and climbing on you in no time.

- Turn around, yell to him, and run away from him. He's likely to give chase.

You've finally got him leashed up, and you want tell him what a bad dog he is for not obeying. *Don't.* The last thing he did was come to you, and he thinks any punishment or reward is for that action. You can't punish him for something he did 5 minutes ago because he won't make the connection. Praise him, tell him he's a wonderful dog, and take him home for more recall practice.

YOU AND YOUR PUPPY

You'll be having a lot of fun with your puppy this month, especially going out more in public with you, so he needs to wear identification in case he gets lost.

He also needs some attention and guidance to keep your friendship on the right track. His busy antics might frustrate you at times, so prepare yourself with items like food-dispensing toys that will occupy him when you need a break. The kids also need guidance on developing a good relationship with their new puppy.

IDing Your Pup

Identification is your puppy's ticket home if he gets lost. When your Golden Retriever reaches 4 months, he has had his rabies vaccine, and most communities require that he be licensed. An ID tag includes your personal contact information, and a license has the animal control jurisdiction's info—both means of getting in touch with you if your pup is found. In addition, if you haven't already, now is the time to microchip your puppy and register the number, another link to you.

The well-dressed Golden Retriever should always wear his ID tag, which should include your name and phone number, including the area code. Consider putting both your mobile and home phone numbers on the tag so if someone finds your puppy, you can be contacted wherever you are. If the sound of jingling tags bothers you, order a collar with your phone number printed on it or use a pouch that attaches to his collar and holds all his tags quietly. Or purchase tags that slip onto and lie flat against his collar. A bonus: flat tags are less likely to catch on something and get lost.

TIPS AND TAILS

The lettering on plastic ID tags wears down quickly, and as the plastic ages, the likelihood of it breaking increases. Engraved metal lasts much longer. Whichever type you use, be sure it has a heavy ring or S hook. Put each tag on a separate ring, so if one is lost, the others are still attached.

There are many good reasons to license your Golden Retriever. Anyone who finds your dog will be more willing to handle him if they know his rabies status, and if he bites someone, his vaccine record is on file. Animal Control will notify you and hold your dog longer than they will an unlicensed dog. Some jurisdictions also give your dog a free ride home. Penalties for having an unlicensed dog are much higher than the cost of the original license, so take the time to get your pup licensed.

All 50 states have dog-licensing laws, and either city or county agencies issue the license. You'll submit his rabies vaccine certificate with the license application. Your vet might even send it in for you.

If your dog loses his collar, a microchip provides lifetime identification he can't lose. In fact, many breeders have the microchip implanted in their puppies before they leave for their new homes. (You have to add your info after you adopt your pup.) The chip, which is the size of a piece of rice, is encased in biocompatible glass to prevent infection and is injected between your pup's shoulder blades. The chip operates on a radio frequency, is not a tracking device, and doesn't require a power source to be activated. When someone runs a scanner over your dog, it reads the chip like a UPC code on an item at the grocery store.

When the chip is implanted, you pay a nominal one-time fee for lifetime registration with a national registry such as American Kennel Club Reunite (akcreunite.org), American Veterinary Identification Devices (avidid.com), or HomeAgain (public.homeagain.com). When the chip number is registered with a national database, it can be traced back to you. Most registries provide a collar tag so whoever finds your dog knows to have the dog scanned. Shelters, veterinarians, and rescue groups usually have their own scanners. If your dog is lost, contact the registry immediately. Most have a 24/7 telephone hotline.

TIPS AND TAILS

A microchip does *not* include your personal information, just a number. If you don't register your dog's microchip, the shelter can't find you and the chip is useless. Before you register the chip, find out what registry your local shelter uses. Many people designate their veterinarian or breeder as the secondary contact. Be sure to update your contact information with the registry if you move or get a new phone number.

Numerous manufactures make microchips, and in recent years, universal scanners have been developed that can read most brands and frequencies. These scanners are labeled "ISO compliant" by the International Organization for Standardization. Be sure the chip you purchase is compatible with ISO scanners. More than 160 countries follow these standards, and dogs have been reunited with their owners from around the world. Some countries even require a microchip before you can import a dog.

Shelters usually scan the dog all over because some microchips migrate elsewhere in the body, like down his shoulder or leg. Newer chips have a small hook that anchors the chip, and layers of connective tissue grow over it to hold it in place. Ask your vet to scan the microchip during your dog's yearly health checkup to be sure the chip is still in place and active.

Global positioning systems (GPSs) for dogs are becoming quite popular. With these, a small tracking device is attached to his collar and interacts with satellite and cell phone towers to follow his movements. You download an app to your smartphone and receive an email or text message if your dog leaves the designated safe area you've set up. The prices for these devices have fallen dramatically in the past few years, so it might be something worth considering.

Frustrated Owner = Confused Puppy

A new Golden Retriever puppy can be a shock to the household, especially if your last dog was very old and you've forgotten what it's like to have a puppy. Or maybe this is your first dog and you had no idea he was going to be this active … or destructive. When the cute factor wears thin, usually right after he chews up the couch pillow or committed some similar crime, what can you do?

First and foremost, remember he's still a puppy, and Golden Retriever puppies are especially active. What he's doing—barking, chewing, biting, digging—are all normal puppy behaviors, and he hasn't developed much, if any, self-control yet.

Also know that a tired puppy is a good puppy. Playtime, especially with you, solves a lot of puppy problems as mental as well as physical exercise tires your puppy.

Puppies learn by doing, and this month he's testing his limits. If he doesn't try things, he won't learn. And if you never have to say "no," how will he know the rules?

Remember, too, that one correction doesn't mean lesson learned. He's a baby, and he'll forget. Be patient and consistent, and keep teaching.

When you get angry, your puppy is confused and sees you as unpredictable. He might not understand why you're so upset; he just knows to get out of your way. When his behavior is too much, put him in his crate with a chew toy, hand him off to someone else, or go for a walk by yourself.

Don't give up—get help. Before you get completely frustrated, talk to your veterinarian, puppy class instructor, or someone who can see what your puppy is doing and offer constructive suggestions. Your breeder also can offer suggestions based on her years of experience. What works for one puppy might not work for yours, and there's more than one way to approach any problem.

HAPPY PUPPY

It's bedtime and you're tired, but your puppy won't settle down. What to do? Consider soft music with a low, pulsing beat that simulates his mother's heartbeat. You can buy CDs and videos specially made to comfort and quiet your dog.

Introducing Food-Dispensing Toys

The way to your puppy's heart is through his stomach. Food-dispensing toys entertain your puppy and keep him from wolfing down his food. Many kinds are available, but hard plastic is best for Golden Retrievers. The dispensers come in various shapes—balls, cubes, etc.—so look for one he can't chew up.

Put a mixture of his kibble and treats in the toy. Add one piece at the opening so it falls out right away and he gets rewarded, and he'll soon be batting and rolling the toy all over to make more food come out. (Know that this is a noisy toy if he's on a hard floor.) Separate him from other dogs while he's playing because bigger dogs will probably try to take it away from him—sometimes aggressively—because food is involved.

Another type of food-dispensing toy is an interactive puzzle, such as those made by Nina Ottenson. These toys are graded by difficulty, and some are made specifically for puppies. He has to manipulate the puzzle by stepping on a piece, picking it up, rocking it, or pushing it to get to the food prize.

You can make your own version of a food puzzle. Put kibble or treats in each cup of a cupcake tin, place a tennis ball over each cup, and let your puppy figure out how to remove the ball and get to the treat. Don't be surprised if he figures out pretty quickly that he can dump the entire tin by stepping on it!

Puppy and Kids: Building the Friendship

The bloom is off the rose, and your puppy isn't brand-new anymore. How do you keep the kids involved and build the relationship between your puppy and your children?

When other children come over, tell your kids that your puppy is a baby and can't speak for himself, so it's their job to recognize signals the puppy is tired or doesn't want to play. Explain to them that when your puppy turns his back, avoids eye contact, won't come to them, or tries to leave, he's tired and ready for his nap. A child will proudly assume the role of protector.

It's also important for you to teach your puppy to respect your kids. A toddler or elementary school–age child won't like a puppy who jumps up or knocks them down. The child might try to tell the pup what to do, and your puppy won't listen.

These little people aren't much bigger than he is, and he might see them as littermates. Help your children use their own body language to stop the pup from jumping on them. Put the puppy on leash, and have the kids practice getting him to calm down by standing up straight and still, not looking at him, folding their arms, and ending the game.

Ensure that your puppy responds when the kids say "Sit" or "Down." Let your child reward the puppy while you hold the leash and enforce commands if necessary.

TIPS AND TAILS

Snap a second leash on your puppy so both you and your child are attached to him. Then, when he doesn't listen, you can help your child get him to respond.

Teach your kids to respect your puppy, too. Establish rules for their interactions with the puppy. The puppy will match his energy level to them, and everyone will stay safe. Point out that they wouldn't like it if the puppy did these things to them, so they need to respect the puppy's feelings, too.

Here are some rules to establish with your kids and your puppy:

- No jumping on or falling on the dog.
- No kicking, hitting, or throwing things at the puppy. (When toys become weapons, take them away.)
- No teasing the puppy and enticing him to chase.
- Don't sit on the puppy or wrap your arms tightly around his neck or head.
- Leave the puppy alone when he's in his crate. No poking fingers in the crate. No teasing.
- Leave the puppy alone when he's eating.

A child might become jealous of the attention your puppy gets when guests visit your home. Children might also get jealous of each other if the puppy spends more time with their siblings or with Mom and Dad. To avoid this, involve the children in the puppy's training. They can take turns giving commands, praising, holding the leash, and providing distractions. Help them teach the puppy tricks, like shake, they can demonstrate when people visit. Or move the puppy's crate into different rooms every few nights so he spends time with everyone. You also could have your child prepare the puppy's meal and give it to him. Have your child make the puppy sit before setting down his food bowl.

You can't expect an elementary school–age child to take complete responsibility for the care of a puppy. In fact, if it becomes a required chore, he might resent the puppy. But one very important job, like putting down his food dish, helps him bond with the puppy and also feel a sense of accomplishment.

You can also encourage harmony between your children and your Golden Retriever by encouraging your kids to play games with your puppy. Hide and seek is one option. Have one child restrain the puppy while another child hides and then have the hidden child call the puppy. When he finds him, switch sides.

Find the treat is another fun game for kids and pup. Let the puppy watch the child hide a treat in plain sight. Release him and then praise him for finding it. Gradually hide treats in harder places or out of the room so he has to look harder. You don't want him digging up the couch looking for a treat, so establish some guidelines with the kids about good hiding places.

	SOCIAL	BEHAVIOR	TRAINING	PHYSICAL	HEALTH
MONTH 1			Littermates and mother teach appropriate canine behavior		
MONTH 2	Breeder starts socialization			Rapid growth	
MONTH 3	Socialization at home with new owner and other pets	Fear-imprint period	Begin house- and crate training		1st DHPP vaccine
MONTH 4			Enroll in puppy class		2nd DHPP vaccine
MONTH 5	Socialization in public	Teething begins—heavy chewing period	Ready for basic commands	Switch to adult food	3rd DHPP and rabies vaccines
MONTH 6			Enroll in basic obedience class		
MONTH 7					
MONTH 8				Moderate growth	Sexual maturity
MONTH 9		Adult teeth are in—chewing continues			
MONTH 10			Ready for more advanced training		
MONTH 11					
MONTH 12 AND BEYOND				Slow growth—reaches adult size	Annual vaccinations and checkup

Full Speed Ahead

Between months 5 and 6, your Golden Retriever puppy finishes another growth spurt, and her body starts to balance out.

This is going to be a busy month for both of you. She has endless energy but not much common sense, so you'll spend time reviewing her training and keeping her safe. Socialization is an ongoing process, so you'll continue to introduce her to more places, people, and things.

Your puppy is prone to injuries at this age—some of which can lead to physical problems later in life—so you should prepare a first-aid kit and get ready for emergencies. If it's fall or springtime, you might be experiencing her first major shedding season, so we share some methods to cope with all that dog hair, too.

PHYSICAL DEVELOPMENT

Although your Golden Retriever puppy is looking more like a dog these days, she's still very much a puppy at heart, as you'll see in her behavior this month. You'll also notice that the amount of sleep she needs is changing as she matures.

Looking Less Like a Puppy

A puppy grows rapidly during the first 6 months. At this point, she can look mature and well balanced, or she can still be all legs and tail. She's reached about 75 percent of her adult height by now but only about 60 percent of her adult weight. At 5½ months, a male puppy who will be within the standard at adulthood—22½ to 24½ inches tall at the shoulder—will be 17 to 19 inches and 39 to 48 pounds. A female who will mature to 21½ to 23½ inches will now be 16 to 18 inches tall and 33 to 42 pounds.

Keep in mind this is just an estimate, and some puppies will be taller but might not weigh much more yet.

Her adult teeth are in as well, and they're starting to set permanently in her jaws, so the chewing continues.

All About Sleep

A newborn puppy sleeps 90 percent of the time. She sleeps less as she grows, but even when she's an adult, she'll still get as much as 13 hours a day of shut-eye.

Just like a teenage human, an adolescent dog sleeps more, especially during growth spurts, when she's using energy to build bone and muscles. And considering her high activity level all day, no wonder she's tired at the end of it!

Her sleep is different from an adult's right now. She wakes up more often, and about 25 percent of her sleep can be characterized as "active," where she seems to be dreaming. She twitches and whimpers or paddles her legs likes she's running after that last ball you threw for her. In fact, scientists theorize that because a dog's brain is similar to a human's in some structural aspects, dogs do dream. Stanley Coren, PhD, FRSC, noted that a dog enters the dream phase about 20 minutes after falling asleep, and evidence has shown that she dreams about daily activities. Her breathing becomes shallow and irregular, and her eyes move behind her eyelids, just like the dream phase in human sleep.

If your Golden Retriever lives indoors and doesn't get much exercise, she might sleep more than an active dog. She'll likely adjust her sleep time so she can be active when you're home and rest when you're at work or are sleeping yourself. Some dogs cope with extreme stress by sleeping more.

TIPS AND TAILS
Yawning doesn't necessarily mean your Golden Retriever is tired. It's also a stress response.

Your dog has an internal clock, and a Golden Retriever *never* sleeps through breakfast. In fact, you can be sure she'll wake you up at precisely the same time every morning to ensure you can serve her breakfast. This quickly becomes a habit when you respond positively by getting up and feeding her. So much for sleeping in on Saturdays!

HEALTH

At this stage of her life, an active young Golden Retriever is more likely to be injured than be ill. Reckless and uncoordinated, blasting into adventure with no thought to her own safety, your Golden Retriever puppy can be her own worst enemy right now. She's also getting taller, and she might be able to reach objects on high shelves that were previously out of her reach.

It's essential that you learn to recognize and react to accidents, illnesses, and especially emergencies. Assemble a doggie first-aid kit, or combine it with your family's first-aid kit because many of the items are the same. (More on this in the later "Assembling Your Doggie First-Aid Kit" section.) Being prepared gives you peace of mind and the capability to act when the unthinkable happens.

Getting to Know Your Puppy's Vitals

During an emergency, you need to assess your Golden Retriever's vital signs. You also need to know what her *normal* heart and breathing rates are, and what her gums normally look like, so you can make a comparison.

To check your puppy's breathing rate, lay her on her right side and let her rest quietly. As you watch her chest rise and fall, count the number of breaths in a 15-second period. Multiply that by 4 to get the number of breaths per minute. The normal rate is 10 to 30 breaths per minute for an adult and 15 to 40 breaths for a young puppy. By 6 months, her breathing rate is about the same as an adult's. Her breathing rate is also influenced by the temperature of her surroundings and her activity level, so keep that in mind when measuring or comparing.

To check her heart rate, again lay her on her right side. Bend her left leg until her elbow touches her chest, and put your right hand on her body where her left elbow meets her chest. You should feel her heart beating there. Count the beats for 15 seconds, and multiply that number by 4. Normal resting heart rate for a puppy up to 1 year old is 120 to 160 beats per minute.

Next, look at her gums (mucous membranes). When she's healthy, her gums are pink and wet. Dark red, blue, brown, or very pale gums indicate she's not getting enough oxygen into her blood.

Check her capillary refill time, too. Firmly touch her outer gum with your finger, and release. The gum should be white where you touched it. Watch the white fingerprint turn back to pink; it should take no more than 2 seconds. Too fast or too slow indicates a problem with her blood circulation.

Your Golden Retriever puppy's normal temperature is between 100.2°F and 102.8°F. (See Month 4 for instructions on how to take her temperature.)

Once you understand what's normal for your Golden Retriever, you can more accurately assess her condition in an emergency.

What Is an Emergency?

An emergency is any situation in which you must take action immediately to prevent further injury or death. In some situations, you can treat a problem or observe your Golden Retriever for a while before contacting the veterinarian. If your puppy has stopped eating, for example, you have some time to look at options. If your puppy can't breathe or seems to be choking, however, there's no time to lose, and you must respond without delay.

Potential emergencies include the following:

Trauma: If your pup has been hit by a car or fallen from a high place.

Difficulty breathing or choking: She's gasping for air, pawing at her mouth, panicked, or her gums are turning blue or white.

Seizures: Long or short duration, or multiple seizures.

Excessive bleeding: Characterized by spurting blood or prolonged bleeding you can't stop by applying direct pressure.

Deep cuts: Especially if bones or organs are exposed.

Snakebite: Look for bite marks on your puppy's skin, swelling, bleeding from the bite, trembling or drooling, difficulty breathing, or signs of shock.

Burns: Blisters, swollen reddened skin, loss of skin and hair.

Suspected poisoning: Can present as vomiting or diarrhea; trembling or twitching; seizure; abnormal gum color; heavy drooling or foaming from the mouth; burns on the lips, tongue, or mouth; or bleeding from mouth, nose, ears, or anus.

Broken bone: Look for pain, swelling, lameness, bone protruding from skin, or a limb held in abnormal position.

Heat stroke: Heavy panting, bright red gum color (may turn blue or gray in later stages), body temperature above 104°F, difficulty walking, and even collapse.

Bloat (mostly adult dogs): Indicated by drooling, panting, retching, attempting to vomit, unable to defecate, pacing and restless, distended abdomen, and signs of shock.

Calm, Assess, Call, and CPR

When you've identified an emergency, you need to stay calm, assess the situation, call the vet if necessary, and administer CPR (cardiopulmonary resuscitation) if required.

It's worth repeating: *stay calm.*

Panic can make people do crazy things, and you can't help your dog if you get hurt, too. If she's been hit by a car, for example, don't run out into the road to get her unless it's safe to do so. First, stop and take a deep breath.

Be sure you can approach your puppy safely. A frightened, injured dog, even your own, might bite. Speak calmly and reassuringly to her. Don't make any sudden movements that might cause her to bolt in fear. Use submissive body language: stand or crouch sideways to her, and don't look her directly in the eye.

To restrain your puppy, put the snap end of a leash through the loop for your hand and make a noose. Drop the noose over your puppy's head, and tighten it without touching her.

Muzzle your dog by taking a long piece of gauze from your first-aid kit and wrapping it around her muzzle, crisscrossing it under her lower jaw and tying it behind her neck. You also could use a belt or other piece of fabric to do this.

TIPS AND TAILS

Shock occurs when internal organs don't get enough blood and oxygen. Shock is common after serious injuries, especially if there's been major blood loss. Symptoms of early shock include increased heart rate, pounding pulse, and red gums. Middle stages of shock are indicated by low body temperature, weak and rapid pulse, pale gums, and a woozy and weakened animal. Slow breathing and heart rate, weak or no pulse, depression, unconsciousness, and cardiac arrest can indicate late stages of shock, which leads to death.

Next, assess the situation. Do a visual survey of the scene. Observe your dog's posture, look for blood or vomit, listen to her breathing, and check for any obvious signs of what caused the injury, such as poison or a snake.

Then check her airway, breathing, and circulation—the ABCs of first aid. Assuming you can touch her, does she have an open airway? Check her mouth and throat for obstructions, and clear any if you can, using tweezers or forceps from your emergency kit.

Is she breathing? Look at the rise and fall of her chest. If you aren't sure, put your cheek against the front of her nose and feel or listen for her breathing. If she is, move on to the next step. A dog can be unconscious and still be breathing.

If she's not breathing, start rescue breathing immediately.

Does she have circulation, meaning a pulse or heartbeat? As discussed earlier, lay your dog on her right side, slightly bend her left leg until her elbow touches her chest, and put your right hand on her body where the left elbow meets her chest. Can you feel her heart beating?

To check for a pulse, use two fingers on one of three places:

- High inside either rear leg about halfway between the front and back of the leg where you feel a slight recess
- On the underside of either front paw just above the middle pad
- On the underside of either hind paw just above the middle pad

If you cannot detect a heartbeat or pulse, start chest compressions immediately.

If you're alone, call for help or call the veterinary hospital before you start rescue breathing or CPR. If it's after regular hours, call the emergency animal hospital nearest you. If you have someone with you, let them call while you start CPR. Your advance call enables the hospital to be ready to help as soon as you arrive.

The veterinarian will want to know a few things:

- Is the puppy breathing? Describe her breath.
- Has she vomited or passed any stool or foreign objects?
- What's her pulse?
- What color are her gums?
- Is the puppy bleeding? How much? From where?
- What's her temperature?
- Has anyone administered CPR?

The veterinarian might ask additional questions and give you instructions to help you care for your dog until you can get her to the clinic.

Next, administer CPR rescue breathing or chest compressions if your puppy has no pulse and isn't breathing. This life-saving procedure keeps oxygen in your puppy's system until help arrives. Continue CPR until she regains consciousness or you arrive at the vet's office.

It's essential that you first be certain your dog is actually unconscious. Never perform CPR on a dog who has a heartbeat or is breathing. Try to rouse her by gently shaking her body and talking to her. If that doesn't work, continue with CPR.

First, check her airway: Tilt her head back to align with her neck to open her airway, but do not extend her neck too far up, which might cause further injury. Pull her tongue forward, and remove any foreign objects that might be in her mouth.

Administer rescue breathing: Close her mouth tightly, and wrap one hand around her muzzle to keep it closed. Take a deep breath, and put your mouth over her nose, sealing her nostrils. Exhale firmly. Watch for her chest to expand, or place a hand on her chest to feel if it rises. If the air does not go in, or if you detect some resistance, reposition her neck and try another two breaths.

Remove your mouth, take another deep breath, and repeat four or five times, allowing her chest to return to normal after each breath. Give her about 20 rescue breaths per minute, and continue until she revives or you arrive at the vet.

TIPS AND TAILS

If you can't get rescue breaths into your puppy or you could not remove an object from her airway, you'll have to perform the canine version of the Heimlich maneuver. If she's standing, put your arms around her belly, join your hands, and make a fist. Push firmly up and forward, just behind her rib cage. If she's lying down, place one hand on her back for support and use your other hand to squeeze her abdomen upward and forward. Either way, give five sharp thrusts to the abdomen. Then check her mouth and remove any objects that may have been dislodged.

Perform chest compressions: If your dog still isn't breathing after the first four or five rescue breaths, check again for a pulse or heartbeat. If she has none, her heart has stopped and you need to immediately begin compressions.

With your dog still lying on her right side, position yourself so you face her, and locate her heart (explained earlier). Straighten your arms; cup one hand over the other; and begin rapid, firm compressions—strong enough that your puppy's chest moves about 1 inch. (For an adult dog, the chest should move 1 to 3 inches.) After five compressions, give one rescue breath and check for a pulse. If she still has no pulse, continue the series of five compressions and one rescue breath until she revives or you get to the vet.

When your puppy is breathing and has a heartbeat, transport her to the veterinary hospital as soon as possible. Ideally, have someone else drive while you concentrate on your puppy.

Assembling Your Doggie First-Aid Kit

A pet first-aid kit enables you to respond quickly when your dog needs help. You can buy premade kits for pets or humans and add additional items you might need. Label your kit or storage container clearly, and keep it where you can get to it quickly, possibly in your car. Or keep several first-aid kits in strategic places.

A basic first-aid kit should include the following:

- Your veterinarian's contact info and the phone number and address of the nearest emergency vet hospital

- A copy of your dog's health records

- A muzzle to fit your dog or a long strip of gauze (30 to 36 inches long)

- Antihistamine (Benadryl or equivalent) to treat an allergic reaction (Discuss the correct dose with your vet based on your Golden Retriever's weight. Remember, the dosage will change as she grows.)

- Tweezers, needle-nose pliers, forceps, or hemostat for removing foreign objects from her mouth or throat

- Saline eye wash for flushing irritants from her eye and for flushing wounds

- Mild grease-cutting dish soap (like Dawn) for removing sticky or caustic substances from her coat

- Rubber or latex gloves

- A rectal thermometer and petroleum jelly

- Hand sanitizer

- Antiseptic solution

- Antibiotic ointment

- Elastic bandages

- Veterinary wrap (such as VetRap) to hold bandages in place

- Blunt-nose and pointed scissors

- Sanitary pads to bandage a bleeding wound

- Nonstick bandages

- Various sizes and shapes of gauze pads to clean and protect wounds

- A flashlight

- A first-aid book (You can also get a pet first-aid app for your smartphone. See Appendix D.)

You also might want to keep a leash, several towels, and a blanket in your car or with your first-aid kit. You can use the leash to restrain your puppy or muzzle her. Use the towels to clean up blood or vomit, and use the blanket as a stretcher or to keep your puppy warm.

TIPS AND TAILS

Something else to keep in your doggie first-aid kit is the number for the ASPCA Animal Poison Control Center: 888-426-4435, or the Pet Poison Helpline: 855-764-7661. Veterinarians here are on call 24 hours a day, 7 days a week. You're charged a small consultation fee. Be sure to gather as much information as possible about the poison before you call.

Pet First-Aid Classes

The Red Cross and many private trainers offer pet first-aid courses that cover both dogs and cats. Classes usually last around 4 hours and train you to effectively care for your pet in an emergency situation, including learning how to handle an injured dog, assessing her condition, and safely transporting her to the vet. You also learn what to do in specific situations like a broken bone, heatstroke, snakebite, or excessive bleeding. The course also trains you to do a modified Heimlich maneuver on a choking animal.

One of the key benefits of pet first-aid classes is that you get hands-on practice bandaging, splinting, and performing CPR using CPR mannequins. The Red Cross program also includes a book and DVD you keep with your first-aid kit for reference. The book covers common injuries and emergency illnesses and reviews all the instruction you received in the class.

Check with the Red Cross, your veterinarian, or local dog trainers for pet first-aid courses in your area.

NUTRITION

Speed eating and food guarding, two issues common at this age, can cause ongoing health and behavior issues if not prevented, so we look at dealing with both of those behaviors in this section.

We also look at choosing healthy treats for your Golden Retriever puppy.

Slowing Down Speed Eaters

At 6 months, your Golden Retriever puppy might eat like she hasn't seen a bowl of food for weeks. It starts when she's with her littermates and has to compete for a spot to nurse, and the behavior continues at the puppy bowl when she begins to eat solid food.

A dog who speeds through her dinner also inhales too much air, which causes gas and discomfort. She finishes eating long before her stomach has a chance to tell her she's full, so she often still wants more. Then she gulps down a bowl of water. This all adds up to a tummy ache, and as she ages, this puts her at risk for bloat, a potentially fatal condition.

Here are some suggestions to slow down your speed eater:

- Don't make her compete for her food. If other dogs are in the house, feed everyone in separate rooms so they don't feel their food is threatened.

- Add water to her food and let it soak a bit before you feed her. The water causes the food to expand in the bowl and not in her stomach, so she'll feel full faster.

- Don't use a bowl. Instead, toss her food on the floor and let her scavenge and eat one kibble at a time. Be sure to do this on a clean, hard surface like a concrete patio or kitchen floor because a hungry Golden Retriever will eat gravel, dirt, seeds, and anything else in her path.

- Put a large rock in the dish. She has to eat around the rock, which slows her down. Be sure to use a rock that's too big for her to put in her mouth.

- Break her meal into small portions, giving her just ¼ cup at a time.

- Put her meal in a food-dispensing puzzle so she has to figure out how it works to get her kibble out. This slows her down *and* entertains her.

TIPS AND TAILS

Gas and diarrhea are usually temporary problems, sometimes caused by a sudden diet change and upset tummy. Or your puppy could have eaten something in the yard that didn't agree with her. Flatulence alone doesn't usually indicate a serious health problem, but if you're worried, talk to your vet. If the problem continues and there's no medical cause, examine her dog food ingredients list for ingredients like soy, beans, or cellulose that might cause excessive flatulence. Switching to a different food might solve the problem. Remember to switch foods gradually, because that in itself can cause gas.

Preventing Food Guarding

Your Golden Retriever puppy should feel comfortable when anyone in the family reaches into her bowl, touches her while she's eating, or takes away her food bowl. At the same time, you want to be sure she won't bite you if you need to pick up the bowl. It's always easier to prevent a problem rather than fix one, so it's important you teach your puppy to welcome your presence while she's eating.

Do this exercise once or twice a week, or once every couple days. Don't make a pest of yourself, or she won't be happy to see you coming.

Divide her meal into four or five portions. Give her one portion in her bowl and then sit nearby on the floor, ignoring her. When she's done, pick up her bowl, put more food in it, and again ignore her until she's finished. She'll learn that having you near her food is a good thing because more food is on the way.

Each time you provide more food, also add one special goodie, like a bite of cheese or hot dog. Not only does she get more food, but that food is *great!* She'll start to enjoy this game. Or reach into the bowl while she's eating and add a treat. Touch the bowl while you add treats, or pick up the bowl, add a treat, and give it back to her.

Also touch your puppy's collar while you put a treat in her bowl or pick it up. Hold her collar for a second or two, put the bowl back down, and add the treats.

Be sure you teach your kids the feeding game. When they understand what you're teaching your puppy, they'll enjoy helping.

HAPPY PUPPY

Your puppy needs to feel secure enough that she doesn't have to watch out for flying objects and can eat her meal in relative peace. This isn't the time for a toddler to bother your pup or for any loud noises to occur next to her dish. Be sure everyone in the family leaves your pup alone when she eats. You want to be able to approach her and her bowl, but you don't want the entire family bugging her to a point that she feels the need to protect herself or her food.

Choosing Treats

Just as you check the ingredients in a dog food before giving it to your pup, also look at what's in the treats you give her. Treats might be high in fat, salt, and sugar to add flavor, and the added salt will likely make your dog drink more. Select treats that are the same brand and contain the same ingredients as her dog food—or better yet, use part of her daily food ration for treats.

Soft or semisoft treats often contain added dyes and fillers, and just because something looks like a piece of bacon or beef doesn't mean it is. Binding agents are also often added to make the treat stick together and look like a chunk of meat. Some "bones" are made with vegetables and cornstarch and could break apart quickly in a Golden Retriever's jaws.

Most treats are not intended as a complete, nutritionally balanced food, and this will be noted on the package. A junk-food dog treat can upset your puppy's nutritional balance, especially if she gets too many.

Treats should account for no more than 5 to 10 percent of her total daily intake of food. Be sure to cut back on her kibble if she's getting a lot of goodies.

HAPPY PUPPY

As an alternative to a constant barrage of commercially made treats, use bits of raw carrot or cooked plain chicken—your puppy will love them. Cheese cubes are also good in small amounts, but too much of a dairy product can cause diarrhea.

Just because you have a big dog (or at least she will be soon) doesn't mean she needs a 4-inch-long dog biscuit every time she gets a treat. Break pieces of larger treats to no larger than about 1½ inches. You can give several pieces as jackpot rewards for learning new things.

GROOMING

Golden Retrievers are usually very clean … when they stay out of mischief, that is. Minor dirt and debris brush off of the surface of the Golden Retriever coat, but she'll need an occasional bath, too. And because Golden Retrievers shed, it's important that you learn to take some preventive measures to deal with all that dog hair.

Bathing Your Golden Puppy

You don't have to give your puppy a complete bath the first time you introduce her to the tub. The idea is for her to enjoy a short, fun experience, not necessarily to get her clean.

To do this, confine your pup in a big tub such as a horse water trough (don't use your bathtub unless you don't have anything else; the drain will get clogged with Golden Retriever hair, and when she shakes, the whole bathroom will get wet), have her on a leash so she'll stay in one place, or ask a helper to restrain her while you bathe her. If the tub is slippery, put a bath mat in the bottom. Use cool to room temperature water to wash your pup. Hot water will dry out her skin, and although cold water won't bother her, you shouldn't use ice-cold water, either.

Let your pup sniff the running water (and the hose if you're bathing her outside) and maybe even taste it. Have your helper offer treats throughout the process, too. Place your pup in the tub, and add water until it barely covers her feet. If this is too much, just splash a little on her feet and quit. Let her out when she's calm. She might try to jump out, but restrain her until she calms down and then let her out. Work with her over several sessions until she enjoys the water and looks forward to it.

Try to separate bath time from play-in-the-water time. You don't want your puppy chasing the hose and biting at the water while you're trying to shampoo her.

TIPS AND TAILS

Dilute pet shampoo to 50 percent strength with water, and put it in a squirt bottle. Then you won't have the shampoo concentrated in one spot while the rest of your pup's coat doesn't get enough. It still lathers nicely, and it rinses out much more easily.

When it's time for an actual bath, you can put cotton balls in your Golden Retriever's ears, but don't wet her face or head until later because she'll want to shake. Wet her coat, starting at her tail end and gradually moving forward. Hold the hose nozzle close to her skin so it penetrates her thick coat and she gets thoroughly wet. Most Golden Retrievers have a water-resistant undercoat, so it will take some work to get her wet to the skin.

Squirt a line of shampoo down the middle of her back, and massage it into her coat, adding more when you need to. Take care to wash her belly and armpits, too. The hair on her neck and throat is especially thick, so add water as you wash.

Lastly, put some diluted shampoo in your hand or on a washcloth and wash her face. You might want to put an eye lubricant like mineral oil around her eyes to help keep out the soap. Wipe out her ears, too, but avoid getting water in them.

Rinse her thoroughly, including between her toes, under her belly, and between her legs, until all the dirt and bubbles disappear—which will probably take longer than the washing step. When all the shampoo is washed out, the water will run clear. If you leave any soap residue in her coat, it will irritate her skin, so be sure to rinse very thoroughly.

To rinse her face, hold her nose up while you rinse the back of her head so the water flows away from her eyes and ears. Her ear flaps should prevent water from getting in her ears. Then, using a gentle stream of water, tip her head forward to rinse the front of the head. To rinse her muzzle, hold the hose level and run a gentle stream of water back and forth over her face.

When all the shampoo is rinsed out, apply a coat conditioner, which makes mats and tangles much easier—and less painful—to brush out. Rinse thoroughly, and add some white vinegar to the final rinse to make her coat shiny. Then rinse well again.

Move her someplace dry and towel off the excess moisture. Let her sit for a few minutes with towels draped over her body to absorb some of the excess water, and when you remove the towels, stand back and let her shake! Remove the cotton balls (if they're wet, you need to work on your rinsing technique) and thoroughly dry her ears.

Don't let her run loose to dry because chances are, she'll head straight for the backyard. She'll roll in dirt, and if she got water in her ears, she'll rub her head along the ground. If you let her loose in the house, she'll rub along the walls and against the couch.

Dry your pup thoroughly, especially during winter or shedding season. Moisture under matted fur or trapped close to the skin can cause bacterial infections and hot spots. Also consider using a hair dryer, which helps blow out any remaining loose coat. Turn the dryer on the lowest possible heat setting because a dog's skin burns easily. Your puppy might bite at the air or be afraid of the noise at first, so begin by holding the dryer at arm's length away from her. Never blow the dryer directly in her face, and don't put her in her crate with a dryer blowing on her. She can't move away from the heat if it gets too hot.

TIPS AND TAILS
If you're going to be bathing your Golden Retriever yourself instead of using a professional groomer, consider purchasing a high-velocity pet hair dryer, which makes drying much faster and blows out more loose undercoat. These pet-specific dryers aren't supposed to get as hot as the human versions, but burns are still possible, so be careful.

Dealing with Shedding

A deep, thorough brushing at least once a week makes for a healthy dog and a cleaner house, but it's not enough to prevent shedding and the accompanying mess. Some preventive measures make housecleaning chores less time-consuming.

You'll probably get used to the dog hair and barely notice it after a while. But you'll cringe when Aunt Charlotte comes to visit, sits on the couch, and is covered in Golden Retriever fur when she stands up. Invest in washable furniture covers to protect the furniture. When company comes, uncover the sofa.

You could teach your Golden Retriever puppy never to get on the furniture, but that wouldn't be any fun. Besides, when she lies on the floor in her favorite spot up against the couch, it will still get dirty and hairy. If you really have to keep a room pristine, limit her access with pet gates. For example, let her nap on the sofa in the family room, but keep the living room off limits.

Also, know that a healthy coat doesn't shed as much. If you're feeding a discount or grocery store brand of dog food, you might see a marked difference in your dog's coat when you switch to a premium food.

A clean dog who sleeps on a dirty bed won't stay clean and sweet-smelling for long, so be sure to wash your dog's bedding regularly. Besides getting rid of excess hair, your house also will smell fresher.

SOCIAL SKILLS

A well-socialized Golden Retriever is friendly, confident, and well behaved everywhere she goes. This is no small achievement, and it doesn't happen by accident. It takes ongoing training, and this month is no exception.

Teaching "Off" and "Sit-to-Greet"

Puppies jump up because they want to be near your face and smell your breath to identify you. A cute little 20-pound puppy might not be such a bother when she jumps, but a powerful 70-pound dog quickly becomes a nuisance. You might let her jump on you sometimes, but she can't tell the difference between your Sunday best suit and your Saturday sweats, so she needs to learn not to jump up unless invited.

TIPS AND TAILS

"Off" is the command for four on the floor. Don't use "Down," because you've already taught her that "Down" means something else—"Lie down on the floor." You want your puppy to learn that "Off" means "Get off me." It's not punishment; it's an instruction.

To teach off, you'll first teach her to jump up on command. Pat your chest with both hands and say "Up" just as she starts to jump. Praise her, and as she backs off, say "Off." Add a hand signal as you work: your flat palm toward her with spread fingers.

Meanwhile, as she's learning up and off, don't give her any attention when she's jumping—no eye contact, no touching, no talking. Look away, stand up straight, fold your arms, and turn your back to her. Stand still and wait her out. As soon as she stops jumping, even for a second, praise her and say "Good off." If she immediately jumps back up, ignore her again. When she's got all four feet down, stand quietly and praise her calmly.

Jumping up is a sign of overarousal, so you want her to lower her energy level. If you bend over her or make eye contact, this invites her back up into your face. Ask her to sit when she hits the floor so she has an alternative behavior to keep her busy. When she's first learning and you do pet her, loop two fingers through her collar to help her keep her feet on the ground. Look away and pet her chest so she's more likely to stay in position.

If she doesn't back off when you ignore her, attach a leash to her collar. When you give the "Off" command, give the leash a quick snap to remind her. You can also stand on the leash so she corrects herself when she jumps. If you drag her off you with the leash or use your hands to push her to the floor, she's not learning anything except that you'll do the work for her. Your hands reward her for jumping up, and even though you think it's a correction, she thinks it's a game.

Off is a command you'll use often with your excited Golden Retriever puppy. When she can alternate up and off on command, she understands the exercise. Practice often around the house and outdoors, and have every family member teach her to respond.

Your puppy is now tall enough to begin playing a Golden's favorite sport, counter surfing, and off is useful for objects as well as people. Hook a leash to her collar, and let her drag it in the house. When her paws hit the counter, grab the leash and tell her "Off." A quick tug will get her attention. As soon as she looks at you, praise her and call her to you. Remember, don't drag her off the counter; she must decide to remove her paws on her own.

TIPS AND TAILS

To help avoid counter surfing, clean off your counters. Anything that remotely smells like food should be in a cupboard or on top of the refrigerator, and be sure to scrape dishes and fill the dishwasher as soon as you've finished eating. One successful scavenging operation rewards her for counter surfing, and she'll try again and again.

Your puppy will happily claim the couch or king-size bed for her own, and if you allow this behavior, the family will be left sleeping on the floor. To fix it, use the same method you used for the counters. Let her drag a leash, give the command "Off," and lure her off the couch with a treat. Praise her as soon as she starts to get off. After some practice, hide the treat and don't produce it until she gets off the couch completely.

Invite her up on the bed or couch if you want to. Some dogs get possessive of their favorite spot (usually at about 1 or 1½ years old) and won't want to move, so be sure she willingly gets down when you tell her.

After she learns off, put it to good use. When your puppy charges full speed at you, hold up your palm in the off position and rush at her. Spread your fingers, put your palm right in her face, and immediately ask for a sit. As she gets the idea, use a less-dramatic hand signal and just lean toward her to remind her to stay off and sit. Eventually, she'll decide off is a two-part command—off and sit—and she'll sit every time.

Sometimes a rambunctious puppy doesn't listen, so you need to use stronger measures. Fill a squirt bottle with water, and keep it handy. When she starts to jump up or is charging at you, squirt her in the face or chest. She'll quickly learn to veer off or refrain from jumping as soon as she sees you holding the bottle. Or because she's a Golden Retriever, she'll decide the water bottle is great fun, and you'll have to come up with another method.

TIPS AND TAILS

You might hear about kneeing your puppy in the chest when she jumps on you. *Don't do this.* It could injure her, either breaking her breastbone or hurting her when she falls. You also might hear you should grab her paws and hold on until she struggles to get down. Again, *don't do this.* It could teach her to bite at your hands or be unwilling to let you handle her feet in other situations, like when you want to trim her toenails. Neither method builds a good relationship with your puppy.

A polite puppy greets people she meets with a sit. Once she understands how not to jump on you, expand her lesson and teach her not to jump on anyone else with a sit-to-greet. This is an entirely different exercise in your puppy's mind.

Enlist family or friends to help you. Have them ignore your puppy and make no eye contact. Don't let them greet or pet her until she sits quietly, and once she does this consistently, use this same method when she meets people out in public. People will be amazed at your training skills!

Add sit-to-greet to front-door greetings at home, too. Hang a leash on the doorknob, hook her up as soon as the doorbell rings, and ask her to sit and stay before you open the door. If she starts to get up, shut the door and have her return to the sit. This will take several tries before she remains sitting. When the person comes in the door, you'll have to start all over, asking her to sit and stay. Remember to touch her and say "Okay" when she's allowed to stand up.

When the visitor moves away from the door, walk your puppy quietly to the person to say hello and sit for petting. If she just can't settle down at the door, put her in her crate and let her out on leash after your guest has entered and everything is calmer.

If you see her think about jumping but then think better of it, praise her to the skies because she is definitely the smartest puppy on the planet. She'll remember how happy you are and try to do as well the next time she's tempted.

Going Many Different Places

Continue to take your Golden Retriever to new places this month. Also return to places you've previously visited so she'll remember them.

In preparation for the adolescent crazies, practice her obedience skills everywhere you go. Bring along a chew bone and have her lie quietly at your feet while you relax on a park bench. For a new sensation under her feet, take her to a harbor if you have one nearby, and let her walk on the floating docks. Walk her across a bridge or over a freeway, too.

If you have a beach nearby, take her there. Although you've introduced your Golden Retriever to water at home, and she probably loves it, the family pool and garden hose are a far cry from a lake or beach. Waves crashing on the shore, birds running along the water's edge, the smell of the ocean and seaweed—these are all new, exciting, and potentially scary to your puppy. Bring fresh water with you for her to drink; you don't want her gulping salty seawater, which will quickly dehydrate her. And ponds and lakes might have bacteria and protozoa that can make her sick if she ingests them.

Consider bringing another dog along for your puppy's first beach expedition. Start by allowing your pup to drag a long line. Many dogs are afraid of the approaching water and spook when a wave splashes on their feet. When she sees another dog having fun, she'll be more likely to try it. Start by walking her along the water's edge and letting her get used to the feel of the wet sand. Don't force her into deep water, and do not throw her in.

Bring a ball she can fetch, but keep it on the beach for now. Don't throw it out in the water until she's happily playing in the shallow waves. Then just toss it a foot or so and let her chase it out on a receding wave. When she's comfortable, you don't want her swimming to China, so keep her close enough that you can grab the long line.

When you bring her home, you'll be glad you've been practicing her grooming skills as you hose her down to get the saltwater and sand out of her coat. You also might need to follow up with a full bath, depending on how dirty she is.

TIPS AND TAILS

Teenage Golden Retrievers and retractable leashes are a dangerous combination. The farther away from you she goes, the less control you have. Many of these leashes extend as far as 26 feet, and when she's that far away, she might ignore your call because she isn't used to responding from a distance yet. And one good, hard jerk when she sees another dog a few hundred yards away and she's gone, the leash ripped from your hand and bouncing along behind her. What's worse, if the handle retracts quickly, it could break a bone when it catches up to and hits your pup. *Please*, wait until your dog is at least 3 or 4 years old before trying retractable leashes—if ever.

BEHAVIOR

The training and socialization you've worked so hard on up to this point won't completely prevent your puppy from her madcap adolescent activities, but you do have an excellent head start and might avoid some typical teenage behavior problems. But just in case, let's look at some areas to work on this month.

The Age of Distraction

At 6 months, your Golden Retriever puppy is ready to take on the world, and sometimes she considers that human being at the other end of her leash (you!) a hindrance to her plans. Expect a lot of overenthusiasm and pulling in every direction when she's out in public, and be ready with calm and consistent training and rule enforcement. You might have to stop what you're doing and spend a few minutes to get her attention so she'll listen to you this month. She's strong and determined, and you must be equally so. And always remember, she isn't trying to annoy you—she's a preteen.

She'll use as many tricks as she can to get out of obeying you. You'll ask for a sit, and she'll paw at your leg. When she lies down, she'll roll on her back like she has a tremendous itch that just won't wait. She'll whimper, snort, wrap herself around your legs, and she'll creep forward as soon as your attention wanders. Just patiently use the leash to put her back in position, and release her when you're ready. Repeat the exercise until she does it correctly, but set her up for success by asking for a shorter stay next time. If you give up and quit when she's goofing around, she wins and will try to distract you every time you ask her to do something.

Use your body language to keep your dog calm and focused. Speak softly, stand up straight, and use the leash instead of your hands to correct her or put her back in position.

Dealing with Digging

Golden Retrievers dig for many reasons, but the most common is because it's fun! Digging rewards her with interesting smells, chewy roots, and other garden delights. You can't train your dog *not* to dig, so the solution includes management and prevention. Conduct a regular perimeter patrol to find and fix any loose boards in wood fencing or broken tension wires at the bottom of chain-link fencing. A determined Golden Retriever can and will tear apart a chain-link fence.

Boredom and separation anxiety cause many dogs to take up recreational digging. A young dog left out in the yard all day gets restless and needs something to do, so she makes her own entertainment. She might have seen you working in the garden earlier, so she digs up a spot that still has your scent. If you use bone meal or blood meal when you plant, she could be attracted to that smell. She might dig to bury a bone or toy or to make a cool resting place under a large bush.

HAPPY PUPPY

A young Golden Retriever needs lots of physical and mental exercise. Tire her out before you leave her in the yard alone and then leave food-dispensing toys that will occupy her for an hour or more.

Consider providing your Golden Retriever with her own digging pit. Set aside a small area; fill it with sand (which is easier to rinse off your puppy than dirt); and bury treat-filled toys, bones, balls, and other prizes in the sand for her to find. When you first introduce her to the pit, leave a few goodies sticking out of the sand so she gets the idea.

Of course, some dogs refuse to use your chosen spot, and this is where management comes into play as you make other holes less attractive. For example, fill holes with dog feces and cover them. Put a balloon in a hole so it pops when she digs and scares her. Or place a piece of chicken wire about 4 inches down in the hole and bury it. She won't like snagging her toenails on the wire.

If you have gophers, moles, or other underground pests, your Golden Retriever will do some serious excavating to try to find them. The easiest solution to this problem is to get rid of the critters. Rodent poisons usually contain molasses or bran, so they'll also attract your dog and could kill her if she ingests any. Even if the bait is placed underground, your Golden Retriever might get to it. Check with your local garden center for dog-friendly methods to eliminate pests.

Your dog might dig because she sees other people and dogs walking past your house, gets frustrated, and wants to join them, so she digs under the fence. To solve this problem, you could put up a solid fence, which also reduces nuisance barking. Or line the bottom of the fence with concrete blocks or large rocks. You also could attach a 2-foot-wide strip of chicken wire or hardware cloth along the bottom of the fence. Place it so the top 12 inches attach to the fence and the bottom 12 inches bend out into the yard. Cover the part on the ground with rocks and dirt.

When all else fails, keep your pup indoors or build a dog run for her to stay in when you aren't there to supervise her activities.

Iron Jaws, Soft Mouth

A Golden Retriever is supposed to gently pick up a fallen bird and deliver it to the hunter in pristine condition—she's not supposed to eat it. She should hold the bird gingerly so she doesn't tear it up, crush it, or otherwise render it inedible. Keep in mind that this is the same dog who can turn a tree branch into toothpicks.

Retrievers should have soft mouths, but people sometimes accidentally train their dogs to grab and bite down hard. They worry that she'll bite their fingers as she takes a treat or toy, so they snatch their hand away as the puppy reaches for it. Or they toss the treat on the ground, which encourages the dog to lunge for it. Dogs who are aroused and excited grab in the heat of a game. Competition from other dogs also causes a puppy to grab.

It's important to teach your Golden Retriever to take a treat nicely. Introduce this treat-taking lesson separately from other exercises you're teaching your puppy because if you're asking her to sit, for example, and then correct her for snatching at the treat, she'll get confused.

First, choose a word to use to remind her to be gentle. *Nicely, gently, easy,* or *softly* are all good choices because they're soft, two-syllable words, which are easier for you to say in a calming way.

If your puppy is a real shark, wear garden gloves. Put a tiny dab of peanut butter on the palm of your hand, and offer it to your puppy. If she grabs, simply close your hand over the peanut butter. She needs to lick this treat, not bite at it.

Try again. If she lunges at your hand, quickly push your hand at her about an inch to slow her down. As she licks the treat, use your word, "Nicely," and praise her quietly. Say "Nicely" in a calm and friendly voice while she's eating the treat. This isn't a command or a warning.

When she's taking the peanut butter off your palm politely, try it with a piece of her kibble. Hold your thumb over the treat and let her chew it out of your grasp. Correct her with "Ack!" if she bites your fingers, but don't snatch away your hand.

Next, switch to holding treats between your fingertips. As she reaches in for the treat, push the treat about an inch into her mouth. She'll feel your hand coming at her and back off slightly. Also hand-feed your puppy her meals (or even a portion of her meal) for a few days, practicing her new manners. Then incorporate "Nicely" into your daily routine and training sessions.

TIPS AND TAILS

A puppy who grabs treats probably also grabs toys and holds them in an iron grip. Avoid teaching your Golden Retriever to bite hard. As she grows up and gets stronger, you won't be able to out-muscle her. Don't play tug-of-war games in which you encourage her to hang on and not let go. And don't pull toys from her mouth; her natural reflex is to bite down and resist. Trade her for a treat or another toy instead.

The "Give" command comes in handy around the house. You'll have a much easier time wrestling the remote, the phone, or other contraband from her mouth using "Give" than trying to pry something from her grip.

This lesson is easier to introduce at eye level. Attach a leash and present your pup with a toy you know she'll want. Be sure to use something you can take without sticking your fingers in her mouth. A tennis ball, for example, might be too small, so choose a stick or retrieving *bumper* instead. Use "Nicely" to encourage her to take it gently, just like she did with food. When she has the toy in her mouth, show her a treat or another highly desirable toy, and say "Give" as she lets go of the first toy.

She might drop the toy or release it into your hand. Whichever she does, praise her and then repeat the lesson several more times. Once she gets the idea, introduce the command "Take it" as you present the toy.

DOG TALK:
A **bumper** is a long, narrow rubber or canvas retrieving toy used for training hunting dogs. Due to their length, they stick out of either side of a dog's mouth so you can take them easily. Rubber bumpers are covered with raised knobs that prevent the bumper from sliding around in your pup's mouth, which would encourage her to chomp down and hold it even more tightly. Canvas bumpers are usually filled with hard foam and sometimes contain weights. Take bumpers away from your dog when you aren't using them because she'll shred them easily.

Golden Retrievers love to retrieve, and they love games. To get a really fast release when you say "Give," throw the other toy for her to retrieve as a reward for giving up what she has in her mouth.

TRAINING

Diligent training is your goal for this month. Your pup is capable of performing at least 10 obedience commands by the time she's 6 months old. She'll be easily distracted, however, so give her plenty of reminders. With practice, she should be able to do a 1-minute sit stay and a 1- or 2-minute down-stay by the end of this month.

Keep your training lessons interesting and fun by teaching your Golden Retriever new skills and polishing old ones.

Basic Obedience Review and Hand Signals

Your puppy should have learned the following commands so far:

Sit: Put your rear end on the floor and don't move. Hand signal: scoop one hand upward, palm up.

Down: Lie down, roll on one hip, and don't move. Hand signal: push your flat hand, palm down, toward the ground.

Okay: You're finished; relax. This command releases your dog from whatever she's doing. Hand signal: toss your hands upward happily, palms up.

Come: Stop what you're doing and come here. Signal: wide open, welcoming arms.

Let's go or **walk:** Pay attention, we're going for a walk. Signal: step off on your left foot (when she's at your left side).

Stay: Don't move until I come back and touch you. Hand signal: flat palm in front of the puppy's nose as you step off on the foot farthest away from her. For example, if she's on your left side, step off with your right foot.

Off: Put all four feet on the floor. Hand signal: flat palm, fingers spread, pushing toward the dog.

Take it: Take an item, such as a toy, that I present to you. No hand signal.

Give: Open your mouth and release an item. Hand signal: flat open hand (like a plate) in front of her mouth.

TIPS AND TAILS

Because dogs are so visually oriented, they read your body language before they pay attention to what you say. A hand signal or other cue from you helps your dog understand what you want. You can use the ones described here or make up your own.

Training Problems

She was doing so well with her training, and now she seems to have fallen completely apart. Who is this disobedient puppy? When you lose mental control of your distracted preteen Golden Retriever, retain physical control by keeping her on a leash. Insist that she comply with every instruction, even when she gives you a "What? You talkin' to me?" attitude. Training problems might actually be attention problems rather than willful disobedience.

If you slack off and let her respond slowly or get away with not responding at all, you'll slowly lose control over your dog, just when you need it most. That should be enough to motivate you work through any training issues you're encountering. Don't reward your puppy if you have to ask twice or physically force her to do what you've asked. Show her the treat but then put it away.

Do, however, reward every sincere try. Remember as you work together that you're not angry at your puppy; you're teaching her. Her behavior right now is part of the learning process.

HAPPY PUPPY

It takes at least three repetitions before your dog starts to understand what you're teaching her. Stick to numerous 2-minute practice sessions over several days instead of one ½-hour session every day. A puppy gets tired and loses interest after a few minutes, and she's most likely to remember the last thing you worked on and nothing else.

Dole out your praise and treat rewards according to her response. When she's done especially well, give her several treats and big, happy praise. When she responds slowly or late, give her mild praise with a small token treat. She'll soon learn by your reaction which responses earn treats and exuberant praise and her performance will improve.

Why is she testing your patience this month? Several reasons could be to blame. For example, she has reached a *learning plateau*. It takes about 6 weeks before a dog's brain converts a behavior from short-term to long-term memory and it becomes a habit. As she's processing the change, she might act like she's forgotten a simple command. Just keep reviewing, and she'll catch up.

DOG TALK

A **learning plateau** occurs when your puppy suddenly seems to have forgotten everything you've taught her. It's common in adolescent dogs and often happens around week 5 in obedience class. The phase might last 2 days or 2 weeks, but it does pass, and you'll see a surge in her progress once she's through it.

She might also be confused. Take a step back in her training and treat her like she's learning it for the first time. Remember, she'll get mixed up if you ask her to do something in a new place or if someone new asks her to do it. Even a simple sit might befuddle her. What's more, if she's uncertain, and that makes you uncertain, she senses your confusion and delays her response. When you're sure she understands what you're asking, act like you expect her to respond.

Or she might be testing you. She could be bored with lessons or just distracted by adolescent energy. If this is the case, you'll see her offer avoidance behaviors—refusing to look at you, barking at you, or bouncing around. Call her bluff, persevere, and reward her when she gives in. For example, if she sits but pops right back up, wait a second. If she doesn't settle back into the sit, walk her around you and ask again. Take a few steps and command "Sit" again. Don't give her a treat until she sits promptly the first time you ask her.

If she rolls around and paws at your feet when you tell her "Down," don't touch her, and do not offer any praise, treats, or comments. Remain calm and firm, get her attention back on you, and try again until she responds. Praise her and then quit.

If she won't come when she's called, attach a long line and reel her in. Be sure she complies every time, and don't call her if you can't enforce it. Always praise her as soon as she looks at you, and encourage her all the way in. Don't wait until she gets to you.

Enrolling in More Obedience Classes

Your Golden Retriever graduated with honors from puppy kindergarten; she's learning all these things you've been teaching her; and she's growing into a beautiful, well-behaved young dog. So why invest time and money in another obedience class? Beginning obedience might appear to be a review of the things she already knows, but it offers other benefits as well.

You could be ahead of the curve this month, but adolescence approaches, and your puppy still has a lot to learn about self-control and good behavior. Obedience classes give her the opportunity to socialize and hone her skills in a controlled environment with new dogs and people of all ages.

As a bonus, the structure of a class motivates you and the rest of your family to continue practicing with your puppy. You'll have the opportunity to ask questions and try different methods if something you're doing isn't working for your particular pup. There's probably going to be at least one other Golden Retriever in your class, so you'll be able to watch how other owners deal with the same challenges you've encountered. In addition, watching other sporting breeds who also mature late and are very active like Goldens gives you insight to your own dog's personality.

Plus, your puppy gets the opportunity to practice things she knows in a new place, and you'll find out if she really understands what you've taught her so far. The instructor offers new and different distractions to challenge her, too.

Once basic class is completed, you can move up to the next level, where you prepare your Golden Retriever for off-leash control.

Teaching the Automatic Sit

While walking your Golden Retriever, tell her to sit every time you come to a stop. Pretty soon, she'll automatically sit for you. As always, when she's first learning this skill, give her a treat and praise as soon as she sits. As she gets the hang of it, you can continue to praise and *fade* the treats. Ultimately, you won't have to say "Sit" when you stop walking but she'll still take a seat.

DOG TALK

When teaching a new behavior, you reward with a treat every time your puppy complies. When she knows a skill, you can wean her off, or **fade,** the treats by skipping an occasional treat reward while still using verbal praise. Eventually, she'll get a treat only once in a while for her best effort. If her response isn't reliable, you might be reducing the number of treats too quickly.

Teaching "Leave It"

The "Leave it" command is different from the "Off" command. With leave it, you want your puppy to turn her attention to you and away from whatever she's interested in. The idea is to prevent her from doing something before she gets too involved with it. You'll use this command in many situations, such as when you drop a cupcake on the floor, when she focuses on the cat across the street, or when she thinks about rolling in horse manure.

To teach leave it, put her on a leash and walk her past a treat or toy on the floor. As soon as she notices the item, say "Leave it," turn sharply, and walk away while making happy talk and luring her attention back to you. If she gets the item before you can say "Leave it," you're too close, so walk by the item farther away next time.

When she focuses on you instead of the item, praise her and give her a treat from your hand. Don't let her have the treat or toy on the floor. Practice several times, and she'll soon look at you for a treat as soon as you command "Leave it." She'll be more motivated if the treat in your hand is one she likes better than the one on the floor.

Practice several times a day and with many different items. When she's reliably looking to you, try the same exercise without turning away. Just keep on walking while saying "Leave it." When she responds to your command, praise her and give her something else to do, like come or sit. If you release her, she'll just dive for the treat.

YOU AND YOUR PUPPY

Raising a Golden Retriever puppy shouldn't be all work and no play. Teach her to enjoy fun activities like swimming, but remember to enjoy some quiet time together, too. Your pup is ready and willing to do whatever you have in mind.

Having Fun in the Pool

Golden Retrievers are born water dogs. Their webbed feet and water-resistant coat makes them naturals at a pool party. But wait! There's one detail you might not be aware of: puppies, even Golden Retrievers, are not born knowing how to swim. You have to teach them. Once your pup gets the hang of swimming, you'll have hours of fun together in the water.

TIPS AND TAILS

Never give your puppy access to a pool until she can swim the length of it and knows how to get out on her own. Even then, you should always be present. If you have a pool cover, don't let your puppy play on or under it. And never throw your puppy in the pool. It won't force her to swim, and instead, she could drown. At the very least, she might never enjoy the water again, which is a tragedy for a Golden Retriever.

Start by letting your dog play in water up to her chest in the bathtub or a kiddie pool. If she's been to the lake or ocean, this will speed up the process. Keep lessons short—maybe only 5 to 10 minutes the first day. Swimming is tiring, and it likely will frighten her until she's used to it.

First and most important, teach your pup how to get out of the pool. Have her on a leash if you need to; if you have a puppy lifejacket, put it on her. Get in the pool with her, sitting on a step and holding her while letting her stand on the step. Pat the edge of the patio or deck outside the pool, and use a few treats to encourage her to jump out of the water. Repeat until she starts to understand how to get in and out of the pool.

Now take your pup a foot or two away from the edge and hold her up in the water with your arms under her belly. Most pups start paddling with their front feet immediately in this position, like they're trying to walk. If you don't hold her up, she'll be vertical, rear feet and tail deep in the water, pawing with her front feet as she tries to get out of the pool. She can't swim until she learns to level herself and get her rear up as high as her front.

Continue to hold her stomach up and let her paddle to the steps and get out. If she's willing, take her back in the water and do it again. Always turn her so she's swimming toward the steps. You want her to think that's the only direction to swim.

After a few tries, give her front end less support as she paddles. Pretty soon, you'll notice she's holding up her front end and her rear feet are paddling, too. Gradually, you'll be able to give her stomach less and less support as she learns to hold herself up. The process may take a day or it may a week. Work with her as long as it takes to ensure swimming stays fun and isn't frightening.

Wait until she's completely comfortable swimming and getting in and out of the pool on her own before you let her jump off the edge into the water. Practice with other people in the pool and a lot of commotion around her, too.

Enjoying Quiet Time Together

You probably have fantasies of spending a cold winter's night in front of a roaring fireplace, reading a good book while your devoted Golden Retriever sleeps curled up on the rug at your feet.

It's probably hard to reconcile that picture with the active puppy you have today. But even a puppy needs some downtime, and so do you. Evenings are also a perfect time for her to quietly keep the kids company while they do homework or watch television. She needs to learn that life goes on around her and she doesn't need to be in the middle of everything that happens. If you respond every time your little tornado asks for attention, she'll just pester you more and more.

Your puppy should be able to lie at your feet without being crated or tethered all the time. As with everything else, practice makes perfect. The first few tries might be more training than relaxation, but she can learn it. If she's restless, be patient. You can start by having her on leash at your feet for just 5 or 10 minutes each night. Give her something to chew on to help keep her occupied. It might take her a few minutes to settle down, but once she understands the nightly routine, she'll happily comply.

A balance of training, play, and quiet companionship marks the beginning of the partnership you and your Golden Retriever will enjoy for years to come.

	SOCIAL	BEHAVIOR	TRAINING	PHYSICAL	HEALTH
MONTH 1			Littermates and mother teach appropriate canine behavior	Rapid growth	
MONTH 2	Breeder starts socialization				
MONTH 3	Socialization at home with new owner and other pets	Fear-imprint period	Begin house- and crate training		1st DHPP vaccine
MONTH 4			Enroll in puppy class		2nd DHPP vaccine
MONTH 5	Socialization in public	Teething begins—heavy chewing period	Ready for basic commands	Switch to adult food	3rd DHPP and rabies vaccines
MONTH 6			Enroll in basic obedience class		
MONTH 7		Adult teeth are in—chewing continues		Moderate growth	Sexual maturity
MONTH 8					
MONTH 9			Ready for more advanced training		
MONTH 10					
MONTH 11				Slow growth—reaches adult size	Annual vaccinations and checkup
MONTH 12 AND BEYOND					

7

The Silly Tweenager

Do you remember being in the seventh grade? Every day was full of drama and excitement. You weren't quite a teenager, but you weren't a little kid anymore either. Your body was changing, and you practiced acting like an adult, unsure about this new role.

Think of your Golden Retriever puppy going through this same experience. At 6 or 7 months old, he has the emotional maturity of a 12-year-old child, but his physical maturity is dawning. He'll be reckless and uninhibited but also insecure and clingy. Most of all, he'll be a whole lot of fun.

PHYSICAL DEVELOPMENT

Although your puppy might not be fully sexually mature this month, his or her related hormones are developing. Soon you'll recognize changes in your Golden's appearance and behavior.

Understanding Female Sexual Maturity

Female Golden Retrievers can mature anywhere from 6 to 14 months of age, but most have their first *heat* between 7 to 12 months. The heat cycle is a clear signal of sexual maturity. (In males the onset of puberty is much more uncertain.) Most female dogs go into heat twice a year, although some take longer to cycle. During this time, you must keep her away from *intact* males to prevent pregnancy. An unneutered male will travel several miles to get to a female in season.

> **DOG TALK**
> **Heat** is the period when a female dog is receptive to breeding and capable of getting pregnant. Also referred to as "in season," the cycle lasts 18 to 21 days. **Intact** refers an unneutered male or unspayed female dog.

But before you start thinking you'll breed your Golden Retriever puppy now, know that a teenage dog is too young to breed. She's not yet physically or emotionally mature enough to deal with a litter, and she might harm or abandon her puppies if she has them this young. In addition, the health testing she should have before being bred doesn't provide accurate results until she's at least 2 years old.

Now, back to her heat cycle. The first stage is called proestrus and lasts about 9 days. During this time, she will emit an odor that attracts males but reject any who come near her. Her vulva swells, and there's a slight bloody discharge. The first hint you might have that she's in heat is the gang of male dogs hanging out in your front yard.

The second stage is estrus, when the discharge increases and is pink in color. This period lasts about 7 days, during which she'll accept a male for breeding. This is when she can get pregnant, and keeping her confined is critical. A chain-link fence isn't enough. A determined dog will breed *through* a fence. Keep her safely indoors.

Diestrus is the final stage of active heat, and it starts about day 14 but could be as late as day 20. The discharge is redder, the vulva returns to normal size, and she no longer accepts a male's advances. Diestrus lasts 60 to 90 days or until the female gives birth, approximately 63 days after conception. When the discharge and swelling have ended, the heat cycle is complete.

A Golden's heat cycle gets messy. Doggie diapers and pads are available to protect your house, but you should also wipe away the discharge regularly, and during the height of her heat you might want to clean her twice a day. Besides keeping your house cleaner, this prevents skin irritation from excess moisture. She might also get cranky, mount other dogs, or try to escape and breed during this time.

Estrogen is the primary female sex hormone. It maintains the female's sex organs and contributes to the development of a feminine appearance. Because of her estrogen, she has finer bone structure, is shorter, and weighs less than most males.

Understanding Male Sexual Maturity

Over the past several months, your male Golden Retriever's testicles have developed and begun to produce sperm, and soon he'll be capable of siring puppies. Male dogs have an increase in testosterone levels at 4 or 5 months, reaching a peak at 8 to 10 months. His testosterone levels taper off to normal adult levels at around 18 months.

Males don't have heat cycles like female dogs do. Once they reach maturity, they're always fertile. However, like a 6-month-old female, he's too young to be bred now. He doesn't have to raise a litter, but he's not old enough to have health clearances that ensure he won't pass on genetic defects to his offspring.

A sure sign of puberty in the male dog is when he starts lifting his leg while urinating. He also might be more aggressive with other dogs and mount them during play.

An intact male develops distinctly male physical characteristics as he matures. He has heavier bones than a female; a bigger, blockier head; and more muscle.

TIPS AND TAILS

To calm down an intact male dog when an in-heat female is near, dab a bit of pure vanilla extract (natural, not synthetic) or Vicks VapoRub around his nose to interfere with his ability to smell. To help mask the smell of a female in heat, put some Vicks on the fur around her tail. You can also give her one chlorophyll tablet twice a day during her heat cycle. These actions decrease her attractive scent but won't totally remove it.

HEALTH

Pet Golden Retrievers should be spayed (females) or neutered (males). Like any issue regarding your dog's health, you should understand why and when it should be done so you can make an educated decision.

In this section, we also take a look at some more external parasites that might plague your pup, along with some genetically inherited Golden Retriever health issues.

Spaying and Neutering

The reasons to spay or neuter your dog are many, and the reasons to keep him or her intact are very few. The main reason to spay or neuter is to prevent adding to pet overpopulation. Shelters and Golden Retriever rescue groups have hundreds of wonderful Goldens available for adoption, sometimes even puppies. Even if you don't purposely breed your Golden Retriever, mixed-breed puppies from an accidental breeding have a slim chance of successfully remaining in the same home throughout their lives.

As you learned in previous chapters, being a responsible breeder is expensive and time-consuming. A breeder must ensure both parents must have health exams and genetic tests and then spends weeks caring for the mother and her puppies. If something goes wrong, the costs can be huge. The breeder also keeps in touch with the new owners, answers their questions, and takes back a puppy any time during his life if the owner can no longer keep him.

Your breeder probably sold you your puppy on a limited registration, which means any puppies your Golden Retriever produces cannot be registered. Goldens are the third most-popular breed in the United States. A lot of study goes into breeding dogs, and only the best of the best should be bred.

Besides the social issues, a spayed or neutered (altered) dog is simply much easier to live with. Your Golden will be more focused on you and less on other dogs. On the practical side, most doggie day cares and many kennels won't accept unaltered dogs.

Male Golden Retrievers

As sex hormones develop in your male Golden Retriever, they affect his behavior. He'll be easily distracted, less focused on you, harder to handle out in public, and more likely to *mark* indiscriminately. He also might not get along as well with other dogs. He'll try to escape, too, and roam when he senses a female in heat, even if she's miles away. An unneutered male is also more susceptible to several kinds of canine cancer.

DOG TALK

A mature dog **marks,** or deposits urine, so other dogs can identify him and determine his age or readiness to breed. Marking also establishes territorial boundaries.

Although a neutered male might still mark, he won't do it as often or in as many inappropriate places as an intact dog. Neutered males are less of a threat to other male dogs and, therefore, aren't challenged as often as they would be if they were intact.

Neutering a male dog consists of the surgical removal of both testicles. Unless the testicles have been retained in the abdomen, it's a simple procedure and your Golden Retriever will go home the same day. The vet uses surgical glue or sutures to close the incision, and your pup will have to wear an Elizabethan collar (head cone) for a few days to prevent him from chewing at and ripping open the incision. The testicular pouch usually remains and shrinks up into the abdomen over time.

Most dogs are able to resume normal activity within a couple days, but don't allow him to exercise too hard. Watch the incision for swelling, discharge, discoloration, or odors that might indicate an infection. It'll take several weeks for the testosterone level in his system to decrease.

TIPS AND TAILS

Spaying/neutering affects your Golden Retriever's sexual behavior but not his ability to learn. He can still hunt, compete in obedience, or participate in any other activities you choose. In fact, he'll perform *better* because his raging hormones won't distract him.

Female Golden Retrievers

Female dogs also behave differently when they're intact. They're more likely to be aggressive toward other dogs, especially females. When in heat, a female is easily distracted, will try to escape, and will mark more to advertise her availability, bringing intact male dogs from miles around to your house. As her heat ends, she'll be aggressive to males, too. Her housetraining also might lapse during this time.

When a female is in heat, she undergoes physical and emotional stress and a complete upset to her usual personality and health. She might not be able to participate in her regular activities like hunting, service, or therapy work.

Intact females are susceptible to more health problems than spayed females. They're prone to mammary cancer, pyometra (uterine infection), and other maladies caused by excess amounts of estrogen in their systems.

A spayed female's personality doesn't fluctuate wildly when she doesn't have the seasonal upset of heat cycles. One health issue that occurs in a few spayed females is urinary incontinence, and she might leak a little urine while she sleeps. This condition is easily managed by inexpensive medication.

Spaying a female dog involves an abdominal incision to remove the ovaries and uterus, so it's more invasive than neutering a male. She'll probably have sutures, which need to be removed after 10 to 14 days. She also will need an Elizabethan collar to prevent her from tearing out her stitches while they heal. Her activity should be restricted for the first few days.

The lack of estrogen after spaying does increase some dogs' appetites, so the old wives' tale about altered dogs getting fat is partially true. Ensuring she gets regular exercise and monitoring her weight should keep her as trim as she needs to be with no problem.

When to Spay/Neuter?

For the past 20 years, animal shelter veterinarians have performed spay/neuter surgeries on dogs as young as 8 weeks old. Their motivation is clear: to prevent pet overpopulation. You shouldn't alter your Golden Retriever at such a young age though. When considering when to alter your dog, long-term health effects of the surgery play an important role.

Veterinarians recommended that dogs be altered before puberty, meaning before a female has her first heat or before a male starts lifting his leg. Today it's believed there are some benefits to waiting. Weigh these against your Golden's behavior and the inconvenience of having an unaltered dog before you make your decision, and discuss the risks and benefits with your veterinarian.

In both sexes, an early spay/neuter surgery could cause a dog to grow taller than if he or she was allowed to mature. During puberty, the *growth plates* of your dog's limb bones grow quickly, and he gets taller. After puberty, the cartilage in the growth plates turns to bone, no new cartilage forms, and your dog stops growing. After the bones reach their full adult length, they expand and become wider, denser, and better able to support the adult dog's weight. A Golden Retriever is usually full height by 10 or 12 months old, but the growth plates don't close until 12 to 14 months.

DOG TALK

Growth plates are discs at the end of each limb composed of soft cartilage. Growth plates are located in the hips, knees, elbows, and wrist bones. Older cartilage is eventually replaced by bone as your pup grows.

Spay/neuter surgery removes the source of hormones that causes the growth plates in your dog's long bones to stop growing. If these hormones are removed, his bones continue to grow. So a dog neutered early is taller and lankier than he would be if he was neutered later. In most dogs, this doesn't matter. But the growth plates in a dog's body close at different rates. If some close before your dog is altered and some afterward, he might develop odd proportions that impact the long-term functioning of his joints.

In males, early neutering prevents some of the male sex characteristics from developing. A mature, unneutered male Golden Retriever has heavier bones and shoulders and a blockier head than a neutered male. Females don't develop these characteristics anyway, so it isn't a consideration. Early spaying in females slightly increases the risk of genital problems like vaginitis, due to the incomplete development of the external sex organs.

Recent studies have suggested there are some benefits related to leaving your Golden Retriever intact. Certain cancers and orthopedic injuries might be more common in spayed and neutered dogs in some families. Other concerns include the risk of bone cancer, the effect on the development of hip dysplasia, and reduced bone mass in the spine. Discuss the timing of spaying and neutering, and whether it should be done, with your breeder. However, know that if you choose to leave your puppy intact, your responsibility as an owner greatly increases.

Dealing with Mites and Mange

During month 7, your puppy might have some pests you have to deal with. Although he can be affected by some of them at any time during his life, this is the age when you might encounter these parasites for the first time.

Demodectic mange (demodicosis): The *Demodex canis* mite is present on all dogs, but it doesn't cause problems unless the dog has a weak or compromised immune system. And it's not all that common in Golden Retrievers. When it is, the mother passes the mites to her puppies during the first few days of life. An active case is caused by abnormally large numbers of mites or by stress, which weakens the immune system. It most often shows up in puppies, who go through a tremendous number of changes in their early months: teething, vaccines, moving to a new home, hormonal changes, neutering, spaying, worming, and more.

Localized demodex is concentrated on the face and forelegs and is characterized by scaly reddened skin, hair loss, pustules, and plugged hair follicles. Symptoms often resolve and disappear on their own by 6 or 7 months of age.

Generalized demodex is much more rare in dogs, but it's much more serious. It develops from localized demodex and usually appears before 18 months of age. Symptoms include patchy hair loss, inflamed skin, enlarged lymph nodes, and severe itching, especially on the feet. Infected dogs are at risk of developing secondary bacterial infections.

Your vet diagnoses demodex by taking a skin scraping and examining it under a microscope. Sometimes the mites are difficult to find, and a skin biopsy is necessary for diagnosis. Treatment of generalized demodicosis includes miticidal dips and oral medication. Your vet will prescribe antibiotics for secondary skin infections.

Canine scabies (*Sarcoptes scabiei*): Also called sarcoptic mange, these mites burrow under your dog's skin and cause intense itching. This highly contagious parasite affects young dogs more often than mature canines. Direct contact with an infected dog or infected wildlife transmits the mite to your puppy, where it immediately burrows into the outer layer of skin and lays eggs.

In addition to constant, intense itching, your dog develops crusty pustules and hair loss, particularly on the elbows, tummy, edges of his ears, and front legs. Severe scratching and biting also cause infection.

Sarcoptic mites are much harder to see under a microscope, so diagnosis often is based on symptoms. Some oral flea and heartworm medications kill mites on your dog before an active infestation can occur. Treatment includes medicated shampoos, miticidal dips, and a course of ivermectin. Your vet might prescribe anti-inflammatories as well to make your pup more comfortable.

Sarcoptic mange is a zoonotic disease humans can get from their dogs. In people, the mites die out on their own and no treatment is necessary.

TIPS AND TAILS

Unlike other types of parasites, sarcoptic mange is highly contagious. An infected dog must be isolated from other dogs and even cats until he's cleared of the mites.

Cheyletiellosis (*Cheyletiella yasguri*): These mites are most often seen on young and adolescent puppies. Infection is easy to prevent because the same insecticides that kill fleas work on these pests. The mites live on the skin's surface, and the main symptom is dandruff (scaling and crusting) along the dog's back. They can also cause itching and enlargement of the lymph nodes.

Cheyletiellosis mites are diagnosed by examining a skin scraping. Your vet will prescribe shampoos and miticidal dips. Other dogs and cats in the family should also be treated.

Ear mites (*Otodectes cynotis*): Ear mites cause a buildup of a reddish, waxy-looking substance in the ear. It can become so severe that the ear is blocked with debris. Symptoms of ear mites are similar to those of an ear infection: head shaking, scratching, and tilting of the head. Even a small number of mites can set the stage for yeast or bacterial infections.

Once your veterinarian diagnoses ear mites, your dog needs a miticide to kill the mites and a prescription antibiotic or anti-inflammatory ointment to cure any resulting infections. The vet might also prescribe an ear wash. Your Golden's ears might be painful, and he'll resist letting you touch them. Some dogs are in so much pain, muzzling is necessary so you can administer the medication.

Golden Retriever Health Challenges

In recent years, researchers have made great strides identifying the genetic components of inherited diseases in Golden Retrievers. But testing isn't available yet for every inherited health issue. You might have received copies of health clearances for the parents of your puppy from your breeder (see Months 1 and 2), so you know your own Golden has a lower risk of developing some of these conditions. If you didn't get clearances, here are the diseases, their symptoms, and their treatments:

Hip dysplasia: Hip dysplasia develops as the dog matures and the head of the femur (ball) no longer fits properly into the hip socket. Symptoms can appear as early as 6 months of age, when a dog might show lameness in his hind legs, possibly caused by overactive play. When a veterinarian manipulates the rear legs, the dog will show evidence of joint pain. X-rays are used to confirm the diagnosis. The vet will prescribe crate rest and analgesic drugs, but the pain and lameness will reoccur as soon as the puppy is active again.

Hip dysplasia ranges from mild to severe. Some dogs never show symptoms even though they're mildly affected. Others develop symptoms as they age because the hip joints develop osteoarthritis.

In a young dog 8 to 14 months old, surgery might be an option. A triple pelvic osteotomy (TPO) is a procedure in which the surgeon cuts the hipbone in three places and rotates it so it will heal in a better position, supporting the ball of the femur. As long as arthritis hasn't already developed, most dogs can return to normal activity. This is major surgery, and the recovery time is several months, during which your dog must remain inactive for long periods, working back up to normal exercise slowly.

For an older dog, total hip replacement surgery is an option. The ball and socket are removed and replaced with metal and plastic, similar to the same procedure in humans. This option also involves a long recovery period.

For dogs who aren't candidates for surgery, owners can take steps to make their Goldens more comfortable, like avoiding high-impact activities such as jogging or anything else painful for the dog. Low-impact exercise like walking and swimming help build muscle mass, and anti-inflammatory drugs ease the pain. These dogs shouldn't be allowed to become overweight because obesity is hard on joints. Many people give their dogs supplements like glucosamine and chondroitin to lubricate joints and ease arthritic symptoms.

A responsible breeder waits to breed until her dogs are 2 years old and have been x-rayed and cleared to minimize the possibility of producing puppies with hip dysplasia. However, there's a slight chance two parents who are clear can still produce hip dysplasia.

Elbow dysplasia: This inherited disease is caused by abnormal development of the three bones that make up the elbow joint, which leads to formation of bone chips and areas of loose cartilage. You won't know your dog has elbow dysplasia until you notice front lameness, usually after exercise. He might also move with an unusual gait in front, throwing his elbows slightly out.

TIPS AND TAILS

Although symptoms can start as early as 4 months, most Golden Retrievers don't show signs of hip or elbow dysplasia until they're older and the condition causes arthritis in the joints. If your puppy has symptoms, have your veterinarian examine him to correctly diagnose any problems.

Treatment of elbow dysplasia is similar to that for hip dysplasia. Walking, swimming, and other non–weight-bearing exercise, and keeping your Golden Retriever at a lean weight reduce pressure on the joints and help build muscle strength. Anti-inflammatory medications ease the pain, and joint supplements also might help. Arthroscopic surgery can remove the bone chips in the elbows to make your Golden Retriever more comfortable.

As with hip dysplasia, breeding dogs should be x-rayed at 2 years of age and not bred if they show signs of the disease.

Progressive retinal atrophy (PRA): This retina disease afflicts many breeds of dogs, and Golden Retrievers are affected by a specific mutation known as prcd-PRA (progressive rod-cone degeneration). It's not common in the breed, but it does occasionally occur. In PRA, the cells of the retina die and eventually cause blindness. First, night vision decreases, then daytime vision diminishes, and ultimately the dog's eyesight fails completely. Goldens don't usually show symptoms until they're middle-aged, at about 4 to 6 years old. Dogs adapt well to blindness, and you might not notice your dog is affected until you move the furniture from its usual place or take him somewhere where he's unfamiliar with the room layout.

An ophthalmologist can diagnose PRA in a puppy or adult, although there's no treatment. Fortunately, the genes causing PRA recently have been discovered and a test is available to identify dogs who carry or are affected with the disease long before they show any symptoms so they can be removed from a breeding program before they produce affected puppies.

Cataracts: Cataracts are opaque spots in the lens of the eye that interfere with the dog's sight. Hereditary juvenile cataracts can cause mild vision problems. As the dog grows, the spots stay the same size, so his vision might actually improve.

Nonhereditary cataracts often appear in older dogs and can lead to blindness if not removed via surgery. You might not realize your dog has cataracts unless his vision deteriorates and he starts bumping into things.

Entropion, ectropion, distichiasis: Entropion and ectropion are inherited defects of the eyelid. In entropion, the edge of the eyelid turns inward, causing the eyelashes to rub against and irritate the cornea. In ectropion, the eyelid rolls outward, exposing the eye surface to irritation. Either of these defects can be surgically corrected.

Distichiasis is a condition in which the eyelashes grow in unusual directions and rub against the surface of the eye, which causes tearing and inflammation and can permanently injure the cornea. Surgery can correct this condition.

If your puppy's eyes are always runny or he has tear stains on his face, have your vet examine his eyes to rule out these problems.

Pigmentary uveitis: Also called Golden Retriever uveitis (GRU) because it almost exclusively affects Goldens, this painful eye disease leads to blindness and can also cause cataracts and glaucoma. Usually, the disease develops in older dogs with symptoms such as red, runny eyes. If caught early and treated, the dog's vision may be saved.

Hypothyroidism: Hypothyroidism is the underproduction of thyroid hormones. Symptoms include low activity level, weight gain, thinning hair, and thickened skin due to fluid retention. Your veterinarian will run a blood test to diagnose the disease. Up to 25 percent of Golden Retrievers are affected by hypothyroidism, which isn't curable, but it is manageable. An affected dog will have to take an inexpensive daily pill for the rest of his life but should suffer from few, if any, symptoms when treated.

Ichthyosis: This is an inherited skin condition that causes excessive dandruff and darkened, scaly skin in Golden Retrievers. It's often misdiagnosed as seborrhea, a similar skin disorder. Before the disease was identified, it was sometimes called puppy dandruff because pups would often have it but then outgrow it. With ichthyosis, the skin becomes thick, scaly, and inflamed, often on the abdomen. Many affected dogs never show any symptoms, while others are moderately affected. There's no cure, but moisturizers and essential fatty acids are often prescribed to help manage the condition. Affected dogs are susceptible to bacterial and yeast infections that cause severe discomfort and require treatment.

Megaesophagus: Megaesophagus causes paralysis of part or all of the esophagus and usually affects puppies, although adult dogs sometimes develop the disease too. The dog will regurgitate his food and might become severely underweight. An affected dog can be fed from an elevated bowl, which helps the food go down. Surgery might help, but aspiration pneumonia is always a threat.

Subvalvular aortic stenosis (SAS): SAS is an inherited narrowing below the aortic valve that causes the heart to work harder than normal to pump oxygenated blood. The disease varies in severity, and in some dogs, it never progresses beyond puppyhood. An affected dog might pant, show signs of weakness, and have less stamina. A veterinarian might detect a heart murmur, but examination and testing by a cardiologist is necessary for a full diagnosis. In severe cases, the condition can cause fainting or even sudden death.

Bleeding disorders: Golden Retrievers are susceptible to von Willebrand disease and hemophilia A. Both cause excessive bruising and bleeding due to insufficient clotting factors in the blood. There is no cure, and even minor injuries must be carefully treated.

Masticatory muscle myositis (MMM): This autoimmune disorder causes jaw muscle pain, and an affected dog will suddenly become unable to open his mouth. MMM can occur in dogs as young as 4 months old. The condition is usually treated with steroids.

TIPS AND TAILS

This list of genetically inherited conditions sounds scary, but don't panic. Golden Retrievers are generally healthy. By learning about these diseases, you'll recognize any symptoms that show up in your puppy and be able to get an affected dog treatment before he becomes seriously ill.

NUTRITION

As you look at the myriad choices available in the pet food aisle, choosing the right food for your Golden Retriever can seem confusing and even overwhelming. How do you figure out the differences between brands or decipher the label information? With a little education, you can make an informed decision and choose what's best for your pup.

All dogs have the same basic nutritional needs—protein, fiber, moisture, vitamins, minerals, carbohydrates, and fats (see Month 2)—and most dog foods contain these essentials, but that's where the similarity ends. Any one food on the market won't meet the nutritional needs of every dog. The following sections outline some basic facts to help guide you through your options.

Who's in Charge of Pet Foods?

Pet food companies are required to list ingredients and meet manufacturing standards regulated by several federal organizations. Individual states get in on the act, too.

The Food and Drug Administration (FDA), through its Center for Veterinary Medicine (CVM), regulates which ingredients are allowed in pet food, the manufacturing process, and what health claims a manufacturer can legally make. The FDA, working with the U.S. Department of Agriculture (USDA), defines the exact requirements for terminology used on labels. (The USDA also is involved in establishing regulations for identification and approval of pet food ingredients.) The FDA, along with state and local agencies, also inspects manufacturing plants to ensure compliance with labeling laws. The actual food itself does not have to be preapproved by the FDA.

The American Association of Feed Control Officials (AAFCO) is comprised of officials from local, state, and federal agencies who enforce laws regarding production, labeling, distribution, and/or sale of pet foods. AAFCO specifies the minimum and maximum percentages of nutrients that must appear in a food to be considered "complete and balanced." It also designates requirements regarding product names, flavor designations, and ingredient names that appear on the label. In addition, AAFCO publishes testing requirements manufacturers must follow to meet safety and nutritional standards.

The FDA, USDA, and AAFCO are the heavy hitters, but a few other groups are also involved. The Federal Trade Commission (FTC) works to prevent misleading advertising by requiring manufacturers to conform to truth-in-advertising standards. The Pet Food Institute (PFI) is a lobbying group that represents pet food manufacturers.

What's on a Label?

With so many regulators involved, the information that appears on a pet food label can be hard to understand at first glance. Just remember that a pet food package is primarily a marketing tool, with the secondary function of accurately disclosing any information required by law. When you see pretty pictures of raw beef, colorful carrots, peas, and corn in an attractive arrangement on the bag, the graphics are designed to convince you to buy that brand. The wording, however, is strictly regulated.

The product name: Several rules exist regarding the name:

○ A product can only be named *chicken* if it contains at least 95 percent chicken.

○ A product labeled *beef dinner for dogs* must contain at least 25 percent beef (excluding water sufficient for processing).

○ If the name is *beef formula* (or *recipe, platter,* or *entrée*), the product is only required to contain 3 percent of the named ingredient.

○ If the label states *with beef,* it's required to have at least 3 percent beef.

○ A product labeled *beef flavor* must have enough beef to make it taste beefy. Manufacturers are allowed to use artificial flavoring or a small quantity of extract from beef tissues. There may be no actual beef at all.

Guaranteed analysis: This list states the minimum percentages of protein and fat and the maximum percentages of fiber and moisture in the food. These are not exact numbers, so you're getting only a rough idea of the percentages. Companies are not required to list the percentage of carbohydrates, and the guarantee says nothing about the quality or digestibility of the ingredients that make up the food.

Compete and balanced: In addition to percentages, to declare a food is complete and balanced, manufacturers must show their food meets the nutrient requirements in one of three ways:

○ Through actual feeding trials. This might sound like the best method, but there's debate over how realistic this testing is. Dogs eat the tested food for a period of time, and their health is then measured.

○ By formulating the food to meet AAFCO's minimum and maximum standards, confirmed by laboratory testing.

○ By stating the food is a "family member" of another of the company's foods that has passed feeding trials or met formulation standards.

Life stages: A dog food is labeled either complete and balanced *for all life stages, growth,* or *maintenance.* There is no designation for senior foods.

TIPS AND TAILS

Some foods are not meant to be fed as a complete diet but instead are suggested for supplemental feeding. The label will state *complete and balanced* if the food is formulated for complete nutrition.

Miscellaneous: The company's name and address are required. Many also include a phone number, email address, and website so consumers can contact them with questions. The bag is also printed with the disclaimer that it contains dog food, not food meant for people, along with the net weight of the contents.

Expiration date: The "best by" date is a stamped or printed code that tells you the latest date food should be used. Some companies include the manufacture date so you can estimate the food's shelf life. Naturally preserved foods don't last as long as those that contain artificial preservatives, but most foods are safe if used within 1 year of manufacture. If a food is close to its "best by" date, you know it's been sitting somewhere for a while.

Ingredients list: This is the most important part of a pet food label. Like human food, pet food ingredients are listed in order by volume, from the most to the least included in the food. It can be tricky to decipher what you're actually reading here. The first six ingredients are by far the most meaningful, but you should look for some other key things, too.

Deciphering Ingredients

The first ingredient listed on your dog's food should be an animal protein source. *Meat* could mean cow, pig, goat, or sheep. You could also find poultry, venison, bison, and fish listed. Ideally, you want to know what kind of animal the protein source is from.

The meat used in dog food has had much of the water cooked out. Meat meal (or chicken meal, etc.) is made of meat, bone, skin, fat, and connective tissue from which the water has been removed, so it contains more protein per pound than just meat. If meat meal isn't listed first, look for it as a second or third ingredient. Meat makes the food taste good; meat meal boosts the animal protein content. Meat by-products are less desirable and can include things like heads, feet, hooves, hide trimmings, and more.

Another source of protein is plant proteins, which are less expensive. When you see corn or wheat *gluten* on a label, that's a plant protein source and could be harder for your dog to digest.

DOG TALK

Gluten is a mixture of two proteins found in processed grains like wheat or barley. Derived from the Latin term for "glue," gluten literally helps food stick together and adds a chewy texture.

When you look at the first three or four ingredients on a dog food label, you might see chicken, corn gluten, wheat gluten, etc. Although chicken is listed first, the combination of the second and third ingredients might contribute a larger percentage of protein than the chicken.

Also look for whole vegetables, fruits, and grains, which contain vitamins, enzymes, and antioxidants that haven't been stripped by processing. Dogs are primarily carnivores, but they eat both plant and animal products. They've been eating grains for as long as commercial dog food has been around, and grains are a source of carbohydrates as well as protein. Wild canines also scavenge plant materials. Cereal grain–based carbohydrates are fine for many dogs, but others might have trouble digesting them. Whole grains are more digestible than processed grains like wheat flour or rice flour. Additional healthy carbohydrate sources include beans, sweet potatoes, and apples.

Farther down the ingredients list, you'll find the preservatives. Preservatives extend the shelf life of food, preventing vitamin loss and rancidity from the fats. Natural preservatives like vitamin C and mixed tocopherols are more desirable than synthetic preservatives like BHA, BHT, and ethoxyquin.

When you see little green things that look like peas and orange bits of so-called carrots in your dog's food, don't be fooled. They're not necessarily peas or carrots. Manufacturers add dyes and binders to make kibble look like vegetables to appeal to you, not your dog. If vegetables are included, they're either part of the mixture that makes up the kibble or mixed into the food after the kibble is made.

GROOMING

You continue your Golden Retriever puppy's education this month by teaching him to allow you to brush his teeth—a critical chore that has major health consequences if neglected.

Also in this section, we look at an often-neglected grooming (and health-care) chore: caring for your dog's paws.

Brushing Those Pearly Whites

Now that your puppy's adult teeth are in, they need regular attention, just like your own teeth do. You want your puppy to enjoy, or at least tolerate, having his teeth brushed because you're going to be doing it every week (or more often) for the rest of his life.

Many dogs have gum disease by the time they're 3 years old, so early care is essential. Although some wear and tear is inevitable as your puppy ages, you can help ward off gum disease by establishing good brushing habits early.

Although Golden Retrievers like to chew and that removes some *dental plaque,* it's not enough. Chewing on hard surfaces like bones only cleans the exposed areas of the teeth. Chewing also is the main cause of broken teeth, which can get infected. A Golden who chews throughout his life can completely wear down his teeth to the gum line and expose the nerves. Even chewing tennis balls is bad. Even though they're soft, constant chewing can wear down his teeth.

DOG TALK

Dental plaque is a buildup of bacteria on your dog's teeth that, if allowed to remain and harden, discolors and turns into tartar.

Gum disease causes severe pain and infection, which can spread through your dog's system, into his body, and even cause kidney or heart disease. If his gums aren't healthy, they recede, causing pockets to form at the base of his teeth where bacteria collect and cause infection. You'll notice that his gums are red, inflamed, and bleed easily. Bad breath can also be a sign of infection or gum disease. To keep his gums healthy, massage them with the toothbrush while you brush his teeth.

Besides cleaning his teeth and massaging his gums, regular brushing gives you the opportunity to inspect your pup's mouth for broken teeth and tumors or look for bits of bone, slivers of sticks, or dog food stuck between his teeth. If your dog seems to have trouble eating, suspect a broken tooth or gum problems. (Dogs don't usually get cavities like humans do because they don't eat as many sugary treats.)

Although your dog will probably need a professional teeth cleaning at some point, it will take much less time and be less painful for him if you practice regular dental care at home. The doctor will anesthetize your dog, remove the tartar, and polish his teeth, while cleaning thoroughly beneath the gum line. The doctor will also remove cracked or loose teeth and check for abnormalities.

Your Golden Retriever won't automatically allow you to mess with his mouth, especially in this new, unfamiliar way. But you can get him used to it with some muzzle-touching lessons. If you've been practicing handling him since he was a baby, you're ahead of the game. But still, he'll probably try to turn it into a play session.

Put your hand gently over his muzzle from the top. Just touch it for a moment and release so he won't have a chance to struggle. Don't clamp your hand on his muzzle at first. It's normal for him to resist; this is a move his mother used to discipline him. Feed him a treat with your other hand while you're lightly touching him.

As you work up to more pressure and longer time, he might flip his head around. Don't let go. Just follow his head and reward him by releasing when he stops. Ultimately, you want to be able to put your fingers behind his upper canines and open his mouth. This lesson also makes it easier for your vet when he needs to examine your Golden's mouth. In addition, you'll use it later if he has a run-in with a porcupine or gets something stuck in his mouth.

To brush your pup's teeth, you can use a toothbrush made for humans, a fingertip brush, or even a piece of gauze wrapped around your finger. Human toothpaste can cause a serious stomach upset if your Golden Retriever swallows it, so purchase meat-flavored doggie toothpaste. Or use a paste made of baking soda and water.

HAPPY PUPPY

Let your Golden hold a ball or big chew toy in his mouth while you brush his back teeth.

Begin by massaging your puppy's mouth with your finger so he'll get used to the sensation. Next, add some doggie toothpaste so he can learn to enjoy the taste. Gradually transition to using a toothbrush instead of your finger, brushing along his front gum line using small circles and covering both his teeth and gums. Hold the bristles at a slight angle so it isn't abrasive on his gums.

Brush his back teeth, holding the brush at an angle while using back-and-forth strokes. Concentrate on the molars in the back, where food gets stuck between his teeth and cheek. The inside of his molars won't have as much plaque buildup because his tongue washes away excess food. Do a portion of his mouth each day until he's used to the routine and accepts it.

Caring for Your Pup's Paws

Your puppy's feet are exposed daily to extreme heat, pesticides, fertilizers, and uneven surfaces that could bruise his paw pads. His feet also are constantly getting wet as he runs through grass, leaves, and streams, and mud can accumulate between his toes and dry into clumps. In the summer, dogs sweat through their paws, which creates the perfect environment for bacteria to grow. If he's licking his paws constantly, something is irritating them. The best way to prevent problems is to keep his paws clean and dry.

Hot asphalt or newly blacktopped streets can burn your pup's delicate paw pads. And he can get road burn—when the bottoms of his feet are rubbed raw—from running on hard surfaces. Treat raw feet with a foot soak (more on soaks later in this section) and antibiotic ointment or aloe vera gel. You'll need to bandage his feet to keep him from licking off the ointment. Place a gauze pad on the bottom of his foot, and tape it in place. Put an old cotton sock over the foot, and tape the top to his fur. A liquid bandage product is another way to help treat his feet.

Golden Retrievers can get dry, cracked skin and calluses on their paw pads, too. After a foot soak, apply a small amount of vitamin E oil to help heal his skin. To keep him from licking it off, put it on his feet just before mealtime, so he'll be occupied long enough for it to soak in. Don't apply too much because it will stain your carpet if he walks on it. You also don't want his feet getting too soft because that will make it easier for them to be reinjured.

If you need to wash chemicals, antifreeze, road salt, or cleaners off your puppy's feet, use liquid dish detergent or vegetable oil to completely remove it. Then rinse and dry thoroughly.

TIPS AND TAILS

Be careful when removing goo or hair from between your puppy's toes, and don't use scissors. Golden Retrievers have webbed feet, and you could accidentally cut him.

Do your puppy's paws smell like corn chips? You read that right—corn chips. If so, that means he has yeast growing between his toes. Wash his feet in Betadine solution. Betadine is a 10 percent iodine-povidone antiseptic that kills bacteria and prevents skin infections. You can purchase it at a pharmacy or tack and feed store.

For general paw relief or for a Betadine treatment, teach your pup to love a foot soak. Soaking penetrates all the nooks and crannies of his feet better than washing with a cloth. To prepare a soak, add 1 or 2 inches of water to a kiddie pool or plastic tub and then add the solution. Have him stand in the tub for a minute or two and then rinse his paws and dry them with a towel.

Consider adding green tea, either bags or brewed tea, to a foot soak. The antioxidants in the tea soothe his skin. Chamomile tea also has soothing properties. Apple cider vinegar is another topical disinfectant. Between soaking sessions, rinse his feet with cool water to remove the irritants, and be sure to thoroughly dry them afterward.

Trimming Your Pup's Feet

By this age, your Golden Retriever likely is getting a lot of fur between his toes and paw pads. He almost looks like he is wearing bunny slippers! Although this might look cute and funny, it's not a good situation because he could slip and fall due to a lack of traction. It's time for a trim.

If you're worried about cutting his skin, use blunt-tipped scissors, and don't clip between his toes. Push the fuzzy hair down between his toes and clip everything that sticks out from the bottom of his foot, even with his paw pads. Then clip around the outside edge of his foot. Then push the excess hair between his toes back up to the top of his foot. Finally, brush the hair straight up, and trim it short.

SOCIAL SKILLS

As your Golden Retriever speeds toward sexual maturity, he needs to continue meeting and interacting with other dogs. He's changing as he grows, other dogs will sense that difference and treat him differently, and he'll need to adjust his behavior accordingly. A dog who stays in the backyard for the next few months will be in for a rude awakening when he finally ventures out in public.

Enrolling in Doggie Day Care

Doggie day care is a great place for your Golden Retriever to have supervised interaction with other friendly dogs. If you select a facility staffed by conscientious professionals, he'll have fun, burn off endless energy, and polish his dog manners. Regular attendance 2 or 3 days a week is easier on your dog and less disruptive for the facility because the dogs all know each other and don't have to get reacquainted each time they visit.

There's no legal requirement that dog day-care facilities must be certified in any way or that employees demonstrate dog-handling skills. No national oversight organization exists either. Anyone can hang out a sign and offer day care. The local health department usually monitors cleanliness and hazardous materials compliance, and sometimes local animal control requires a kennel license, which specifies standards for the facility, not the staff.

When you contact a prospective dog day care, expect to fill out an application and attend a get-acquainted visit with your dog. The facility will require up-to-date shot records for DHPP, rabies, and bordetella (kennel cough). They also might require proof of a clear fecal test from your vet, showing your dog is free of internal parasites. Your dog should also be on a regular flea and tick preventative. Most day cares require your dog be spayed or neutered after a designated age as well.

While the manager is busy checking out you and your dog, ask some questions of your own. You might not be allowed to enter the playroom. Don't take that as a red flag; a stranger walking into a room full of dogs can cause an uproar, and scuffles or fights could break out. You won't be able to see the dogs at normal play firsthand.

Instead, many day cares have a doggie webcam or a one-way mirror so you can see the playroom.

Here are some points to consider when checking out doggie day cares:

- How many dogs does the facility allow per day?
- Are there separate groups for high-energy and low-energy dogs?
- Are small dogs separated?
- What is the staff-to-dogs ratio?
- What training have employees had regarding dog handling and behavior?
- What are the hours? Are there limited drop-off and pickup times? What about Saturdays?
- Are any special pricing packages available? Are ½-day rates offered?
- Do the dogs play all day, or is there a specified nap time?

If you can, watch the employees, too. Are they paying attention to the dogs, or are they in the corner, texting or chatting with other employees?

No facility, and no dog, is perfect. Accidents can happen, and occasionally a dog is injured by an inadvertent bite during play or a scuffle. Who is responsible for the vet bill when an accident happens? How do they decide if the offending dog will be allowed to come back? Be sure to ask these questions while you're there.

If you choose carefully, dog day care can be a rewarding experience for you and your pup.

Teaching "Wait"

The "Wait" command helps your Golden Retriever puppy refine his manners. Ask him to wait before he goes through a doorway, before he eats dinner, and before he jumps out of the car. Wait means he's not allowed to move forward until he gets an okay from you. He doesn't have to sit; he doesn't have to lie down. Different from stay, with wait, he doesn't have to remain in place until you touch him. This is a temporary pause, not a stay.

Teach this skill with your dog on a leash, and start in a doorway. As the two of you start through, your pup will undoubtedly try to rush ahead. Say "Wait," and give him the hand signal you use for stay—an open palm in front of his nose. Walk through the door, and if he doesn't try to follow, tell him "Okay," and let him walk through after you. If he does try to follow you, body block him with your hip and turn to face him. Continue to block his way through the door until he stops trying and is still, whether standing or sitting. He'll probably look at you, which is what you want. Now tell him "Okay," give him a treat while he's still on the other side of the doorway, and let him walk through.

Practice this many times in many different doorways. Practice in the car, both getting in and getting out. He'll try to read your body language for a signal he can move. Practice moving around a little without letting him through so he learns he has to wait for your "Okay" release word.

It's tempting to say "Wait … wait … no … stay … *WAIT!*" while you're teaching this command, but don't. That will just confuse him—is he staying or waiting? Dogs really do learn the difference. When you give the command multiple times, he anxiously watches you instead of relaxing and waiting for the release word.

The learning curve might be long and trying for this lesson. It's an advanced concept, but he's old enough to understand it now.

Introducing New Animals

When your Golden Retriever was just a pup, you introduced him to the cat, rabbit, pet snake, and any other animals in the house. He should continue to meet different species as he grows so he remembers and is able to deal with other new animals he encounters throughout his life.

If you have the opportunity, visit a place where he can meet some really big "dogs." Donkeys, sheep, goats, cows, horses and ponies, peacocks, or geese are all critters he can get to know. (Be sure to have someone restrain the other animal so he can't run away or attack.)

Use your jolly routine, treats, and patience while your puppy checks out the animal from a short distance. Don't approach until your pup is calm. Barking, lunging, and raised hackles will only scare the other animal. Have the owner move the other animal around a little so your pup sees it walking and realizes it's a living being.

When he's ready to approach, keep the leash loose so he doesn't feel trapped. If he lunges, turn away, start farther back, and keep trying until he can restrain himself. This might be all you can do on the first encounter. If so, practice with a number of animals so he learns this is the proper way to respond to a new animal.

A friendly horse will put her nose down and say hi to your pup. They'll also sniff each other's breath. Don't let your puppy jump up against the fence or the horse, though. When you're done, praise your pup and walk away.

TIPS AND TAILS

If the horse or other animal is frightened, keep your distance. A scared horse will strike out with her front feet. It could be that the horse is learning, too.

Playing Too Rough

Your preteen Golden Retriever loves to play, and you love to play with him. But even though you're just playing games, he's learning which behaviors are allowed and which aren't. Be careful what you teach him.

Between 6 and 7 months, your puppy is figuring out how strong he is, and he'll naturally try to use his body in his dealings with others. In his childish enthusiasm, your Golden Retriever sometimes forgets himself, bowling over smaller or weaker dogs and body blocking his way across the playing field. His newly raging hormones encourage him to try a new behavior, mounting. Play that was fine in a 12-week-old puppy is now too much for many of his peers. If he's allowed to roughhouse, he'll decide it's okay.

His playmates will tell him when he's played too roughly. They'll growl, snap at him, and chase him away. This helps him learn to mind his manners. Watch these interactions closely, and intervene if your puppy isn't getting the message. You want other dogs to discipline him, but you don't want an all-out fight.

It's one thing to roughhouse with his buddies, but he also needs limits when he plays with you and your family. At this age, he'll jump on you, crash into you while he runs around the yard, slam into your legs, and grab your arms. You might enjoy the game, but when he crashes into someone else, it won't be so cute. He could injure someone, or he could be injured. He could land wrong and tear a ligament, crack immature bones, or tear muscles.

TIPS AND TAILS

Interrupt active games with some control exercises. Have him sit before he retrieves the ball, and practice off. When kids are playing, slow everyone down and introduce some structured games. Quit or call a time-out when things get overly rough.

Before leaving this section, we want to say a word about tug-of-war. Playing tug-of-war teaches your Golden Retriever all the wrong things: he learns to growl aggressively at you, and he's rewarded for holding on and refusing to let go.

Tug-of-war makes a pushy dog pushier and encourages grabbing, biting hard, and jumping—all things you're trying to gain control over this month. Golden Retrievers are blissfully happy when they can retrieve all day; they don't need over-the-top aggressive games. If you must play tug-of-war with your dog, save it until he's older.

BEHAVIOR

Be patient. This month your puppy will have moments when he seems to have forgotten everything you've so diligently taught him. He might not come when he's called, or he might not fetch because his teeth hurt. Just remember that this, too, will pass.

Dealing with Teenage Behavior Regression

What looks like a regression in behavior to you is more like a new awakening on your puppy's part. Seemingly overnight, your previously well-behaved and adoring pup has transformed into a wild child. His interactions with other dogs might have also deteriorated as he has practiced new ways of dealing with others.

Problem aggression and anxieties might develop during this time, but they also recede as your puppy finds his way. Spaying or neutering makes a huge difference in his behavior, lessening fighting, marking, and bullying among dogs.

Because he's distracted by his adolescence, your puppy's obedience skills might falter, and you'll need to use a stronger hand to control and redirect his behavior. This is the age when many Golden Retrievers are relegated to the backyard or turned in to shelters because of their overly boisterous behavior.

Adolescence might last until your Golden Retriever is 2 or 3 years old. It might be small comfort to know he'll get over it, but if you continue to work with him, he'll get through this period, and so will you.

Here are some of the behaviors you might see:

○ Shyness or fearfulness

○ Destructive, acting-out behavior to satisfy his endless energy

○ Housetraining relapse, marking

○ Aggression

○ Overexuberance

○ Bossiness, rudeness, constant testing of the rules

○ Ignoring commands, distracted

○ No self-control or ability to resist temptation

○ Overprotective

We help you deal with all these issues in this and upcoming chapters.

Working Through a Second Fear Period

The fear-imprint period that was so important during your puppy's first 2 or 3 months might come up again this month. If your Golden Retriever had a bad experience in a particular room when he was 8 weeks old, he might seem to suddenly, fearfully remember that event now, months later.

The adolescent fear period starts between 6 and 14 months and can last anywhere from a few days to several weeks. He's going through major physiological and psychological changes now. The fear period seems to correspond to growth spurts, and his anxiety might vary from day to day. He might spook or bark aggressively at something he's seen a thousand times, like the mailbox at the curb. Don't overreact. In most cases, you can ignore the behavior. As you did when he was a baby, let him approach scary things when he's ready, and don't force him into a situation where he feels overwhelmed.

A well-socialized dog will get through this period much quicker than a dog who has been kept at home and isolated. Your normal, happy, friendly Golden Retriever will grow out of it with less trouble than some other hypersensitive breeds. Just be sure to keep him on leash in public in case something frightens him.

Still Chewing

By 6½ months, your Golden's adult teeth are in, but they won't completely set in his jawbones until 8 or 9 months. So until then, he'll continue to be a chewing machine. And because he's bigger and stronger now, he'll be more destructive.

Many dogs especially enjoy chewing on wood, quickly graduating from sticks in the yard to stair rails, 2×4s, fence posts, shingles, and other things you'd never imagine he'd eat. Invest in some chew-repellent products from your local pet-supply store, or make some of your own with red pepper sauce in a bottle of water. (Watch for potential staining with the latter.)

Chew toys are as important now as they've ever been, and diligent supervision on your part will protect your more vulnerable household treasures. Provide a variety of chewables: stuffed frozen KONGS, tire toys, bully sticks, and heavy nylon bones. He might lose interest in a certain toy. If that happens, put it away for a week or two, and it will be exciting to him when you bring it out again.

When you give your Golden Retriever something new to chew on, supervise him to be sure he isn't going to immediately destroy it and swallow pieces. You can offer some softer toys, like retrieving bumpers, and then put them away when you can't watch him.

Marking

You know your Golden Retriever has reached adolescence when he starts lifting his leg. Testosterone levels start to rise as young as 4 or 5 months old. But it isn't just the boys; females mark, too, just not as often or as obviously.

A male Golden Retriever hikes up his rear leg so his hip is perpendicular to the ground, while a female usually lifts one rear leg forward while still squatting. When they're done, both might kick the ground with their rear legs to spread the scent of their urine. By doing this, your dog is announcing his sexual maturity and laying claim to that territory, whether at home or away.

When your puppy starts marking, the scent of his or her urine has changed, and any other dog who smells it will know there's a new sexually mature dog in town. No longer can he roll over on his back and leak a little urine to get the big boys to back off. Other adult males will know he's an adolescent, and his permission to misbehave is immediately revoked. Many male adults will put a teenage dog in his place before he gets too full of himself and tries to challenge the older dogs.

On your walks, your male dog will mark repeatedly—and often in unacceptable places, like on the neighbor's car. You'll catch him marking over where another dog has just urinated, too. His motives aren't just territorial; dogs read each other's urine like we read the daily newspaper—comedian Dave Barry called it "yellow journalism." They learn who's been to this spot, when, and the other dog's age and sexual maturity. Then your dog leaves his own calling card, often releasing just a tiny bit of urine, like he's saving up so he has enough for the entire trip.

There's no reason to let him get away with impolite marking behavior. Don't stop and wait while he has a good sniff and lines up to pee; correct him and move on. When excessive marking becomes a habit, it's hard to break. Most dogs continue marking after they're neutered, although not as often.

Sexual maturity can also mean a sudden lapse in housetraining. It's not really a housetraining issue; it's marking. Males will lift their leg indoors and out, on any vertical surface they can reach. Females will mark indoors, too.

Treat this like any other accident. Interrupt your dog with a loud "No!" or "Ack!" and go outside with him like you did when he was a baby. Praise and give him a treat when he goes in the proper spot. Go back to supervising him indoors and crating him when you can't. Deal with the problem like he's on his first day of housetraining as an 8-week-old puppy. You can't stop a dog from lifting his leg or marking, but you can teach him where and when he's allowed to go.

TIPS AND TAILS

Golden Retrievers usually aren't a difficult breed to housetrain. If your pup is marking indoors often, he might have a bladder infection, or your spayed female might be suffering from urinary incontinence. Rule out health problems before you decide your dog just refuses to be housetrained.

TRAINING

Training is a lifelong process, but it doesn't have to be misery. You're investing time raising a well-behaved puppy so you can enjoy years of companionship and fun together. Once you lay the foundation, he'll only need an occasional brush-up to keep his skills sharp and his responses eager.

As he reaches adolescence, a Golden Retriever will put your patience to the test. Two or three months now of diligent effort are worth the payoff. And don't forget to keep it fun!

Practice Makes Perfect

Your dog might be an obedience champion when you're in the backyard practicing, but does he really understand the commands? And can he perform out in public when you're under stress and really need him to behave? What's more, dogs depend on body language for much of their communication. What happens if your arms are full of groceries and you can't give him a hand signal along with a command?

Test your dog to see if he really understands sit. Face your dog, ask him to sit, and use your hand signal. If he sits, good. Release him. Now look away, ask him to sit, and stand perfectly still with no body language, eye contact, or hand signal. Did he do it? If not, he still needs some guidance. When he can perform all the commands you've taught him without any visual cues, you know he understands.

When your dog is doing a solid sit-stay and down-stay, it's time to add some distractions. He'll make mistakes and get up when he's not supposed to; that's how he learns exactly what stay means. Here's a progression of increasing distractions to help your Golden Retriever understand stay:

1. Put him in a sit-stay. While you're still holding the leash, start to walk around him. His head will follow you, and his natural response will be to stand up as you leave his field of vision. Touch his muzzle with your hand to remind him to stay in place as you move.

2. Once he can stay with you circling him while he's on leash, drop the leash and try it again.

3. Circle in the other direction.

4. Circle farther away.

5. Turn your back on him, and walk away several steps before turning to face him.

6. Crouch down without saying anything. Don't look at him. You're not trying to lure him out of place; you want to help him succeed.

Every time he stays in place, verbally praise him from a distance. You don't want him to get excited and get up, but you do want him to know he's done it correctly. He also has to learn that praise doesn't mean you're finished. Always end up at his side, touch him, and say "Okay" to release him. Then have a party! When he makes a mistake, just put him back and continue. No scolding. Take plenty of breaks between tries, and quit when he's done something especially well.

The ultimate practice is to make obedience commands part of everyday life, at home and in public. Practice on walks, at the park, and wherever else you take him. At home, he should sit for his dinner, while you brush his teeth or clip his nails, and when you put a leash on him. He should do a down-stay while you do dishes, brush him, or eat dinner.

Your Golden Retriever should walk nicely on a leash wherever you take him. He should wait politely at doorways and wait for permission to jump into and out of the car. Take time to train throughout the day, and pretty soon it won't be training anymore and you'll have a well-behaved Golden Retriever.

HAPPY PUPPY

Many behavioral problems evaporate after some basic obedience training. Issues like barking, digging, and chewing might cure themselves when your dog is comfortable with his position in the household, knows the daily routine, and understands what's expected of him.

Teaching Cooperation, Not Confrontation

A puppy who misbehaves isn't engaging in mutiny; he's just being a teenager. The only way to respond is with consistent guidance and training. Your dog adores you, but he actually will behave better with discipline and structure. As he challenges you, look for opportunities to build your relationship.

Reward your dog throughout the day, not just during training sessions. You might not have noticed that perfect sit he offered while you were fixing his dinner, or the way he went to his crate at bedtime without being told. Make a deposit in the bank of goodwill, and praise him when you see he's on his best behavior.

If you correct him or interrupt an unwanted behavior, always give him a chance to do something right and earn rewards. Say "Good boy!" when he stops whatever he was doing that you didn't like. Then ask for sit or down, just so you can praise him. No one, even a dog, likes to be yelled at all the time.

Be fair to your dog, too. Be sure he understands what you want him to do before you get frustrated because he didn't do it. Help and reward him, and always set him up for success. Don't expect him to do something perfectly—like a down-stay—the first time company comes over. Put him in his crate, tether him, or hold on to the leash so he can't make a mistake. He'll try harder for you next time.

Teaching the Retrieve

One day you'll look at down at your Golden Retriever pup and find he has dropped a big stick at your feet. His wagging tail gives away the game. "Throw it!" he's saying, his body quivering with excitement. And so it begins; you have a retriever.

For more than 100 years, Golden Retrievers have been hard-wired to retrieve. If you've ever watched a hunting dog at work, you can see he loves it, happy and intense, tail wagging, nose to the ground. You don't have to teach your dog to retrieve; you just have to teach him to bring it back to you.

It's important that you control the game—when it starts, when it ends, and who keeps the toy at the end (you). If your pup gets tired and quits, pick up the ball and put it away until next time. He needs to know it's your toy. This is a subtle message that you're in charge, not him. Although it's a game, you're teaching your dog to cooperate with you and respect your leadership. If you let him decide when to quit and take the ball under a bush for a good chew, he's in charge.

For this example, we'll assume he's retrieving a ball. Golden Retrievers have endless variations on returning the ball, none of which including giving it to you. Why would he bring it back when you're just going to take it away from him again?

This makes perfect sense to him. He'll invite you to chase him, he'll stop just out of your reach, and he'll drop the ball and grab it as soon as you reach for it.

Attach a long line—about 20 feet of clothesline or other light rope—to your dog's collar. When he's running around the yard after picking up the ball, reel him in, take the ball, and throw it again immediately. He doesn't need treats as a reward; throwing the ball is what he wants. The longer you hang on to the ball, the less of a reward it is for him, and the less likely he'll be to return it next time. Still, occasionally wait a few seconds before you take the ball from him.

Never go to him to get the ball—he just taught you to chase him. If he drops the ball before he gets to you or stops just out of reach, take a few steps backward or turn and run away from him.

And don't keep throwing until he's bored. Always leave him wanting more. Keep track of how many throws he retrieves before he gets tired, and quit before you get to that point next time.

You taught your Golden Retriever the "Give" command in Month 6, and fetching is a good time to use that skill. If you're going to hunt with your dog or compete in formal obedience, you'll want him to release the ball directly into your hand rather than drop it. If you don't care, it's fine if he drops it instead.

When he won't give up the ball, show him another ball. He'll usually give up the one he has and take off after the new one. Don't throw it until he drops the first ball, or he'll take it with him.

YOU AND YOUR PUPPY

Don't expect a lot of downtime this month. He's still very young, and he'll play hard until he collapses and falls asleep. You also can play brain games to wear him out if he just isn't ready to settle down.

Continuing to Play

The games you played with your Golden Retriever puppy—hide and seek, find it, and others—will still entertain you both, and you can make them tougher now to challenge him. Teach him to find a person by name, for example. Have the person hide, and while restraining him, tell your puppy to "Find Joe." Have Joe then call your puppy. He'll quickly learn to find multiple people, one after the other.

Your Golden Retriever is probably great at retrieving by now, so this is the perfect time to teach him to retrieve multiple objects, not just a single tennis ball or bumper.

As you throw the item, name it for him, and soon he'll learn to identify which item you want him to retrieve by name.

Hit a ball with a tennis racket to send it farther, and make him hunt to find it. Toss a stick in a creek, and watch him search and bring back the right one. Swimming is excellent and tiring exercise.

Learning Easy Tricks

When training seems like a chore, switch to teaching him tricks and bring the fun back into your time with your puppy. The whole family can participate.

"Shake" and "Roll over" are two easy tricks you or anyone else in your family can teach your puppy.

For shake, get down on the floor with your pup and have him sit. Don't say anything; just reach out and tickle the back of your puppy's front foot just above the floor. He'll lift the foot off the ground. When he does, say "Good," and reward him with a treat. After a few tries (always reaching toward the same foot), he'll lift his foot when he sees your hand coming. Fantastic!

Now give it a name; it doesn't have to be "Shake." You could say "High five" or "Go team" or anything you want. As he lifts his paw, say your word and take hold of his paw. Give him a treat from your other hand while you're still touching him, and release. Work up to where he'll let you shake his paw.

When he's really good at shake, you can work on variations. You can teach him to put his paw in your open hand or lift his other paw to shake. Give these new behaviors a different name and hand signal. For instance, use a different hand when you want to him to shake with the other foot, and use an open hand when you want a high five. Teach just one behavior at a time until he understands it completely. Later, you can alternate which behavior you ask for.

For roll over, have your puppy lie down and roll on one hip, like he's going to do a down-stay. Put a treat in front of his nose, and move it back and toward his spine so he twists his head as he follows the treat. Pull the treat far enough back that he has to put his head on the ground to follow it. As he lies flat on the ground, roll his legs up and over with your other hand and then give him the treat. He'll quickly get the idea after a few repetitions. Add the word you choose for the command.

Both of these tricks are easy for your Golden Retriever to learn in just a few days. Alternate tricks with obedience commands to keep training time fun and interesting for both of you.

	SOCIAL	BEHAVIOR	TRAINING	PHYSICAL	HEALTH
MONTH 1			Littermates and mother teach appropriate canine behavior	Rapid growth	
MONTH 2	Breeder starts socialization				
MONTH 3	Socialization at home with new owner and other pets	Fear-imprint period	Begin house- and crate training		1st DHPP vaccine
MONTH 4			Enroll in puppy class		2nd DHPP vaccine
MONTH 5		Teething begins—heavy chewing period	Ready for basic commands	Switch to adult food	3rd DHPP and rabies vaccines
MONTH 6					
MONTH 7	Socialization in public		Enroll in basic obedience class	Moderate growth	Sexual maturity
MONTH 8		Adult teeth are in—chewing continues			
MONTH 9			Ready for more advanced training		
MONTH 10					
MONTH 11				Slow growth— reaches adult size	Annual vaccinations and checkup
MONTH 12 AND BEYOND					

MONTH
8

Adolescence

Your Golden Retriever is anxious to grow up, and you're scrambling to keep up with her this month. Between 7 and 8 months, you'll have moments when you feel like you have a new dog you've never seen before. Her personality changes as she inches toward adulthood and she discovers she has to deal with other dogs differently from when she was a puppy. She'll temporarily forget a lot of her training, too.

All is not lost, however. Most of her behavior is typical teenage mischief and not a cause for major concern, as long as you deal with it and don't let it become habit. The training you've done up to this point gives you the tools you need to handle her behavior. Basic obedience practice solves many seemingly unrelated difficulties, and you'll spend a lot of time this month reinforcing her training and teaching her self-control and manners.

Her teenage exuberance provides hours of fun and laughs for you and your family, and you'll enjoy even the most challenging times with your Golden Retriever puppy.

PHYSICAL DEVELOPMENT

Her body is ahead of itself this month, and she can't figure out where those long legs came from. Her behavior strays into uncharted territory, and she often leaps before she looks, so be prepared for lots of action!

Understanding Dog Adolescence

In Golden Retrievers, adolescence lasts from about 7 months until 2 to 2½ years. With that kind of time span, it's not a phase you can just wait out, but if you're prepared to deal with it, you'll emerge at the other end with a well-behaved adult dog.

Enjoy her youthful enthusiasm and energy now, though. She loves to do things and thrives on the attention you give her.

Hormones play a big role in your puppy's adolescent behavior. This is the time when her sexual maturity is way ahead of her mental and emotional maturity. If your pup has already been spayed or neutered, you're not completely off the hook because brain development also plays a role. Like human teenagers, she doesn't have enough experience yet to make mature choices, and she doesn't understand the consequences of her changing body. But of course, she wants to be all grown up and do what the big dogs do, so she plays the role of an adult and learns from her mistakes.

The first thing you might notice is that she asserts her independence. She "forgets" her name, takes off, ignores you at the park, and refuses to obey obedience commands. She grabs your shoe and plays keep-away to get out of doing what you've told her to do. Treats don't always work anymore, and her appetite fluctuates from day to day.

Your Golden has had 7 months to learn to read your body language and facial expressions. She knows if you mean it when you say something to her, and she's at the stage where she'll call your bluff. To deal with this, use authoritative posture—stand tall and straight when you're dealing with her to help her understand that you mean it.

You'll find her bossy barking at you when she wants something or urine-marking your belongings as she tries new behaviors—bullying, marking, mounting, and maybe some aggression. She'll take teenage rebellion to new extremes, becoming possessive of her toys or barking at or ignoring you when you tell her to get off the couch. She's also suddenly overprotective of her territory and barks at every car driving by or person coming to the door.

She's conflicted, trying to balance teenage insecurity with her endless energy. She still depends on you, but she also needs to rebel. She does remember what you've taught her, but she needs to be reminded that there are consequences when she misbehaves. Purely positive training might not be enough to keep her attention, and firm *but kind* discipline has its place this month. What works today might not work tomorrow though, so keep trying different things.

Helping Your Puppy Gain Coordination

An adolescent Golden Retriever doesn't know she has hind legs, and when she remembers, she trips over them. She runs with her front legs, and her back end just kind of follows. To improve her overall coordination, you can run her through activities that require her to concentrate on her feet and legs when she moves. You'll be surprised how hard it is for her.

The ladder walk: For this exercise, place a ladder flat on the ground. Put your pup on leash and have her walk through the ladder to the other end. She'll be impatient and want to leave, so you might need someone on her other side to keep her from jumping out of the ladder and walking beside it. Encourage her with treats in front of her nose as she practices lifting her feet to go over the rungs. After a few tries, she'll be pretty good at it.

Cavalettis: Place some pieces of 2×4 lumber on the ground about as far apart as her stride, and walk her over the boards. She'll stumble at first, unaware that the boards are even there. Adjust the distance apart so she can comfortably trot over the boards. When she's mastered the task at ground level, put them up on bricks, about 3 inches off the ground, and try again.

The platform: Place a 2×2-foot piece of plywood on blocks. Have her jump up, guide her with a treat to turn around in a circle once, and sit.

Fast and Fearless

Teenage Golden Retrievers are big, strong puppies, and they know how to use their strength. They're pushy and impulsive at this age, and they have no maturity to hold them back. Your little bull in the china shop isn't intentionally torturing you, she's just acting her age. When you get frustrated, she'll do her best to make you laugh.

The same adolescent who reacts fearfully to fireworks will be strangely oblivious when plunging through brush and brambles, icy water, and other physical challenges. Her common sense is on vacation for the next few months, so you have to protect her from herself. You don't want her to learn the hard way that some things, like ice-covered lakes, are actually dangerous.

HEALTH

From dangerous weather conditions to holiday safety hazards, your Golden Retriever needs to be protected from an assortment of seasonal mishaps. By educating yourself and taking precautions each season, you'll keep your canine buddy safe.

Spring Safety Hazards

It's the season to begin hiking, camping, and enjoying outdoor activities. Do some shorter conditioning hikes with your pup before you head out for long expeditions to get her muscles in shape. Even then, remember she's still a puppy so don't overdo it. If she'll be carrying a backpack, build up the weight gradually, and check with your vet to determine the maximum weight she can safely carry at this age.

Your dog's paw pads are soft and susceptible to cuts and scrapes at the beginning of the season. Walking on asphalt or concrete can cause road burn, so build up slowly while her feet toughen.

As the weather warms up, fleas, ticks, and poisonous snakes become active. Be prepared for these pests by using preventatives on your puppy. Consider rattlesnake avoidance training and a rattlesnake vaccine for your dog if you live where these snakes are common.

TIPS AND TAILS

Snake avoidance training has become popular in many areas of the southern and western United States where people and rattlesnakes live in close proximity. Training methods vary but have the same general goals: dogs are exposed to live snakes whose mouths have been taped shut or are otherwise disabled so they can recognize the sight, sound, and smell of a snake and alert you to its presence even if she can't see it. Most trainers use electronic collars during this training.

Mosquitoes are at their worst during humid summer months, and that increases your puppy's risk of contracting heartworm. If she's not already on a preventative, you need to have her tested for the parasite before you can safely put her on a heartworm prevention program. Take care of this chore by mid- to late spring, or keep her on a preventative year-round.

At Easter time, keep wrapped candy, Easter baskets, fake grass, and chocolate bunnies out of your dog's reach. Most varieties of lily, Easter or otherwise, are toxic to your pup. If she eats a petal, leaf, or even just the pollen, it can cause an upset stomach; if she eats enough, kidney damage could result. Make generous use of your puppy's crate during the holiday to keep her safe and out of trouble.

Springtime also means gardening season, when lawns are fertilized and gardens are sprayed with pesticides. Anything from weed control to garden mulch can be toxic to your pup. Cocoa mulch, for example, which contains the same poisonous ingredients as chocolate, is particularly deadly. If you fertilize or spray, follow the manufacturer's guidelines carefully, let the grass dry completely before letting your puppy walk on it, and wash her feet if you think she's been exposed. And don't let her eat plants or mulch.

Although you take these precautions to protect your dog at home, public parks and other neighborhood homes also might have these hazards—sometimes unbeknownst to you. Always be aware when you're out and about, and ask to be put on notification lists about spraying in public areas where you frequently walk. Also see Appendix C for a complete list of household and yard hazards.

Summer Health and Safety Hazards

Heat exhaustion is the single most dangerous summer hazard for a dog, and your Golden Retriever's body temperature can rise to unsafe levels and result in organ failure. Humidity increases the risk of heat exhaustion.

Dogs have a limited number of sweat glands, they perspire mainly through the pads on their feet, and they pant to cool themselves. When you're out and about, ***never leave your pup in a hot car.*** Any temperature above 70°F is too hot to leave your dog in the car, even if you've parked in the shade with the windows open. The car can heat up to 100°F in 15 minutes or less. Being left in a hot car is the most common cause of heatstroke in dogs.

Lightly exercise with your dog in the early morning or evening, and keep her indoors during the heat of the day. Too many owners innocently assume their dog can jog or hike with them on a hot day without consequence, and your Golden Retriever will do her best to keep up. But remember that she's still too young for hard running on solid surfaces. Place your hand on the sidewalk, sand, or road where you'll be walking with your pup. If it's too hot for your hand, it's too hot for your dog's paws. She can be seriously burned.

HAPPY PUPPY

Always keep cool, fresh water available for your Golden Retriever. In fact, consider putting out two water bowls in case she dumps one during the day, or tie a full bucket to a fence so she can't drag it around and play with it. Many puppies love an ice cube treat on a hot day, so add crushed ice or ice cubes to her bowl. Or leave a faucet dripping into her bowl so she can get water even if she runs out. Be sure she also has access to cool shade if she's outdoors and it's too hot in the garage or doghouse. It doesn't have to be fancy; a beach umbrella is sufficient. A kiddie pool filled with a couple inches of water gives her a cool spot to beat the heat.

It's important that you learn to recognize and treat heatstroke. A tired and overheated dog usually will try to stop and rest. Don't force her to keep going. Find some shade, give her a drink of water, and wet her paw pads to bring down her body temperature. A dog in serious distress will pant heavily, drool thick saliva, have bright red gums and tongue, have an increased heart rate, and may stagger drunkenly or appear disoriented. As symptoms progress, she might vomit or have diarrhea (with or without blood in it), collapse, go into shock, and fall unconscious. In advanced stages, her gums will turn pale gray or blue.

Your first priority is to safely cool your puppy. Lay her on a cool floor, and turn on a fan if possible. Wet her body with cool water from a garden hose, or place cool, not cold, wet towels on her feet, head, neck, tummy, and especially her groin area. Let her drink if she's able. If you can take her temperature, do so. Anything over 104°F is an emergency, so get her to the vet immediately, even if she appears to recover, because this is a life-threatening situation. Dogs who have previously suffered from heatstroke are at increased risk for a second occurrence.

More dogs are lost, killed, or injured on the Fourth of July than any other day of the year. And it's not just one day. People shoot off fireworks for a week or more before and after the holiday. (If you live near the local high school, fireworks are part of many halftime shows and homecoming games. New Year's Eve is another noisy, terrifying night for many dogs.)

A panic-stricken dog afraid of fireworks will do things she'd never consider any other time: rip the leash out of your hands, jump a fence, or run into the street. Many dogs don't react until something blows up right in front of them. Protect your puppy by keeping her at home and indoors on the holiday.

If your Golden Retriever is frightened by the noise, take steps to relieve her anxiety. Some dogs are happiest in their crates in a quiet place. You might need to outfit her with body wrap products like ThunderShirt that soothe your dog by putting pressure on acupuncture points. Or turn on the television or stereo to mask the sounds from outdoors. An exceptionally terrified dog might need medication. Plan ahead and visit your vet for a prescription or to find out about the use of essential oils or aromatherapies. Don't use over-the-counter sedatives on your dog though.

HAPPY PUPPY

Don't comfort your puppy or try to soothe her when she's frightened of fireworks or thunderstorms. Your anxious tone and body language tell her she really does need to worry. Act happy and confident so your dog will realize nothing is wrong.

You can desensitize your dog to the sound of fireworks or thunderstorms. In the off season, play a tape of the sounds at low volume, and entertain your Golden Retriever with a game or otherwise distract her while it plays in the background so she learns to associate the sound with fun or a chew toy. You might have to start at some distance away from the sounds. When she reaches a point where she recognizes the tape and looks to you for her reward, you can increase the volume slightly and move closer to it.

Fall Safety Hazards

As cold weather approaches and drivers winterize their cars, beware of antifreeze in driveways and on the roadways. This greenish liquid's sweet taste is especially attractive to dogs, and your pup can lick enough off her paws to cause kidney failure and even death. If you think your dog has stepped in antifreeze, wash her feet with Dawn dish detergent or olive oil and then call your veterinarian.

Halloween can be a challenge to your pup. Remember when you were socializing your puppy and invited your guests to wear big hats and raincoats? For your dog, Halloween is all those scary-looking people times 10. Trick-or-treaters wear wings and masks and carry large, flapping bags. If your pup barks when the doorbell rings, this is either a great time to practice her obedience or a better time to put her in her crate in the back bedroom.

Burning candles, jack-o'-lanterns, and other flammable decorations tempt your Golden Retriever to investigate. Costumes for pets and people can include choking hazards like string and ribbons. Wooden sticks from caramel apples, candy wrappers, and gum can cause serious injuries. And poisonous chocolate lurks in those goodie bags.

Winter Safety Hazards

If your puppy must be outside for a few hours in extremely cold weather, be sure she has access to a doghouse or other protection from the cold and dampness. Remember, she's still a puppy, and even if she does have the Golden Retriever double coat, she doesn't have enough fat to stay warm.

Even a Golden Retriever can get hypothermia if she gets wet to the skin. The first sign is shivering, a physical reaction that helps her retain heat by elevating her metabolism. Take your puppy indoors immediately if you see her shivering, and warm her body by drying her and wrapping her in blankets. Take her to the vet immediately.

When a dog is hypothermic, her blood retreats to the main trunk of her body to protect and heat her internal organs. That means her paws, tail, the tips of her ears, and other extremities are susceptible to frostbite. A dog with frostbite might limp, and the affected area will be pale and hard to the touch. Dry and warm the area with warm, not hot, compresses. Take her to your veterinarian for further care.

When you exercise with your puppy outside in cold weather, don't overdo it. Cold air and high altitude cause your puppy to burn more calories and get tired faster. Also beware of frozen water and thin ice. Be sure you know where rivers, ponds, and streams are located, and keep your puppy away from them. If she does fall in icy water, don't go in after her. Send for help instead. Adult dogs can survive in freezing water longer than humans can. Puppies are more vulnerable.

Monitor your pup when she's outside in cold and snowy weather. Snow hides familiar landmarks, and your pup might not realize she's left her own yard if you're not there to show her the way. She can't distinguish the curb or driveway, and she might wander into the street. Snowplows have a hard time spotting dogs when they're plowing, and light-colored Golden Retrievers are particularly hard to see in the snow. Also, put your Golden Retriever inside when you use the snow blower. She'll want to be where you are, and as much fun as she might have chasing it, the hard-thrown snow could injure her.

TIPS AND TAILS

After winter outings, wash your dog's feet to prevent irritation from road salt. Salt dries out your pup's paws pads and leads to painful, cracked skin. If her feet are really dry and irritated, apply vitamin E oil or a lotion with lanolin.

It might not look pretty, but during her first few winter holidays, it might be a good idea to deck the halls with exercise pens and pet gates. And beware: your adolescent male might pee on the Christmas tree—after all, it's okay to urinate on trees when he's outdoors.

Decorations make fun, crunchy noises when they break in her mouth, and crinkling cellophane sounds like a package of dog treats, but ribbons can tangle in her gut and cut off her circulation. As she makes her way to her favorite spot at the window, she could get tangled in extension cords and crush gifts. Decorations look like toys to her, and candles can light her fur on fire when she stands too close.

Food is equally hazardous this time of year. Cakes and candies wrapped under the tree don't fool her nose; she knows there's food in that box. Chocolate is especially dangerous, remember. When food is set out for guests, block your pup's access.

Leftover turkey is also tempting. You might want to feed her table scraps, but don't. Fatty meat, skin, and gravy can cause pancreatitis, a potentially fatal disease, so dispose of the carcass where she can't get to it. Remember, poultry bones are brittle and can break in your dog's mouth, throat, or stomach, causing life-threatening injuries. Freeze them until trash pickup day if you have to.

NUTRITION

You go to a lot of trouble selecting the right food for your Golden Retriever puppy, and what does she do? She eats kitty litter! As frustrating as that can be, continue to adjust her food according to her growth, and be prepared for her to make some unusual diet choices of her own.

How Much Food Does Your Pup Need?

Although her growth is slowing down, your Golden Retriever is still eating more than she will when she's an adult. When she reaches 75 to 80 percent of her adult weight, she'll still need up to 125 percent of the calories she'll require when she's mature.

How much she needs to eat varies by her size and activity level. In spring and summer, when she's most active, she'll burn more calories. In the fall, a working hunting dog might need more food than at any other time of year. In the winter, she'll burn more calories outside because of the cold; but on the other hand, she'll spend more time indoors and not be as active overall.

Goldens vary so much in size that it's hard to recommend an absolute amount of food for every dog. Whatever your Golden's size, she doesn't need 5 or 6 cups of food a day as an adult. Unless she's 100 pounds (which some Goldens are), she needs between 2 and 3 cups of food a day.

The type of food you feed is another factor to consider. Premium foods offer more condensed nutrition, so you don't have to feed as much.

The best way to decide how much food is enough for your puppy is to keep track of her condition and weight. See Appendix B for instructions on how to determine if your Golden Retriever is overweight, underweight, or just right. When in doubt, consult with your veterinarian.

The Icky Things Goldens Eat

Although dogs eat things we think are disgusting, to a dog, they are delicious. Dogs have been natural scavengers since before they were domesticated, eating waste left behind by the nomadic tribes they followed. Today, when your dog eats cat litter or horse manure—or even her own feces—she's just repeating behavior that's been part of her nature for tens of thousands of years. Because she considers it completely normal, punishment doesn't usually eliminate the problem.

Dogs have fewer taste buds than humans and aren't as discriminating about what they eat, and there are nutritional as well as behavioral reasons for why they eat feces. If she isn't digesting all the nutrients in her food, they're passed through her body and out into her stool. The stool then becomes a source of additional nutrition. Feces are also a natural source of digestive enzymes and B vitamins. A mother dog eats her puppies' feces to clean the den, hide their scent, and protect them from predators. Puppies often eat the stool of older dogs and their littermates; it's a natural way to establish their intestinal *microflora*. Stool-eating is self-rewarding and may become a habit. When dogs don't get enough exercise and live in a relatively boring environment, they might pick up this habit. The best defense is to pick up feces as soon as your pup deposits it.

DOG TALK

Microflora are microorganisms that live in an animal's digestive tract and perform various functions, such as building the immune system, producing vitamins, and preventing growth of harmful bacteria.

Cat feces have a high protein content that's attractive to dogs. But if a dog ingests clumping kitty litter, it could cause an intestinal blockage. The easiest way to avoid this problem is to use pet gates to block your puppy's access to the litter box and be sure the box is clean.

If you want to use aversion training and make her avoid the feces, use a foul-tasting liquid like bitter apple or pepper sauce. Spray some in your puppy's mouth so she'll recognize the taste and smell and want to avoid it and then spray it on the feces. If you don't introduce her to the taste beforehand, this method doesn't work very well.

Dogs who eat horse and cattle manure are searching for another type of nutrition. Manure is full of digested vegetable matter, like hay and grass. Alfalfa hay also is a source of protein. Dogs are carnivores, but they do include plants in their diet. Dogs might eat manure if they aren't getting enough plant matter in their diets, or just because it's a natural instinct, like stool-eating.

Whatever kind of poop your Golden Retriever chooses to eat, she runs the risk of picking up intestinal parasites. One more reason to prevent this nasty activity.

When Your Pup Eats Grass

All dogs eat grass; it's a perfectly normal behavior. Grass provides nutritional value in your dog's diet and is a source of fiber and roughage high in potassium and digestive enzymes. Your only concern should be if your lawn is chemically treated with fertilizers, herbicides, or pesticides that could make her ill.

Your dog might vomit after eating grass. If this happens a few times a year, it isn't anything to worry about. A dog with a tummy ache occasionally eats grass to make herself throw up whatever is irritating her. This might prevent her from getting seriously ill from something she ate.

If your dog eats grass and vomits every week, there might be a more serious reason. It could mean gastric upset, parasites, nutritional deficit, or food sensitivity. She might be trying to compensate for something that's missing in her diet. Try switching brands or flavors of food. A different protein or carbohydrate source might work better for her. You also could add some lightly steamed vegetables such as carrots, kale, or zucchini to her diet.

GROOMING

Golden Retrievers can suffer from occasional coat problems, and a hundred different causes could be to blame. Besides adolescent hormonal fluctuations, let's look at some other possible reasons for coat problems and how to treat hot spots.

Addressing Skin and Coat Problems

A healthy coat is a sign of a healthy dog. Your dog's coat should be shiny and her skin should be clear, with no dandruff, red spots, or scaling. Some problems, like allergies, can be inherited. (See Month 12 for more information about allergies and treatments.)

During the transition when your Golden Retriever sheds out her puppy coat and her adult coat comes in, her fur might look pretty scruffy. A dull, dry coat along with dandruff or inflamed skin indicates that more than just the semiannual shedding is taking place. A health problem such as chronic allergies, hypothyroidism, ichthyosis, poor nutrition, or liver disease could be the issue. Make a vet appointment.
After your vet rules out health concerns, you can look for other problems that could be the cause.

Too-frequent baths can remove natural oils and lead to a dry coat. If you need to bathe your pup often, don't use shampoo every time, just when she really needs it. The other times, just rinse her well with water. Be sure to use a dog-specific shampoo when you use one. Human shampoos dry out the coat more than those made for dogs. Frequent brushing distributes oils, removes dirt, and makes her coat shine. That might be all she needs on a regular basis.

If your dog swims in a pool, chlorine can dry out her coat. Salty seawater also dries her coat. Be sure to rinse her thoroughly after she swims in either type of water.

Your pup's food might not contain enough of the nutrients she needs to keep her coat healthy. For example, a protein deficiency can cause dryness, excessive shedding, and ear infections. The problem could be caused by grain rather than meat as the primary protein source in the diet. Fat or fatty acid deficiency can also cause a dull coat, dry skin, and itching.

External parasites like fleas or sarcoptic mange make your Golden Retriever scratch constantly, leaving patches of bare skin. It only takes saliva from one flea to cause an intense reaction in some dogs.

Another parasite, demodectic mange, is passed down from the mother to her puppies during the first few days of life and is aggravated by a depressed immune system. It doesn't necessarily cause itching, but it does affect the coat dramatically, causing patches of hair loss and red crusty skin.

TIPS AND TAILS
Cool water relieves itchy skin, while warm or hot water aggravates the itching. Antihistamines like Benadryl can provide some relief. Your veterinarian can tell you the appropriate dose for your Golden. For more serious itching, the vet might temporarily prescribe corticosteroids or antihistamines.

Internal parasites (worms) also can affect a coat's condition, making it feel wiry and dry. Your vet can analyze a stool sample to identify and treat worms.

Dealing with Hot Spots

A hot spot is a moist, inflamed circle of skin your dog licks or scratches until it's raw. A hot spot could have one of many causes, such as allergies, flea bites, flea dirt, or a vaccine reaction. They usually develop in warm weather and rarely in winter. They can appear anywhere on the body, but you'll often find them behind your dog's ears, on the ruff of her neck, and on her belly at the top of her legs—all places where her fur is thick and easily mats.

Always dry your Golden Retriever thoroughly whenever she gets wet. A Golden's top coat traps moisture, and a damp spot can cause bacteria to grow on an already dirty spot on the skin, which then festers and becomes a hot spot. If not tended to, the hot spot will get larger and more irritated as your dog continues to bite at it. You might have to put an Elizabethan collar on her to prevent licking, as chewing and licking can cause a secondary infection that must be treated with antibiotics.

To treat the hot spot, apply cool, wet compresses to loosen the crusty outer layer and soothe the skin. If it's not too painful for your pup, trim the hair around the spot and clean it twice daily with mild, nonperfumed soap or antiseptic solution.

Here are some more suggestions to relieve hot spots:

- Wash with cool green or black brewed tea. The tannic acid in the tea helps dry out the spot so it can heal.

- Apply aluminum acetate solution (available from your pharmacy) three times a day using a spray bottle or compresses. This also helps dry out the spot and speeds healing.

- Add hydrocortisone cream to relieve itching. Apply just enough to rub in completely. Don't use too much, or your pup will lick it off.

- Use aloe vera cream or gel to ease pain and help hot spots heal.

If the hot spot does not respond to treatment in a day or two, a visit to your veterinarian is in order.

SOCIAL SKILLS

Socializing your Golden Retriever is an ongoing process, and when she reaches adolescence, she goes through some major changes. This is a critical time for your dog's development, and she needs to continue her socialization.

Preventing Desocialization

Socialization was an easily acquired skill when she was a puppy, and most Golden Retrievers are naturally friendly throughout their lives. But during adolescence, your pup undergoes so many hormonal, physical, and emotional changes, sometimes it might seem like it's too much trouble to take her out much in public. Continue taking her out, though, because the consequences of not socializing your dog now are hard to overcome.

If your puppy is isolated during adolescence, she quickly becomes desocialized. She's no longer positively reinforced for friendly encounters with other dogs and people, she has no way of working through her lack of confidence, and she cannot develop the social skills an adult dog needs to get along in the world.

Your Golden Retriever is developing a healthy sense of caution at this age that will serve her well in adulthood, when she's learned there are consequences to leaping without thought into every situation. You might think your dog is overly careful, but she's practicing the art of self-preservation and will grow more confident as she settles into her new role as an adult dog.

Dealing with Dog-to-Dog Aggression

Your Golden Retriever's relationship with other dogs changes dramatically as she reaches adolescence. No longer on her "puppy pass," she can't just roar up to other dogs and expect them to love her. She has to learn new methods for interacting with other dogs.

Other dogs will treat her differently when she reaches puberty. She'll be more assertive as she tries to establish herself as an equal and no longer a puppy in the group, and she'll be challenged by older dogs and put in her place. These are natural behaviors, and your dog needs to experience them. If she goes unchallenged, it reinforces any aggressive or pushy tendencies and she never learns she has to restrain herself around other dogs or mind her manners.

For males, it starts with competition for females. He's interested in them in a different way now, and play behavior turns into courtship behavior. The females won't put up with it, and the other males aren't going to let him take over their turf. Intact females are the least likely to get along with each other. They also compete, and rather than flirt with males, they'll argue with each other.

Altering prevents some conflicts among dogs. Once a Golden Retriever is neutered, he's no longer competing with the other males so they don't challenge him. Spayed females don't provoke competition among themselves, either. But altering isn't a substitute for continued socialization. You'll still observe marking, mounting, and pushy behavior, even in altered dogs of both sexes. If you start seeing aggressive behavior in your Golden Retriever, male or female, consider altering now.

TIPS AND TAILS

Play is important during adolescence and allows your pup to develop her canine instincts. Stalking, chasing, mounting, and other natural doggie behaviors all are part of puppy play sessions. These activities take on new meaning in adult play though. Dogs trade roles as they play and relearn how to interact, but adolescent dogs sometimes don't know when to stop, and they might not read their playmate's body language correctly in the heat of the moment. Be sure to supervise so play doesn't get too rough.

Even the best-socialized dogs can lose their temper and get in a spat. Dogs' personalities vary, and not everyone is meant to be best friends. Puppies who formerly played well together might have the occasional dustup. It's almost inevitable that your Golden Retriever will get in a few tussles during adolescence. The question is how serious are these encounters?

Many dogfights are simply arguments, not real fights. Everyone makes lots of noise, but no one has a mark on them when all is said and done. You also might see some competitive growling and snapping over preferred sleeping spots or a favorite toy. One dog usually gives in, and it's over. In these cases, the puppies have learned effective bite inhibition from other puppies.

That doesn't mean fighting is okay. When two dogs clearly don't like each other, there's not much you can do about it except separate them. It's important to continue socializing your dog to other friendly dogs, however, so don't give up.

You can help prevent dog aggression when your pup meets new dogs. New encounters can be high-stress situations, filled with excitement, anticipation, and frustration. The worst thing you can do is hold the leash taut while the dogs sniff each other. If you do, your dog thinks she's restrained and can't escape. She assumes you're tense, too, which could trigger a fight. It's hard to make yourself do it, but relax your hold and let the leash hang loose from her neck.

Introduce unfamiliar dogs on neutral territory, not at home. If both people are holding back their dogs, the dogs will explode at each other when you let go. Instead, go for a walk with the other owner and their dog. Start the dogs far apart, and as everyone calms down, walk closer together.

Don't reward an aggressive reaction, and don't comfort your dog, either. Use your jolly routine and treats, and only reward her for good behavior and for paying attention to you.

If you feel your Golden Retriever is developing a real aggression problem or that it's escalating, work with a trainer or behaviorist. Someone who is experienced in evaluating dog behavior can give you a realistic picture of what's going on, and together you can develop a plan to prevent aggression from becoming a habit.

TIPS AND TAILS

Life on a chain is a miserable life for a dog. A dog who spends the day tied up outside gets frustrated. She can see things, but isn't able to get to them. She can't escape if an animal or person comes in the yard, and feels she has to defend herself, which can cause chronic aggression in an otherwise nice dog. A lonely, bored Golden Retriever barks all day. She can also get tangled in the chain and strangle herself, get wrapped around a tree, or otherwise get injured. Find another way to confine your Golden Retriever.

Hopefully you'll never encounter an aggressive dog, but if you do, you need to know how to handle the situation. When you're out with your Golden Retriever, carry treats to toss away from you and distract the aggressor. Speak in a high, happy tone, and yell "Treats!" "Cookies!" or some other term you hope he'll recognize.

Also carry pepper or citronella spray. Be careful when you aim at an oncoming dog, though, because you don't want it blowing back in your face.

Pay attention to the dogs in your neighborhood so you know if any are a threat. Some might be territorial and bark every time you walk past their house. If they're in the front yard, they might consider the sidewalk and street their territory, too. They might be all bluff and bluster, but they might not be. Either way, try to avoid aggressive dogs. Cross the street or turn around if you can.

If you do encounter a strange dog, speak firmly to him and tell him to sit. He might stop in his tracks and obey. If he's really agitated, though, don't run. This encourages him to chase you and triggers his prey drive. Remember how you learned to catch your runaway Golden Retriever in Month 5? You ran so she'd chase you. In this case, that ploy works against you.

Stand sideways and don't look the aggressor in the eyes. You'll be much less threatening, and he might go on his way after he decides you're no harm. If your puppy is still small, pick her up. With bigger dogs, drop the leash. This might diffuse the situation because your dog isn't getting signals from tension on the leash. If they're going to fight, you don't want to be tangled up in the middle of it. If a dog does attack you, curl up in a ball and protect your face and neck.

If the worst happens and your dog gets in a fight, think twice before jumping into the fray. Most fights are over in a few seconds and you won't have to intervene. If the dogs are really fighting, you're risking your own safety if you try to stop it. In the midst of a fight, instinct takes over, and a dog will bite anything that gets in her way. The worst thing you can do is grab a dog by her collar during a fight. She won't realize it's you, and she might turn and bite you, thinking another predator is attacking her from behind. Keep your hands and body out of the action.

If you decide to try and stop a fight, here are a few tips that might help you stay safe:

- Bang together two metal dog dishes or cooking pots. When the dogs are startled by the noise, they might separate long enough for you to intervene and safely remove your dog.

- Avoid screaming or hitting the dogs. They don't hear you or feel the blows. And if they do, it just adds to their arousal.

- Spray water from a garden hose at the face of the attacking dog.

- If you're indoors, wedge a chair or broomstick between the dogs to pull them apart.
- Lift the aggressor by his hind legs to throw him off balance, which might force him to let go. If someone is there to help you, have her do the same with the other dog.

When the dogs are separated, leash them and take them out of each other's sight. It might not be safe to touch your dog by the collar yet, so put the end of the leash through the loop at the end to make a noose to slip over her neck, and tighten.

When everyone has calmed down, inspect each dog for injuries. You might be surprised to find no large bite wounds. Still, look carefully around your dog's neck and face. Small puncture wounds are hard to find in heavy fur, and they might not bleed. Look for punctures in pairs from the canine teeth.

If you do find a bite wound, treat it immediately. Puncture wounds close up and trap the bacteria in the wound. Because a dog's mouth contains a lot of bacteria, bite wounds usually get infected. Clip the hair around the wound, and wash and rinse the wound thoroughly with water or antiseptic solution. Then take your dog to the vet immediately because she will need antibiotics.

Larger bite wounds, even just an inch long, might need stitches. Your vet might even put a drain in the wound for a few days to allow the bacteria to escape.

BEHAVIOR

One day your Golden Retriever is a cyclone whirling through the house. The next, she sleeps all day. One day she is the perfect obedience student. The next, she seems to have forgotten everything you've ever taught her. All this is typical for her age. She hasn't forgotten her lessons, but they're submerged under a wave of adolescent distraction.

Although she's testing her limits—and your patience—this month, your pup needs her family to fall back on when adolescence overwhelms her. The rules and structure in her life are her safety net. Be sure you're there to remind her.

Being Proactive (Rather Than Reactive)

A teenager in the house means something's always happening, and it's a challenge to stay one step ahead of her this month. By taking a few preventive measures and limiting her freedom a bit, you can prevent her from getting into mischief, keep her safe—and save yourself a lot of angst.

Just because she's a teenager, this isn't the time to give her the car keys. You have to assume she'll get into mischief. She's still a puppy, so continue to crate her at night and when you can't supervise her. Look at things from her perspective, and set her up for success. She can't chew up your clothes if you shut the bedroom door, for example. And she can't get into the trash if you keep the wastebasket in a closet.

Continue to reinforce her training because her knowledge will deteriorate if you don't reinforce her skills during this turbulent period. Enforce the household rules, and remind her when she forgets. You've probably relaxed a little because you know she knows what she's supposed to do, but remember that she's testing the waters right now. If you slack off, she'll take advantage of every opportunity. If she discovers she can get away with jumping on you occasionally, for example, she'll keep trying.

HAPPY PUPPY

If you've just adopted or rescued a young Golden Retriever, congratulations! Goldens are adaptable and can love their new family with incredible devotion. This is the age when many Golden Retrievers change homes because of behavior problems. Although an untrained teenage Golden can be a handful, she's far from a lost cause. Enroll in an obedience class, and read through this book from the beginning like you just adopted a small puppy. Take advantage of this honeymoon period when she's soaking up information about her new surroundings, and teach her house rules from the first day, and she'll be a treasured family pet in no time.

Dealing with Mounting

Adolescent dogs, both male and female, begin mounting when they reach sexual maturity. Mounting is normal canine behavior, just like barking, digging, or chewing. It's less acceptable because it embarrasses you when your dog mounts a guest's leg or humps a stuffed animal in the middle of the living room. Owners often assume the reason is sexual, but there are other reasons, too. You need to look at the context of each incident to understand what's really happening with your dog.

Anxiety and arousal (excitement, not sexual) contribute to a dog's actions. Mounting is a form of *displacement behavior,* a way of acting out to relieve her energy or stress. If she's uncertain of how to react to a situation, or if she's overly excited about the arrival of guests, mounting relieves her tension.

DOG TALK

Displacement behavior is an act that occurs out of context in response to an internal emotional conflict such as stress or anxiety.

Sometimes a dog engages in mounting hours after the exciting event, particularly if she's still anxious after being punished for misbehavior she doesn't understand. For example, you might come home and find she's been emptying the wastebaskets. You're angry, and whether you punish her or not (you shouldn't), she's worried. She needs an outlet to release that anxiety.

She also might learn that mounting works as an attention-getting device. You immediately react and try to stop her, and she learns to use the act as means to get you to interact with her.

Try to anticipate when she'll mount someone or something, and step in to interrupt the behavior. If she's mounting people, attach a leash to her when company comes, and direct her to her toy or pillow instead. Spaying or neutering decreases mounting behavior but doesn't eliminate it completely.

Getting Her Enough Exercise

Golden Retrievers were bred to be workers, but dogs today spend long hours at home alone. They don't get enough stimulation, mental or physical, and they have no outlet for their energy. Your canine athlete needs daily exercise to develop her muscles and her mind.

If you can find a large, fenced field with plenty of interesting smells, she'll entertain herself tracking rabbits, birds, and other scents. Free-ranging exercise such as this isn't as stressful on young bones and joints.

Don't forget to give her short breaks during her exercise. She'll run until she collapses just to please you, so be sure to quit while she still wants more. Take it easy during hot, humid weather because she'll tire quickly. Also remember that repetitive pounding on hard pavement or jumping on hard surfaces could injure her.

Too much exercise can come back to haunt you. As your puppy builds stamina, she'll need even more exercise to tire her out. If she doesn't get what she needs, you suddenly might have an obsessive retriever, for example, who just can't seem to get enough. For a dog like this, a 15-minute aerobic session followed by calmer problem-solving games works best.

TRAINING

While you train your Golden Retriever during the coming months, you'll develop the fine skill of infinite patience. She'll challenge your skills and creativity as you endure her endless puppy antics. Have a good laugh, and keep training because she's learning even when she's not listening very carefully.

Working with a Hyper Dog

Owners of teenage Golden Retrievers often conclude their dog is abnormally hyperactive. An adolescent male fidgets, can't relax, and is *always* moving. It seems like he can't concentrate, has trouble learning, and doesn't remember what you taught him from one day to the next. Females aren't exempt from hyperactive behavior either.

Golden Retrievers don't completely mature until they're 2 or 3 years old, and within the breed, there's a huge variation in energy level, so you can't predict how your particular Golden will behave. Other factors contribute to a hyperactive personality, too. Her environment, health, socialization, training, and the amount of exercise she gets all play a part in her activity level.

TIPS AND TAILS

At home, practice sit and down dozens of times a day with food treats. It doesn't have to be a stay. You just want her to respond and have enough self-control to stay put for a few seconds. Down is more difficult for her, but she'll get better as you practice. Put her dinner kibble in your pockets, and spend the evening doling it out while you work together. You'll hold her attention and keep her occupied. Soon she'll be following you around, offering sits and downs when you didn't ask for them!

Spaying and neutering helps reduce a dog's frenzied behavior. Once the sex organs and the accompanying hormones are removed, she's not as distracted or constantly on the lookout for intact dogs.

If your Golden Retriever is counter surfing and raiding the trash, lunging at everyone and everything while on walks, and too excited to even notice you giving her commands, ask yourself some questions:

○ Are you accidentally rewarding her with attention when she misbehaves? Even yelling is attention.

○ Did you encourage exuberant greetings and wild play when she was little? If so, she's just doing what she was taught.

○ Is she getting adequate exercise every day?

HAPPY PUPPY

The absence of bad behavior is hard to recognize sometimes. Pay attention so you catch her doing something right and reward her. She'll learn what behaviors get attention when you consistently reward her for good behavior.

Teaching Self-Control

Unfortunately, when the adolescent crazies hit, some owners give up on their puppies. What was previously cute is no fun anymore. Your Golden Retriever is wild in the house, dragging you on walks, and rudely jumping on everyone she meets. She's too much trouble to deal with. The less you take her out in public or allow her indoors, the more her behavior declines, and she ends up in the backyard or, worse, a shelter.

Self-control is a developed skill, similar to when you build muscle memory by practicing a sport. Your Golden Retriever is currently in "react-first, think-later" mode, and she needs to learn to think first, even when she's excited. Help her make correct decisions rather than trying to control her behavior by manhandling her. An excited dog needs calm handling, but many owners instinctively react by yelling and grabbing their dog, which just fires her up more. She learns that you will stop her; she doesn't learn to stop herself. By moving slowly and speaking quietly, you tell her there's no reason to act wild. That advice is easy to give, but it's hard for almost everyone to do. Rather than try to defuse a situation in the heat of the moment, practice when you're not in the midst of a crisis.

Practice the sit and down while on your walks so she starts to expect you'll occasionally ask her to do something. When you take her out—which you should do every day no matter how hard it is—watch for opportunities to practice her self-control. You might not walk more than a block, but that doesn't matter.

For example, if you see someone walking toward you, focus your Golden's attention on you by asking for a sit and rewarding her before she notices the oncoming person. Start your routine far enough away that your dog can be successful. Once she gets the idea, start closer on future walks. With enough repetitions, she'll see an oncoming person and look to you—an occasion you should mark with a huge jackpot of treats and praise.

TIPS AND TAILS

The middle of a hyperactive frenzy is not the time to teach your dog a settle-down cue. Instead, practice with your dog in a quieter setting so she can learn it without distractions. It's easy to ignore your pup when she's quietly sitting or lying at your feet, but this is the behavior you want, so watch for it and reward her when you see it.

Teach your puppy to settle down on command. It's probably easy to get her mildly riled up with a tennis ball or toy. Then simply stop. Hide the toy in your pocket. Don't look at her. Ignore her. Cross your arms. At some point she'll be puzzled and stop jumping around. She might even offer a behavior to get a reaction from you. Ignore her until she sits. Praise her quietly and bring the toy out again. Repeat this sequence several times, and you'll soon discover that she sits faster each time because that makes you produce the toy.

Give both the active and the quiet phase a name, like "Whoopee!" and "Cool it." Gradually extend the settle period to a few seconds and work up to a minute or more. Always praise her for settling, even when you don't have a toy. You can now transfer this behavior to a situation where you need it. She won't be perfect the first time, but with practice, she'll learn.

Using Equipment to Control Your Dog

Ideally, you should be able to control your dog with training, rewards, and discipline. But Golden Retrievers are strong, and if she's out of control to the point you can't handle her, you might decide to employ some equipment to help manage her.

Some items, like head halters and no-pull harnesses, might provide a much-needed breakthrough in dealing with your dog. Work with a professional trainer, and use these tools while you're teaching your teenager to listen to you. Just remember these are tools, not solutions. You can't stop training because you have a new collar. After all, you don't want to have to use special devices throughout her life.

Head halters: These work on the same principle as a horse's halter. By controlling your dog's head, you control her movement. You can't out-muscle a horse, but a halter gives you the control you need. The same is true for your dog. With the halter, you can steer her gently, but she can't drag you. The halter's straps go over her muzzle and behind her ears, join with a ring in the throat area where you attach the leash, and the straps tighten over her muzzle when she pulls. There's also often another strap you can hook to your pup's regular collar so she can't escape if she rubs and removes the head halter.

Most dogs resist head halters at first. She'll pull away, dance around, and paw at it, so expect to spend several short sessions working with it before she's accustomed to it. Add a second leash attached to her regular collar to give you more control if you need to. Once she accepts the halter, it works well.

The halter requires some finesse on your part for correct use. If you yank on it or drag your dog, you can twist and injure her neck. Never leave a head halter on your puppy.

There's a downside to using head halters. When you meet a stranger, they'll assume your dog is muzzled. Their next assumption is that she's dangerous and will bite. Therefore, you might have to educate the people you encounter.

No-pull harnesses: A dog who pulls on the leash will cough and gag from the pressure of the collar on her trachea. That leads some owners to try a harness, which relieves neck pressure because the straps lie across her chest and rib cage instead. A traditional harness (like you see on toy poodles) triggers an opposition reflex in a large dog like a Golden Retriever, and your dog will instinctively resist the pressure. That's why a sled dog wears a harness—it makes her pull. It actually triggers the same reflex in a small dog, but because the owner is stronger than the dog, it doesn't matter as much.

No-pull harnesses were developed so an owner with less strength or with an untrained dog could still walk her dog. Several styles are available. Some attach the leash to a ring on a chest band, while others have straps that go under the dog's legs and fasten behind her shoulders, where the leash attaches. They tighten when the dog pulls and give the owner more control.

Equipment to Avoid

The following sections cover a few devices you *should not* use without a trainer or behaviorist's guidance because they can damage your relationship and actually injure your dog: chain collars, prong collars, and shock collars.

TIPS AND TAILS

In the hands of an inexperienced person, any tool can hurt a dog. If you feel you need special equipment to control your Golden Retriever, first consider working with a trainer or behaviorist to evaluate the situation. Then learn how to use any equipment you both decide is necessary safely and without ruining your relationship with your dog.

Chain collars: Chain collars have fallen out of favor over the past two decades. The training method of choice since the 1950s was what trainers now refer to as the "jerk-and-pull" method. Owners spent their time in obedience classes learning how to give their dogs a "proper" correction, which entailed a quick, hard jerk on the chain and an equally quick release. The method worked, but owners didn't like hurting their dogs. As a result, more positive training approaches have taken its place. Unfortunately, many dog owners still use these collars.

Also called choke collars (for good reason), chain collars tighten when your dog pulls, which can choke her or injure her trachea. This collar should *never* be left on a dog for any reason. Your dog could get caught on a branch or fence and choke to death.

Prong collars: A prong collar is a correction device, not a training tool. The prongs go entirely around the dog's neck, which evens out the pressure applied when the dog pulls or the handler makes a correction. Thus, there isn't as much risk of injuring the trachea as with a chain collar. But if the prong collar is too tight or the owner uses too much force, the prongs can puncture the dog's neck. People without enough strength to control their dog often use a prong collar to give themselves some leverage.

Ideally, a dog self-corrects with a prong collar—you don't have to do anything. The effect when a handler makes a correction is instant and extreme, and it really hurts. A sensitive dog might react aggressively in self-defense or fear. Other dogs become increasingly stressed while wearing one. A prong collar can destroy your relationship or save it. Never use one without expert help.

Shock collars: The manufacturer of electronic or "shock" collars call it a "stimulation" collar to sidestep the negative image of you shocking your dog. But that's exactly what it does, and it has its place in certain types of training.

Hunters who train their dogs to take commands from a distance make use of these collars. When a person understands the scientific principles of negative reinforcement and uses the collar correctly, the dog can learn. But if you hit the button at the wrong time, all you've accomplished is confusing, hurting, and frightening your dog. For pet owners, there's no practical purpose in using these collars.

Knowing When You Need Help

Pet owners are not professional dog trainers and shouldn't have to be. A frustrated owner with a frustrated dog won't make much progress. If you just can't handle your wild Golden Retriever yourself, get help from a trainer or behaviorist. Many options are available.

You could sign up for a beyond-the-basics class and repeat it if you need to. You'll absorb more information now that you've had more real-life experience with your puppy. Agility classes will burn off some of your Golden's energy, although she's too young to do any jumping on hard surfaces. If you're looking for a professional dog trainer, check with the Certification Council for Professional Dog Trainers (ccpdt.org) or the Association of Professional Dog Trainers (apdt.com).

Private lessons might be necessary. Sometimes it helps to have a trainer come to your home, where the problems are occurring. You spend time working together on the particular issues you're having with your Golden Retriever, and the entire family gets individual attention and can try different solutions.

Sending your young Golden Retriever to boot camp, a board-and-train program, might seem extreme, but professional trainers get quicker results. If you're an inexperienced dog owner, it'll be easier for you to learn to handle your dog if she's already had some training—then you both aren't beginners. If you decide to go this route, be sure you get instruction as well, and ask about training methods and types of equipment used. A puppy doesn't need to be trained with electronic collars or other harsh devices, for example. Get references from other clients, too.

If you're dealing with aggression or other potentially serious behavior in your Golden Retriever, consult an animal behaviorist or other professional with advanced training in behavior modification. A qualified consultant can evaluate your situation and help you work through your dog's specific issues.

Several types of consultants are available, and each has an advanced level of education and experience. Specific organizations train and certify these experts, and they often maintain a database of professionals you can contact for help. Here are some of the organizations and associations you might hear about:

International Association of Animal Behavior Consultants (iaabc.org): A member of the IAABC has been tested and certified in assessment, counseling, and behavioral science. Members also must submit references and case studies demonstrating their skills.

The Association of Companion Animal Behavior Counselors (animalbehaviorcounselors.org/acabc_members): The ACABC certifies specialists at several levels: Certified Professional Dog Trainer (CPDT), Certified Canine Behavior Counselor (CBC), and Board Certified Companion Animal Behaviorist (BCCAB). Each requires increasing levels of education and continued training in the field, along with supervised internships.

Certified Applied Animal Behaviorist (certifiedanimalbehaviorist.com): CAABs have an advanced degree (an MS/MA or PhD) in the science of applied animal behavior and have demonstrated expertise and experience in diagnosing and treating behavior problems.

Veterinary behaviorist: This is a board-certified veterinarian who has a specialty in animal behavior and has completed a 1- to 3-year residency program in veterinary behavior. He has conducted research, published his findings in academic journals, and passed a 2-day exam. These are the only behavior specialists who can prescribe medication for your dog. The American College of Veterinary Behaviorists (dacvb. org) maintains a database of behaviorists in the United States. You'll need a referral from your veterinarian.

TIPS AND TAILS

No magic pill fixes behavior problems. If you spend a lot of money on professional advice, also commit to working with your dog until her issues have improved to an acceptable level.

Clicker Training

Many training methods are available. In recent years, positive reinforcement instead of punishment methods have gained favor, and with good reason. It's much more fun for you and your puppy if you're rewarding her for doing something right rather than punishing her all the time for doing something wrong.

Clicker training, in which you use a handheld clicker as a signal to your dog that she's done the right thing, is one such positive reinforcement training method. Besides being fun, clicker training is based on scientific principles and research developed decades ago with dolphin training. It's based on Ivan Pavlov's famous operant-conditioning research, where he rang a bell before feeding a group of dogs. The dogs associated the bell with food and salivated in anticipation.

The idea behind clicker training is simple: you can't force a dolphin to do something. You can't lure her or shape her into position to show her what you want. So instead, trainers "marked" the correct behavior with a click, followed immediately by a food reward. (Sound familiar? That's what you're doing when you praise your dog while she's sitting and then give her a treat. The click, or your praise, marks the sit and tells the dog food will follow.) The trainers took a sound that had no meaning to the dolphins and gave it meaning. The dolphins knew a treat was coming when they heard the conditioned reinforcer, or the click.

Timing is critical in clicker training. It's impossible to deliver the praise and food reward at the exact second the correct behavior occurs. Therefore, you must click as your dog performs the behavior so she understands what brought her the food reward. Your puppy will happily run through her entire repertoire of behaviors until she finally does the one thing you were waiting for and get the click.

To use the method effectively, we recommend you find a good book and a trainer to get you started. Any lesson can be broken down into steps and taught with clicker training, and many owners find it a lot of fun and much easier for teaching their puppy.

YOU AND YOUR PUPPY

When your teenage Golden Retriever slows down enough to notice you, seize the opportunity to enjoy her company.

Time for a Belly Rub!

Teenagers need a lot of rest, and after a frantic day of running and playing, your Golden Retriever needs some quiet time—although she might not think so. As long as you'll play, she'll be up for a game, so quit before she exhausts herself.

If you cut off the activity cold turkey and expect her to settle down, she won't. She's still wound up and ready to go. Instead, after an active play session, take her for a quiet walk or, better yet, give her a belly rub or a massage. It will relax you both at the end of a long, active day.

Living with a Teenage Golden Retriever

Attitude is everything when you have an adolescent Golden Retriever, so don't take it personally.

Remember when you were a teenager? You stayed out late, didn't listen to your parents, had to be doing something with your friends every minute, and thought you were invincible. That's what your puppy is going through now. She's full of life and having a blast, so you might as well sit back and enjoy it. When she rips up the couch, take a photo so you can laugh about it later.

TIPS AND TAILS
Write down the stories of your pup's crazier moments. Golden Retriever owners love sharing puppy stories.

	SOCIAL	BEHAVIOR	TRAINING	PHYSICAL	HEALTH
MONTH 1			Littermates and mother teach appropriate canine behavior	Rapid growth	
MONTH 2	Breeder starts socialization				
MONTH 3	Socialization at home with new owner and other pets	Fear-imprint period	Begin house- and crate training		1st DHPP vaccine
MONTH 4			Enroll in puppy class		2nd DHPP vaccine
MONTH 5		Teething begins—heavy chewing period	Ready for basic commands	Switch to adult food	3rd DHPP and rabies vaccines
MONTH 6	Socialization in public		Enroll in basic obedience class		
MONTH 7		Adult teeth are in—chewing continues	Ready for more advanced training	Moderate growth	Sexual maturity
MONTH 8					
MONTH 9					
MONTH 10					
MONTH 11				Slow growth—reaches adult size	Annual vaccinations and checkup
MONTH 12 AND BEYOND					

In Search of a Leader

Your adolescent Golden Retriever is beginning to look like an adult, but he's still very much a teenager. Around this time you'll see his attention span improve, he'll be pushy but not as aggressively as some breeds, and he'll be more watchful and protective of you. Yet he still needs your leadership to maintain his good behavior.

Enjoy his company and the challenges he presents. He's a lot of fun, and he joyfully delights in his time with you.

PHYSICAL DEVELOPMENT

Between 8 and 9 months, you'll see subtle differences in your Golden Retriever's physical appearance. His growth has slowed dramatically, even though he isn't yet his full adult height. He might grow an inch in a week and then stop altogether for the next 2 weeks. His coordination also improves.

Internally, his bones are developing and hardening. He might still look light-boned and slightly out of proportion until he's 13 to 18 months old because he hasn't developed much muscle mass yet. He's at extra risk for injury this month, as his rapid growth stresses his bones and ligaments. His teeth have all broken through the gums, and by next month, most of his teething pain will end as his teeth have set in his jaws. And as he closes in on maturity, his second puppy coat has come in and he looks gorgeous.

Males Looking More Masculine

If he's neutered, he'll mature differently from an intact male. A dog of either sex stops growing at some point, and his bones begin to harden and thicken. It's the sex hormones that put the brakes on the height, and if a dog is altered, he'll continue to grow a bit taller and lankier than he would have if left intact. This appears to be more obvious in neutered males because females have naturally lighter bone structure.

Last month, he still looked a little gangly and his body might have seemed longer than it should be. His back legs probably looked like they were higher than his front legs, too. This month he starts developing more muscle in his rear, and as he does, his body starts to look more in proportion. His rib cage fills out and broadens. His head becomes larger as it grows in width and breadth. His neck thickens, and the coat around his neck gets heavier. Again, if your dog is neutered, these changes aren't as dramatic.

Females Looking More Feminine

While males look obviously male, females are harder to define based on looks because they don't change dramatically like an intact male does as he reaches maturity. Most of the female characteristics stay the same whether or not the dog is spayed because it's the absence of testosterone that makes them look female.

Coat differences exist between males and females, but this month they look quite a bit alike. Also, females have a feminine head when compared to a male, as well as overall lighter bone structure. Although if spayed early, female dogs might get taller like neutered males.

HEALTH

There's a lot going on inside your puppy's body this month as he continues to grow and develop. His energy level may differ wildly from day to day, and you'll need to watch for signs of injury or other limb problems that might develop.

Occasional Lack of Energy

Glucose is the form of sugar found within the bloodstream. It's formed from carbohydrates during the digestion of foods and is then used as energy. Puppies digest their food faster than adult dogs, and this sometimes prevents absorption of all the nutrients in their food. What's more, a puppy who overexercises expends the nutrients in his body faster. The combination of the two can cause low blood sugar (hypoglycemia), which makes him tired.

If your puppy is eating a poor-quality food, the carbohydrates in his diet might not be as easily digestible as they should be. This can affect his ability to produce enough energy to keep up with his needs. If your pup seems to have a frequent problem with low energy, look at his food to see if it might be contributing to the problem.

Your young Golden might be tired for other reasons, too. During growth spurts, he uses a lot of energy to build his muscles and bone, and he might need more food. Don't let him get fat, though. If he looks like he's getting heavy, cut back on the amount you're feeding him. His caloric and energy needs may vary from week to week this month, so pay attention and feed accordingly.

Parasites like intestinal worms or heartworm also can contribute to a puppy's lack of energy. Look for other symptoms, like a dull coat, coughing, or watery eyes.

TIPS AND TAILS

If your puppy seems overly tired all the time, take him to the vet for a checkup to rule out serious disease and treat parasites.

If Your Puppy's Limping

A puppy might limp for several reasons. He could have slipped and twisted a leg while playing, for example, in which case the limping might go away in a few hours. Or it could be something more serious, as several conditions can occur in adolescent Golden Retrievers. Pay close attention to your dog's symptoms, and take notes on what you see so your veterinarian can make an accurate diagnosis.

Most bones start off as cartilage, a flexible connective tissue that gradually hardens and is replaced by bone. The longest bones in your puppy's body are his limbs. These long bones must grow longer so your puppy can get taller and wider to physically support his adult weight.

We talked about growth plates in Month 7 and the effect the spay/neuter surgery has on the timing of when the plates close. Here, we want to look at this and other problems that might cause lameness in a young Golden Retriever. Some scientists believe that feeding a food too high in calcium or one that promotes fast growth could be a contributing factor in any or all of these conditions—a good reason to switch from puppy food to an adult formula if you haven't already. (Remember, Golden Retriever puppies should switch to adult food at 4 or 5 months old.)

TIPS AND TAILS

A dog shouldn't run or jump on hard surfaces like asphalt until he's at least 18 months old and his growth plates have closed. Because their bones are still soft, teenage dogs are especially prone to leg and growth plate fractures. Such fractures could affect the final length and angle of the bone when he matures, and he may permanently move with an uneven gait. He'll also be more susceptible to arthritis in the joint where the fracture occurred and in other joints affected by his off-balance movement. A fractured growth plate must be surgically repaired.

Osteochondritis dissecans (OCD): Your puppy also might face osteochondritis dissecans; young, rapidly growing Golden Retrievers 4 to 8 months old are especially susceptible. A predisposition to OCD can be inherited and affected by factors like excess trauma to a dog's shoulders. Immature cartilage is fractured from the bone and sometimes floats loose in the joint fluid. Hard-pounding exercise contributes to the risk, so if you have slick floors, put down runners so your pup won't slip and injure his fragile bones.

The first symptoms of OCD might show as your dog being stiff and sore or limping after exercise. OCD can affect one or both shoulders, and if untreated, the lameness will become permanent as arthritis sets in. X-rays are used to diagnose the condition, and treatment consists of 4 to 8 weeks of complete crate rest and anti-inflammatory medications. Surgery to remove the loose cartilage is also an option.

Panosteitis: Also referred to as "growing pains" or wandering lameness, panosteitis affects the humerus in the front legs and the femur in the rear. Common in young, rapidly growing breeds like Golden Retrievers, panosteitis causes lameness that often switches from one leg to the other every few days. It's sometimes misdiagnosed as elbow dysplasia, an inherited condition (see Month 7). At the first stages of panosteitis, your Golden's legs are sore and he might be unwilling to play or appear depressed. He also might not feel like eating and could have a fever. X-rays will show changes in bone density.

Treatment includes restricting your dog's activity, plenty of crate rest, and analgesic drugs. The condition isn't hereditary or caused by injury, it usually resolves itself in 4 to 6 weeks, and there are no long-term consequences if he receives treatment and injuries are prevented.

Torn anterior cruciate ligament (ACL): A torn ACL is a soft tissue injury rather than a bone problem. A hard-playing Golden Retriever can leap up to catch a ball or flying disc and land wrong, tearing this knee ligament. Other causes include making a sudden turn while running, slipping on a hard surface, or being hit by a car. Overweight dogs are at higher risk because their knee joints are weaker from carrying too much weight. With a torn ACL, your puppy will be in intense pain and limp because the tear allows the tibia and femur to grind against each other.

A partially torn ACL might heal with treatment, including limiting his activity for 8 to 12 weeks and low-impact exercise like swimming or walking when he's ready to start moving again. Your vet will also prescribe anti-inflammatory medications.

At this time, the only treatment for a completely torn ACL is surgery, which involves a recovery time of at least 6 to 8 weeks, during which time your pup is restricted to leash walking with very limited exercise.

If the injured ACL isn't treated, the dog usually develops arthritis. Also, because the one leg is injured, the opposite leg bears more weight, which sometimes causes the ACL to rupture on that side, too.

The Nose Knows

Hunting for a fallen bird in heavy cover or water, trailing the scent of a lost person, finding traces of arson after a fire—you'll find Golden Retrievers and their keen sense of smell in each of these situations and more. Scientists estimate that a dog's scenting ability is millions of times more advanced than that of his human companions, and up to one third of his brain is devoted to scenting and analyzing what he smells. And that's something Goldens have at birth, so your puppy can already smell thousands of things you can't.

The canine nose is divided into two cavities with a vertical dividing wall of tissue called the nasal septum. The nasal cavity contains a maze of bony structures that, along with the sinuses and nasal septum, communicates with the olfactory nerve, which sends scent information to the brain. Often a dog will "lick" the air with his tongue and bring the scent to his nose to absorb it.

When a scent reaches the brain, it goes to areas that process memory, pleasure, and emotions, making associations between them. As your puppy encounters new smells, he builds a memory bank of scents and what they mean to him. Just like you remember the smell of Thanksgiving dinner and all the fond memories associated with that experience, your puppy learns that some smells mean good food, some mean a thing tastes bad, and others signify a memorable experience. But with the ability to process thousands or even millions of scents, by the time he's an adult, he's a virtual encyclopedia of scents!

Your puppy's nose is ideally constructed for poking around in the dirt. When he sniffs, his nostrils dilate and mucus in his nose filters out bacteria, dirt particles, and other matter, which he then exhales.

As if that wasn't amazing enough, a structure called Jacobsen's organ (vomeronasal organ) resides in the nasal cavity. This organ communicates with different parts of the brain and can process "smells" that aren't actually odors but actually chemical messages passed from one animal to another. It's the Jacobsen's organ that makes a newborn puppy able to recognize his mother's milk and allows her to recognize her own puppies. It also enables a dog to recognize the "scent" of fear in humans.

Pheromones play a big part in communication between dogs, and Jacobsen's organ is able to detect and interpret quite a bit of this information. For example, one dog can recognize if another is an adult or puppy, male or female, altered or intact, or ready to breed.

DOG TALK
A **pheromone** is a chemical secreted by an animal (including humans). Other animals, usually of the same species, can interpret this chemical.

The length of your dog's nose also has an effect on his scenting ability. Breeds with longer noses, like Golden Retrievers, have more scent-reception cells.

Alternative Health Care

Dog owners who want to treat their pets with natural remedies or who find conventional medicine isn't working for their dog might look to alternative or complementary medicine for treatment. Although your pup is probably years away from serious illness or age-related disease, some forms of alternative treatment can be used to heal injuries or in cases of behavior-related problems.

Most veterinarians practice Western medicine, and some incorporate complementary therapies into their treatment plans. There are also purely *holistic veterinarians and practitioners,* who treat patients solely with herbal or other alternative therapies.

DOG TALK
A **holistic veterinarian or practitioner** addresses the whole dog, including mental and social factors, instead of limiting treatment to the symptoms of disease.

Acupuncture: Acupuncture is an ancient Chinese practice that's been successfully used on animals and people for thousands of years. Its goal is to correct energy imbalances in the body and promote healing. Acupuncture addresses pain and inflammation from injuries, arthritis, hip or elbow dysplasia, neurological disorders, and digestive disorders.

The practitioner inserts into the skin or muscles fine needles that stimulate predefined acupuncture points. These points lie along meridians, or energy lines, that travel through the dog's body. The meridians contain nerve endings, connective tissue, and blood vessels that release endorphins and other mechanisms to relieve pain and trigger healing. Some acupuncturists add electrical stimulation to the needles.

Your veterinarian might recommend acupuncture in addition to physical therapy or conventional medicine. The treatment usually takes 20 to 30 minutes per visit, and dogs accept it with minimal discomfort. In fact, they tend to relax noticeably during a session. To find a veterinarian who provides acupuncture for dogs, visit the American Academy of Veterinary Acupuncture at aava.org.

Acupressure: Similar to acupuncture, acupressure works the same energy meridians on the body, but instead of needles, the practitioner uses pressure on the acupuncture points, similar to massage, to treat allergies, diarrhea, digestive problems, ear infections, respiratory problems, and more. Your veterinarian might teach you how to use acupressure at home on a daily basis to treat your dog. Most practitioners recommend 5- to 10-minute sessions. If you find your dog resists the pressure, winces in pain, or otherwise tries to avoid the session, stop and consult with your vet.

TIPS AND TAILS

Veterinarians have advanced degrees and are licensed and regulated by law. No similar system exists for credentialing nonveterinary alternative practitioners. It's up to you to investigate treatments and the people who supply them to be sure you're getting safe and appropriate care for your dog. Do some research, or ask for recommendations and check references if you're thinking of using an alternative practitioner. Also visit the American Holistic Veterinary Medical Association at ahvma.org for more information.

Chiropractic: Chiropractic therapy can relieve pain and improve a dog's movement. During a session, the practitioner adjusts the dog's vertebral joints, extremity joints, or head. It's often used to treat injuries, arthritis, and hip and elbow dysplasia.

The American Veterinary Medical Association recommends you have a vet examine your dog before you pursue chiropractic treatment. X-rays and other tests will help you and your pup's doctor choose an appropriate treatment plan. Opt for a chiropractor who specializes in animals and is a member of the American Veterinary Chiropractic Association (avcadoctors.com).

Massage: Massage and other body manipulation techniques are helpful for some dogs. Traditional massage helps improve circulation, relieve pain and stiffness, improve flexibility and range of motion, and restore proper functioning to joints and limbs.

TTouch is particularly beneficial. Linda Tellington-Jones originally developed this therapy for horses, but it has been used on all species of animals. Moving her fingers in circular motions, the practitioner works different parts of the body to promote healing and behavior modification by opening the body's awareness and releasing tension. You can learn to use the technique to relax your puppy and help improve problem behaviors when incorporated into training programs. Find out more at ttouch.com.

Homeopathy: *Homeopathy* is based on the law of similars and the concept of "like produces like." In homeopathic therapy, practitioners use a substance that in undiluted form causes a particular symptom; in a highly diluted homeopathic formula, the same substance relieves the symptom. Remedies are usually diluted with alcohol or distilled water, and most are administered to your dog in the forms of drops you put in his mouth.

DOG TALK

Homeopathy is the practice of using herbs, minerals, and natural compounds to strengthen the body's natural defenses and cure disease.

Homeopathic remedies are used to treat a variety of health problems, such as pain, inflammation, fluid in the lungs, bruises and wounds, bleeding, skin problems, respiratory illness, allergies, and more. Some remedies address a variety of health problems at once. Practitioners do not claim to cure diseases like cancer or arthritis, but they do strive to help your dog attain the best possible overall health so his immune system can fight these diseases.

The Food and Drug Administration (FDA) classifies homeopathic remedies as drugs but does not evaluate them for safety or effectiveness. Therefore, do careful research and buy only from a homeopathic practitioner or use a well-known brand name. To find a veterinarian who uses homeopathic techniques, visit the Academy of Veterinary Homeopathy at theavh.org.

Considering Natural Remedies

Natural remedies make use of plants and other natural substances for healing health and behavioral issues. Although they've been successfully used for centuries, they shouldn't be considered a substitute for veterinary care.

Although owners generally regard natural remedies as safe and effective, always consult with your vet and research potential side effects before giving anything to your dog. The quality and concentration of ingredients varies dramatically from brand to brand, and a remedy might not have the same effect on every dog.

TIPS AND TAILS

Neither the FDA nor any other government authority regulates natural remedies, and manufacturers' claims about their effects have not been scientifically proven.

Supplements: Glucosamine and chondroitin are compounds found in cartilage and are sometimes added to dog food, especially senior formula dog foods, to improve joint health. Dogs with arthritis due to hip dysplasia, injuries, or aging can experience increased mobility due to a decrease in inflammation and pain with treatments of these supplements. For example, if a young dog is diagnosed with hip dysplasia, glucosamine can help prevent cartilage breakdown, while chondroitin contributes to the creation of new cartilage. These supplements can cause stomach problems like nausea and diarrhea, so be sure to consult with your vet before giving them to your dog.

Herbal remedies: For centuries, humans have taken advantage of the healing properties of herbal remedies, using roots, flowers, stems, or leaves dry or made into teas, juices, or tinctures. In a tincture, the herbs are combined with alcohol, soaked, and the liquid drained off. You can make your own remedies or purchase them in tablets or capsules.

Herbs contain nutrients and chemicals that can aid healing in dogs, too. They sometimes work much more slowly than traditional medicine, and it's not unusual for one to take several months before you see any effects. Some remedies target a specific illness or emotional state; others boost the immune system and overall health. Thousands of plants contain medicinal properties. Some commonly used herbs include the following:

- Chamomile, for its calming effect
- Alfalfa, as an anti-inflammatory
- Ginger, for carsickness

○ Echinacea, to boost the immune system

○ Nettle, as an antihistamine

It's important to remember that herbal remedies are medicines and can have harmful side effects if used incorrectly. Remember, too, that some plants are poisonous to animals (see Appendix C), so do careful research or work with a veterinary herbalist. Learn more about herbal remedies from the Veterinary Botanical Medicine Association at vbma.org.

Flower remedies: Also called essences, flower remedies are homeopathic remedies made from flowers or parts of flowering plants formulated to treat health and behavioral issues. Probably the most well known is Rescue Remedy, used to treat stress and anxiety. Developed by Dr. Edward Bach in the early twentieth century, each Bach Flower Remedy includes several flower essences formulated to treat imbalances in the body and spirit. Rescue Remedy, for example, includes several flower essences, including star of Bethlehem, clematis, impatiens, rock rose, and cherry plum. The remedies were developed for use in people, but many are also used for dogs, administered with an eyedropper, either directly into the dog's mouth or added to his water or food. Because they're homeopathic, they're highly diluted, so you just give your dog a few drops.

Essential oils: Also from the plant kingdom, essential oils are made from roots, leaves, flowers, or seeds and used to heal wounds, repel insects, and treat skin problems. Unlike other remedies, these aren't taken internally; they're applied to your dog's skin or fur. One of the most well known is citronella, which is made from lemongrass and repels mosquitoes. Tea tree oil (from the melaluca tree) is another popular oil known for its antiseptic, antibacterial, and antifungal properties. Some essential oils formulated specifically for animals treat skin irritation and repel ticks and fleas.

TIPS AND TAILS
Investigate essential oils carefully, because many are safe for people but not for dogs. Also, some oils that are safe for dogs are not safe for use on cats.

Pheromones: As mentioned earlier, pheromones are naturally produced chemicals dogs can sense in another animal, usually of the same species. Synthetic dog appeasing pheromones (DAP), similar to the pheromones a mother dog releases to calm her newborn puppies, are recommended for fearful or anxious dogs or dogs with aggression issues. DAP is widely available as a spray, collar, or mister.

NUTRITION

Dog food can influence your puppy's behavior, as mentioned earlier, so it's important that you know what you're feeding your puppy and serve him the best food possible.

The Links Between Food and Behavior

Puppies who are fed diets high in cereal grain carbohydrates sometimes have signs of hyperactivity, are unable to concentrate, don't retain what they've been taught, and just can't seem to hold still. Although a teenage Golden Retriever certainly exhibits all these symptoms regardless of what you feed him, you might see a noticeable improvement in his behavior simply by changing his food.

Protein contributes to the *serotonin* levels in your dog's body. Just like in people, serotonin affects his mood, sensitivity, and sleep cycle. Serotonin is produced by tryptophan (the chemical that makes us sleepy after we eat a big turkey dinner on Thanksgiving), and tryptophan comes from eating meat. If too many carbohydrates replace protein in his diet, it can cause a shortage of serotonin in the body, which results in hyperactivity, aggression, and restless sleep.

The types of carbohydrates in food also play a role in your pup's behavior. Carbs with a high *glycemic index* raise his blood sugar rapidly and cause a sugar high, a sudden increase in energy followed by a dramatic letdown and sleepiness. Rice and corn are two carbohydrates with a high glycemic index, and both are common dog food ingredients because they're inexpensive.

DOG TALK

Serotonin is a neurotransmitter involved in the transmission of impulses between nerve cells. It's found in the brain, blood platelets, and intestinal tract. The **glycemic index** is a scale that measures the speed at which the body converts carbohydrates into sugars.

Carbohydrates with a lower glycemic index digest slowly and are easier to digest. This provides a balanced blood sugar level, which evens out your dog's behavior. Oatmeal, apples, barley, and beans are all low–glycemic index foods.

The Debate Over Foods

You want to give your dog the best care possible, and feeding a quality food is part of that mission. But it's not easy to know if you're feeding the right food. The choices are endless, and marketing claims and pretty packaging don't always tell the entire story.

If you've chosen to feed your Golden Retriever commercially made dog food—which is how most people feed their dogs—it's important that you educate yourself about the food, but be skeptical. Don't believe everything you hear or read. Many passionate people fervently believe they know how your dog should be fed. Most aren't scientists and might not have facts to back up their claims. Therefore, consider the source, and make your own decision.

Dogs were fed table scraps or horsemeat from the local butcher until the early twentieth century, when Ken-L Ration introduced the first canned dog food in the 1920s. Quality wasn't much of an issue in those early time-saving and convenient foods, and pet food companies didn't invest in much research. Easily available, inexpensive ingredients like wheat and surplus horse and mule meat were the basis of most dog foods. Things soon changed as horses became scarcer with more cars on the roads. During World War II, tin was scarce, so canned dog foods were less available. By the 1950s, kibble was on the market. Convenient and sold as "better than table scraps," it soon took over the pet food industry.

Today's dog food manufacturers spend millions of dollars researching ingredients as well as canine health. They've developed unique protein sources like duck and lamb plus veterinary diets that address particular health problems like allergies and kidney disease.

The manufacturing processes used today are a mixed blessing. Although you get a food with quality ingredients, the process used in making the food destroys some nutrients. Most modern pet foods are cooked under pressure at such a high temperature that it kills some minerals, enzymes, and vitamins. The manufacturer then has to add ingredients like fat and other nutrients back into the food after cooking, along with preservatives to prevent rancidity. They also often use synthetic chemicals, which are harder for your dog to digest, as well as artificial flavors and coloring.

Cost is a huge factor in dog food manufacturing. Some companies use less-expensive ingredients like cereal grains, by-products, and meat that's not fit for human consumption. Leftover ingredients from processing human foods, from slaughterhouses, and imported from overseas, where countries have less-stringent regulations, are also sometimes included.

Although there had been dog food recalls over the years, the 2007 recalls involving Menu Foods brought the issue of pet food safety to the public's attention. At that time, the FDA forced a recall of more than 100 different brand-name products. More than 6,000 pets became ill, and more than 3,000 died because wheat gluten imported from China was contaminated with melamine. Soon after, contaminated corn and rice gluten were also discovered.

TIPS AND TAILS

Since 2007, recalls have affected many brands of dry food, wet food, and treats. The FDA maintains a database of all recalls at fda.gov. Log on and search for "dog food recall" to find a complete list sorted by brand name.

Commercial food manufacturers aren't trying to kill our pets with tainted ingredients. Although not all food is made with high-quality ingredients, remember that dog foods must reach minimum nutritional standards set by the Association of American Feed Control Officials (AAFCO) and other federal and state agencies. Price is one factor you can look at, but the quality of the ingredients is the key factor.

Grocery store and generic (private label) brands are usually the least expensive and include grains and by-products as their main protein sources. Artificial colors, flavors, and preservatives are often used, too. Many dogs are just fine on these foods, but some develop skin or digestive issues.

Premium foods contain a wide variety of ingredients, and some are better than others. They might still contain synthetic preservatives or other chemicals. The price is higher, and most of these foods are found in pet supply or feed stores.

Super-premium foods are usually made with the best ingredients. You might still find some artificial additives, but on the whole, these brands strive to use healthy ingredients. Many varieties and mixtures of ingredients are available in this category.

Natural foods cannot claim to be natural if any synthetic chemicals or additives are used during processing. The FDA doesn't regulate the use of the word *natural* but states: "natural can be construed as equivalent to a lack of artificial flavors, artificial colors, or artificial preservatives in the product." AAFCO regulates the use of the term, but their regulations allow a lot of leeway. If a label says, for instance, "Natural, with added vitamins," the vitamins could be synthetic.

Organic foods earn this designation based on the way the plant and animal ingredients were raised. Although the U.S. Department of Agriculture doesn't specifically certify organic pet food at this time, most companies follow the guidelines for human organic foods. To be labeled organic, the food must contain at least 95 percent organic ingredients, and the other 5 percent must consist of approved ingredients. Organic foods must be raised with no fertilizers, pesticides, growth hormones, antibiotics, or genetically modified sources.

HAPPY PUPPY
Feed your Golden Retriever twice a day. A dog who eats just once a day can suffer from low blood sugar and hunger, which can contribute to stress, irritability, and aggression.

With all these choices and factors to consider, choose a food based on your budget and your dog's overall health.

GROOMING

This month your Golden Retriever's "second puppy coat" comes in full and thick, much like his adult coat will be, although it might be a lighter color than his coat will ultimately be at 2 or 3 years old. He looks beautiful this month, but don't get too attached to this look because his coat will shed out again by month 12.

To keep him looking his best and make brushing easier for both of you, you'll want to neaten his coat by trimming excess hair on a regular basis. Also, professional groomers are important allies now that your pup requires more coat care.

Trimming Your Pup's Coat

By now your Golden Retriever has started growing a full coat, and you might want to trim it a little to keep him neat and help prevent matting. And if your dog plays in heavy brush, less hair means fewer foxtails and other debris in his coat.

To neaten up his legs, trim some of the feathers off the back of each leg, as high as you prefer. Many people also shorten the belly hair and trim some of the feathering from his rear end and tail to keep his coat neater and easier to maintain. Using thinning shears can help you achieve a more natural look instead of an abrupt, straight cut.

Goldens have a lot of hair in and around their ears, and there's a big clump in front of the ear. Removing some hair in and around his ear allows air to get into the ear canal and helps prevent ear infections. Use thinning shears to help prevent matting, or clip it completely short so it blends in with the face. Behind the ears, you can use thinning shears, clip the hair short, or even shave it off. If you leave the hair, be sure to brush and comb it often, because these areas mat easily.

Employing Professional Groomers and Dog Washes

Even if you brush your Golden Retriever regularly, you could still get your pup professionally groomed occasionally, especially during shedding season. If you aren't keeping up with grooming chores yourself, professionals recommend you have your Golden groomed every 6 to 8 weeks, no matter what time of year it is.

This doesn't mean you can brush your dog less. Groomers will appreciate your work when they don't have to snip or brush out mats. If your groomer is able to use good conditioning products, managing the coat and preventing mats—especially on the long feather hairs on the legs, belly, front mane, and tail—will be easy with a slicker brush 3 to 5 days a week.

Groomers have powerful forced-air dryers that blow out more hair than you can remove at home using a regular hair dryer. Their specialized tools remove mountains of undercoat, too. The groomer uses a raised table with a harness to restrain your pup while he works, which might be easier—and cleaner—than your home setup.

Groomers also have shampoos and conditioners that soothe a dry skin and coat. If your dog gets skunked, your groomer might be able to remove the odor with a powerful enzymatic cleaner. If your dog gets into something especially disgusting in the middle of winter and you don't want it all over your bathroom as you attempt to bathe him, take him to a groomer. If you don't like to or are unable to trim your dog's toenails, a groomer can do the job for you. They usually trim nails à la carte, without requiring a full bath and brush. Some groomers even offer teeth brushing or scaling.

TIPS AND TAILS
On grooming day, wash all your Golden Retriever's bedding and clean her crate to remove fleas and odor.

Mobile dog-washing companies come to your door and bathe your dog in their van. They supply everything, even the water. This is less time-consuming and more convenient for you—and less stressful for your Golden Retriever—than spending half a day at a grooming shop. Check your phone book or ask other dog owners you know to find a good mobile groomer if this interests you.

Do-it-yourself dog washes are another option for stress-free grooming. They supply a wide variety of shampoos, conditioners, and towels, and you have access to the facility's high-powered sprayers, raised tubs, power dryers, and grooming tables to make the job easier.

SOCIAL SKILLS

Your puppy is growing and doesn't look so much like a puppy anymore. Strangers often don't react to an adult dog like they do a puppy, and your Golden Retriever needs to learn how to interact with people differently now that he's bigger. Pay attention to how other people greet your dog, and ensure his safety and theirs.

When People Don't Like Your Dog

How could anyone not love a Golden Retriever? Well, it happens. Respect the feelings of others, and don't force your dog on anyone. If someone appears to be afraid, don't try to talk him out of it; you don't know their history or fears. Avoid the person, keep your dog at a distance, and let them approach you when and if they choose to do so.

You can help ward off fears and prejudice by tying a bright bandana around your pup's neck, tucking a flower on his leash, or having him wear a bright cape. You'll break down barriers just by having a friendly looking dog.

TIPS AND TAILS
Some people are afraid of dogs, especially big dogs. A lunging, barking Golden Retriever is not a good canine ambassador. You can help put others at ease if your dog is well behaved and polite when he meets people.

Meeting New People

So many people, especially children, want to rush up and pet or hug a strange dog. Protect your Golden Retriever from their ill-informed enthusiasm by introducing your pup to new people so both parties are comfortable—because even the nicest dog likes to take his time to get acquainted. Instead of allowing the onslaught of enthusiastic greetings, say "Let me introduce you" to those who want to meet your Golden Retriever.

Always allow your dog to approach the person. A large human looming over a dog's is scary. (Remember the socialization process in Months 1, 2, and 3?) Think of how you'd feel if someone much bigger than you got in your personal space. You'd probably immediately back up until you were comfortable. A dog interprets someone coming straight at him as confrontational; likewise, to him, someone who looks straight into his eyes and holds his gaze is challenging him. He might even see it as an attack on you and try to protect you. This viewpoint is noble, but it's still inconvenient if he defends you from the wrong person.

You might find your Golden Retriever purposely stands between you and the person you're talking to. In this case, he's being protective of you, and you need to alleviate his fears. If you stand face to face with the other person, he might see them as a threat, so walk side by side with the person so your dog sees you are friends.

A person meeting a new dog should never put her face right in the dog's face … exactly what a child does when she hugs a dog. As she throws her arms around your dog, he'll feel trapped and unable to leave. Many Goldens love the attention and will wiggle and kiss their new friend, but don't take that chance. Your dog might someday decide he doesn't care for the stranger who's mauling him with affection. Or when he doesn't feel well, or the person steps on his toes, pulls his sore ear, or otherwise accidentally hurts him, he might not remember his manners when responding.

When you meet someone who doesn't feel comfortable with an overly assertive dog, have her stand sideways to your dog, which makes her seem smaller and less threatening, and tell her not to make eye contact. To encourage a shy dog to approach someone, have the person crouch on the ground while still facing sideways. Invite the person to scratch your Golden's chest rather than pat him on the head. Patting is annoying, and stroking is much more pleasant for your pup. And a hand coming at your dog from below is less threatening than a hand approaching his face.

Every outing is an opportunity to practice your dog's social skills. Continue to incorporate obedience commands into your walks so he'll respond to you when he has the chance to show off for someone new.

Getting Out and About in Nature

A well-socialized city dog might be terrified during his first hike in the woods, or he might love it. The safest way to hike is with your Golden Retriever puppy on leash until he knows his way around the area and you're sure no predators are nearby. Wild animals move silently in their natural environment, and you might never realize they're close. Your dog can sense them, though. Snakes, bears, crocodiles, mountain lions, coyotes, poisonous toads, and even raccoons can seriously hurt you or your Golden Retriever. If he appears anxious or reluctant to go on, listen to him and turn back.

Many parks require that dogs be kept on leash to protect both you and the wildlife. Early in the morning, the scent from all the nocturnal creatures who were out and about the night before will be heavy, and your dog will love absorbing all the new smells … until he encounters a deer. He might react fearfully and bark, or he might get excited and chase. Either way, if he took off running, he could easily get lost. Always keep him on leash until you're sure he's well-enough trained to stay with you. And never let him off leash in areas where that's prohibited.

If he's never seen one, an encounter with something as harmless as a tree stump can cause your dog to approach cautiously until he's familiar with his surroundings. Teach him to climb over logs and cross streams, and get him used to carrying a backpack, and soon he'll be an eager companion for your days outdoors.

BEHAVIOR

As your teenager develops, he'll undoubtedly test your patience and misbehave. If you continue to work to establish a good relationship with your Golden Retriever and pair that with calm and consistent leadership and discipline (not necessarily punishment), your pup will trust you and behave properly.

How Adult Dogs Show Leadership

Adult dogs earn a puppy's respect and compliance by using gentle but firm discipline. They chastise unruly puppies with just enough aggression to make their point and no more. A mother plunks a paw on top of a pup to stop him from harassing her, puts her mouth over the puppy's muzzle, or gets up and leaves when a puppy bites on her teats too hard. A puppy who oversteps his bounds with other adult dogs receives a snap and a roar that sends him packing. The adult settles back into her nap, and the pup minds his manners from then on.

When a dog rolls another dog over or pins him to the ground, she's either playing or putting an offender in his place because he was too pushy. A submissive dog rolls over voluntarily and shows his tummy to appease the aggressor; he isn't forced. That's usually the end of the discussion. Pinning a dog to the ground and holding him there or grabbing his neck is likely to start a fight.

We'd do well to follow the example of our canine friends. Discipline misbehavior with the minimum amount of force needed to stop the behavior, and no more.

Is *Dominance* a Dirty Word?

Dog behavior is often compared to that of wolves in a pack. The example given is usually one of a dominant wolf who rules the pack and forces the others to submit to him in order to retain his position.

In recent years, wolf-pack theory, especially as it relates to dogs, has been disproven. The concept of an alpha wolf who is *dominant,* with the rest of the pack deferring to him, was based on observation of unrelated wolves living in captivity. These wolves were thrown together in an artificial situation and had to establish a social order of some sort in order to get along.

DOG TALK

According to the American Veterinary Society of Animal Behavior, **dominance** is a relationship between two or more individuals established by force and submission in order to gain power over resources.

In the wild, wolves live in family groups with a dynamic entirely different from that of captive wolves. Their relationship is one of cooperation and respect, not aggression and violence. A breeding pair of wolves leads the pack, and youngsters are born, grow, and leave the pack to form their own family units. Oftentimes the pack includes a very young litter of infants and older adolescents who haven't left the pack yet. Leadership shifts among members of the pack all the time, depending on what they're doing. The females are in charge when it comes to caring for the pups, and the males are in charge when it's time to forage for food.

Dominance has become a controversial term in dog training and behavior, and experts debate the meaning and how it applies to our relationship with our pets. You might have been told you have an "alpha," or dominant, dog and you must be the dominant one or he'll take over the household and become aggressive. You might think you have a permanent problem that can't be fixed. Not necessarily. What you probably have is a silly adolescent Golden.

Being a Kind and Fair Leader

Rather than think of yourself as having to be dominant over your dog, think of yourself as his leader, much like parents act toward their children. A parent leads the family and provides resources: food, clothes, money, and shelter. The child looks to her parents for care, education, and protection and respects their authority. That's really what we do for our dogs, too.

What is a leader, and why does your dog need one? A good leader is respected. His followers listen to him and go along with his example. A leader sets limits, establishes rules, and enforces them consistently and fairly. When your leadership is well established, your dog feels secure and happy because he knows what's expected of him. Your puppy has had rules since he was in the litter with his mother and siblings, and he learned early what he could and couldn't do.

A dog without a leader feels he has to make decisions for both of you, and they will be doggy decisions, not necessarily what you would choose. Your puppy needs you to step in when you see him taking over a situation. This reassures him that you will protect him and he doesn't have to respond to every little thing.

Dogs thrive on consistency. Your Golden Retriever learns how to earn what he wants through good behavior. You might not be thinking about a being a leader all day, but your dog is watching you 24/7, taking mental notes. What should he do? What do changes in your behavior mean for him? Should he test the boundaries to see if the rules have changed?

You love your dog, and it's tempting to spoil him, or at least be lenient when he's misbehaving. After all, he's still a puppy. But spoiled dogs are like spoiled children—they always want more. The more you cater to your dog, the more he'll demand to be petted, fed, entertained constantly, etc. And he'll throw a tantrum or act out when he doesn't get his way.

Leaders love their dogs. They aren't overly harsh or dominant. Being a leader doesn't mean you can't pet your Golden or hug him, either. When you have a problem with a rude, hyper, or misbehaving dog, that's when you have to reinforce the rules and reestablish your authority. Leadership and respect are earned, not a gift.

TIPS AND TAILS

Your household is not a dictatorship. Every member of the family should be a leader in your Golden's eyes, and he should respect the children as well as Mom and Dad. He'll quickly learn who he can manipulate. Avoid conflict by having a family agreement that everyone enforces the rules the same way.

Think of a reestablishing your leadership program as "no free lunch"—a concept introduced by canine behaviorist William E. Campbell decades ago to help owners deal with doggy dictators. Dole out your attention and resources. If he sticks his head under your hand to be petted, ask him to sit first. When he wants to come indoors, have him do a down. Before you present his food dish, have him perform a trick. Ask for something meaningful so he has to make some effort to respond. Sometimes a sit is just too easy and he'll impatiently offer 20 sits in a row just to say "Get *on* with it, already." In this case, you can work on sharpening his skills. Be sure his elbows touch the ground during the down or his rear stays on the floor for more than a nanosecond during the sit.

Be clear when you respond to his behavior. Say "Yes" or "No," and don't ignore him or avoid an issue. Use your body language to show you're confident and in control. Don't beg him to comply, and don't repeat yourself. *Tell* him; don't *ask* him. Practice dozens of downs, sits, stays, leave its, and waits—all commands you've been working on and he should know. Two minutes once a day and scattered moments throughout make a big difference in how he responds to you.

Don't get angry at him; it just confuses him and makes him think you're unpredictable. Aggression in the form of hitting, yelling, grabbing, or throwing him down on the floor is likely to be met with aggression in return. He sees it as protecting himself from an irrational attacker. Golden Retrievers are very sensitive, and any kind of negative handling or yelling can cause them to become skittish and lose confidence, and the next thing you know, you have a fear-biter.

A good leader does *not* throw his dog on the ground in an *alpha rollover* to prove he's dominant and that the dog must submit. How would you feel if your boss threw you against the wall when you disagreed with him? That's an exaggeration, of course, but a good example of how your Golden feels if his beloved owner is suddenly aggressive and cruel. There are better ways to earn your puppy's respect.

DOG TALK

An **alpha rollover** is a punishment that's supposed to mimic how wolves establish their dominance over each other. A person forces his dog to the ground and holds him on his side or back until the puppy "submits" and stops fighting. *Do not try this at home, and don't let a "trainer" do this to your dog.* Trainers who years ago advocated the alpha rollover now have retracted their endorsement. If you try it, you're more likely to get bitten than earn your puppy's respect.

Dealing with a Rude Dog

Does your teenage Golden Retriever block your path as you try to walk? Does he crash through doors ahead of you? Lean on you? Charge out of his crate? Counter surf? Grab food? If so, he's rude, and he needs to know who the leader is at your house.

When your space invader crowds you, do it right back to him. Lean toward him; don't bend over, just push slightly with your body, and he'll back off. Don't move out of his way or go around him if he blocks you. Shuffle your feet and keep moving forward in short steps to push him out of your way. Don't use your hands; he sees hands as the human version of mouthing and playing. He understands a body block because that's what he does. Remember, he reads your body language before he hears what you say.

TIPS AND TAILS

Horse trainers have perfected the art of using their bodies to move a horse. By moving toward the horse's back hip, they can move the horse forward. By putting on "pressure," or leaning forward toward the horse, they make him back up. The same type of movement works with your Golden Retriever.

When you see a total body block coming at you full speed, take a couple quick steps toward him and aggressively push your hands toward him in a "Stop!" motion. This should startle him and make him veer away. You don't want to turn it into a game, so don't reward him or praise him a great deal. Just say "Good dog" and move on to another activity, like asking for a sit. When he's pestering you for attention, stand with your arms folded and ignore him. Tilt your chin up, and turn your body away.

Doorways are a big issue for dogs. Fights often start between dogs as they jostle with each other, trying to crowd through the door at the same time. Your puppy's excited to go out or in, and he doesn't want to be left behind. He's impolite and impatient, and as soon as he sees you head for the door, he leaps up and gets there before you.

Teach your puppy that calm behavior gets him what he wants. As soon as he starts to rush the door, stop and walk away. When he comes back in and settles, start again. After a few tries, he'll watch you carefully. If he runs up behind you, block his way to the door. Without saying anything, herd him back into the room with your body, not your hands or the leash. If you drag him by the leash, he's not learning anything except that you'll do the work. He'll soon figure out that he has to wait behind you. It's not an instant process, but eventually he'll understand.

Here's another exercise you can try: with your Golden on leash, open the door and as he dashes out, shut the door behind him with you still on the inside holding the leash. Whoops! That isn't the result he had in mind! In a few seconds, he'll whimper or scratch at the door. He can't leave because he's still attached to you, but he's not actually with you, either. Let him in and try again. After a few tries, he'll hesitate and look at you. Praise him when he does, walk through the door, and let him follow you. Remember that you taught your pup to wait in Month 7. This is the perfect time to use that command.

If he charges out of his crate the second you open the door, that's the next behavior to address. Never open the crate door for a dog who's whining, scratching, or otherwise demanding to be released. Ignore him because if he sees he has your attention, he'll continue fussing much longer. Wait until he's quiet. When you open the door, don't let him come crashing out. Quickly shut it in his face if he tries to charge. Do this as many times as you need to until he hangs back. Then quietly let him out and calmly go about your business.

Continuing Use of the Crate

This is the age of mischief for your puppy, and the crate is an important tool for preventing trouble during adolescence. Your puppy looks grown up, and he sleeps through the night without incident, so you might be tempted to leave him loose at night or in the house during the day. Don't.

A 9-month-old Golden Retriever isn't mature enough to handle the responsibility of entertaining himself for long periods of time alone. By putting him in his crate, he'll feel secure, and he won't feel like he has to investigate every sound. When he's excited in anticipation of your return, he won't be able to act out by tearing up a pillow or blanket that smells like you. If he gets hungry, he can't raid the trash. When he realizes he can't act on his adolescent impulses, he gives up and takes a nap. He also learns self-control in the process.

TRAINING

Continue to develop your Golden Retriever's skills this month with more advanced challenges. He's capable of learning more complex concepts because his attention span is no longer that of a little puppy. He can remember his new lessons much better for the same reason.

Solving Problems with Leash Walking

By 9 months old, your Golden Retriever is really strong. You can't drag him or hold him back when he's distracted—and at this age, *everything* distracts him. Walking quietly at your side is not a natural canine behavior, and when you don't let him rush off every time he sees something that interests him, he's likely to mutiny and try all kinds of different maneuvers to get out of walking at your side.

Solving this problem requires your full attention. This is not the time to be pushing a baby stroller or talking on your cell phone.

First, use a 4-foot leash, or take up the slack in your 6-foot leash, so he doesn't have as much length available for his antics. The clip on the leash should hang down, and the rest of the leash should form a U shape. If you let too much length hang down, he'll walk over it and become tangled. Hold your hands at waist level, where you'll have more control.

If you continually hold the leash tight, you're doing his thinking for him. He assumes the leash is supposed to be that way, he doesn't have to pay attention to you, and he knows right where you are. When he's on a loose leash, he makes mistakes and learns from them, and in the process, he learns self-control. When he's walking at your left side, you're tempted to pull tighter if you hold the leash in your left hand. Take your left hand off the leash, and hold it in your *right* hand at your waist.

When he balks, stands up on his rear legs, or refuses to go forward, start walking in the opposite direction. Turn around, walk right past him, and keep going. If he still doesn't follow you, walk in a circle around him. If he's still dancing around at the end of the leash, stop and work with him until he sits. When you resume walking, stop after just a few steps and ask him to sit again. Reward him when he does what you ask. You can use treats if that helps keep his attention.

When your pup cuts in front of or behind you, block him with your leg, calmly turn into him, and start walking in another direction. If he runs behind you from the left, pull the leash in front of you to the right so he can't get clear around you. Then do an about-turn and walk into him. This also works if he tangles himself in the leash or wraps it around your legs.

TIPS AND TAILS

When walking your Golden Retriever, start calm and end calm. He must sit quietly while you put on the leash and walk politely out the door. If he starts acting wild, you must stay calm or his behavior will escalate. When you get home, he must sit politely while you remove the leash.

Your Golden Retriever might take the leash in his mouth because he knows you're going to give him a correction and he wants to avoid it. This is a telling action. Have you jerked on the leash too often? Are you nagging him? The simplest solution is sometimes the best—let him carry his bumper or another toy in his mouth while you walk. If that doesn't work, spray the leash with pepper spray or chewing repellent before your walk. Spritz a little in his mouth, too, so he recognizes the taste and smell.

If you try to jerk the leash out of his mouth, he'll quickly turn it into tug-of-war. To combat this, you might want to switch to a chain leash, which hurts his teeth when he bites it. Chain leashes are chew-proof, but they're also uncomfortable on your hands, so consider wearing garden gloves with them. Horse-supply stores have stud chains for horse leads that are 12 to 18 inches long. You can attach one to his collar and then attach the leash to it.

Does your pup bump into you as you walk? You might think he doesn't realize he's bumping into you, and sometimes he's certainly oblivious to his own body. But most of the time, he knows exactly what he's doing. Bump him back, but overexaggerate the move. Don't be subtle. Bump him to the left or make a hard turn or about-face to the left. Don't lean back into him, or you both will be thrown off balance. His motivation is similar to pulling on the leash here: he keeps track of where you are, but he doesn't have to pay attention. He's also being very pushy and rude!

Your puppy also might lean against you when you're standing still. Or he'll put a paw on your foot. Again, by doing so, he knows right where you are so he doesn't need to pay attention. He's also invading your space. Step away quickly so he loses his balance. He won't fall all the way to the ground, but he will pay closer attention to you.

Maybe you've seen other Golden Retrievers dragging their people down the street, or maybe your pup has done this to you. This is the most common problem, but it's also the toughest to fix. While you work on correcting this, your walks might not take you very far from home as you practice sits, downs, and short stays. Do plenty of U-turns so he has to pay attention and see what you're going to do next. As you turn, talk and joke with your Golden, saying "Hey, you missed it! Where'd you go?" Make it a game. Every once in a while, when you do a sudden turn, pull out his favorite toy or treat and reward him with it when he follows.

To prevent pulling, you need to be more interesting than his surroundings. You get to decide when it's time to stop and sniff, not him. If you see something you know will make him pull, turn his attention to you and reward him before he starts pulling. If you need to, lure him with a treat right in front of his nose as you walk past the tempting distraction. You can reward him for his good behavior with "Go sniff!"

If one method isn't working for you, there are other ways to teach your dog to walk nicely. For example, stand still and don't move a muscle when he hits the end of the leash. Hold the leash at your waist, and don't pull back against him. Make no eye contact, and ignore him until he looks at you to see what you're doing. Then calmly praise him. If he immediately lunges ahead, stop again.

Or if your dog is pulling ahead, stop and back up slowly. With this, instead of reaching his goal, he's moving farther away. When he stops pulling, you can start walking forward again.

If you're using a no-pull harness or a prong collar, you and your dog might become dependent on these tools. Practice with a trainer so you both can learn to walk without them. If you have to use severe equipment to control your Golden Retriever, you'll never get to the point where you can let him off the leash because he isn't listening to you.

Teaching "Watch Me"

When your Golden Retriever is distracted, the "Watch me" command helps him focus on you. Goldens don't take much of anything seriously, so this is an entertaining way for him to learn to pay attention, too. There are several ways to teach the command.

Place treats or kibble in both of your hands, let your dog see them, and then hold your arms out sideways at shoulder level. He'll probably sit in front of you or leap at your hands to get the goodies. If he does, wait. At some point, he'll stop focusing on the goodies and look at you. When he does, praise him and deliver a treat immediately. After a few tries, he'll be staring at your face to get those treats, ignoring your hands completely. Now you can use the words "Watch me" just before he makes eye contact and praise him for looking at you.

You could also hold a treat right in front of your dog's eyes. Bring the treat up to your face, saying "Watch me." When his eyes shift from the treat to your eyes, praise him and give him the treat. If he looks away before you can give him the treat, don't give it to him. He only gets a treat when he maintains eye contact. Do this only a few times and then quit. You don't want to fill him up on treats.

Once he's paying attention, back up while moving the treat to your nose. This helps him pay attention to you while you're moving. Then you can add zigzags, circles, and other variations.

You also can teach him to watch while he's sitting at your side so he doesn't have to swing in front of you. Then he'll know how to keep his eyes on you when you're out on a walk and you ask for his attention.

Teaching "Stand" and "Stand-Stay"

When your veterinarian is examining your Golden Retriever, wouldn't it be nice if your he'd stand quietly while being handled? Beginning obedience competition requires a stand for exam exercise during which your dog must stand still while the judge runs her hands over him. Advanced competition requires a moving stand, where the dog stops while walking and remains in a stand-stay as you continue moving forward.

To teach your Golden to stand, kneel facing his side while he's sitting. Tweak his skin where his rear leg meets his belly, and lightly poke him up into a standing position while saying "Stand." He'll quickly learn to stand when you touch that spot.

You also can lure your dog from a sit into a stand. Stand facing him as he sits, take one step back while holding a treat just out of reach, put pressure on the leash, and tell him to stand. Once he knows the command, turn the motion of luring him with a treat into a hand signal.

YOU AND YOUR PUPPY

Earlier in this chapter, you learned about your Golden's incredible nose and talent for scentwork. In this section, you learn how to harness that talent by developing his brainpower and putting his scenting skills to good use—all while having some fun together.

Challenging Your Golden Retriever's Mind

Scientists have shown that dogs can learn up to 300 words. With that potential, your Golden Retriever's brain is full of opportunity. Think about what a hunting dog is capable of doing: marking the fall of three different birds, remembering where he saw them, figuring out how to pick them up in the order they fell, and returning the birds to his master. Assistance dogs must learn to turn on lights, pick up keys, alert their owners to the doorbell, and other specialized skills. Future service dogs already know at least 30 commands by the time they leave their puppy-raiser to go into training. Your Golden Retriever is capable of such great things and, like a child, he must practice using his brain to develop these skills.

Challenge your Golden Retriever with puzzle games. Present him with interactive games, and he'll figure out how to slide open a compartment to find a treat. Teach him the names of different objects during scenting and retrieving games as well as the names of specific locations in the house. Surely he recognizes the words *walk* and *dinner* by now. Teach him to go to his bed or crate, to ring a bell hanging from a doorknob to go outside, or to fetch the morning paper, all by just saying key words.

Challenging Your Golden Retriever's Nose

You might not be interested in or ready for competitive sports, but there are many other ways to have fun with a young Golden Retriever.

Nosework: An activity you can enjoy together at home, in public, or in classes and workshops, nosework is a fun, easy way for both of you to learn search dog skills as you train your dog to search for his favorite treats and toys. You don't need a lot of equipment or training; all you need is a motivated puppy and his favorite food or a toy reward.

Nosework starts out easy, with your Golden Retriever searching for his toy that's hidden under or in one of a group of cardboard boxes. The challenges get progressively harder as your dog builds his skills and learns the game.

If you're interested, you can check out training workshops and trials where your dog can earn nosework titles searching for a specific scent such as birch. For more information, visit the National Association of Canine Scent Work at nacsw.net. The first step is an odor recognition test (ORT), during which he demonstrates he knows how to search for a scent. Then your Golden can earn titles beginning with Nosework 1 (NW1), where he identifies one target odor, up to NW3, where he identifies three target odors under increasingly difficult conditions. Dogs can continue to get elite titles for multiple qualifying rounds as well as titles for identifying different elements like anise and clove.

HAPPY PUPPY

Nosework, tracking, search and rescue, and barn hunts are sports your Golden Retriever can begin as young as 6 or 7 months old. He's too young to do a lot of strenuous jumping or running at this age, so scentwork is a perfect outlet for his energy. He gets to use his mind, build his confidence, and spend time with you, and you learn to read your dog's subtle communication signals and recognize when he realizes he's on the scent.

Tracking: Tracking was one of the first performance events held by the American Kennel Club (AKC), back in 1936. Originally part of what were called Obedience Test Field Trials, tracking became a separate event in 1947. Today's rules remain similar to the original tests: your Golden demonstrates his scenting ability by following a human scent and finding "lost" articles, such as gloves, dropped by the tracklayer along the way. The handler (you) has no idea where the track goes, so it's completely up to your dog to find and follow the trail.

Before your dog competes in an actual test, he must earn a certification to compete. He completes a basic Tracking Dog (TD) track while being observed by an AKC judge. If he completes it successfully, he's eligible to compete in official AKC tracking tests. Unlike the other canine sports that require several outings and qualifying scores, a dog earns his AKC title after one successful track. The levels are Tracking Dog (TD), Tracking Dog Excellent (TDX), and Variable Surface Tracking (VST).

For a TD, the dog must follow a track in an open field that's 30 minutes to 2 hours old and 440 to 500 yards long. A flag marks the beginning of the track, a second flag marks direction of the first leg, and the track includes three to five legs, or changes in direction. An article such as a glove or wallet is placed at the end of the track, and at the beginning of the test, the dog is presented with another article that contains the scent he's supposed to track.

When he moves up to TDX level, your Golden must follow a longer and older track: 800 to 1,000 yards long and 3 to 5 hours old. A TDX test includes five to seven changes of direction and two crosstracks made by humans. No flag indicates the direction of the first leg of the track, and four articles are placed throughout—one at the starting flag, one at the end, and two more along the track itself. Whereas a TD is conducted on an open field, a TDX might contain natural and man-made obstacles along way such as gullies, plowed land, woods, vegetation, streams, fences, bridges, or lightly traveled roads.

In the VST, dogs face a much more difficult challenge. The track is 600 to 800 yards long and presents a varied tracking environment. The dog trails a scent 3 to 5 hours old in an urban setting rather than in the wilderness over at least three types of surfaces, such as concrete, asphalt, gravel, sand, or mulch. Tracks may be laid along the sides of buildings and fences, through buildings with two or more openings, breezeways, shelters, or roofed parking garages. There are no obstacles, as on a TDX track, and a VST track contains four articles along the way—one each of leather, plastic (rigid or semirigid), metal, and fabric.

A dog who has earned all three titles becomes a Champion Tracker (CT).

The AKC also offers an optional tracking title, the Tracking Test Urban (TDU), in which the track is plotted on surfaces like roads, pavement, and parking lots. This test is less difficult than the VST in that the track is shorter (400 to 500 yards) and the track is only aged 30 minutes to 2 hours. The TDU does not count toward the Champion Tracker title.

TIPS AND TAILS
You can get started with tracking by taking classes offered by local obedience clubs. Your breeder may know of a tracking group in your area, and the AKC website also lists tracking clubs by state.

Search and rescue: Golden Retrievers make excellent search-and-rescue dogs and also can work with professionals as arson dogs, drug dogs, and in many other capacities. If you've enjoyed tracking and want to volunteer with your dog, this is an excellent way to give back to your community.

Rescue teams work with law enforcement agencies and must be available to join a search at a moment's notice, day or night. Search dogs must be able to concentrate on a single scent that might be days old while blocking out distractions such as traffic, crowds, food, and other animals.

To qualify, you and your Golden must undergo extensive training and you must be certified in various skills such as CPR, canine and human first aid, radio communication, map reading, and crime scene preservation. You can participate in urban and wilderness searches or human remains searches or serve as a first responder in case of a national disaster. The National Association for Search and Rescue offers more information on how you can get involved at nasar.org.

Barn hunts: Barn hunts are an exciting dog sport for all breeds, not just for terriers. Both the Barn Hunt Association and United Kennel Club offer barn hunt titles to all breeds. (The AKC recognizes titles but doesn't offer barn hunt.)

A barn hunt tests the hunting and teamwork of dog and handler. The dog follows a scent through a maze of straw bales to find a rat (safe in a protected, aerated tube) at the end within a set amount of time. Dogs who complete the challenge are awarded a leg toward their title. Dogs can start by taking the Barn Hunt Instinct Test (RATI). Judged on a pass/fail basis, the dog has 1 minute to get to three tubes laid out side by side and to correctly identify the one tube containing a rat.

For the Novice Barn Hunt (RATN title), the dog must qualify at three different hunts. In each, the dog must enter an official tunnel, climb over bales of hay, and indicate the correct tube containing the rat, all within 2 minutes. Besides earning a qualifying leg toward a title, first through fourth place ribbons are awarded based on the fastest times.

For the Open Barn Hunt (RATO), the time increases to 2 minutes, 30 seconds; the tunnels are more complicated; and there are two rats to find.

At each level the difficulty increases, and your Golden Retriever can earn additional titles: Novice Barn Hunt (RATN), Open Barn Hunt (RATO), Senior Barn Hunt (RATS), Master Barn Hunt (RATM), Barn Hunt Champion (RATCh), and Master Champion (RATChX). To learn more about barn hunts, visit the Barn Hunt Association at barnhunt.com.

	SOCIAL	BEHAVIOR	TRAINING	PHYSICAL	HEALTH
MONTH 1			Littermates and mother teach appropriate canine behavior	Rapid growth	
MONTH 2	Breeder starts socialization				
MONTH 3	Socialization at home with new owner and other pets	Fear-imprint period	Begin house- and crate training		1st DHPP vaccine
MONTH 4			Enroll in puppy class		2nd DHPP vaccine
MONTH 5	Socialization in public	Teething begins—heavy chewing period	Ready for basic commands	Switch to adult food	3rd DHPP and rabies vaccines
MONTH 6			Enroll in basic obedience class		
MONTH 7		Adult teeth are in—chewing continues	Ready for more advanced training	Moderate growth	Sexual maturity
MONTH 8					
MONTH 9					
MONTH 10					
MONTH 11				Slow growth—reaches adult size	
MONTH 12 AND BEYOND					Annual vaccinations and checkup

In Transition

Although your Golden Retriever isn't quite full size at 10 months old, you can still get a good idea of what she'll look like as an adult. It's hard to remember she's still a puppy, but she hasn't lost her sense of fun and teenage mischief. As she participates in more activities, she's prone to injuries, so it's important that you know some basic first aid. Seasonal grooming also needs your attention.

You should be able to control her exuberance better now as she learns more advanced obedience skills and starts to listen to you more consistently. Golden Retrievers aren't pushovers, though, so you continue to work with discipline and preparation for off-leash privileges.

At this age, she can start preparing for her Canine Good Citizen certificate, so we share information on that and take a look at some activities your dog and your children can participate in together.

PHYSICAL DEVELOPMENT

Variation exists from dog to dog, but there are reasons why Golden Retrievers look the way they do. The originators of the breed put a lot of thought into what would, in their minds, make the perfect retrieving gundog, and the breed has been developed carefully over 150 years to produce the characteristics seen today.

Looking at the Breed Standard

Breed standards are written descriptions breeders can follow that define the function, ideal structure, size, proportions, coat characteristics, and temperament for a specific breed of purebred dog and how those features relate to the function of the breed. In other words, the Standard describes the features that make a Golden Retriever look like a Golden Retriever. If the dog had upright ears or a short, smooth coat, she wouldn't resemble the Golden Retriever described in the Standard. If she weighed 25 pounds or was white with black spots, she wouldn't look like a Golden, either.

The Kennel Club of England first recognized Golden Retrievers as a specific breed in 1911, naming them Retrievers—Golden or Yellow and redesignating them Retriever—Golden in 1920. Goldens arrived in Canada first, before they came to the United States, in the early 1900s. The first Golden registered in the United States was Lomberdale Blondin, in 1925. The AKC recognized the breed in 1932, and the Golden Retriever Club of America was formed in May 1938.

Golden Retrievers rose rapidly in popularity due to their gentle temperament and trainability. From the beginning, Goldens were superior gun dogs and excellent family pets. Over the years, breeders have been able to retain these traits, and Goldens have remained in the top 10 most popular AKC breeds for several decades.

TIPS AND TAILS

The latest version of the American Kennel Club (AKC) Breed Standard has been in effect since 1990. To read the complete Golden Retriever breed standard, visit the Golden Retriever Club of America at grca.org.

At dog shows, dogs are judged on how well they conform to the Standard physically and temperamentally. There's no such thing as a perfect Golden (or a perfect dog of any breed), so the dog who wins on a particular day is the one who, in the eyes of the judge, appears the closest to the description of the ideal Golden Retriever.

Some parts of the breed standard are purposely vague. There can be acceptable variations in the characteristics that define a Golden Retriever, so the breed standard has to allow for those differences. Although conformation judges look at the total dog, judges might differ in their priorities regarding the importance of specific points of the Standard. For instance, when evaluating two good examples of Goldens and trying to decide between them, the judge might see that one moves better than the other, so the better mover gets the top award that day. Another judge might put more emphasis on head and coat character.

When a judge looks at a Golden Retriever, he evaluates features like the dog's stride, the length of her forearm, and if the angle of the shoulder is correct. Is this Golden built to work all day over rough terrain? Will her coat protect and insulate her from cold water? Are her jaws strong enough to carry a duck or pheasant? Does she have the correct number of teeth? Is her temperament correct, meaning does she appear to be friendly, reliable, and trustworthy, as stated in the Standard? The breed standard defines all these characteristics.

Comparing Your Puppy to the Standard

Although your Golden Retriever hasn't reached maturity yet, you can have fun comparing her to the breed standard. Ask your puppy's breeder for a conformation evaluation. Even as puppies go through their awkward growth stages, you can learn about general characteristics such as how tall your dog will be and what she'll look like when she's fully grown. Your breeder can tell you if your puppy is a show prospect when she's as young as 8 weeks old. Puppies can be shown in AKC-approved conformation events at 6 months old.

Even if your puppy doesn't look like a show dog, to you and your family, she'll seem just as beautiful as any Golden Retriever who wins ribbons. In the long run, it won't matter much to you if she's too tall or is missing a tooth. In fact, some quirks make her that much more endearing to you.

Let's explore some of the terms used in the breed standard and get a better understanding of what to look for in your Golden Retriever.

This is the first paragraph of the Standard:

General appearance:

> *A symmetrical, powerful, active dog, sound and well put together, not clumsy nor long in the leg, displaying a kindly expression and possessing a personality that is eager, alert and self-confident.*

As you see, this description defines a dog built for physical work, with a lively and willing temperament.

> *Faults: Any departure from the described ideal shall be considered faulty to the degree to which it interferes with the breed's purpose or is contrary to breed character.*

You'll see *faults* mentioned several times in the Standard. A fault is a physical or temperamental deviation from the ideal Golden that, at the judge's discretion, is penalized in the show ring. A disqualification, on the other hand, is specifically defined and the dog is eliminated from competition on that day. The only disqualifications in the Golden Retriever Standard pertain to incorrect bites (alignment of the teeth) and height. However, a Golden who growls or bites a judge in the ring would also be disqualified.

In addition to the breed standard, the AKC has rules that disqualify dogs whose appearance has been altered in any way by artificial means, such as a surgical correction of an eyelid abnormality, or a male who does not have two normally descended testicles.

Head:

> *Broad in skull, slightly arched laterally and longitudinally without prominence of frontal bones (forehead) or occipital bones. Stop well defined but not abrupt … no heaviness in flews.*

Using a profile picture of a Golden Retriever's head, if you draw a line from the back of the skull to the dog's nose, you'll see a definite "break" in the line at the eyes, at roughly the center point. This is the Golden's eyebrow, or stop, a transition from the back skull to the foreface. The head shouldn't have overly pronounced bone structure. Many Goldens have an obvious occipital bone, the knobby joint on the back of the head where the skull meets the spine.

Flews are the dog's upper lips, and they shouldn't hang loosely or be too long. The Standard doesn't specify how long they should be, so "heaviness" is left up to the judge's discretion.

Ears:

> *Rather short with front edge attached well behind and just above the eye and falling close to cheek. When pulled forward, tip of ear should just cover the eye. Low, hound-like ear set to be faulted.*

A dog with long, floppy ears would have a fault and be penalized but not eliminated from competition. *Ear set* refers to where the top of the ear begins. Correct ear set keeps water out of the ears while the dog swims, an important characteristic for a retriever. If the ears are set too low, water can get in and cause ear infections.

HAPPY PUPPY

Just for fun, check your Golden's ears to see if they cover her eyes when pulled forward. Make it a game of peek-a-boo!

Teeth:

> *Scissors bite, in which the outer side of the lower incisors touches the inner side of the upper incisors. Undershot or overshot bite is a disqualification. Misalignment of teeth (irregular placement of incisors) or a level bite (incisors meet each other edge to edge) is undesirable, but not to be confused with undershot or overshot.*

This explains how the teeth meet in the mouth. A scissors bite is when the top teeth are in front of the bottom ones, which is correct in Golden Retrievers. If the teeth meet evenly, this is called a level bite, and the teeth wear faster as the dog ages. An underbite, where the bottom teeth are in front of the top teeth, impairs a Golden's ability to carry game.

Tail:

> Carried with merry action, level or with some moderate upward curve; never curled over back nor between legs.

When your Golden Retriever puppy is excited, you'll likely see a happy tail carried up, higher than her body. But when she's moving naturally, a correct tail is carried straight out from or just slightly higher than her rump, never curled.

Body:

> ... well-balanced, short coupled, deep through the chest.

Short-coupled refers to the area between the last rib and the point of the hip. Why is this important? A short loin, or short-coupling, provides a strong connection between the front and rear parts of the skeleton and uses less energy for movement, which helps increase stamina, an important characteristic for a retrieving gundog.

Coat:

> Dense and water repellent with good undercoat. Outer coat firm and resilient, neither coarse nor silky, lying close to body; may be straight or wavy. Untrimmed natural ruff; moderate feathering on back of forelegs and on under-body; heavier feathering on front of neck, back of thighs and underside of tail ... Excessive length, open coats and limp, soft coats are very undesirable.

The coat is an essential characteristic of the Golden Retriever. An open coat is fluffy, doesn't lie flat against the body, and usually doesn't have much undercoat. It wouldn't keep a dog warm while retrieving a bird from a field or body of water. The lovely coat is probably one of the reasons you chose this breed.

Color:

> Rich, lustrous golden of various shades. Feathering may be lighter than rest of coat ... Predominant body color which is either extremely pale or extremely dark is undesirable.

As mentioned earlier, very pale, almost white, Golden Retrievers are popular in Europe, but they're penalized in U.S. show rings. Color has no effect on temperament or your dog's ability to be a wonderful pet.

Temperament:

Friendly, reliable and trustworthy.

The Standard defines more than just a Golden Retriever's ideal physical characteristics. This is the essence of the dog you know and love.

Disqualifications

1. Deviation in height of more than one inch from standard either way.

2. Undershot or overshot bite.

Except for these two disqualifying faults, evaluating a dog according to the Standard is very subjective. Beauty is truly in the eye of the beholder, meaning the judge has plenty of leeway when selecting the winning dog.

The Conformation Assessment Program

The Golden Retriever Club of America (GRCA) offers a Certificate of Conformation Assessment any Golden over 18 months old can earn—even one who's spayed or neutered. The dog must be registered with the AKC or Canadian Kennel Club (CKC), or have a Purebred Alternative Listing (PAL) or Indefinite Listing Privilege (ILP) number.

The program is noncompetitive, meaning dogs are evaluated against the breed standard rather than other dogs. Owners receive written assessments of their dog they wouldn't get from a show judge, and the records are archived for historical and reporting purposes.

The test contains 10 categories (general appearance, head, neck and topline, body, forequarters, hindquarters, coat and color, gait and coordination, temperament, and overall impression—the same qualities a judge would evaluate in a conformation show) in which an evaluator scores a dog from 1 to 10 points each. A dog is required to have a total score of at least 75 out of 100 points and receive a qualifying score from three different evaluators to earn the title.

Conformation assessments are held in conjunction with events such as breed specialty shows, hunt tests, field trials, agility or obedience trials, and during the national specialty each year. To learn more, visit the GRCA website at grca.org.

HEALTH

You learned about CPR and dealing with life-threatening emergencies in Month 6. Now let's look at some other injuries and health problems you might encounter with your Golden Retriever and how to treat them.

Treating Injuries

When your puppy is injured, it can be easy to panic. But your cool-headedness is important to ensure his safety. Here's what to do:

Bleeding: If a wound is deep or spurting bright red blood, apply direct pressure and take your dog to the vet immediately. This is an emergency. She could have a severed artery, which quickly causes major blood loss. And don't wash the wound. That could prevent clotting. Less-drastic wounds bleed slowly, ooze dark red blood, and stop bleeding within 5 minutes.

If possible, elevate the bleeding area above the heart to reduce blood flow. Apply direct pressure with a clean cloth, sanitary pad, nonstick gauze bandage, or paper towels. When the bleeding stops, don't remove the cloth because it could cause the bleeding to resume. If one bandage becomes soaked through, add another bandage on top of it rather than remove the first. If the bleeding doesn't stop, have a second person apply pressure just above the wound. Secure the bandage by wrapping it against the dog's body, and get your dog to the veterinarian.

Bleeding ear: A cut on the ear bleeds a lot, and your Golden might make it worse by shaking her head. The good news is that ear wounds usually look worse than they really are. Place a gauze bandage or small sanitary pad on either side of the ear, and apply pressure for several minutes to stop the bleeding. Without removing the bandage, fold the ear up against your dog's head, and secure the ear to her head by wrapping a length of gauze or panty hose over her head and ear and under her chin. Don't wrap too tightly or interfere with her breathing in any way. You should be able to slip two fingers between the bandage and her chin.

Within 24 hours, check the wound (be careful—ear injuries can reopen easily), clean it, and apply antibiotic ointment. Take your dog to the vet if you feel it needs more attention or might get infected.

Bleeding tail: If her tail is bleeding at the tip, she might have whacked it against a wall or fence repeatedly. Elevate the tail to minimize blood flow, and apply pressure to the underside of the tail at the base, near the anus. This is a pressure point that helps slow the bleeding.

The hardest part of treating a tail wound is keeping it bandaged so she doesn't break it open again every time she wags her tail. Clip away fur from the open wound, and wash the area with saline solution or antiseptic soap.

TIPS AND TAILS
To make saline solution, combine 1 teaspoon salt with 1 quart warm water.

You want to bandage the tail, but don't do so too tightly because you could cut off blood circulation and cause severe injury. Put one long strip of adhesive tape against each side of the tail, extending several inches below the wound and above the wound off the end of the tail. Wrap the tail and the tape with gauze, starting well below the wound and ending just past the end of the tail. Fold the tape back over the bandage, and twist the tape so the sticky side adheres to the bandage and past it, adhering to the hair, too. By sticking the tape to her hair, the bandage is better anchored so it won't slide off the end of her tail. Place an elastic bandage (like VetRap) over the gauze wrapping, ensuring the wrap sticks to plenty of hair. To keep your dog from chewing off the bandage, you might have to put an Elizabethan collar on her.

If the injury is severe or isn't healing, take her to the vet. Most Goldens with tail injuries end up at the vet anyway because it's so hard to keep their tails bandaged.

Bleeding paw pad: Your puppy's paw pads contain many blood vessels, and they bleed profusely when cut.

Be sure you remove all the glass or other matter from the bottom of your puppy's foot (see the later "Object imbedded in body" section), flush the foot with running water to wash out any remaining debris, wash the area with saline solution or warm water, and dry the foot. Bandage the foot to keep dirt and debris out of the wound, using a similar technique as for bandaging a tail injury. Put one strip of adhesive tape against each side of the foot, extending several inches above and below the foot, and wrap the foot and the tape with gauze, starting at the toes and ending just above the ankle. Fold the tape over the bandage, and twist it so the sticky side adheres to the bandage. Place an elastic bandage (like VetRap) over the gauze, wrapping from the toes to the ankle, tight enough to stick but not so tight that it cuts off circulation. Check after a few minutes to be sure your pup's toes aren't swollen; if they are, the bandage is too tight.

Then, take your Golden to the vet. She might need antibiotics or further treatment.

Broken limbs: A fracture might mean one or more broken bones, usually to a leg. Suspect a broken bone if your Golden is holding her leg in an abnormal position, she appears to be in extreme pain, or she's unable to put weight on the limb.

TIPS AND TAILS

When she's hurt, you might need to muzzle your dog so she doesn't bite out of fear or pain. If you don't have a muzzle, wrap a long length of gauze around her mouth and tie it behind her ears. Double the gauze for added strength. Make a loop in the center of the length of gauze, slip it over her nose, and tie a knot on the top of the muzzle. Wrap the gauze under her jaw, and tie again. Then pull the ends behind her ears and tie. Do not cover her nose so she can still breathe.

Before you transport your puppy to the vet, put her in a crate or immobilize the break with a splint. The splint must cover the joints above and below the break to safely protect the limb. If your dog struggles too much, she risks worsening the injury. In that case, forego the splint and transport her to the vet as soon as possible.

When splinting a broken limb, do not reposition the bones. Place a rigid magazine, yardstick, or rolled newspaper on either side of or around the limb to prevent movement, and keep the splint in place using multiple pieces of tape wrapped around the splint and leg. Don't wrap too tightly. If you can't find any splinting material, use the opposite leg to stabilize the fracture, putting a piece of cloth or some kind of pad between the two legs before wrapping the legs together.

If a bone is protruding from the skin, you need to take additional precautions. Don't move the bone, or you could cause internal damage or bleeding. Wash the area with saline solution, cover it with a sterile nonstick gauze pad, secure the pad with a covering of cloth or gauze, and tape it a few inches above and below the exposed bone. Immediately transport your dog to the veterinarian. A broken bone requires professional treatment.

Burns: Cooking accidents or caustic chemicals can cause painful burns and permanent scars. Your dog's fur might mask the seriousness of a burn, so take her to a vet after you've performed first aid, even if the burn seems minor. First-degree burns are the least serious and usually just cause redness and pain. Second-degree burns cause blisters and swelling. Third-degree burns, the most serious, damage the skin, hair, blood vessels, and deeper tissue.

To treat a burn from fire, steam, or hot water, flush the burned area for 5 to 10 minutes with cool water. This reduces the temperature of the skin and prevents further tissue damage. Don't submerge your dog's entire body in water, or you risk sending her into shock. Cover the burned area with a nonstick bandage or torn, clean cloth. Don't use any type of material that might stick to the burn, and don't apply any ointments or creams. If the burn is near your dog's neck or head, remove her collar in case the skin swells so it won't restrict her breathing. Seek immediate veterinary attention.

To administer first aid for chemical burns from products like bleach, pool chemicals, battery acid, or weed killers, first protect yourself with rubber gloves, a facemask, eye protection, and protective clothing before treating your dog. If your dog tries to shake off the chemical and you're not protected, you could be burned, too. Then, restrain and muzzle her so she won't try to lick off the chemical. Remove her collar if the burn is near her neck.

A chemical burn will continue to burn into the tissue long after it makes contact with her skin, so flush the burned area with cool water for at least 20 minutes. If the chemical is oily, add mild dish soap to the rinse. For powder burns, attempt to brush off as much as you can before rinsing. With either kind of burn, take your dog to the vet immediately.

TIPS AND TAILS

To prevent burn injuries, keep your Golden Retriever out from underfoot when you're cooking, whether you're in the kitchen or outdoors. The smells entice her to investigate, but you might not see her when you're carrying hot pans. She also might try to stick her nose in an open oven to see what's cooking.

Electrical cord/shock: Even though you puppy-proofed your house, your teenage Golden Retriever might have found an unprotected electrical cord somewhere. If she bites it, she could get electrocuted and collapse, have a seizure, or experience other severe symptoms as a result of contact with electricity. If you see any of these, consider it a life-threatening emergency. If she stops breathing, perform CPR (see Month 6), and take her to your vet immediately.

Most electrical injuries are less severe, and consist of a mild burn on his lips, tongue, or mouth, for example.

If your dog is still touching the cord, put on rubber gloves and disconnect the power before you touch her, move her away from the cord with a broom or wooden chair, or trip the main circuit breaker. Avoid stepping in water, which conducts electricity.

Keep your dog as calm as possible to keep her breathing normally and prevent her from going into shock. Flush burns in her mouth with cool water, and apply an ice pack to burned lips. Then take her to the veterinarian immediately. She could have internal damage that isn't immediately apparent.

Insect bites or stings: When a curious puppy approaches something buzzing that's new to her—like a bee, wasp, or hornet—the result is often a sting on the face or nose. Unless she has an allergic reaction or multiple stings, these usually aren't life-threatening.

To treat minor stings, remove the stinger as quickly as possible if it's still embedded in your Golden's skin. Pull it out with tweezers, or scrape it with a credit card (you'll squeeze less venom into the wound this way). Soothe her skin with a paste made of baking soda and water, hydrocortisone cream, aloe vera gel, or cold compresses.

TIPS AND TAILS

When you travel, carry a bottle of meat tenderizer in your first-aid kit. You can mix it with water to make a paste to apply to bug bites or stings. (This remedy works great on people, too.)

If the sting is on or near her face and starts to swell dramatically, your puppy could be having an allergic reaction that might interfere with her breathing. Take her to the vet immediately.

Object imbedded in body: When your puppy comes running up to you with a stick protruding from her side, resist the urge to pull it out. Muzzle her because while she's in pain she could attempt to bite you. Wrap cloth around the base of the object without repositioning it, and tape the cloth in place to stabilize it. Keep your dog calm and as immobile as possible, and take her directly to the vet.

You can remove smaller objects like splinters, thorns, or porcupine quills with tweezers, a needle, or pliers. If a splinter is completely under the skin, sterilize the tweezers or needle before using them by dipping them in alcohol or running them through a flame. Grasp the object as close to the skin as possible, and pull it out slowly. After you remove the object, soak the area with a mixture of warm water and Epsom salt for 15 minutes. The Epsom salt, made of magnesium and sulfate, absorbs into the skin and reduces inflammation. Repeat daily until completely healed.

Glass or small sticks might break if you try to remove them, and you'll need to have her examined by a vet to be sure no pieces remain in the wound.

If your dog has been stuck with more than a few porcupine quills, she'll need to go to the vet to have them removed and her wounds thoroughly cleaned.

Fishhook in the skin: She can get a fishhook imbedded in her face or lips while tasting bait or fish. If your Golden has done this, push the hook farther through her skin so the barb is exposed, cut off the barb with wire cutters, and pull out the hook the way it went into her skin.

If there's no exit wound, take your pup to the vet for removal. She'll probably need antibiotics to prevent infection.

TIPS AND TAILS

Removing a fishhook deserves special attention because pulling out a hook incorrectly can do a lot of damage to your puppy's skin.

Torn dewclaw or toenail: If your dog's nails grow too long, they risk being snagged and torn. The front toenails seem to be more at risk for injury; dewclaws are loosely attached, so the entire toe is in danger of tearing. Because the nail quick is comprised of living tissue, a torn nail can be very painful. Your dog might need to be muzzled and restrained while you treat the injury.

Stop the bleeding by applying pressure with a cloth or your finger. The dead portion of the nail might be split or torn, so trim it off if you can. Then apply styptic powder, cornstarch, or flour to help the blood clot.

If the dewclaw is injured, wash the area, dry it completely, apply antibiotic ointment, and tape or wrap it against the leg to keep it from flapping around and reopening the wound. Wrap the foot and take her to the vet for treatment if the tear is deep or involves the flesh on the dewclaw. She might need antibiotics or stitches to prevent infection and repair the tear. If the dewclaw is badly injured, it might need to be surgically removed.

Treating Symptoms of Illness

When you realize your puppy is not well, you can take steps to treat the problem while you evaluate how serious it is. Some issues, like diarrhea and vomiting, could be minor and respond to treatment quickly. If these conditions don't resolve, or accompany other troublesome symptoms, a vet will need to investigate further. Others, like seizures, might be a symptom of a much more serious problem and require immediate veterinary treatment.

Diarrhea: If your puppy is vomiting at the same time she has diarrhea, she could be seriously ill. If there's blood in the stool, either fresh (bright red) or digested (dark red or black), take her to the vet immediately. Take a stool sample with you for the vet to examine.

At the first onset of diarrhea, you can give your puppy antidiarrheal medication. Check with your vet to find out what brand to use and the proper dosage. To prevent dehydration, be sure your Golden Retriever has plenty of water available. A pediatric oral electrolyte solution can replace some of the nutrients and moisture she's lost. You'll find this product in the children's section at your grocery store or pharmacy.

Temporarily switch to a high-fiber or bland diet. You can purchase a prescription diet from your vet or make your own by combining cooked white rice with boneless boiled meat or chicken with the fat drained off. If the diarrhea subsides, slowly switch your puppy back to her regular food. If the diarrhea lasts longer than 48 hours or is combined with vomiting, see the veterinarian for further care.

Seizure: Witnessing your dog have a seizure is frightening. Before a seizure, she might seem dazed or anxious. During an active seizure, she might twitch and fall over, lose control of her bowels or bladder, and not recognize you. Afterward, she might appear dazed and disoriented, or she could seem just fine. The length of the seizure can vary dramatically. A seizure lasting longer than 2 minutes is an emergency and can cause high fever or brain damage.

To protect your dog from injury during a seizure, move her away from stairs or furniture so she won't fall or hit anything. Don't disturb or restrain her during the seizure. She won't swallow her tongue, so don't put your hand in her mouth because she could accidentally bite you.

If this is your dog's first seizure, have her examined by a vet immediately. Make a note of how long the seizure lasted, the time of day, the date, and when she last ate a meal.

There are many possible causes for seizures in dogs, include poisoning, a tumor, bacterial infection in the brain, organ failure, diabetes, and epilepsy. If your vet can identify the cause, he may be able to treat the condition and your dog may never have another episode. The cause is often hard to identify, though, as is the case with epilepsy. Some animals will need antiseizure medication for the rest of their lives.

Vomiting: When your Golden Retriever eats something yucky (as puppies so often do), she might vomit to get it out of her system before it makes her sick. She could have a simple gastrointestinal upset, or she might have eaten an inedible object like a toy. If she doesn't pass the object in her stool, she'll get increasingly ill. Serious infections like pancreatitis can also cause vomiting. If your Golden Retriever is lethargic or has a fever, take her to the vet immediately.

Rapid dehydration is the biggest risk when your dog is vomiting over a period of hours. Withhold food, but offer her small amounts of water or ice chips if she'll take them. If she seems otherwise healthy, after 12 hours, reintroduce food in small amounts—about ½ cup at a time. If she continues to vomit, she might need to visit the vet for antinausea drugs and fluids.

NUTRITION

We've talked about dog food before, but it's such a vast topic, it warrants further discussion.

From ingredients to nutrients to calorie count, it might seem like there are a hundred different ways to evaluate dog foods and figure out what's best for your Golden Retriever. Try to balance the information you gather from each method without relying too much on any one absolute formula. And remember, the best way to decide if you're feeding correctly is to look at your dog, not the label on the dog food bag.

Counting Calories

As you learned in Month 7, dog food manufacturers are required to include information about ingredients, nutrient percentages, serving sizes, etc. on the label. They're not required to list the calorie count, but many do. That's how many people keep track of their own diets, so it makes sense to look at your dog's caloric requirements, too. There's no one correct calorie amount your dog should consume each day. Quality of ingredients, premium or generic brands, your dog's activity level, and her health all play a part in determining her recommended daily amount.

Recommended calorie counts are based on the measurement—for example, 1 cup is 400 calories. A healthy Golden Retriever who weighs 50 pounds and maintains an average activity level needs about 1,000 to 1,400 calories a day. A 70-pound dog needs about 1,400 to 1,800 calories.

In general, most adult or large dog formulas have between 350 and 400 calories per cup. Premium brands have a higher calorie count than other foods, so you should feed less of these. "Light" or weight-loss formulas vary dramatically. Some have as little as 50 calories fewer than the regular formula, and some have more than 100 calories fewer per cup. Nutrient percentages may vary, too, with some containing less fat and more fiber. (For more about treating obesity in Goldens Retriever, see Month 12.)

You need to know the exact calorie count of the specific formula you're planning to feed. If it's not listed on the bag, call the company or visit its website to find the information you need.

Choosing Training Treats

For training sessions, many Golden Retrievers are happy with bits of their regular dry food. But to really motivate your dog, choose a high-value treat that's especially tasty to her. Look for treats with the highest meat content available and human-grade ingredients.

Dehydrated and freeze-dried treats are convenient and don't make a mess in your pocket. You should be able to cut up the treats so you can feed tiny amounts during training sessions. Remember, treats should make up no more than 5 to 10 percent of your dog's total daily calories. To keep her from gaining weight, use part of her daily food ration for training mixed in with special goodies.

HAPPY PUPPY

Your dog needs to respond to you even when you don't have food, so mix up her training rewards with toys and games. The latter are sometimes more valuable to her.

GROOMING

In addition to your regular grooming routine that includes brushing her coat, cleaning her teeth, and trimming her toenails, pay attention to your dog's seasonal grooming needs. Although grooming is a year-round chore with Golden Retrievers, they need some extra care during different times of the year. Let's take a look at what your dog needs each season.

Spring Grooming Needs

Spring is the heavy shedding season for Goldens, and you might need to brush her every day to keep her fur from taking over your house.

After outings in spring and summer, check your puppy carefully for foxtails, especially if she's been in unmown grassy areas. One blade of grass can let lose hundreds of tiny barbed seedlings, and dried foxtails are most dangerous because they're sharp and can easily penetrate her skin. Foxtails are so small they're often hard to see, and to make it more difficult, they're the same color as your Golden's coat.

To deal with them, inspect your dog's entire body every day, including her ears, rear end, between her toes, in the folds around her neck, and her armpits.

During heavy exercise, the vocal folds that protect your dog's windpipe won't close completely when she exhales, which increases the chances she could inhale foxtails or other foreign bodies. If your puppy suddenly develops an explosive sneeze, suspect a foxtail or other foreign body in her nasal passage. She might rub or paw at her nose, have a nasal discharge, or get a nosebleed. A foxtail can also penetrate the skin and migrate into her bloodstream, eventually lodging in her lungs, causing an abscess and serious illness. If you suspect this, schedule a vet visit to have the foxtail removed before it causes serious problems.

If your dog has seasonal allergies, she might show signs during the spring when plants and grasses are in bloom. Rinsing her off with cool or distilled water can ease the irritation.

A dog's eyes are vulnerable to seasonal pollens and debris, too. A bit of grass can severely irritate her eye, scratch her cornea, or cause other eye injuries, and she might rub at her eye, blink a lot, or squint. If you see a discharge from her eyes, or they appear excessively watery, inspect them to be sure nothing is under her eyelids. You might be able to remove any offending matter by pulling out her lower eyelid and sweeping it with your finger or a wet cotton swab. Be careful not to scratch the eye itself as you do this though.

Use an eye rinse or artificial tears (saline solution) to wash out your puppy's eye to remove small irritants. This cleanses the surface of her eye as well as the surrounding tissue. Wipe the skin around her eyes with a towel to remove any discharge. If her eyes are still irritated, use a cool, wet compress on one eye at a time. If this doesn't clear up the problem, have your vet examine her to rule out an injury. Eye irritation might also be a symptom of allergies, and your vet can help you determine what the problem is.

Your vet might prescribe an antibiotic ointment to heal your puppy's injured eye. To administer the ointment, pull down on her lower eyelid and apply the ointment on the inner surface of her eyelid, not on her eyeball itself. Rub her eyelid gently over her eyeball to spread the medication.

TIPS AND TAILS

Your Golden Retriever might love riding with her head out the car window, but that's not a safe idea. She's at risk for an eye injury from flying debris and dust.

Fleas and ticks are coming out about now, too, so if you discontinued preventatives during the winter, restart them now.

Summer Grooming Needs

Your Golden Retriever is probably quite active during summer months, so she'll need more baths to keep her clean and smelling nice. Always rinse her off after she swims in a pool, ocean, or lake. Chlorine and salt water are both extremely drying to her coat, and fresh water carries bacteria and parasites that can make her sick.

During your weekly grooming sessions, check her mouth to be sure no bits of sticks, seeds, and other debris are stuck between her teeth or lodged in her mouth.

A dog's fur usually protects her from direct skin contact with two summertime hazards, poison oak or poison ivy, whose the leaves and branches contain an oil that can cause allergic reactions. Learn what these plants look like, and keep your dog away from them. If she runs through the woods, gets the oil on her coat, and you touch her later, you can be infected, too. Be sure to first put on gloves and then thoroughly bathe your puppy if you think she's been exposed.

If she does get the oil on her skin, she might get an itchy rash, just like you would. Especially vulnerable are areas where her hair isn't as thick, such as her tummy, inner legs, and muzzle. If your dog ingests some of the plant, she can suffer from vomiting or diarrhea, or her airway could swell. If this happens, take her to the vet immediately.

Fall Grooming Needs

Golden Retrievers shed their summer coat in the fall and grow in a heavier winter coat. During this time, she'll need extra brushing for several weeks to remove the loose hair. Her coat will pick up more debris during the fall, too, like fallen leaves and dead flowers.

Fall outings mean she'll also track in mud and dirt. It's easier to brush out of her coat when she's dry, if you can wait.

Winter Grooming Needs

If you live where the white stuff falls, your Golden Retriever will love romping in the snow. Clean her feet after these chilly outings to remove ice from between her toes and road salt from her paw pads. Don't leave her wet, especially if she's gotten soaked to the skin. Dry her well with towels, and use a hair dryer on low temperature to finish the job. If you have a forced-air dryer made especially for dogs, even better.

Your Golden may get a dry coat from being in a heated house all day during the winter months. Regular brushing helps distribute the oils in her skin and coat. A humidifier might also help her dry skin.

SOCIAL SKILLS

We each have our own ideas about what makes a well-behaved dog and how we would like our pet to act in public. The AKC has created a program that outlines canine good citizenship to help owners reach their goals for a well-socialized and welcome canine member of the community.

As more and more laws are enacted restricting dogs' access to public places, we all have a duty to be sure our dogs aren't part of the problem, but part of the solution.

The Canine Good Citizen Program

The AKC Canine Good Citizen (CGC) program was developed to encourage responsible dog ownership and praise owners for their training efforts. It also recognizes dogs who have good manners at home and in the community. For families just starting out with a new puppy, the program provides a clear definition of what makes a well-behaved dog and offers goals for you to strive for when you begin training. While learning the exercises for the CGC, you enjoy time with your dog, exercise her mind, and forge a deeper bond. The best benefit is that a dog who has passed the CGC exam is a joy to live with.

The CGC is accepted throughout the United States (34 states now have CGC resolutions on the books) and the whole world as evidence that your dog is well behaved and you are a responsible owner. Carry the certificate with you when you travel to present to hotels and other public facilities. Therapy dogs often must pass the CGC test as part of their certification for visits. Animal-control agencies might require owners and their dogs to earn a CGC certificate when issues arise with the dog's behavior in public.

Many obedience instructors use the CGC program as the basis for their beginning obedience classes and incorporate the test into graduation. Check with local trainers to find classes for the CGC test. The AKC website lists evaluators you can contact for more information and posts a schedule of upcoming tests in your area.

The CGC Test

The CGC test has two versions, the original CGC and the new added Canine Good Citizen Urban (CGCU), which is formatted for city dwellers and the unique challenges their dogs face. To earn a Canine Good Citizen certificate, your dog must demonstrate her training and good manners during a 10-step evaluation by an AKC examiner. At the same time, you sign a pledge to be a responsible dog owner.

The test for either version is challenging and requires practice before you both are ready. Passing is an achievement you and your Golden Retriever should be very proud of.

The CGC test is made up of 10 challenges:

1. Your dog accepts a friendly stranger who approaches and speaks to you. The evaluator ignores your dog while greeting you in a friendly manner, shaking hands, and engaging in conversation.

2. Your dog must sit politely for petting by a stranger. She must sit at your side and show no aggression or resentment while a stranger pets her on her head and body.

3. Your dog accepts grooming and handling by a stranger and is presented in clean, healthy, and well-groomed condition. Your puppy must permit a veterinarian, groomer, or other person to groom or examine her. This also demonstrates that you provide good care for your Golden Retriever.

4. Your dog walks nicely on a leash at your side. This test shows that you can control your dog. She must be attentive to you and respond to your changes in direction to turn left, turn right, halt, and do an about-turn.

5. You can walk your dog through a crowd and keep her under control without her showing excessive shyness or resentment around strangers. Your Golden Retriever demonstrates that she's under control and polite in public places. She shouldn't jump on anyone or strain on the leash.

6. Your dog will sit and down on command and stay in place while you walk 20 feet away and return. This exercise demonstrates that your Golden Retriever has been trained and will remain in position. You first show that she'll do both a sit and a down. Next, you replace her leash with a 20-foot line and ask her to do either a sit or down (your choice). She must stay in position until the evaluator instructs you to release her.

7. Your dog comes when called. She's still on a long line, and you walk 10 feet away, turn to face her, and call her to you.

8. Your dog demonstrates a polite reaction to another dog while owners greet each other and walk together. Two handlers and their dogs approach each other from about 20 feet away, stop, shake hands, and speak to each other. Both then continue on another 10 feet.

9. The dog demonstrates confidence when faced with a distraction she might normally encounter, such as someone dropping a chair or rolling a cart past her. Your dog can express interest or be startled, but she shouldn't panic, try to run away, bark, or show aggression.

10. Your dog tolerates separation from you without becoming overanxious while someone else holds her leash. This test shows that your dog can be left in someone else's care and maintain her training and good manners. The evaluator takes hold of your dog's leash while you leave and go out of sight for 3 minutes.

The CGCU Test

The CGCU recognizes that city dogs sometimes need extra skills to be a truly canine good citizen. Here are the 10 tests your dog must pass:

1. Your dog exits/enters doorways with no pulling.

2. She walks through a crowd on a busy urban sidewalk.

3. Your dog reacts appropriately to city distractions such as horns, sirens, etc.

4. Your dog waits on leash and crosses the street under control.

5. She ignores food and food containers on the sidewalk.

6. She allows a person to approach her on the sidewalk and pet her.

7. Your dog performs a 3-minute down-stay in the lobby of a dog-friendly building.

8. She safely negotiates stairs and elevators.

9. You can confirm your dog is housetrained.

10. Your dog enters and exits or rides dog-friendly transportation (car, subway in a carry bag, cab, etc.).

If you successfully complete either test, congratulations! You have a well-trained Golden Retriever.

The Responsible Dog Owner's Pledge

Think about all the work you've put into raising your Golden Retriever. You deserve recognition for the care and training you provide. The Responsible Dog Owner's Pledge represents the promise you made to your puppy when you added her to your family:

AKC CGC Responsible Dog Owner's Pledge

I understand that to truly be a Canine Good Citizen, my dog needs a responsible owner. I agree to maintain my dog's health, safety, and quality of life. By participating in the Canine Good Citizen test, I agree that ...

I will be responsible for my dog's health needs:

- Veterinary care, including check-ups and vaccines.
- Adequate nutrition through proper diet and clean water at all times.
- Daily exercise and regular bathing and grooming.

I will be responsible for my dog's safety:

- I will properly control my dog by providing fencing where appropriate, not letting my dog run loose, and using a leash in public.
- I will ensure that my dog has some form of identification, be it include collar tags, tattoos, or microchip ID.

I will not allow my dog to infringe on the rights of others:

- I will not allow my dog to run loose in the neighborhood.
- I will not allow my dog to be a nuisance to others by barking in the yard, in a hotel room, etc.
- I will pick up and properly dispose of my dog's waste in all public areas, such as on the grounds of hotels, on sidewalks, parks, etc.
- I will pick up and properly dispose of my dog's waste in wilderness areas, on hiking trails, at campgrounds, and in off-leash parks.

I will be responsible for my dog's quality of life:

- I understand that basic training is beneficial to all dogs.
- I will give my dog attention and playtime.
- I understand that owning a dog is a commitment in time and caring.

BEHAVIOR

Your Golden Retriever's behavior improves every day, but you sometimes still suffer through moments of regression, when she reminds you she's still an adolescent. As much as you want to use positive methods to train your dog, Golden Retrievers sometimes need a firmer hand to deal with their behavior.

Barking Barking Barking Barking Barking

Problem barking often begins during the teenage months. Your Golden Retriever goes through periods of uncertainty, and one way she expresses that concern is to bark. The more socialization she has had up to this point, the less fearful she will be.

Golden Retrievers aren't usually chronic barkers, but if yours is barking a lot, you don't want it to become a habit. Barking is a natural behavior you can never entirely eliminate, but if you get it under control now, it won't become a bigger problem later, when she matures and becomes more territorial and protective.

Manage your puppy's surroundings, and figure out what makes her bark, to discourage and prevent excess barking. For example, if she barks in the yard, limit her view. Put up a solid fence instead of chain link, don't let her out on the upper deck where she can see the neighbor kids playing, or bring her in when kids are walking home from school. If she barks out the living room window, don't let her in the living room, or close the drapes.

TIPS AND TAILS

You want your Golden Retriever to bark occasionally. Check out what she's barking at and then quiet her and redirect her to another activity. She's done her job, and now you've taken over.

Does she bark every time the doorbell rings? Think about how she sees it: you jump up and head for the door, so she does, too. She could be either excited or frightened, but either way, it's a big deal in her eyes. Teach her to sit quietly when the doorbell rings or go to her crate. (This lesson might require a helper.) Put a leash on her before you open the door, and practice her sit-to-greet. Give her a toy if you need to. After all, when she has a toy in her mouth, she can't bark!

Does she bark aggressively at the neighbor through the fence or someone at the front door? She's most likely afraid of the person. She's too young to be overprotective (something that happens closer to 18 months old), but this type of barking can turn into an ugly habit. Have the person toss a treat in her direction, and after a few treat sessions, your Golden will be happy to see the person and engage in an entirely different type of barking.

Maybe you have a bossy barker. She wants in, so she barks. She knows it's close to dinnertime, so she barks. She wants to play fetch, so she drops a toy at your feet and barks. It's time to wake up, so she stands by the bed and barks. See the pattern? You might inadvertently teach your dog to bark at you by responding to her every request. Make her earn your attention instead. Ask for a sit or a down before you give her what she wants. Keep in mind, too, that down is a subordinate position, and most dogs don't bark while lying down. She might not want to lie down when she's excited and wants something, but that's all the more reason to insist on compliance. Don't reward her or let her up until she calms down. Put her on a leash if you have to, or give her a 5-minute time-out in her crate if she's barking at you to do something. If bossy barking is really getting to be a problem, have her do many 1-minute downs throughout the day.

Another tactic is simply to ignore her barking. This is really hard to do, but if you can hold out, she'll give up eventually. The barking will get worse before it gets better, though, as she gives it one last over-the-top burst of effort right before she gives up. This is when many people cave in and respond. If you do, she'll bark much longer next time. Reward her when she stops barking even for a few seconds.

Some people yell at their dog to be quiet, but she has no idea what that means. She figures you're just barking with her. The more excited you are, the more excited she gets, so stay calm.

Teach her to bark on command. Catch her when she's barking and praise her, saying "Good bark!" or whatever word you want to use (*speak* or *talk,* for example). As soon as she breaks off, say "Good quiet" and reward her. She'll learn to respond to "Bark" and "Quiet."

Try to head off barking binges before they get started. If you see something you know is going to make her bark, call her and get her attention on you. Practice when there are no distractions by rattling a treat shaker (a small container of kibble) and calling her. When she learns that something good happens and she gets treats, you'll be able to call her away from that exciting thing before she starts barking.

TIPS AND TAILS

Golden Retriever rescue groups report that behavior problems are the main reason Goldens are given up for adoption—usually between 1 and 2 years old. The time you spend training and resolving behavior issues while your dog is still young helps ensure you have a well-behaved family member throughout her life. If you've adopted a rescued Golden, it's never too late, but training will take a little more time and patience on your part. Golden Retrievers are especially resilient and forgiving, and they adapt quickly to their new environment and new rules.

Disciplining Your Golden

Most people agree that physical punishment can destroy your relationship with your dog, but what are you supposed to do when positive methods don't work and you need to discipline your dog?

When your Golden Retriever was a puppy, it was enough to stop her and redirect her to an acceptable activity. You can still do this, but you'll have to use a lot more conviction. Stop her by saying, "No!" or "Ack!" Your tone of voice conveys your displeasure, and for some Goldens, that's enough.

Be sure your dog realizes why she's being disciplined. You must catch her in the act or she won't understand what she did wrong. Dogs live in the moment. She won't comprehend why she's being punished for something she did 2 hours, or even 5 minutes, ago. If you come home and find she's destroyed the couch, she'll look guilty because she knows you're mad, not because she knows she did something wrong. To effectively discipline your dog, use the same methods you use in obedience training. Praise her while she's doing it right so she understands exactly what action earned the praise. Punish her *during* the misbehavior, not after, so she knows what caused your anger.

Give your Golden Retriever an opportunity to earn praise right after you discipline her, and she'll forgive you instantly. Try a few obedience commands she can easily perform.

Consider this example: you're walking with your Golden, and she rudely jumps up on a woman in dressy clothes, frightening and angering her. A voice correction ("Off!" or "No!") is appropriate, but that might not be enough. You might have to give a firm pop on the leash to force her to drop to the ground. Then immediately have her do a down stay. After everyone has calmed down, release your dog and ask for a few sits and downs so you can praise her for listening. Once she puts her brain back in obedience mode, she'll listen to you better and you can stop misbehavior before it happens.

One good strong correction is better than nagging. "Puppy, no, honey, come here, sit down, good girl … no …" isn't even going to get your Golden's attention, and it contains so many contradictions, any dog would be confused. Repeated nagging corrections teach your Golden Retriever to ignore you until you get really mad. Then she knows you mean it, and she complies. A correction should last 1 or 2 seconds and no longer. Make it as firm as it needs to be for the situation, quickly said, done, and over with.

TIPS AND TAILS
When you need to discipline your dog, use the *minimum* amount of force necessary to stop the behavior.

Never hit your Golden Retriever. Hitting her only makes you look unpredictable, and you don't want a relationship based on fear. Even the best-trained dog may at some point decide she has to defend herself, and you don't want her to ever feel she has to bite you or anyone else. When you lose your temper, give yourself a time-out from your dog so you can cool down.

Environmental corrections help discipline your dog when you aren't around so she doesn't associate the correction with you. For example, if she puts her paws up on the counter, booby trap it with cans full of pennies. When she hits one, it'll fall off the counter and startle her. Other environmental-correction devices include ultrasonic buzzers that make an unpleasant noise when she barks, a ScatMat or battery-operated mat that gives her a mild shock when she jumps on the couch, and a bitter spray that tastes terrible when she chews on something she shouldn't.

TRAINING

Teaching your Golden Retriever self-control continues this month, and although you probably don't dare let her off leash yet, you'll enjoy teaching her the basic principles so she'll be ready when her brain catches up to her body.

Teaching the Emergency Drop

If your Golden Retriever dashes into the street, she could be hit by a car and killed. When she decides to chase a cyclist down the road or bound into the woods after a bear, your dog needs to respond to you instantly. If she breaks her collar and takes off, you need tools to catch her.

A life-saving command, the emergency down is a lightning-fast version of down. When you give this command, sometimes called "Drop," she'll probably be running away from you, so it takes some practice for her to understand it.

Start by speeding up the down. If she can't drop quickly in front of you, she won't be able to drop from a distance. Practice the down when you're in different positions—at her side, in back of her, with her in back of you (use a mirror so you can see her comply)—and finish the exercise when she drops. Once she understands the concept, you can use the word "Drop," which has a popping sound at the end of the word to help get her attention. When she gets confused—and she will—go to her and put her in the down. Then release her by tossing her a treat.

She can't read your body language to figure out what to do next, and she won't have time to look back at you in an emergency. Practice while you're standing and sitting so she doesn't learn to look at you for physical cues. Always toss a treat behind her to release her. You don't want her to automatically think she's supposed to come to you unless you call her. In an emergency, you'll either call her or go to her, so she needs to learn both scenarios.

Now you're ready to add movement. While walking alongside her, suddenly point to the ground, yell "Drop!" and pivot in front of her to stop her forward movement. Use an urgent tone of voice; this is an emergency. Release her by saying "Okay," tossing a treat away, and letting her run to get it. Practice just a few times. For the next step, attach her to a long line, and as she's wandering around a few feet from you, give the drop command.

This exercise is very stressful for your Golden Retriever, so don't train for more than a few minutes per session. She'll build up a lot of excitement as you work; take advantage of her energy and make it a game. Toss treats, and let her chase them and come back to you. Occasionally, on her way back, give the drop command and rush toward her a few steps to encourage her to stop and drop. Then toss a treat behind her and let her go.

When she can drop while coming toward you, teach her to drop from any position. As she's running around chasing treats, occasionally throw in a drop command. Give her a jackpot once in a while: pull her favorite toy from your pocket or feed her a full handful of treats.

The emergency drop takes hundreds of repetitions and regular practice for your Golden Retriever to be reliable with it. Use the command often during play sessions and walks to be sure she understands it.

Preparing for Off-Leash Control

A 10-month-old Golden Retriever is not ready for the responsibility of being allowed off leash. Reliable off-leash control takes a long time to develop. Your goal is to ensure that, when she's mature enough to handle it, she's had the training that makes it possible.

Answer these questions before deciding if your Golden is ready for off-leash freedom:

○ Is her recall ("Come") always perfect and immediate? Does she consider it a positive command?

○ Does she know and reliably perform the emergency drop?

○ Is her obedience reliable on leash? Can she ignore distractions and respond when you ask her to?

○ Do you have off-leash control in the house? In the backyard?

If you answer "No" or "Most of the time" to any of these questions, polish her skills until you can answer "Yes" to all of them.

When your dog is off leash, you must pay attention and be ready to intervene before she does something impolite or dangerous. If your Golden Retriever is defiant and sometimes purposely ignores your commands, that could have fatal results.

TIPS AND TAILS

Many trainers offer a beyond-the-basics course that starts teaching owners and their dogs off-leash control. It's a course you can take as many times as you like after you've completed a beginning obedience course.

You'll need two training tools: a 15- to 20-foot light line and a 6- to 8-inch short leash or line. The 15- or 20-foot line is for outdoor training. The short line is a handle you can quickly grab when you're close to her. It should be so light she doesn't feel the weight. You want her to forget it's there.

You've been working on indoor off-leash control since the day you got her, but now she needs to perfect her responses in anticipation of new and bigger responsibilities. You can let her drag a shorter line that's maybe 6 to 8 feet long while she's indoors. If there's no loop at the end, it's less likely to tangle in furniture. (For her safety, never leave any kind of training line, collar, or leash on your dog when you can't supervise her.)

Tie her loosely with the long line to a tree or fence post in the backyard, walk about 10 feet away, and give her an easy command like "Sit." At first, she'll be confused because she's not used to responding to you from a distance. If she doesn't respond, move closer and try again. When she does, praise her and try something else, like "Down." Once she gets the idea, you can try commands at different distances and positions, like you did when teaching the emergency drop.

Next, untie the line and let her drag it. Walk around the yard and give an occasional command from a distance. Include come and the emergency drop. Use the line to reel her in or detain her if she stops paying attention to you.

Teach her to check in with you, similar to when you practice the recall, and drop the line and let her wander. When she's in the midst of something, call her to you and enforce the command. Her reward for coming is that you let her go back to what she was doing. Find fenced areas away from home where you can practice this that might be especially enticing to her.

When you're comfortable that she no longer needs the long line, attach the 8-inch light line and work with her close to you. You can hold the light line and she won't feel the weight of a leash, so she might try to take off, thinking you can't control her. She'll soon learn.

YOU AND YOUR PUPPY

Your children are a big part of family life, and they can enjoy spending time with your Golden Retriever puppy in many ways. Organized activities introduce them to dog sports and pet care. At the same time, your kids learn how to be good pet parents and about the many facets of dog ownership and care. They can even explore careers with dogs.

Boy Scouts, Girl Scouts, and 4-H

Children of all ages can participate in activities with their Golden Retrievers. Besides organized activities like scouting and 4-H, many animal shelters offer day-camp programs and workshops for groups of kids working on badges and awards.

Boy Scouts can earn several different badges while learning about their pets. To earn the Pets merit badge, a child must care for his dog for 4 months, write a report about it, keep records, and read a book about their breed or other aspect of pet care. He also participates in an activity like a dog show with his Golden Retriever or teaches his dog tricks. The Dog Care merit badge introduces boys to responsible dog ownership. They learn about different breeds and track the care and health of their dogs. They also teach obedience commands and learn how to perform pet first aid. The

Boy Scout must also visit a shelter or veterinary hospital. And to earn the Veterinary Medicine merit badge, the Boy Scout learns about veterinary care for many different species, observes at an animal hospital, and explores other aspects of veterinary care and careers.

Girl Scouts can earn animal-related badges at each level. Brownies can earn a Pets merit badge by learning about and practicing pet care skills. Juniors earn the Animal Habitats badge by learning about wild animals and how to protect their habitats. Cadettes earn the Animal Helpers merit badge by studying how dogs and other animals help people in fields like search and rescue, therapy visits, and as service animals. Senior scouts earn the Voice for Animals badge, for which they learn about volunteering and animal welfare.

Your local Cooperative Extension generally offers dog 4-H programs for your county. Kids can participate in Grooming and Handling, Obedience, Rally, and Agility. Some counties offer additional classes such as freestyle, or dancing with your dog. 4-H'ers learn to keep records about their dog's care and training, develop public presentations, and compete at county and state fairs.

Junior Showmanship

Children between ages 9 and 18 can participate in Junior Showmanship at AKC conformation and performance events. Juniors show their own or a relative's Golden Retriever and have the opportunity to learn more about dogs and dog shows, develop handling skills, and learn about good sportsmanship while enjoying time with their dogs. In conformation, beginners compete in Novice classes. Once a child has received three first-place ribbons in novice, he or she can move up to Open competition.

Children are judged on their ability to present their dogs in a similar fashion as dogs in the breed ring at a conformation show. The quality of their presentation is judged, not the quality of the dog. Juniors learn to groom their dogs and present them to a judge, conduct themselves properly, and dress appropriately for judging. Top-winning juniors from around the country travel to the Westminster Kennel Club Show and AKC/Eukanuba National Championship to compete for honors.

Attend some dog shows with your family and watch the junior showmanship competition to learn more about it.

In addition to conformation, the AKC has recently introduced recognition programs for children who compete in performance events like obedience, agility, and tracking. The AKC also offers other activities for juniors, along with extensive educational materials and scholarship programs. Learn more at akc.org/kids_juniors/jr_getting_started.cfm.

	SOCIAL	BEHAVIOR	TRAINING	PHYSICAL	HEALTH
MONTH 1			Littermates and mother teach appropriate canine behavior	Rapid growth	
MONTH 2	Breeder starts socialization				
MONTH 3	Socialization at home with new owner and other pets	Fear-imprint period	Begin house- and crate training		1st DHPP vaccine
MONTH 4			Enroll in puppy class		2nd DHPP vaccine
MONTH 5	Socialization in public	Teething begins—heavy chewing period	Ready for basic commands	Switch to adult food	3rd DHPP and rabies vaccines
MONTH 6			Enroll in basic obedience class		
MONTH 7					
MONTH 8		Adult teeth are in—chewing continues	Ready for more advanced training	Moderate growth	Sexual maturity
MONTH 9					
MONTH 10					
MONTH 11					
MONTH 12 AND BEYOND				Slow growth—reaches adult size	Annual vaccinations and checkup

Putting Your Golden to Work

When your Golden Retriever reaches 10 or 11 months, he's ready to start practicing canine sports like hunting, agility, and obedience. Goldens are incredibly smart and willing to do almost anything you could ask of them, so the two of you have a lot of choices of activities you can do together. He'll relish having a job to do, exercising his mind and body while building his skills.

Meanwhile, prepare yourself for his adventures by establishing a pet disaster preparedness plan, considering pet health insurance, and beginning to take him traveling with you.

PHYSICAL DEVELOPMENT

Your Golden Retriever puppy might reach his full height this month, but his still-growing bones aren't strong and fully developed yet. Continue to limit his running on hard surfaces, and don't let him jump much for a few more months.

His teeth are almost fully in and not as painful as they have been. They'll continue to develop strength until he's 3 years old, and he'll continue chewing during that time, too.

Now that your pup is almost full size, so is his tail. It's always wagging, and he has no idea what it's doing back there, so clear the coffee table and protect your valuables situated within tail reach. And if you hear strange thumping sounds in the night, look for the tail.

He'll start looking more coordinated this month as his proportions even out and he gets comfortable using his adult height and body. He'll dive into activities with great enthusiasm—in fact, he'll be hard to hold back!

HEALTH

Both hunting dogs and pet Golden Retrievers are at risk for contracting internal parasites, and humans risk contacting these pests from their dogs. It's important that you learn to recognize the signs of infestation so you can treat these conditions.

Anal glands are an unpleasant subject but one that's important to discuss for your puppy's comfort and health.

Also in this section, we show you how to plan ahead for your puppy's care in case of natural disasters, and we investigate pet health insurance to cover major illness or accidents.

Dealing with Internal Parasites

You'll spend a lot of time out in nature with your Golden, swimming and retrieving in lakes, tromping through the woods, and other fun activities. And during those times, your dog could be exposed to internal parasites that could make him ill—and could even infect you.

Giardia: A single-celled protozoa, giardia is most often found in contaminated water like streams, lakes, and rivers, but your dog can pick it up anywhere. Wild animals such as coyotes, rabbits, raccoons, and beavers carry giardia—in fact, it was originally called "beaver fever." An infected animal carries the giardia cysts in its digestive tract and sheds them in its feces. If your dog ingests the stool, drinks infected water, or steps in it and then licks his paws, he can pick up the parasite. Once giardia is in your dog's system, it attaches to the walls of his intestine and reproduces, forming cysts that he then sheds in his stool.

The main symptom of giardia is loose stools or diarrhea. This often goes away in a few days, and it's easy to assume your dog just ate something wrong, but he can carry the parasite for years with no symptoms. Long-term effects of giardia include weight loss, damage to the lining of the intestine, and *malabsorption*. Repetitive bouts of diarrhea are the most obvious sign of a problem. You won't see any signs of giardia in your dog's feces, because it's a microscopic organism.

DOG TALK
Malabsorption is the inability to process and use nutrients in food.

Your veterinarian performs a fecal flotation test in the clinic to check for giardia. A fresh stool sample is required to look for this parasite. The giardia cysts are not shed in every sample, so it might take more than one test to diagnose. Also, before your veterinarian rules out giardia completely, she might send out a stool sample to a medical laboratory for more extensive testing. Treatment consists of a simple round of medication, but reinfection is a risk every time you take your dog out into nature.

Giardia is a zoonotic disease, meaning the disease can infect people as well as animals, if you remember from earlier chapters, so you need to protect yourself, too. Take care not to touch your face while you're outside, and thoroughly wash your hands after outings. Also carry drinking water for you and your Golden when you go on hikes.

Coccidia: Another single-celled parasite, coccidia most often affects young dogs. It's sometimes found in raw meat, dirty kennel situations, or animal shelters. Livestock are often infected, and a dog can ingest coccidia from manure and grass in pastures. Cockroaches, mice, and flies also transport and spread coccidia.

As an adult, your dog might carry coccidia in his intestines and shed the cysts in his feces, but if he has a healthy immune system, he can fight off severe symptoms. Stress can trigger symptoms if a dog has coccidia present in his digestive tract. A major infestation can cause damage to the intestines.

The primary symptom of coccidiosis is diarrhea. It could be minor or severe, and it might contain blood or mucus. The symptoms for coccidia are similar to those of giardia and parvo infection. A fecal flotation test identifies the parasite, and medication stops reproduction of the organisms but does not kill them, so a complete cure takes several weeks. The biggest challenge is protecting your Golden from reinfection. To prevent this parasite from taking hold, practice diligent sanitation, including cleaning with ammonia disinfectants and picking up feces.

Coccidiosis is not a zoonotic disease, so you are not in danger of becoming infected.

TIPS AND TAILS

You can help prevent infestation by giardia and coccidia. Don't allow your dog to eat or lick other animals' feces, and don't let your dog drink from unfiltered sources of water.

Anal Gland Care

The anal glands, also called anal sacs, are two tiny glands just inside your dog's anus. The fluid in these glands contains pheromones, and when a dog defecates, the pressure of firm stool pressing against the glands expels the fluid. The pheromones enable other dogs to "read" the feces (using Jacobsen's organ located in the nose) for information about the other dog's age, gender, and sexual status.

A problem arises when a dog has soft stool or diarrhea that doesn't force the glands to empty. If the soft stool continues too long, you need to work with your veterinarian to figure out what's causing the bowel problem. Other issues that cause the anal glands to become impacted include inflammation in the gastrointestinal tract, allergies that cause your dog to scratch and chew at his anus, or infection. A small minority of dogs has improperly positioned anal glands; in some cases, surgical removal is the only option.

If you see your Golden Retriever scooting his butt on the ground, biting at his rear, sitting in an odd position, or in obvious discomfort, suspect impacted anal sacs. If his anal glands are impacted, your veterinarian can express them during an office visit. No sedation is needed.

Occasionally, in a highly stressful situation, your dog might suddenly expel the anal sac fluid. You'll know when this happens because the smell is extremely offensive.

A healthy dog doesn't need to have his anal glands emptied for him. In fact, emptying the sacs too often causes trauma to the ducts, closing the anal glands so they can no longer expel fluid on their own. Don't have the procedure done unless your dog actually needs it.

Planning for Disasters

Most likely, you have an emergency plan in place for your family. If it doesn't already, it also should include provisions for your Golden Retriever's health and safety. When disaster hits and you have to evacuate, you might not be allowed back into your neighborhood for days, so always take your dog with you. *Always.* Leaving him in the house or turning him loose could be a death sentence.

Some Red Cross evacuation shelters allow dogs, but most don't. During a crisis, hotels might relax their pet policies, and places that do allow pets will require them to be crated. Before a disaster strikes, make a list of pet-friendly hotels, boarding kennels, and veterinarians within 100 miles of your home. You don't know how far you'll have to travel when you're forced to leave, and it's best to be prepared with locations you know you can go to with your pup. Also line up friends who can take your dog in an emergency. And be sure to make arrangements with a neighbor to evacuate your dog if disaster strikes while you aren't at home.

HAPPY PUPPY

Your Golden Retriever will adjust better to the stress of emergencies or travel if he's already used to spending time in his crate.

If you live in an area at risk for floods or hurricanes, purchase a neon-colored life vest made especially for dogs. If you get separated from your Golden Retriever in a disaster, he'll be easier for rescuers to spot if he's wearing a bright vest. If you have a two-story home, buy a canine evacuation harness similar to the ones used by search-and-rescue organizations. Keep it under your bed so if a fire breaks out downstairs, you can lower your dog out the window to safety. Practice putting these devices on your Golden when everything is calm. In a disaster, you'll be fumbling and in a hurry and will appreciate the practice. Be sure the vest and harness fit and can support his weight.

If you can't evacuate, plan a safe area within your house. If it's a basement or similar room, be sure no hazardous materials are nearby that can harm your dog. As soon as you know a storm is coming, find your dog, be sure he's wearing his leash and collar, and keep him indoors with you. Frightened animals often wander away during the commotion and become disoriented. Then, after the storm has passed, nothing looks or smells the same, and your dog might not be able to find his way home.

During disasters, keep a leash on your Golden, even when he's in the car, and keep him crated as much as possible. He'll be as anxious as you are, he'll feel safer in his crate, and you won't have to worry about keeping track of him. After the crisis passes, keep your dog leashed and with you until you're home and safe.

When planning your dog-friendly disaster kit, include the following:

- Your dog's microchip and license information, your contact info, emergency caretaker phone numbers, your dog's medical records, a photo of your dog, and feeding and care instructions, all inside a waterproof bag or container

- Extra leash, trash bags, poop scoop supplies, and towels

- Food and water bowls

- Food and water for 3 days

- His crate, marked with your cell phone number and emergency contact info

- ○ Calming medication or herbal/flower formula, like Rescue Remedy or chamomile tea bags to add to your dog's water
- ○ First-aid kit
- ○ Medications, including heartworm and flea control products

Store your kit in an outdoor shed, near an exit door where it's easily accessible, or in your car.

Considering Pet Health Insurance

Should you purchase health insurance for your puppy? If so, should you buy it now or wait until he's older and more likely to get sick? You have many considerations when making the decision whether to purchase pet insurance. No one wants to be faced with the horrible decision of euthanizing their dog because they can't afford a procedure that could save his life. Lesser expenses add up, too, and you might decide the expense of coverage is worth it for your peace of mind. By removing financial pressure from the equation, it frees you to make better decisions about your Golden's care.

Insurance companies offer many different types of pet coverage. Depending on what you're willing to pay, almost any type of coverage is available. The most inexpensive plan is usually a major medical plan that only covers accidents and major illnesses like cancer or heart disease. More comprehensive plans include hereditary diseases and routine care like vaccines, spay/neuter, and teeth cleaning. Most plans don't cover preexisting conditions, or they have a waiting period before a previously cured disease is covered. Behavioral problems, parasites (like heartworm), and special veterinary food are also excluded from most policies. In one policy we examined, hip and elbow dysplasia and anterior cruciate ligament injury are specifically *not* covered.

TIPS AND TAILS
Examine pet insurance plans carefully to be sure you completely understand what is and isn't covered.

The following is a sampling of claims filed by dog owners over the past several years with a national pet health insurance company (all these dogs survived with no lasting effects):

- ○ Cali, a 5-year-old Golden Retriever, ate 5 pounds of marinated London broil off the kitchen counter and got a case of severe gastritis.
- ○ Roxy, a German Shepherd, crashed into a sliding glass door, shattering it.

- Luke, a Lab, retrieved a golf ball and swallowed it.

- Macie, a Lab, got her leash tangled in a bicycle tire while out with her owner. She was run over by the bike and suffered a broken leg.

- Dingo, a mixed breed, ate rising bread dough from two dozen rolls and got alcohol poisoning. The warm, moist environment of his stomach caused the yeast to ferment.

- Chance, a Lab, was head-butted by a goat, hit a fence, and got a bacterial infection from his injuries.

Note that some of these emergencies could have been prevented with better supervision and management.

TIPS AND TAILS

Although not mentioned on this list, the insurance company reported that ingested socks are the most common emergency requiring surgery. Another reason to train your pup to leave your socks alone—and for you to pick them up!

When researching pet insurance policies, here are some good questions to ask:

- Is there a deductible?

- Will the price increase as my dog ages?

- Will the price increase if he's diagnosed with a chronic disease?

- What illnesses or injuries are *not* covered? What *is* covered?

- Are hereditary conditions covered, even if my dog shows no symptoms now?

- Is there a waiting period before some chronic, hereditary, or preexisting conditions are covered?

- May I choose my own vet?

- Are diagnostic tests covered?

With most pet insurance policies, you, the owner, pays the bill, submits a claim and receipts, and is reimbursed by the insurance company. The veterinarian doesn't get involved in billing or receiving payment. Some plans have a set amount they reimburse for each type of illness or injury, so that's something to keep in mind, too.

NUTRITION

Your Golden Retriever might be perfectly healthy on a diet of dry food, but other options and supplements are available. As you ponder the multitude of choices at the pet store, you might worry you aren't doing enough for your beloved pup.

The best advice is, if it works, don't try to "fix" it. If your Golden Retriever has a healthy and shiny coat, clear eyes, and healthy skin; if he's the appropriate weight; and if he enjoys good health, he probably doesn't need anything added to his diet. This might change as he ages, but most Goldens live long, healthy lives by eating a diet based on a quality dry dog food.

Looking Beyond Dry Food

Should you add canned or semimoist foods to his meals? Or should you feed wet food exclusively? Or maybe you'd like to give him a daily bowl of wet food as a treat. Dogs certainly seem to love it.

Canned dog food contains up to 78 percent water, which helps fill your dog. It usually includes more protein, fat, and animal-based ingredients than dry dog food and less grain. Overall, the ingredients are usually better quality than you'll find in most dry foods, but read the ingredients on the label to be sure, and look for named meats and minimal grain. The nuggets, chunks, and other shapes you see in some canned foods aren't actually meat. They're formed from textured plant proteins or sometimes (although rarely) natural meat tissues. Some foods also contain "vegetables" that look like carrots and peas. These might be real or artificially colored and shaped.

There are advantages to feeding canned food. If your Golden has kidney problems or is constipated, he'll need extra moisture, and canned food is one way to provide it. Canned food also contains fewer preservatives because the can is an oxygen-free environment, which, when properly sealed, does not allow bacteria to grow. (Be sure to refrigerate leftovers to avoid spoilage.) Canned food is more expensive, however, so you probably won't want to feed him an exclusively canned diet.

Semimoist foods, usually packaged in foil packets, contain lots of additives, particularly sugar, for taste and to solidify the food. These are generally the least-healthy diets you can feed your pup. Although semimoist foods contain more moisture than dry food—about 25 to 30 percent—they're extremely expensive in comparison. Reserve semimoist food for treats, if you use it at all.

What About Nutritional Supplements?

If your puppy is eating a quality dog food and is in good health, you don't need to add supplements to his diet. In fact, too much supplementation can throw his system out of balance and cause health problems. And too much of a nutrient is just as bad as too little. But once in a while, supplements can be beneficial to your dog's health. Owners who feed raw or home-cooked diets need to give their dog supplements to be sure he's getting the vitamins, minerals, and other important nutrients he needs.

Work with your vet or consult a nutritionist to determine when and how to add supplements to your dog's diet because some can interfere with medications he's taking. And be sure you use products specifically meant for dogs because a dog's nutritional needs are different from a human's.

Nutritional supplements are not subject to evaluation by the Food and Drug Administration for their purity, safety, or ability to improve your dog's health, and not all supplements are necessarily equal or risk free, so do some research and purchase only brands you trust. The National Animal Supplement Council (nasc.cc) certifies manufacturers' products and awards a seal of quality to those that meet their standards of safety, quality, and accuracy.

TIPS AND TAILS

If you feel your dog needs supplements with his food, consider switching to a different or better-quality food rather than oversupplement. Most of the supplements discussed in this section are already included in commercial dog foods.

Probiotics: Probiotics contain beneficial bacteria that can bolster your Golden's immune response to harmful bacteria in his intestinal tract. Probiotics are an important contributor to your puppy's overall health because 70 percent of a puppy's immune system is found in his digestive tract. When added to your dog's diet, probiotics help return his system to a normal state by restoring the balance between good and bad bacteria.

Many things can affect your dog's gastrointestinal health. Eating a poor-quality diet, consuming unclean water, eating feces or grass, or ingesting fertilizers or pesticides all can introduce bacteria to the gut that throw it off balance and cause problems like diarrhea and incomplete food absorption. Stress caused by a change in routine, such as travel or boarding, also can be a factor. Diseases like inflammatory bowel disease, colitis, or kidney disease can affect the balance of bacteria in his body as well. Antibiotics and cortisone can kill good bacteria as well as bad bacteria, and for this reason, some veterinarians prescribe probiotics for your dog if he's on antibiotics.

Antioxidants: Antioxidants such as vitamins A, C, and E; beta-carotene; and other compounds help support your puppy's immune system and protect him from disease. Antioxidants protect cells against the effects of free radicals, which cause cellular damage and are produced when the body breaks down food or is exposed to pollution, cigarette smoke, or other environmental toxins. You might want to add antioxidants to your dog's diet if he's suffering from cancer or heart disease. But always check with your veterinarian first because too much of some items can be toxic.

Digestive enzymes: These are sometimes packaged with probiotics because both affect your dog's gastrointestinal health. Digestive enzymes break down nutrients in food so the body can absorb them. When commercial dog foods are cooked at high temperatures, these enzymes are killed and must be added back into the food. Dogs also produce their own digestive enzymes in their saliva glands, pancreas, and stomach. Yogurt is an excellent source of digestive enzymes. Purchase one with live, active cultures. A dog's production of digestive enzymes is affected by aging, and sometimes older dogs benefit from their addition to his diet. A young, healthy Golden shouldn't need these.

Bone meal: Bone meal adds calcium to the diet, which is something young Golden Retrievers don't need. In fact, breeders recommend you *not* feed him puppy food or any dog food high in calcium because it causes orthopedic problems later in life.

Vitamin and mineral supplements: These are necessary for dogs eating home-cooked or raw food, but they're usually unnecessary for Goldens eating a commercially made food. If you feel you need to give your dog additional vitamins and minerals, choose those made especially for dogs. And don't oversupplement any vitamins or minerals because they can have toxic effects.

Fatty acids: Fatty acids must be added back to dry dog food after cooking. If your dog has a dry, dull coat, a supplement in the form of fish oil or cod liver oil can provide essential fatty acids (linoleic acid) and vitamins A and D. Flaxseed is also high in beneficial fatty acids. Some of these are high in calories, so be careful not to give your pup too much.

Whole foods: If you give your dog whole foods to supplement his diet, you're less likely to overdose him on any specific nutrient because his body expels the excess as it digests the food. Foods such as carrots, cottage cheese, apples, bananas, blueberries, green beans, dandelions, and kelp all provide extra nutrition. Be sure the foods you choose are beneficial and not toxic to dogs (see Appendix C).

Prepackaged whole-food supplements are also available. Missing Link is a well-known, established brand. When in doubt, consult your veterinarian and research different product lines before adding a supplement to your Golden's diet.

Glucosamine and chondroitin: Both of these exist naturally in the body, but when a dog has arthritis, his body might not make enough of these substances. Glucosamine helps build connective tissue and stimulates the growth of healthy new cartilage, and chondroitin protects joints and slows the breakdown of existing cartilage. The two supplements are usually taken together and are often added to senior formula dog foods. It takes several weeks to see the effects, but many dogs enjoy greater mobility and less pain on these supplements.

GROOMING

Most dog owners are a bit more tolerant of the smells and messes their dogs make than people who don't have dogs. By keeping your Golden Retriever and his bedding clean, a guest shouldn't be able to smell a dog in your house.

And because your teenage Golden is pretty inquisitive, in this section, we help you prepare for the most obnoxious grooming chore ever: bathing a skunked dog. What's more, that lovely, long coat can collect anything from burrs to bubblegum, so we look at how to remove the goo without ruining his good looks.

Dealing with Doggie Odor

Some folks are more sensitive to doggie odor than others, but Goldens shouldn't smell bad by anyone's standards. If you do detect strong odors, they could be caused by health problems such as ear infections, tooth decay, gum disease, skin disease, or kidney problems, so your smelly pup might need a vet visit.

If your puppy rolls in something disgusting, swims in foul water, or just generally makes a stinky mess of himself, add vinegar to your rinse water when you bathe him or use an enzymatic odor-removing shampoo, like Nature's Miracle. The skunk bath explained in the following section also works very well.

Skunked!

Few odors are worse than the smell of a freshly skunked dog. You let him out for a last pee of the night, and when he comes back in … ack! Run for the tomato juice! But wait. There are more effective ways to remove the skunk smell than tomato juice, which will stain his coat. Instead, bathe your dog in a mixture of the following:

1 quart 3 percent hydrogen peroxide

¼ cup baking soda

2 teaspoons Dawn dish detergent

Mix the ingredients just before using, and lather your Golden's *dry* coat thoroughly, down to the skin, and rinse well. Be sure to keep the mixture out of his eyes because the hydrogen peroxide will burn. Use a soapy washcloth around his head, and rinse his face carefully.

You'll know immediately if the smell is dissipating. You might have to repeat this treatment several times, so be prepared to make more of the mixture. And because the mixture doesn't keep, always make a fresh batch.

Removing Sticky Stuff

Just like children get chewing gum in their hair, puppies get tree sap, tar, or other sticky things in their fur. Home remedies such as vegetable oil, peanut butter, and mayonnaise contain enough oil to break down the gummy texture so you can scrape or comb out the gunk, and they won't irritate his skin. Commercial products like Simple Green and some orange oil cleaners are nontoxic for use on pet fur.

If your Golden Retriever has gum in his fur, put an ice cube on the gum to harden it enough that you can chip it off. Tar and tree sap or pitch may be tough to remove so apply vegetable oil and let it soak on the area for 24 hours. You might want to put a T-shirt or Elizabethan collar on your dog so he won't lick it while it works. Paint is easier to remove if you let it dry and harden and then chip it off.

Sometimes you just can't lubricate, wash, or soak the crud out of your dog's coat, and at these times, you'll have to cut out the offending substance. Use blunt-nose scissors or grooming clippers, and be very careful, especially when working close to his skin. Don't use regular, pointed scissors because they could too easily cut him.

TIPS AND TAILS
Never use gasoline, kerosene, turpentine, or solvents on your dog. These products can severely burn his skin and are toxic if he ingests them.

SOCIAL SKILLS

Your Golden Retriever is a member of the family, and he'd love to tag along when your family goes on vacation. With a little preparation and planning, your best friend can get away from the hustle and bustle of everyday life with you. While on vacation, no one has to go to work or school or other activities, and you all have more time to relax with each other and with your puppy.

Most buses and trains won't accept dogs, so to travel with your pup, you must go by car or airline.

Traveling by Car

When he's in the car, restrain your Golden Retriever. A dog who leaps around in the car can cause an accident, hit you in the face with his tail, or knock the gear shift out of gear. And as much as he might love it, don't let him hang his head out the car window. Bugs or flying debris could hit him in the eyes and injure them. If the window is down far enough, he could jump out and be badly injured.

If you have room for it, the safest place for him is in a crate. Prevent the crate from tipping over when you go around corners by either tying it down or wedging it between your luggage. If your car isn't large enough for a crate, use a seatbelt harness. Special car harnesses are made for pets, or you can make one with a harness and short leash. And put him in the backseat so he won't be injured by the airbag if you're in an accident.

HAPPY PUPPY

It gets hot in the back of an SUV or van, even while the car is running. As you travel, be sure your Golden is shielded from direct sun and has plenty of air circulation back there. Stop often to give him water and ensure he isn't overheated. You can purchase small battery-operated camping fans to provide extra ventilation if necessary.

Flying with Your Golden Retriever

Most airlines don't allow online reservations for pets, so call the airline directly to schedule your Golden Retriever's flight. Transporting a large dog is expensive, and his ticket might cost as much as yours. Make your reservations early because spots for pets are limited, and reconfirm your reservation with the airline 24 to 48 hours before you leave. Your Golden Retriever is too large to travel in the cabin, so he'll have to be shipped in the cargo hold. If you're taking an international flight, research the regulations at your destination because there might be a long quarantine period. Hawaii also has strict guidelines when it comes to bringing animals to the islands.

Check the weather forecast before you leave home. When the ground temperature is too high or too low, some airlines refuse to fly with animals (more on this coming up). Try to schedule an overnight or late-night flight if you're traveling in the summer so you can avoid extreme heat and humidity. Avoid traveling on holidays or weekends, and try to book a nonstop or direct flight so your dog doesn't have to switch planes.

Your Golden's shipping crate must conform to the airline's regulations and the standards developed by the International Air Transport Association. It must be sturdy plastic (not wire); properly ventilated; and large enough that he can stand, turn around, and lie down. Many airlines require metal doors rather than plastic to prevent the dog from chewing and escaping from the crate. In addition to including your name and address on your dog's kennel, you must use arrows or stickers to indicate the top.

TIPS AND TAILS

Airline policies for traveling with pets vary, so check with your carrier for its specific requirements. To view the pet policies for specific airlines, visit pettravel.com/airline_rules.cfm.

Fasten empty food and water dishes inside the crate door so they're accessible from outside. Attach a food and water schedule, and tape a bag of food to the outside of the kennel. The crate must not be locked in case someone needs to remove your dog in an emergency, but it must close securely with a latch that can be opened without tools. You cannot leave a leash with the kennel, but be sure to take one with you so you can take your dog out of the crate for a walk. Airline security will inspect your Golden Retriever and his belongings like any other passenger's.

Most veterinarians and airlines recommend you don't tranquilize your dog before flying. Tranquilizers and sedatives can affect your dog's equilibrium, breathing, and ability to regulate his body temperature. He also might be more likely to have a bad reaction due to the altitude and change in air pressure. A fully awake dog is usually safer.

If you're not traveling with your dog, he'll ship as cargo. You'll deliver him to the freight terminal, which is in a different part of the airport from where passengers go. Because you won't be at the airport to claim him when he arrives, mark the crate with the phone number of a person at your destination who can be contacted about your dog. Also find out where the freight terminal is at the destination airport so you know where to pick him up. Get the direct phone number at your departure site and any connecting airports so you can confirm your dog has made all his connections and arrived safely. Most airlines have complete instructions for shipping pets posted on their websites (see Appendix D).

Staying at Pet-Friendly Accommodations

Plan in advance to stay at pet-friendly hotels and campgrounds. Most major chains accept dogs, but call ahead to be sure. Pet-friendly hotels might have a limited number of rooms available, while others designate their smoking rooms as dog friendly. Some hotels charge an extra fee for dogs, require a deposit against damage, or don't accept dogs above a certain size. Many facilities offer extra amenities for dog owners, like dog day care, play yards, dog walkers, and treats.

Some hotels don't allow guests to leave their dogs alone in their room. Housekeeping personnel might be frightened if a big dog greets them at the door, and your Golden Retriever could escape. If you are allowed to leave your dog in the room, crate him while you're not there to watch him. Don't leave him alone for too long, especially if he might bark in the crate and disturb other guests. Leave the TV on to keep him company when you go out.

TIPS AND TAILS

Feed your dog in the bathroom of your hotel room so he doesn't damage or dirty the carpets while he eats.

Don't allow your dog to relieve himself right outside the door, where the stains and smell might offend other guests. Take him away from the building instead. Some hotels have designated pet areas or may be able to guide you to nearby dog parks or walking trails. Always pick up after him, too.

When investigating dog-friendly campgrounds and RV parks, ask if there are any size restrictions on the dogs allowed or if you have to pay extra fees to bring your pooch. Clarify if your dog is allowed in all parts of the park or if he must stay at your site. Dogs are allowed in most national parks, but they must be kept in your car, on the roadway, or in parking lots, and they aren't allowed on hiking trails at all. National forests do allow on-leash dogs to hike on the trails. The rules vary at different facilities, so contact each one to confirm that you can bring your Golden with you.

To find dog-friendly accommodations, log on to petfriendlytravel.com, petswelcome.com, and dogfriendly.com. While you research hotels and camp-grounds, you also can find lists of dog-friendly beaches, dog parks, and other areas and activities. Local dog day cares might allow you to leave your Golden Retriever temporarily while you spend the day at an amusement park, and some large parks, such as Disney, provide kennels for your dog to stay in while you enjoy the park.

Preparing Your Dog for Travel

Before you travel with your dog, ensure he's healthy and safe for his vacation, review his doggie manners, and be sure you take all the necessary precautions and requirements.

Health certificate: If you take your dog across state lines or fly him anywhere, you must carry a health certificate, a veterinarian-signed document that certifies your dog is healthy enough to travel and is current on your state's required vaccines. (All 50 states require a rabies vaccine.) Some airlines also require an acclimation certificate, which states he's allowed to travel when the temperature is below 45°F. Both certificates must be signed by a federally accredited veterinarian. No acclimation certificate is available pertaining to hot weather, although airlines usually don't accept pets for transport in the cargo hold when the temperature is above 84°F.

Identification: Be sure your puppy's tags are securely fastened and that the lettering is legible. Consider adding a tag with your cell phone number and emergency contact information on it, too. If he isn't already microchipped, do so before you travel, and be sure he has a tag that states he's microchipped so anyone who finds him will know to scan him. Dogs traveling internationally should have a chip that meets ISO standards, an internationally recognized frequency. Check with your microchip registry to be sure your contact information as well as your backup information is up to date.

Heartworm preventative: If your Golden Retriever isn't already on heartworm preventative, have him tested and on medication before you leave. In almost any area of the country, he'll be exposed to heartworm, especially in the summer, when mosquitoes are common.

Training: You've probably already taught your dog to eliminate on different surfaces, but if he needs more work, do so before your trip. If he's used to going on grass only, he might not want to go in a strange place or on a new surface. Many dogs who stay in kennels don't like to relieve themselves on concrete nor where they sleep.

Review his other obedience and manners, too, and practice skills like sitting to greet people, leave it, and walking nicely on leash. Refresh his memory so he'll wait to jump out of the car or go through a door. He could be lost if he rushes off when you're in a strange place. Also revisit his crate training if you haven't been using it much. He might have to spend more time in the crate—in the car, in a hotel room, on a plane, or at your host's home—while you're on vacation, and he should feel comfortable and safe in it.

TIPS AND TAILS

Teach your pup to eliminate on cue, and give it a name, like "Go potty," or "Hurry." Praise and give him a treat when he goes, and he'll soon associate the word with the action, making your rest stops much shorter.

It's inconvenient, if not impossible, to leave food down for your Golden Retriever while traveling. Most owners can't free-feed (leave food down all day for him) or they'd have a 200-pound dog, so train him to eat within 10 minutes. If he doesn't eat, pick up the food and put it away until the next meal. He'll quickly learn to eat when it's put in front of him.

If you'll be using fold-up travel bowls or giving him water from a bottle, teach him to use them before you leave home. Many dogs refuse to stick their noses in a canvas bowl or other tight spot. Drinking from a water bottle is an acquired skill, and it might take a few days for him to get the hang of it.

Packing for Your Pup

Pack a suitcase for your Golden Retriever when you're packing for yourself. If you're traveling by car, you'll be able to bring more of his supplies with you. Here's what to pack:

Health certificate: If you're flying or crossing state lines, this is required.

Microchip information: Bring the chip number, brand name, and registry contact information.

Photo of your Golden: If your dog gets lost, you'll need a photo to identify him and make posters.

Food and treats: You might not be able to find the same brands, and a diet change could cause a stomach upset.

Water: Water from an unfamiliar place can cause diarrhea. If you can, take some of your own from home.

Leash and collar: Always leash your Golden Retriever in public. Bring a regular leash rather than a retractable one because in most places, the latter is impractical and dangerous. Have identification on the collar with your travel contact info.

Crate: If you're traveling by air, be sure the crate is airline approved. Familiarize your dog with the crate before you travel if he's not already.

Bedding and toys: Things that smell like home will make your Golden more comfortable in strange places.

First-aid kit: Include medication to treat carsickness. Over-the-counter medication for humans that contains the active ingredient meclizine is safe for dogs, but check with your veterinarian to find out brand names and dosage amounts. Ginger (as in gingersnap cookies) also helps prevent motion sickness.

Cleanup supplies: Bring disposable bags and paper towels.

Travel Tips

You and your Golden Retriever must mind your manners in pubic places. If you don't see signs prohibiting dogs, that doesn't necessarily mean they're welcome. Keep him under control at all times, and prevent him from jumping on or sniffing strangers. And don't leave him tied up outside a building; he could be stolen or someone might accuse him of biting.

Highway rest areas often designate doggie relief areas. Keep your Golden on leash, and clean up after him, even in designated doggie zones. If there's a fenced dog area, patrol the field for scattered food, wrappers, trash, broken glass, and waste left by other dogs before you turn your dog loose. Wild animals often scavenge at rest areas, so be on the lookout for raccoons, possums, rats, mice, and coyotes. Rattlesnakes nap under picnic tables, in the restrooms, or under nearby bushes.

Being left in a hot car can kill a dog, so eat at drive-through restaurants while traveling with your Golden Retriever. Stop at public rest areas to use the restroom, too. The disabled stall is usually big enough for both of you.

Wherever you go, and however you get there, always be a good citizen so dogs continue to be welcome in public places.

When He Has to Stay Home

If your pup can't travel with you, you have several options for dog care while you're gone. You can board him in a kennel, hire a pet sitter, or have family or friends care for him. Wherever you leave him, it will be a stressful time for him, especially if he goes to a place he's never been before.

A young, active Golden Retriever should probably be boarded in a kennel for his own safety. If you leave him at home and have someone come in to see him twice a day, that leaves him with more than 20 hours a day to entertain himself—and by now you probably know what that entails. After a few days of isolation, a lonely Golden Retriever will do things he'd never do when you're home. Although you might leave him alone while you're at work each day, that's much different from leaving him to his own devices for a full weekend or more.

Kennels provide safety and a choice of amenities for your Golden Retriever. He'll be confined or supervised at all times, and you might be able to add extra activities to his daily routine, like exercise, walks, doggie playgroups, or swimming. Although there's usually an extra charge for these services, your dog will adjust better and suffer from less stress if he can get out of the confined kennel each day. Some facilities might offer deluxe suites for your Golden Retriever that mimic a home environment with a couch, TV, and real walls instead of chain-link or plastic panels. Although Goldens are adaptable and happy dogs who adjust well to almost any situation, kennels are noisy and stressful places, no matter how well they're operated. Your dog might come home extremely tired.

A boarding facility requires proof of DHPP, rabies, and bordetella (kennel cough) vaccines. The kennel cough vaccine should be given at least 1 week, and not more than 6 months, before you board your Golden Retriever. By giving the vaccine a week in advance, your dog has time to absorb the protection of the vaccine into his system.

You'll have to sign a contract and a liability release in case your Golden Retriever bites someone or injures another dog. Provide your veterinarian's contact information, too. Be honest about any behavioral problems your Golden Retriever has, like separation anxiety or fear of men. Kennel staff are trained professionals and can take precautions to prevent injuries or extreme stress.

Ask for a tour of the facility when you visit so you can see where your dog will stay. Ask some questions as you look around:

- Will he be housed with another dog in the same kennel?
- Can you bring his food or a bed that smells like home?
- Is someone on-site 24 hours a day?
- What veterinarian is used in case of an emergency or illness?
- Are there extra charges for administering medication or feeding your own food?

TIPS AND TAILS

Alert your veterinarian that you'll be away and leaving your dog home, and authorize them to treat your dog or give information to the kennel, caregiver, or another clinic should the need arise.

Boarding your Golden Retriever with friends or family puts a lot of responsibility on people who might not be able to handle a big, active dog. If your Golden knows them well, they have another dog he knows, or if he has spent time at their house with you, the arrangement might work out.

Think carefully before you impose on your acquaintances. If something happens to your dog, it could ruin your relationship. Dogs often escape from private homes—they're in a strange place, anxious, and want to go home. A dog who never digs could dig out of the yard or jump the fence. Your friends don't know your dog or his habits, and their children could inadvertently leave a gate open.

A pet sitter is a better option for an adult Golden Retriever who has matured and settled down. You might already have a sitter who regularly walks your dog while you're at work. Remaining at home is less stressful for your dog, as long as you trust him to behave. If you have multiple pets, this is also a less-expensive option than boarding.

With a professional pet sitter, you'll sign a contract and liability release. Because she'll be providing more than just a daily walk, ask some in-depth questions:

- How much experience does she have caring for Golden Retrievers? How does she deal with their activity level and strength?
- Does she have liability and property damage insurance?
- Does she do each visit herself? Does she have employees?
- How long does she stay each visit?
- Are there any extra charges you should know about? Any extra services she provides?
- Does she provide references? Could you call other Golden Retriever owners whose dogs she cares for?
- Does she know pet first aid? Has she completed a pet first-aid course?
- Is she a member of any professional associations?
- How would she handle a personal emergency? Does she have backup help?

Some pet sitters board dogs in their home. In this situation, your dog is in a cage-free environment and treated like a member of the family. In-home or cage-free boarding services vary. Some operators take only a few dogs, while others operate more like a doggie day care and crate or kennel all the dogs at night.

A house sitter is another option. When interviewing a house sitter, ask many of the same questions you'd ask a potential pet sitter, with extra attention given to the house sitter's personal routine while in your home. Some sitters only stay overnight and go to another job during the day. Some guarantee they'll stay in your home a certain number of hours each day. Be sure to clarify these details.

Also be clear about sleeping arrangements, food, cleaning, and whether the house sitter can have guests over. Some house sitters treat their time at your house as a personal vacation; be sure they understand they are there to care for your Golden Retriever and spend time with him.

BEHAVIOR

Even a well-adjusted, happy-go-lucky Golden Retriever will sometimes be anxious or afraid. He might react to new situations, people, or something that has frightened him in the past, possibly during one of the fear-imprint periods in his youth. The situation could be temporary and easy to deal with, or it could have catastrophic results.

Respect your puppy's stress or fear. Protect him from real danger, and acclimate him to safe situations where he's reacting poorly using the socialization methods you've practiced in previous months. In rare situations, medical help or behavior counseling might be necessary to cure symptoms of an emotional nature.

Recognizing Signs of Stress

Stress can be good or bad, and Golden Retrievers are especially sensitive. Trying to hold a sit-stay could be stressful to him, and your arrival at the end of the day is stressful, even if in a good way. While a short burst of stress causes an adrenaline rush (a flood of stress hormones) that results in a temporary but sometimes extreme reaction, low-level chronic stress can cause serious health problems in your dog.

Your puppy might exhibit subtle signs of stress that you won't recognize unless you learn to read his behavior:

Ears pinned back: This is a classic sign your dog is worried. Watch how his ears perk up when he's interested in something, how they appear when he is resting, and how they fall down and back when he's unsure.

Yawning: Many times he's not yawning because he's tired. Yawning is a stress-relieving mechanism.

Licking his nose: He might be gathering scent and pheromones so he can further evaluate the situation.

Teeth chattering: This can be a sign of excitement.

Turning his head away: He refuses to look at the thing that bothers him. Dogs often avoid eye contact to deflect a confrontation with another dog.

Panting: This isn't his normal panting in hot weather or after exercise. You'll see rapid stress-related panting even in cool weather.

Drooling: While he drools, he also might lick his lips or his feet, have sweaty paws, or whine.

Wide, round eyes: The white haw in the corner of his eye will show (referred to as whale eye), or he'll have dilated pupils.

A dog subjected to chronic stress with no relief will develop physical symptoms:

Stomach upset: He might vomit or have chronic diarrhea.

Hyperactivity: He might suffer from an inability to settle down or listen to you, be constantly vigilant, and overreact to everything around him.

Obsessive-compulsive behavior: Symptoms include chronic licking or chewing on himself to the point of leaving permanent, open sores; tail chasing; barking; or pacing.

Separation anxiety: He might be destructive when left alone or howl or bark the entire time you're gone.

The Fearful Golden

A frightened or extremely anxious dog responds in one of three ways: freeze, flight, or fight. He freezes to evaluate what's happening, maybe lying down and refusing to move or appearing not to recognize you. Next, he flees by either running away or frantically struggling to escape. If he runs away, he's not paying attention to where he's going or what hazards are in his way. He fights if he's cornered and feels he has no other options, starting with a warning snap or growl. If that doesn't work, a full-on bite is his next line of defense.

The signs of stress listed in the previous section tell you he's worried. Don't comfort him if you see him exhibiting these symptoms. For example, if his hackles go up and he starts barking as you approach a mailbox he's sure contains something scary, don't pet him and tell him not to be afraid. He could interpret your tone of voice as confirming there really is something to worry about. By petting him, you also inadvertently praise him for his fearful reaction.

Keep the leash slack so he never feels trapped by a scary thing. Let him observe from a distance and approach only if he wants to. Don't bribe him either; he'll endure his terror just to get the treat. Instead, use your jolly routine and get his attention on you. When he sees you think that scary thing is no big deal, he'll learn to look to you for your reaction before he decides to be afraid.

HAPPY PUPPY
Got a tense puppy? Herbal or flower remedies like Rescue
Remedy might help calm him.

If your dog is chronically afraid, work with a behaviorist to develop a program to improve the situation. Counterconditioning and desensitization are two treatment options. You can't force him to face his fears, and he'll only become more and more terrified if you try. You might not think they're rational, but they are very real to him.

TRAINING

As you might know by now, Golden Retrievers are willing to work hard and learn complex tasks. If you enjoy training your dog and would like to try more challenging things together, competitive obedience and hunting tests might be fore you. These activities make use of your Golden's natural abilities while honing his skills. And you'll enjoy training as much as competing and make many like-minded friends along the way.

Rally and Obedience Competition

Are you and your dog enjoying obedience training? The American Kennel Club (AKC) offers two types of competitive obedience for dog owners, and Golden Retrievers are superstars in both. In fact, you'll see more Goldens than any other breed in obedience trials. The sports require dog/handler teamwork and performance skills and use similar obedience exercises in different ways. Rally and obedience both offer novice A classes for beginning handlers who have never entered trials or earned titles with their dog.

You can take classes just for the fun of working with your dog, and you're not required to enter trials. Although first through fourth places are awarded in each trial class, you and your dog really compete against a perfect score, and if you qualify, you earn a leg toward a title. You can earn a title without the need to compete against another team in a class. At each level, you must achieve three legs—a qualifying score—to earn a title.

Rally and obedience trials are usually held in conjunction with conformation events. Golden Retriever *specialty shows,* in which only Golden Retrievers compete, might offer an obedience or rally trial at the same time. Sometimes a specialty trial is open to all breeds, while others are for Goldens only. To start training or learn more about rally and obedience, find a local obedience club or dog trainer who teaches competition classes.

DOG TALK

A **specialty show** is a conformation dog show for a single breed of dog held by a breed club. In a Golden Retriever Specialty, the breed club often also conducts obedience, rally, hunting tests, and agility trials.

Rally is a good place for a newcomer to start in competitive obedience because it's less structured than traditional obedience, yet it's still a step up from the Canine Good Citizen test you read about in Month 10. You and your dog move at your own pace through the course, completing challenges at individual stations. Each station has a sign with instructions regarding the skill you are to perform. Scoring isn't as precise and rigorous as in regular obedience, and you're encouraged to talk to your dog and have fun while you're going through the course.

A rally course includes 10 to 20 stations, depending on the level of competition, with both stationary and moving exercises. Stationary exercises include halting and sitting your dog, and moving exercises include executing an about-turn and heeling at a fast pace.

The levels in rally are Novice, Advanced, and Excellent. In Rally Novice, there are no more than five stationary exercises, and all are performed on-leash. Dogs earn the Rally Novice (RN) title after three qualifying scores. In Rally Advanced, all exercises are done off-leash, and there are no more than seven stationary exercises. The exercises are more difficult, and one low jump is included. Rally Advanced (RA) is the title for this level. Rally Excellent exercises include challenges like backing up three steps while the dog stays in the heel position and a moving stand while the handler walks around the dog. Rally Excellent includes 15 to 20 stations and no more than 7 stationary exercises. The title earned for this level is Rally Excellent (RE).

HAPPY PUPPY

Both rally and obedience trials test your teamwork as you and your Golden Retriever perform obedience exercises together. Rally is less formal, and you can talk to your dog and praise him in the ring. Obedience is more precise and structured, with strict rules that restrict touching or talking to your dog.

Once you've conquered rally, the Novice class in traditional obedience will seem easy. Rally was officially accepted as an AKC event in 2005, but obedience competition has been part of the AKC since 1936. Golden Retrievers have been winning titles since 1942.

AKC clubs hold all-breed obedience trials and specialty trials, which are usually held in conjunction with conformation events. When compared to rally, obedience competition requires a more structured and precise performance and much less interaction between dog and handler while in the ring.

The exercises in obedience are the same at each trial, whereas courses can vary quite a bit in rally. In the Novice class, handlers and their dogs perform on- and off-leash heeling, figure-eight heeling, stand for examination, recall, 1-minute sit-stay, and 3-minute down-stay. When you and your Golden Retriever have completed three qualifying rounds, he earns the Companion Dog (CD) title.

In the Open class, all the exercises are performed off leash: heeling, figure eight, retrieve a dumbbell, go over a jump and retrieve a dumbbell, drop on recall (a formal version of the emergency drop you taught your Golden in Month 10), broad jump, 3-minute sit-stay, and 5-minute down-stay. Both stays are performed with the handler out of sight. After three qualifying scores, your dog earns the Companion Dog Excellent (CDX) title.

The Utility class is the most difficult. Your dog must respond to hand signals for the stand, stay, down, sit, and come. He also must demonstrate scent discrimination by finding an article with his handler's scent on it from a pile of identical articles. In the directed retrieve, he must retrieve a glove indicated by the handler. The directed jumping exercise consists of the dog going away from the handler and returning over a specified jump. In the moving stand and examination, the handler moves forward while the dog halts and stays standing. A judge walks up to the dog and runs her hand over him, and the dog then must return to the handler on command.

The Utility class requires a high level of teamwork between you and your dog, and it usually takes much longer to earn a title than at the other two levels. The Utility Dog (UD) title is given to teams who successfully qualify in three trials. Dogs can continue to compete and earn a Utility Dog Excellent (UDX) title after qualifying in both Open and Utility classes at 10 trials.

In addition to regular classes, obedience clubs and breed clubs often offer nonregular classes at their trials. Nonregular classes don't count toward titles, but they are fun for you and your dog. You can enter them for fun or while training for the next level of competition. There also are optional titling classes: Beginner Novice (BN), Grad Novice (GN), Grad Open (GO), and Versatility (VER).

HAPPY PUPPY

One nonregular class in particular is fun for Golden Retriever owners: team obedience. Often offered at specialty shows, a team of four Goldens and their handlers perform the novice exercises together in the ring, like a drill team.

Hunting Tests and Field Trials

Plenty of opportunities are available for you to practice hunting skills and compete with your dog, even if you don't want to hunt. The AKC conducts hunting tests and field trials, and the United Kennel Club (UKC) also has a hunting division that conducts tests. Learn about the UKC Hunting Retriever Club and its levels at huntingretrieverclub.org. The North American Hunting Retriever Association also holds competitions (nahra.org). The competitions profiled here are AKC, but all the organizations have similar levels and procedures. To get involved in hunting tests, contact local clubs for a referral to trainers and group practices.

For beginners, the Golden Retriever Club of America, the AKC Golden Retriever parent breed club, offers a Working Certificate (WC) and Working Certificate Excellent (WCX) to test a Golden's natural working ability and retrieving instinct. This gives owners the opportunity to enjoy and experience the work Goldens were bred for, without having to spend months training for competition. It's a great way to see if you're interested in pursuing the sport. Your dog only needs to pass the test once to earn his WC.

To earn a Working Certificate, a dog must do the following:

A land double: Two birds are shot or thrown, your dog watches them fall, and he retrieves them one after another in the order they fell. The birds are in moderate cover approximately 40 to 50 yards away and 90 degrees apart. Besides testing his retrieving ability, your dog must remember where the second bird fell after he has retrieved the first one.

Back-to-back water singles: Your dog executes two retrieves of shot ducks in water from about 25 to 30 yards away. This proves he's willing to swim, retrieve a waterfowl, and reenter the water.

Drop: Finally, he must drop the bird within the boundaries designated by the judge. (He doesn't have to deliver the bird to the judge's hand.)

The Working Certificate Excellent test requires a land triple and a water double as well as an honoring exercise, for which he must come up to the line (starting point) and sit or stand quietly off leash while another dog executes two water retrieves.

Local and regional Golden Retriever clubs hold the tests in conjunction with AKC Hunting Tests or separately if they have enough people entered. You don't have to be a member of a club to enter.

Hunting tests are next step for you and your Golden Retriever. In these noncompetitive events, if your dog completes the retrieves according to the rules, he qualifies and earns a leg toward his title. The purpose of the tests is to evaluate a retriever's ability as a hunting companion. Natural situations are set up on land and water, and dogs must retrieve any type of game bird. There are three levels of hunting tests: Junior, Senior, and Master Hunter.

In the Junior tests, your Golden is judged on his ability to *mark* where the bird falls and remember it, along with his style, perseverance, and hunting ability. He also must retrieve four single *marks*—two on land and two in the water—one at a time. When he returns one bird, he turns and another bird is thrown. He must stay quietly at his handler's side until he's sent to retrieve the bird, return it to the handler, and release it to hand (not dropped on the ground) when asked. The handler doesn't have to actually shoot a bird (throwers out in the field throw or shoot for them), and your dog must have a soft mouth and not damage the bird. After your Golden Retriever qualifies in four tests, he earns the Junior Hunter (JH) title.

DOG TALK

In a hunting test, a bird is thrown or shot and the dog **marks** it by visually recognizing where it fell and remembering the location.

After the Junior Hunter, dogs and handlers can work toward entering Senior Hunter (SH) and Master Hunter (MH) tests, which include blind retrieves, where the dog doesn't see the bird fall. The handler must guide his Golden Retriever using signals to find and retrieve the bird. The handler isn't allowed to touch his dog, and the dog must remain steady—that is, not leave until sent. Advanced tests also include doubles and triples, in which the dog visually marks multiple falls, must remember where each bird is, and retrieve them in the same sequence they fell. Dogs also must honor by sitting quietly while another dog retrieves.

Top trainers and serious sportsmen compete in retriever field trials, which are more competitive and difficult. At a field trial, dogs compete for placements, and only dogs finishing in the top four placements receive points toward their Field Trial Championship. While Hunt Tests strive to mirror realistic hunting situations, dogs in field trials typically retrieve birds shot several hundred yards out in the field—much farther than a hunter could shoot a bird in a realistic hunting situation.

Once the dog achieves a certain number of points in field trials, he earns a Field Champion (FC) or Amateur Field Champion (AFC) titles. The highest honor a Golden Retriever can achieve is Dual Champion, or both a Field Championship and a Conformation Championship.

YOU AND YOUR PUPPY

Finding a job for your puppy means finding something you'll enjoy, too. From dancing to therapy visits, you and your Golden Retriever can enjoy many activities together.

Competitive Dog Sports

You don't have to be a superathlete to compete in most canine sports. In fact, people with disabilities perform in a number of AKC-approved activities. You also can train just for fun and never actually enter a competition.

Some of the sports listed in this section offer AKC competitions, others are put on by the sport's parent organization, and some have several groups that sponsor events, which gives you access to more trials and training.

For AKC sports (referred to by the AKC as companion events), your Golden Retriever must either have registration papers or get a Purebred Alternative Listing (PAL) number, which is available to unregistered dogs and mixed breeds. (The PAL used to be called Indefinite Listing Privilege, or ILP, so you might hear both terms used.) Along with the PAL application and registration fee, you must submit two recent and clear color photographs of your Golden Retriever, one full front view showing the facial characteristics, and one view showing the full side profile of him standing on a flat surface (not grass). Once you've received your PAL number from the AKC, you use that number on the entry forms for events.

Agility: Agility classes are fun and help your Golden Retriever develop his coordination. Similar to jumping competitions in the equestrian world, dogs run an obstacle course and must complete it within a preestablished time frame and without any faults, such as knocking over a jump pole or failing to hit a required contact point on an obstacle.

Although your puppy shouldn't start jumping until his growth plates have closed, he can learn many aspects of agility at this age. Weave poles, the A frame, seesaw, pause table, dog walk, and tunnel are all safe for a young dog's growing bones if you don't overdo it. When he starts jumping, instructors usually set the jumps low while your dog learns. When he's fully grown and able to compete, in the AKC, jumps for

Golden Retrievers are set at one of two heights: 20-inch Class for dogs 22 inches and under at the withers (shoulder) or 24-inch Class for dogs over 22 inches at the withers.

Contact obstacles have painted zones at the ends your dog must touch with at least one paw in order to qualify. Contact obstacles include A frame, dog walk, and seesaw. This keeps the dogs from leaping off the top of an obstacle and being injured.

Seven organizations in the United States offer agility trials, and your dog can earn dozens of titles. The titles can't be mixed and matched with each other, but your Golden Retriever can build an impressive list of initials at the end of his name. Here are the seven groups:

- American Kennel Club (AKC): akc.org/events/agility
- United States Dog Agility Association, Inc. (USDAA): usdaa.com
- United Kennel Club (UKC): ukcdogs.com/WebSite.nsf/WebPages/DogAgility
- North American Dog Agility Council (NADAC): nadac.com
- Australian Shepherd Club of America (ASCA; accepts all breeds for competition): asca.org/programs/agility
- Canine Performance Events (CPE): k9cpe.com
- Dogs on Course in North America (DOCNA): docna.com

The organizations have similar obstacles, levels of competition, and awards. As an example, the AKC offers three levels: Novice, Open, and Excellent. The minimum time allowed and the number of obstacles to complete increase as the level of difficulty increases. Novice dogs compete over 14 to 16 obstacles, and judging focuses on the owner's handling technique while scoring any faults. Open agility consists of 16 to 18 obstacles. They're more difficult than novice and require the handler to use more advanced skills. Excellent, the highest level for AKC agility, consists of 18 to 20 obstacles. The handler and dog must work as a team and have advanced skills to complete the course. In Masters (for dogs who have completed titles), a dog must qualify 10 times in their class. The ultimate title is the Master Agility Champion (MACH) title, requiring multiple qualifying scores tallied on a point system.

The AKC divides the classes into Standard, Jumpers With Weaves (no contact obstacles), FAST (Fifteen and Send), and Time to Beat (T2B). FAST classes include additional challenges so dog and owner can demonstrate speed, handling skill, accuracy, and distance handling. T2B uses obstacles from Jumpers With Weaves, with the option of having one or two contacts included on the course. Each owner has the chance to set the time to beat for each jump height division.

In addition, trials offer the Preferred Class, which offers longer course times and lower jump heights for the regular classes.

Canine freestyle: Dancing with dogs is a fun and increasingly popular activity. You don't have to be a great dancer to participate, and Golden Retrievers love to perform. Based on basic obedience training and dressage, musical freestyle adds music, timing, costuming, and showmanship as you and your dog perform heelwork or dance moves to music. Your dog dances both at your side and away from you.

Both men and women enjoy the sport, and you can see the dogs are having fun and enjoying the crowd's approval. You select the music and develop your own choreography, and once you've developed your routine, you can do demos or compete in freestyle events. For more information about canine freestyle, visit the World Canine Freestyle Organization at worldcaninefreestyle.org or the Canine Freestyle Federation at canine-freestyle.org.

Dock dogs: You might have seen dock dogs at the fair or on television. It's an exciting sport, and easy for a beginner to get started. If your Golden loves to chase a retrieving toy and enjoys swimming, you're ready. All you need is a floating toy he loves, a leash, plenty of towels, and a place to practice. There are clubs all over the United States where you can practice and compete.

Dock dogs compete in three types of games:

Big air, a long jump for dogs, is the event you see on TV. Handlers throw a floating toy in the pool and their dog retrieves it, running the length of a 40-foot dock and jumping into the water. His jump length is measured where the base of his tail enters the water. The goal is jump length; he doesn't have to return the toy to earn a score.

Extreme vertical tests a dog's jumping ability. A toy is suspended 8 feet out and 4½ feet up from the edge of the dock, and dogs have two chances to jump and grab the bumper. If they make it, the bumper is raised in 2-inch increments until all other dogs are eliminated.

Speed retriever is a timed event. You hold your Golden 20 feet back from the edge of the dock, behind an infrared beam that serves as the starting line, and a foam duck toy is suspended at the far end of the pool. When you get the green light, you release your dog, and he leaps off the end of the dock and swims to the duck. The dog is timed, and when he grabs the duck, the timer stops. He doesn't have to bring the duck back to you. The challenge is finished when the timer stops.

Iron Dog is a point system that ranks dogs participating in all three disciplines. To learn about dock dogs and to find local clubs, visit dockdogs.com.

Flyball: Another exciting sport based on speed and retrieving, flyball races consist of two teams of four dogs who compete against each other in relay races. The course is 51 feet long with 4 jumps. Each dog jumps the hurdles, steps on a tennis-ball launcher at the end of the line to release the ball, and returns with the ball. When he crosses the finish line, the next dog is released to do the same thing. Both teams run at the same time, side by side, so competition is fierce and the audience cheers their team on to the finish line. Teams are divided into divisions so they can compete against teams with similar levels of ability.

The hurdle heights are determined by the height of the shortest dog on the team, so you'll often see an odd combo of breeds, such as three tall dogs like Golden Retrievers and a short Yorkie. The start line and timing are measured electronically, and the winning team might win by a thousandth of a second—important when four experienced dogs can finish a run in less than 20 seconds. The North American Flyball Association has more information available at flyball.org/aboutflyball.html.

Conformation: When you see a televised dog show, like the Eukanuba National Championship or the Westminster Kennel Club Show, that's a conformation event. In these events, dogs are judged against the breed standard. Within each breed, judges evaluate dogs in classes separated by gender and then further divisions within each sex. The winners of each class compete against dogs who have earned their championship for the Best of Breed award.

Dogs earn points based on how many dogs they're shown against, and when they've won a certain number of points against a representative number of dogs for the particular breed, they earn their championship. Champion dogs are considered excellent candidates for breeding because they've proven they have the correct structure and temperament representative of the breed. After they have their health clearances, these dogs can go on to produce sound, healthy puppies and improve the breed overall.

Breeds are divided into seven groups in AKC competition. Golden Retrievers are part of the Sporting group, and the Best of Breed Golden competes against other retrievers, spaniels, pointers, and setters for the Best in Group award. The other breed groups (and some representative breeds) are the Working Group (Rottweilers, Boxers), Herding (Collies, German Shepherds), Toy (Maltese, Toy Poodle), Non-Sporting (Standard Poodle, Keeshound), Terrier (Scottish Terrier, Airedale Terrier), and Hound (Bloodhound, Dachshund). The winner of each group then proceeds to the Best in Show ring, where a judge chooses a winner among the seven top dogs from that day's competition.

If you're interested in conformation, talk to your breeder. Your Golden Retriever may or may not be a show-quality dog, and an expert will need to go over him to confirm whether he should be shown. Conformation dogs must be intact (not spayed or neutered). Also, you'll need to learn about handling your dog in the ring, grooming, nutrition, conditioning, and pedigrees so you can be competitive. Many breed clubs have fun matches in which you can practice and take classes, and some breeders will mentor people who are new to the sport.

Therapy Dogs

Accompanied by their owners, therapy dogs make visits to schools, nursing homes, rehabilitation hospitals, libraries, and other facilities to the cheer patients, residents, and staff. Golden Retrievers are naturally suited for this kind of work.

Most facilities require that you and your dog be trained and certified through a recognized therapy dog organization, and local and national groups offer training and testing. Therapy Dogs International (tdi-dog.org) and Pet Partners (petpartners.org) both have local chapters all over the United States that train and certify animal-assisted therapy dogs. Pet Partners also offers a home-study course to prepare you and your dog for visits.

Many therapy groups use the Canine Good Citizen test as the basis for certification and expand it to include exposure to wheelchairs and hospital situations. Dogs with more advanced training can participate in animal-assisted therapy, attending actual physical or psychological therapy sessions. For instance, a patient in a rehab hospital could relearn to use her hands by brushing your Golden Retriever, throwing a ball for him, or opening a can of dog food. Or your dog might sit next to a child who is undergoing a frightening procedure to calm her. In schools, a child could read to your dog while working on her reading skills.

TIPS AND TAILS
Therapy dogs must be immaculately groomed for their visits. Their toenails must be cut short, for example, so they don't tear the skin of fragile or elderly patients. They also must be healthy and free of parasites because they'll be around patients with compromised immune systems.

To find a therapy dog group near you, ask local obedience trainers or hospitals to refer you to a group. Or contact the national organizations and see if there is a local chapter in your area.

	SOCIAL	BEHAVIOR	TRAINING	PHYSICAL	HEALTH
MONTH 1	Breeder starts socialization		Littermates and mother teach appropriate canine behavior	Rapid growth	
MONTH 2					
MONTH 3	Socialization at home with new owner and other pets	Fear-imprint-period	Begin house- and crate training		1st DHPP vaccine
MONTH 4			Enroll in puppy class		2nd DHPP vaccine
MONTH 5	Socialization in public	Teething begins—heavy chewing period	Ready for basic commands	Switch to adult food	3rd DHPP and rabies vaccines
MONTH 6					
MONTH 7			Enroll in basic obedience class		
MONTH 8		Adult teeth are in—chewing continues	Ready for more advanced training	Moderate growth	Sexual maturity
MONTH 9					
MONTH 10					
MONTH 11				Slow growth—reaches adult size	
MONTH 12 AND BEYOND					Annual vaccinations and checkup

Your Golden Grows Up

Golden Retrievers have an extended puppyhood, and yours won't settle down much until she's 2 or 3 years old. Some Goldens are quiet and mellow, but most keep their happy-puppy attitude well into old age. You have many years of laughter to look forward to as your pup matures.

PHYSICAL DEVELOPMENT

Over the next 2 years, your dog will continue to physically mature, although the changes will be nowhere nearly as dramatic as those you've seen during her first year.

Changes from 1 Year to Adulthood

Your Golden Retriever will look like a teenager until she's about 18 months old. Then she'll fill out and look fully mature and balanced between 2 and 3 years old. The growth plates in her limbs will close between 10 and 18 months, and her height will stabilize. Her legs will grow stronger and sturdier, and for a male, characteristics like a broader head and chest will develop if he's not yet neutered. Females won't look a lot different when they reach maturity, but they, too, will stop growing and fill out a little.

Your 11-month-old Golden Retriever has the maturity of a 15-year-old child. She's still very much a puppy, with a teenager's exuberance and energy level, and she might not have much common sense yet. By the time she's 18 months old, she'll have matured a bit. She'll be less frantic but still very active.

Adult Sizes and Weights

Your Golden Retriever probably won't grow more than another inch between now and full maturity. She'll add on a few pounds, and she'll eat like a horse, but don't excuse weight gain as filling out. Continue to check her body condition (see Appendix B) and adjust her food accordingly.

Remember that an adult male should weigh between 65 to 75 pounds when he's 3 years old, so depending on his height and build, he should be less than his expected weight now. A female should be 55 to 65 pounds at 3 years old. When in doubt, keep your Golden Retriever lean rather than heavy. A lighter weight puts less stress on her joints and she'll be at risk for fewer health problems.

HEALTH

With a little attention, your Golden Retriever should be healthy and active for many years to come. Schedule regular wellness exams with her veterinarian as well as the necessary vaccines. And watch for signs of health problems so you can catch them before they get serious.

When Are Her Next Vaccinations Due?

Assuming your puppy had her rabies vaccine and final DHPP booster at 4 months, she should need her next inoculations at 16 months, or 1 year later. Consider waiting a week or two between the DHPP and rabies vaccines to avoid overloading her immune system though. After this round of vaccines is completed, you shouldn't have to revaccinate her for 3 years.

TIPS AND TAILS

In 2003, the American Animal Hospital Association changed its vaccine guidelines, recommending veterinarians vaccinate dogs only every 3 years. Research has shown that yearly vaccines are unnecessary because most animals retain the immunity from the initial vaccines for many years. There are also indications that overvaccination is potentially harmful. Adverse long-term effects are still being studied, but researchers suspect excessive vaccination could contribute to anaphylaxis, immunosuppression, autoimmune disorders, infections, and other disorders.

Your dog also might have had other noncore vaccines such as those for Lyme disease, coronavirus, or leptospirosis. Discuss optional vaccines and the risk of contracting the diseases in your area with your veterinarian.

If you'll be boarding your dog, the bordetella vaccine is required and must be given on a 6-month or yearly basis, depending on the kennel's requirements.

If you take your dog to the veterinarian for a suspected illness and her vaccines are ready to be updated, wait until she has recovered from whatever ails her. Her immune system is compromised when she's ill, and the vaccine might not create the protective immunity it's supposed to provide. Likewise, as your dog ages, consider her health status before administering vaccines. It's possible that older dogs with diabetes, hypothyroidism, glaucoma, or any other chronic medical condition should no longer be vaccinated. Explore this option with your veterinarian when the time comes.

Titers

A *titer,* an alternative to boostering vaccines, is a blood test that confirms if a dog has responded to a specific vaccine and still has that immunity. If she does, no further vaccination is necessary. Veterinarians usually test for parvovirus and distemper because if the dog is protected from these two, it's fairly certain her immunological status in good shape. Titers should be repeated yearly to detect when or if your Golden Retriever loses her immunity.

DOG TALK
A **titer** measures the amount of antibodies to a particular disease your Golden Retriever is carrying.

Vaccines cost less than running a titer test, but the benefit is that you don't expose your dog to unnecessary vaccines.

The Annual Checkup

Even if you don't vaccinate your dog every year, she still needs an annual wellness exam. Dogs age faster than humans, and your Golden Retriever changes dramatically between vet visits. Dogs also hide pain well, and your vet might discover something you haven't noticed yet.

The annual exam establishes a history so that when your dog does have a problem, the veterinarian has a record of her past health status to compare to. This helps him decide if further tests are needed and aids his diagnosis.

Before you take your Golden Retriever to the vet, make a list of questions about her health, behavior, nutrition, and anything else on your mind. Review her health record so you know the date of her last vaccines and any other treatments she's had. Bring her treats with you to the appointment so you can make the visit a positive experience for your dog. Also bring a stool sample to be checked for worms and other parasites, along with any medications or supplements you're giving her.

During your visit, the veterinarian will examine your dog. He will …

- Check her weight and assess if it's normal or if she's overweight.
- Conduct a nose-to-tail examination, listening to her heart, lungs, and digestive sounds and feeling for any abnormalities, lumps, or signs of pain.
- Test her reflexes to be sure they're normal.
- Examine her teeth to see if they're clean and her gums are a healthy color.
- Draw blood for heartworm test and any other tests indicated, such as testing for tick-borne diseases.
- Administer annual bordetella (kennel cough) vaccine if needed and update any other inoculations as needed.
- Examine her ears to see if they're pink and healthy and free of infection or foreign bodies.
- Renew her prescriptions for flea control, heartworm preventative, and any other necessary medications.

If the vet finds a problem, he might order further bloodwork, x-rays, or other testing.

Common Golden Retriever Ailments

Like all dogs, Golden Retrievers are vulnerable to disease as they mature. Some ailments strike young dogs for no apparent reason. Others are preventable if you take sensible precautions.

Allergies: Research indicates that allergies are the number-one problem Golden Retriever owners must deal with. If your dog is licking her paws, scratching for no obvious reason, chewing the base of her tail, suffering from chronic ear infections, or has dander or flaky skin, she might be reacting to an allergen. A Golden Retriever's allergies could be caused by food sensitivities, flea allergy, or environmental allergies. Just as people do, she might suffer more during certain times of the year.

We've talked about food, noting your Golden Retriever might be sensitive to a particular grain or protein source. Food allergies are actually uncommon in dogs. Careful experimentation with elimination diets might solve this problem, and your vet might prescribe a hypoallergenic food. It can take up to 12 weeks to see a difference in your dog's health if a food allergy is the issue.

Your pup can also be allergic to flea saliva, and it only takes one flea to cause an intense itchy reaction. Check her coat for flea dirt, and bathe her if you see evidence of infestation. Keep her on a regular flea preventative, too. Some preventatives lose their effectiveness because the fleas build up immunity to them, so switch brands if your dog suddenly becomes reinfested. If your dog is clean and in excellent health, she won't be as attractive to fleas.

Environmental allergies are harder to treat because you usually can't eliminate the allergen. Called *atopic dermatitis,* such allergies often start slowly, with just one or two sensitivities, and your dog starts reacting to additional substances over time. Many things can affect her, including pollen, grasses, dust mites, feathers, and mold. As your dog continues to suffer, she might develop thick, greasy-looking skin. Your veterinarian or a veterinary dermatologist can perform skin sensitivity testing and develop injections to desensitize your dog to the offending substances. Unless the allergies are extreme, your best bet is probably to take measures to keep your dog comfortable. Your vet can prescribe antihistamines, antibiotics, and steroids to control symptoms. Be aware that as your puppy scratches, she also might get secondary yeast and staph infections, which also need treatment.

If you think your pup has environmental allergies, keep her indoors with the windows closed when the pollen count is high. (Check your daily paper for that information.) Also keep her indoors during the peak hay fever times of day—early morning and evening. Also rinse her feet and wipe her down with a damp towel or unscented dryer sheet when you bring her indoors.

Even if they don't have a food allergy, some dogs with atopic dermatitis improve when switched to a higher-quality dog food. If your Golden is allergic to house dust mites, they often react with grain mites. In that case, your puppy will benefit from a grain-free canned food or kibble.

HAPPY PUPPY

If your Golden Retriever has allergies or hot spots, give her a cool, medicated bath to soothe her skin. Don't use oatmeal shampoo. Although it soothes the itching, it's a grain, and dogs with grain sensitivities could have an additional allergic reaction.

Keep in mind that not all itching is caused by allergies. Parasites like sarcoptic mange (scabies) cause intense itching. If your dog gets wet and isn't dried thoroughly, she can get hot spots or yeast infections. Your vet can rule out all the possibilities before diagnosing allergies.

Arthritis: Manage your Golden Retriever's exercise for life so she won't be crippled by arthritis as she ages. Whenever possible, have her run and play on soft ground because hard pounding jars her bones and joints. Although arthritis is sometimes caused by hip dysplasia, otherwise healthy dogs can get it due to a previous injury, tick-borne disease, autoimmune disorder, obesity, or cartilage problems caused by poor diet.

If your veterinarian diagnoses arthritis …

○ Manage your dog's weight and provide gentle exercise such as swimming or walking to maintain her muscle tone.

○ Give her glucosamine and chondroitin supplements that lubricate her joints and may relieve her pain.

○ Consider getting her acupuncture to help relieve symptoms.

○ Be sure she has a soft bed that cushions her sore joints.

○ Allow her to stay indoors on cold, damp days.

○ Raise her food bowl if she has a stiff neck.

○ Help her climb stairs and provide a ramp to help her get in and out of the car.

○ Ask your vet about pain-relieving medications.

○ Put carpet runners on hard floors so she can walk more easily.

Bloat: Gastric dilation volvulus, or bloat, most often occurs in large, deep-chested dog breeds, and Golden Retrievers are vulnerable. The risk increases as your dog ages. With bloat, the stomach fills with gas and fluid and swells because the dog cannot expel it (gastric dilation). As a result, the stomach twists (volvulus). Symptoms include drooling, unproductive retching, restlessness, biting at her side, a distended abdomen, and signs of shock. Emergency surgery to relieve the twisting could save your dog's life. If your dog's stomach doesn't twist, her veterinarian might be able to relieve the gas by passing a tube into her stomach.

Dogs who have suffered from bloat are very likely to have another occurrence. To prevent bloat …

○ Restrict access to water for 1 hour before and after meals.

○ Avoid strenuous exercise 1 hour before and after meals.

- Divide her food into three small meals, spaced well apart.

- Do **not** feed her from a raised food bowl. For many years, it was thought that feeding large dogs from raised bowls helped prevent bloat. A 2000 study conducted by Purdue University found that feeding from elevated bowls actually *increased* the likelihood of bloat.

- Avoid feeding dry food that lists fat among the first four ingredients.

- Never let her gulp a large amount of water all at once so she doesn't take in too much air. If she's very thirsty, let her have a quick drink and then wait a minute or so for another one. Repeat as needed to quell her thirst.

TIPS AND TAILS

Bloat is a life-threatening situation, so if your dog shows symptoms, take her to the veterinarian immediately.

Cancer: Cancer is the most common cause of death in Golden Retrievers. Up to 60 percent of the breed dies of the disease, almost double the rate of other breeds. Lymphoma and hemangiosarcoma are the two most common types, and dogs over 7 years old appear to be most susceptible.

Lymphoma is a cancer of the lymphatic system, which transports lymph fluid between body tissues and the circulatory system. The first symptoms you might see are enlarged, hard lumps on her lymph nodes on the throat under the jaw, on her shoulder, in her groin area, or behind her knees. An affected dog also might experience weight loss, lethargy, weakness, and increased water consumption. Your veterinarian will perform a surgical biopsy to diagnose the disease. With chemotherapy, most dogs will achieve remission.

Hemangiosarcoma originates in the endothelial cells that line the blood vessels. This type of cancer can affect any organ, but it most often appears in the spleen. One symptom is periods of weakness alternating with normal behavior and activity. The most common symptom, however, is sudden collapse due to internal bleeding when a tumor ruptures. The veterinarian performs x-rays or an ultrasound to diagnose; a blood test is being developed to diagnose the disease and should be available soon. Surgery to remove the tumor and chemotherapy can slow the progression of the disease.

The AKC Canine Health Foundation, Golden Retriever Foundation, Golden Retriever Club of America, and Morris Animal Foundation have all sponsored extensive research on cancer in Golden Retrievers. They're studying methods of early detection, ways to effectively treat the disease, and what causes these cancers to occur.

Gum disease: Caring for your Golden's teeth and gums is crucial to ensuring her lifelong health. By the time your dog is 3 years old, she might need a teeth cleaning to remove tartar and plaque on her teeth and beneath the gum line where the toothbrush can't reach. Without diligent dental care, she could get a serious infection that could spread through her system and shorten her life.

Although her teeth are beautiful and white now, chewing on sticks and tennis balls can wear them down significantly over time. She might also break a tooth that will need to be removed.

Your veterinarian can determine if your dog needs her teeth cleaned and can show you where plaque has built up or gum disease has started.

Hip and elbow dysplasia: Research has shown that overly rapid growth and obesity, in addition to genetics, play a role in whether your dog will develop these diseases. Dogs suffering from hip or elbow dysplasia develop arthritis, sometimes at a very young age. Puppies don't exercise as hard as adults and don't carry a lot of weight, so symptoms in a severely affected dog might not show up until she reaches her full adult size. Some dogs with hip dysplasia never show symptoms, like gait abnormalities or holding their elbows at an unusual angle, but most develop arthritis in their middle years, between 5 and 8 years old.

One of the keys to slowing the progression of dysplasia is to keep your Golden Retriever at a lean weight. Work with your veterinarian to decide what that weight should be.

If your dog has hip or elbow dysplasia, follow the same tips as given for arthritis earlier in this chapter to make her more comfortable.

HAPPY PUPPY
Arthritis, hip dysplasia, and other ailments can be prevented or at least improved by keeping your Golden Retriever slim and trim.

Laryngeal paralysis: A disease that affects primarily older Golden Retrievers, laryngeal paralysis occurs when a dog's vocal folds, which usually open when the dog inhales, don't open at all or open out of sync with the dog's natural breathing rhythm. Part of a neurological disease process that develops over a long period of time, it can affect one or both vocal folds. A dog who has laryngeal paralysis pants excessively, is overly sensitive to heat, and is easily fatigued. Often her breathing won't return to normal until hours after exercise.

A surgeon can tie back the vocal fold (or folds) to the outer sides of the larynx so the airway will remain open. Although the dog's breathing improves, she's susceptible to aspirating (inhaling) her food. When she eats, she might get food or water in her lungs, which can cause pneumonia.

Lumps and bumps: As Golden Retrievers age, they often get an assortment of lumps on their bodies. This is perfectly normal, but you'll want your vet to take a look at them to be sure they're not something serious. Sometimes he can tell by how the lump is attached to the body what it is. He also might withdraw some fluid or cells from the lump and examine it microscopically to confirm what it is. If the lump is benign, there's no need to remove it except for cosmetic reasons, and you can wait until your dog has to go under anesthesia for another procedure, like teeth cleaning, if you want it removed.

If a lump starts to grow or drains fluid, take your dog to the vet for further testing.

TIPS AND TAILS

Select a permanent guardian for your Golden Retriever to ensure she won't end up in a shelter if something happens to you. In fact, select three people who have agreed to care for your dog. Then, if someone's situation changes and he's unable to fulfill your wishes, someone else can.

NUTRITION

In the previous section, we touched on food allergies. There are other ways your dog's diet can affect her health, too, and we look at those here. We also explore raw and home-cooked diets, along with their benefits and drawbacks.

The Relationship Between Food and Health

Poor-quality food can cause nutritional deficiencies in your pup and lead to major illness. Now that the pet food industry does a much better job of manufacturing complete and balanced dog foods, there's a much lower incidence of diseases caused by nutrient imbalances, but even a food label that states "complete and balanced" might not provide the best nutrition for your dog's particular needs.

Here are some examples of what happens when certain nutrients are out of balance:

- Vitamin A toxicity can occur when too much liver, cod liver oil, or vitamin A is added to the diet. It causes lethargy, loss of appetite, and bone and joint pain.

- Vitamin B_{12} deficiency causes anemia.

- Vitamin D toxicity causes excess levels of calcium in the blood and can lead to kidney stones and organ failure.

- Fatty-acid deficiency causes skin and hair disorders, such as a dry, brittle coat and hair loss. It also causes slow healing from injury or illness.

- Zinc deficiency sometimes occurs in dogs fed poor-quality or generic dog foods or those who have been oversupplemented with other minerals like iron, calcium, and copper. A deficiency causes poor growth in puppies, and too much causes calcium and copper deficiencies.

- Protein deficiency causes infections, weakened immune system, slow healing, hormone deficiencies, and skin problems.

TIPS AND TAILS

If you're feeding your Golden Retriever a raw or home-cooked diet, you are responsible for ensuring she's getting the proper balance of the nutrients she needs.

Dealing with Obesity

Golden Retrievers gain weight very easily, but their fur often covers the evidence. If your dog is 20 percent or more over her ideal weight, then she's not just plump, she's obese. That means an 84-pound dog who should weigh 70 pounds has to lose 14 pounds. Spayed females are the most likely to gain weight, but all Goldens are susceptible. If your pup develops this problem, you're risking serious future health problems, such as arthritis, heart and respiratory disease, hip dysplasia, cruciate ligament injury, kidney disease, cancer, pancreatitis, and a decreased life expectancy by up to 2 years less.

Once you've established that your Golden Retriever is too heavy, work with your veterinarian to put together a realistic weight-loss plan. Before you start anything, have your vet do a complete physical exam. Health conditions like thyroid disease can cause weight gain.

Helping your dog lose weight is similar to going on a diet yourself. To say "less food and more exercise" is simple, but you need to do more. Let's look at productive ways to help your Golden Retriever maintain a healthy weight:

- Cut back on her food gradually so she isn't suddenly starving. If you cut back too fast, her metabolism will slow to compensate for the decrease in food.

- Add beans, pumpkin, and other high-fiber veggies to her meal to help her feel full.

- Switch to a light commercial dog food or a low-calorie, high-fiber prescription diet food. The bulk is the same so she doesn't feel deprived.

- Feed her twice a day, and pick up her food in between.

- Soak her food in water before feeding her so it expands in the bowl and makes her feel full as soon as she eats.

- Eliminate coat supplements that might be high in fat and calories.

- Cut back on treats. A big dog doesn't need giant dog biscuits; a little snack is sufficient. Choose less-fattening treats like carrots, rice cakes, or popcorn (if she isn't sensitive to rice or corn). Give her air-popped popcorn, and don't add butter or salt.

- Avoid table scraps. Those calories add up fast.

- Put her meal in a treat-dispensing toy so she'll be entertained and less focused on scarfing down as much food as possible.

Last but never least, begin an exercise program with your Golden Retriever. Assuming she's healthy enough to exercise, start with walks and work up to more energetic games of fetch or other activities when her fitness begins to improve. Daily exercise builds muscle tone, and muscle tone decreases the amount of fat she carries around. Muscle mass also increases metabolism, which helps burn calories.

HAPPY PUPPY
Swimming is excellent exercise, and most Goldens enjoy it.

Home-Prepared Foods

Today you have more options than ever when choosing food for your dog. Instead of commercially manufactured dog foods, many people opt to feed their dogs raw or home-cooked diets. Many of these owners want to provide their puppy optimum nutrition and have control over the quality and ingredients they're feeding, without added dyes, fillers, or preservatives. Others might have lost faith in commercial foods due to recalls. Some want to try a home-prepared diet to see if they can resolve a health problem their Golden suffers from, like allergies or digestive issues.

Home-prepared foods have advantages and disadvantages, and you'll find plenty of advice in books and online. When you're researching diets, take into consideration the source of the information. This is a subject people get very passionate about, but they're sometimes long on opinions and short on facts.

A poorly prepared, imbalanced diet can cause more health problems than it solves, as you saw in the previous section about the links between health and nutrition. So unless you're a veterinary nutritionist, consider working with one to be sure you're providing the healthiest possible diet for your Golden Retriever. Keep in mind that dogs are carnivores, so whatever type of diet you choose, it should contain about 75 percent meat. No more than 10 percent should consist of grains, and 15 percent can be vegetables and fruits.

TIPS AND TAILS
Feeding home-prepared foods is not an all-or-nothing proposition. You can feed a quality commercial food to be sure your dog is getting sufficient vitamins and minerals and supplement it with raw or home-cooked ingredients.

Monitor your Golden's health to be sure the diet is working for her. Her stools should be smaller because her body is making better use of the nutrients she consumes and she isn't eating too many grains and fillers that are hard to digest efficiently. Her teeth should be cleaner, her gums should be healthier, her skin should be healthy, and her coat should be thick and shiny. Overall, she should appear healthy and happy, with clear eyes and ears and plenty of energy.

If your Golden Retriever suddenly develops diarrhea, vomiting, gas, or a decrease in appetite, discontinue feeding the diet and consult with your veterinarian. It could be due to a single ingredient, or something else might be wrong.

Raw diets are often referred to as BARF (Bones And Raw Food, or Biologically Appropriate Raw Food). The BARF diet was popularized by Australian veterinarian Dr. Ian Billinghurst, who believes dogs should eat the way their ancestors ate. But considering that dogs have been domesticated for more than 10,000 years, this might not be an appropriate comparison. Another way of looking at it is that wolves still eat this way in the wild. Wolves are much different from dogs, and dogs have changed dramatically since they were first domesticated. Wolves don't necessarily get the nutrients they need for good health, and ancient dogs quickly became dependent on humankind for food.

So although the reasoning may be flawed, there are some advantages to feeding raw, whole foods, along with some disadvantages:

Advantages of a raw diet:

○ You have complete control over the ingredients.

○ You can purchase fresh, whole foods and avoid pesticide-treated, processed foods and meat raised with antibiotics or growth hormones.

○ You can experiment with different ingredients and take advantage of seasonal produce.

○ Your dog will have smaller, less frequent stools.

Disadvantages of a raw diet:

○ It's hard to know whether you're feeding a proper balance of nutrients, especially vitamins and minerals. For example, a dog needs a good balance of calcium and phosphorus in her diet. Raw meat provides phosphorus, and raw bones provide calcium, but getting a correct balance is often the biggest problem with a raw diet.

○ Raw meat must be from healthy animals and handled carefully during processing to prevent spoilage or contamination, especially because it isn't cooked, which kills bacteria.

○ Ingesting raw meat can give you or your dog E. coli or salmonella if you aren't careful.

○ Large, raw bones can break a dog's teeth or perforate her stomach or intestinal tract. Small, softer raw bones, like chicken or turkey necks, are safer. If you find bits of bone in her stool, she's not chewing them completely. Grind them smaller as you prepare her food, or discontinue feeding bones.

○ Raw foods are more expensive than feeding commercial dog food and take a lot of planning and preparation time.

○ There's a risk of feeding too much fat, which can cause pancreatitis, a potentially fatal disease.

Home-cooked diets are usually a stew made of meat, grains, and vegetables. Your dog gets many of the benefits of a raw diet without as much risk of contamination, although safe handling practices are still necessary on your part.

Table scraps don't provide adequate nutrition for your Golden Retriever and usually contain excessive amounts of fat. Cooked bones should be removed and discarded after cooking or ground into small, safe pieces.

TIPS AND TAILS
As with any change in your dog's food, make the transition to a new diet gradually to avoid major stomach upsets.

GROOMING

You've taught your puppy to enjoy handling and grooming, and now it's time to make good use of those skills and not let her forget them.

Maintaining a Regular Grooming Schedule

Pick an evening at least once a week, and sit down on the floor for a good grooming session with your Golden Retriever. Sunday night is often a good choice. She's tired after an active weekend and willing to sit still. The more often you practice this, the more she'll look forward to your time together—as well as the multitude of treats she gets when you trim her toenails.

At times, you might need to brush her more often, especially when she's blowing her coat twice a year. At these times, you can break up grooming chores into several shorter sessions during the week. Teeth-brushing Tuesdays, Friday fur-fights—the idea is to be able to look forward to spending this time with your dog while keeping her clean and healthy.

The more time you spend grooming, the more cooperative she'll be. If you slack off for a couple months, maybe in the winter, you'll find she gets a case of the wiggle-butts come springtime when you want her to sit still for grooming.

Shaving Your Golden

A normal Golden Retriever coat, with regular grooming, shouldn't need to be shaved. However, if grooming becomes too much, or your dog is extremely matted, shaving is a reasonable option and much easier than trying to brush out all those mats. If your dog swims in the pool all summer, her coat needs a lot of maintenance—another reason to shave.

It takes months for a shaved coat to grow back in completely, and in the meantime, it might look pretty ratty. The undercoat might grow in first, or the topcoat and undercoat could grow at different rates on different parts of her body. The time of year makes a difference in how her coat grows back. If you shave her in September, for example, her coat will grow in thicker in preparation for winter.

If you let her coat grow back completely, it eventually should return to its former glory. If not, question whether a health issue is causing a problem. Low thyroid or Cushing disease can both affect coat quality.

Performing Weekly Health Checks

Don't forget to perform a weekly health check (see Month 4) during your grooming sessions. Go over your Golden's entire body—her coat, skin, feet, mouth, eyes, and ears—to identify grooming needs and health issues before they cause serious problems.

As your Golden ages, also look for lumps and signs of soreness due to arthritis or other conditions.

SOCIAL SKILLS

You've spent a lot of time and effort raising a well-behaved Golden Retriever, and now it's time to enjoy the fruits of your labor. A backyard dog quickly forgets her manners and social skills, and she redevelops the behavior problems you've worked to avoid. So continue socializing her and enjoying her company.

Enjoying Daily Walks

No matter how old she is, your Golden Retriever always needs some daily activity, both for exercise and companionship with you. A daily walk helps you unwind and gives her some much-needed exposure to the outside world, and you'll enjoy some nice time together. Once around the block won't be enough to wear her out, though. She needs at least a half hour of active exercise and a long walk. A nightly trip to the dog park or a visit to the neighbor dog for a play date takes care of both.

If you don't keep up with walks and exercise, your Golden Retriever will gradually get harder to handle, and her training will deteriorate. The more trouble she is, the less time you'll want to spend with her, and next thing you know, she's spending way too much time alone or in the crate.

HAPPY PUPPY
Remember, your Golden Retriever is still young and needs a lot of exercise, guidance, discipline, and time with you.

Continuing Socialization

As we've mentioned, dogs quickly become desocialized if they don't get out regularly. Plus, at 12 months, males are reaching an age where they might become more territorial and protective, so they still need diligent socialization.

Include your Golden Retriever in activities when company comes to your house so she continues to welcome people into your home. Be sure she also spends time with children if you don't have any of your own. She also needs to continue meeting other friendly dogs of all sizes on a regular basis.

With a little work on your part, her social skills will continue to improve, and she'll remain the friendly, outgoing dog a Golden Retriever is supposed to be.

BEHAVIOR

She might look like an adult, but she isn't quite there yet. Give her leeway as she earns it, but don't be afraid to continue with crating and discipline when she needs it.

If her behavior deteriorates, back up a few steps and put her on a puppy boot-camp program around the house. When her skills have been reviewed, try again to offer her some adult privileges.

Changes as Adulthood Approaches

As your Golden Retriever nears adulthood, she's still your happy-go-lucky puppy, but she's growing bigger, stronger, and more protective of her territory. Although Goldens aren't particularly good defenders, you might find her sounding the alarm well before your doorbell rings. You shouldn't see any aggression like what might appear at this age in other breeds, however, because a typical Golden Retriever is universally friendly.

You'll find her attention span has improved and she concentrates better. She's not as distracted and impulsive as she once was, and she obeys you more readily and accepts your leadership. In other words, although she's still a rambunctious youngster, your pup should be developing into a sociable, well-mannered member of society.

If you haven't yet neutered your Golden, be sure to plan this in the next few months.

Continuing Crating

A 12-month-old Golden Retriever isn't mature enough to have full run of the house when you're not awake or there to supervise her. It's just too much responsibility. Continue crating her at night and when you're unable to watch her. She can't resist temptation yet, and like most teenagers, she always needs to be doing something. She might need to be crated at night until she's past 2 years old.

You'll also find her spending time in her crate by her own choice, so don't worry that you're being cruel by enclosing her. She considers her crate her own safe haven away from the world.

TRAINING

She's still an adolescent, and she will be for many months, so your Golden Retriever puppy might suddenly test the rules when you least expect it.

When you finished basic obedience class, your work wasn't done. A Golden Retriever puppy still has a lot of maturing to do, and her skills need reinforcement on a regular basis. Here are some reminders for how to use training throughout her life and keep her skills fresh:

- Always ask her to sit when you put on the leash and wait for you before going through doors.
- Have her sit to greet people.
- Ask her to do a down-stay while you eat dinner or are out in public.
- Incorporate sits, downs, and stays into your daily walk routine.
- Have her sit or do a down before you give her her food bowl.
- Don't allow her to boss you around, enticing you to play or go for a walk, without asking her to earn her privileges by sitting first.
- Practice self-control exercises. You don't want her to be rambunctious and out of control when you most need her to behave.
- Keep the recall a fresh and happy command so you can always rely on her to come when you call her.
- Even when you're playing a game, enforce commands like give, off, and sit. She'll enjoy the challenge.

Continue practicing, taking her to classes, and adding new skills to her repertoire. Socialization and training go hand in hand, and the more time you invest in both—while having fun with your Golden Retriever—the better companion and pet she'll become.

YOU AND YOUR PUPPY

Your Golden Retriever puppy's first year presented a lot of challenges, and now she's almost grown. All the time you've invested has built a good foundation for your next decade or more together.

Your Changing Relationship

Your relationship with your puppy will gradually change from one of constant supervision and training to one of friendship and understanding. You've spent a lot of time getting to know each other, and your Golden Retriever can read your moods well. And of course, you've learned to read her, too, especially when she's about to take off with your shoe.

Check in with your breeder at least once a year, and give her an update on your puppy. She'll want to know if your dog has any health issues you're concerned about, and she'll be thrilled to catch up on your Golden's activities.

Enjoying Social and Fitness Activities

Hiking with your Golden Retriever can be fun. When she's matured, work up slowly to more challenging hikes so she doesn't get overly tired, heated, or injured. Research hiking trails before you go to be sure dogs are welcome.

Here are some things to take along:

- A quart of water for each of you and a portable water bowl for her
- Snacks for added energy—peanut butter on dog biscuits provides a quick energy boost for her
- Waste bags—be a responsible hiker and pick up her poop
- A first-aid kit that includes Benadryl, eyewash, tweezers, antibiotic ointment, a large bandana for bandaging, gauze pads, insect repellent, and meat tenderizer to put on insect bites
- Leash
- Doggie backpack—be sure you've tested it beforehand and it fits her without rubbing and isn't too heavy

Sometimes it's hard to get yourself off the couch to exercise, but your Golden Retriever can help you get out the door. You two can participate in one of the multitude of doggy fitness classes nationwide. Walking groups, exercise classes, and even doga—yoga for you and your dog—offer the opportunity to strengthen the bond between your and your Golden Retriever while reaping health benefits for you both.

Meetup groups offer get-togethers for like-minded folks in any number of hobbies and activities, including dogs, and you're sure to find a special Golden Retriever meetup group near you. Go to meetup.com, put in your zip code, and see what's happening. Golden owners schedule play dates at local dog parks, beach walks, costume contests, and even "yappy" hours.

Golden Retriever rescue groups always need more volunteers, and members share a common love for their breed. Even if you can't bear to visit a shelter, you can help out with adoption fairs, transport, fund-raising, and other events. Members often bring their own Goldens along, so be sure to take yours, too, if she's well socialized.

You also could join the local or national Golden Retriever breed club, especially if you're interested in activities like obedience, conformation, hunting tests, tracking, or agility. You'll find plenty of fellow Golden Retriever owners to train with, and you'll stay up-to-date on upcoming events and activities.

Outfitting Your Dog

Owning an active Golden Retriever means outfitting her with her own gear for your adventures together. These products make it easier to take your dog along and ensure her safety.

You might need some accessories to take your dog out on the town, or at least for camping and hiking activities. Major sporting goods chain stores and camping and hunting catalogs carry an array of products especially designed to outfit the well-appointed Golden Retriever.

You might remember the search-and-rescue dogs who worked after September 11, 2001. A nationwide campaign gathered donations to supply those dogs with protective boots to wear while searching in the hot, dangerous debris after the disaster. Even if your Golden Retriever isn't a search-and-rescue dog, she might be more comfortable on your adventures if she's got some boots. Protective boots come in everyday lightweight styles that provide air circulation while protecting her paw pads from hot pavement. For snowy, cold weather, tall, insulated boots keep snow out while a textured sole prevents her from slipping on ice. Traction sole boots also help her navigate rocky terrain and slippery boat decks. Whatever your activities together, you're sure to be able to find some appropriate footwear for your dog.

Carrying a backpack gives your Golden a job to do and helps you out, too. She can carry her own gear in the pack, or you can get a special water pack that has two compartments for water—one for yours and one for hers. Start with light loads and get her used to carrying the pack before you take her on a longer trip. She should never carry more than 25 percent of her body weight. For a 70-pound dog, that's 17½ pounds; for a 60-pound dog that's 15 pounds.

If you're boating, kayaking, or hunting from a boat with your Golden Retriever, a life vest will help keep her safe. When wet, a Golden's heavy coat can weigh her down in deep water. Most life vests are reflective so you can easily see your dog, and they have a handle you can use to lift her out of the water.

For use with larger boats, you can buy boat ladders made especially for dogs. More like stairs or ramps with rubberized steps for traction, these helpers make it easier for your wet dog to get in and out of the boat, and you won't have to pick her up.

Hauling a wet dog in the back of your SUV is no fun, but bench seat covers make it a little easier. Removable and washable, they fasten around the seat with straps so they'll stay in place and protect the upright part of the seat as well as the bench.

Here are some other smaller convenience items for Golden Retriever activities you might want to check out:

- Reflective, waterproof collars
- Safety reflectors to hang from her leash or collar
- Bungee leashes you can attach to your waist and to your dog for use while jogging or hiking
- Folding canvas food and water bowls with waterproof inserts
- Crate-cooling fans
- Heated dog beds
- Canvas and rubber bumpers for retrieving

Adopting a Teenage or Adult Golden

Golden Retrievers are given up by their families for a variety of reasons. Rescue groups report that the majority of dogs they get are between 10 and 18 months old, untrained, and ungroomed. Dogs arrive with skin problems and poor manners, like jumping on people and stealing food off counters and many haven't been allowed indoors since they got big and unruly. These are the lucky dogs because they'll readily adapt to a new home with some care and education.

Older dogs arrive with more entrenched behavior and health-care issues, but they're not a lost cause at all. They might have been neglected for a long time, but most thrive with the attention from their new family, love other dogs, and settle in with few adjustment issues.

When you adopt a Golden Retriever from a rescue group, you won't know much about your dog's life up to this point—good or bad. If your new dog has been in a foster home, the foster family can fill you in on what they've learned while she's been staying with them—she's housetrained, friendly toward cats, appears well-socialized, has had some training, etc. She'll have had all her shots and been neutered (or spayed). The rescue group also takes care of any health problems and discloses ongoing issues with you.

Golden Retrievers in animal shelters are usually strays who haven't been claimed by their owners. As a result, you'll have no history on her health or behavior, so getting her off to a good start is especially important.

One thing is for certain: what you do in the first few weeks and months with your adopted Golden Retriever has a big impact. She'll eagerly soak up everything she sees and hears so she can figure out the rules and routine in her new home. Goldens are friendly, adaptable, and anxious to please you—take advantage of that! Many adopters feel sorry for their new dog and whatever previous situation she must have been in and overnurture, allowing her to get away with anything and everything when she first arrives. Don't do this. She'll get confused by the sympathy and attention, especially if there are no rules or a structured routine she can quickly learn to count on. Once the newness wears off and the rules change, she'll be even more confused. It's no wonder new dogs chew and otherwise misbehave.

Don't assume your rescued Golden Retriever was abused. She likely just didn't get adequate training and socialization. Still, she might react fearfully or even aggressively to unfamiliar things. Honor her fear, and back off until she's comfortable. Take it slow, start training and socializing like she's a young puppy, and don't overwhelm her.

Positive reinforcement training is very effective with rescued dogs. Gradually introduce her to unfamiliar things so she's comfortable in new situations, and reward her with treats when she's brave. If you punish her or force her to confront something scary, she'll become even more afraid. As she learns to trust your judgment and understand that you won't force her, she'll look to you for guidance. Your happy voice and unconcerned body language will reassure her.

Enjoying Your Best Friend

The loving companion you envisioned sleeping at your feet in front of the fireplace is well on her way to growing up—or is further along if you adopted or rescued an older dog.

During your time together so far, she's probably given you lots of laughs, made you want to tear out your hair, eaten your prize rosebush, and vomited at the foot of your bed. She's also probably snuggled with the kids and dried your tears with her big, sloppy tongue while knocking over your favorite lamp with her tail. Maybe it's her sense of humor that's made you love her so much, but you can't imagine life without her now, and why would you want to?

We hope you'll enjoy your Golden Retriever's youth and exuberance, her maturity and loyal companionship, and her devoted old age. She'll be your best friend through thick and thin, always ready to play, always happy to see you come home. Include her in your life and allow her to love you. There's something about a Golden Retriever that's made the breed one of the most popular in the United States year after year, and you are lucky enough to find out why.

Glossary

alpha rollover   A punishment that's supposed to mimic how wolves establish their dominance over each other. A person forces his dog to the ground and holds him on his side or back until the dog "submits" and stops fighting the handler. Do not try this at home, and do not let a "trainer" do this to your dog.

antibody   Large proteins the immune system uses to fight disease-causing bacteria and viruses.

bitch   A female dog.

breed standard   A description of the ideal Golden Retriever as developed by the Golden Retriever Club of America, the parent club of the breed in the American Kennel Club (AKC). The standard specifies guidelines for size, color, structure, and temperament.

breed type   The qualities that define a Golden Retriever and make him different from other dog breeds as set forth in the breed standard.

bumper   A rubber or canvas retrieving toy used for training hunting dogs. Bumpers are long and narrow enough that they stick out of either side of the dog's mouth so you can take them from your dog easily.

call name   The everyday name you use for your Golden Retriever. It may or may not have anything to do with his AKC registered name.

"come"   The command that means "Stop what you're doing and come here, to me, right now."

conformation   The shape or structure of a dog. Judges at a dog show evaluate the conformation of the dog against the breed standard.

dam   The mother of the litter.

dewclaw   A vestigial toe and toenail dogs have partway up each front leg.

displacement behavior   A behavior that occurs out of context in response to an internal emotional conflict.

dog   A term that can mean any dog or specifically refer to a male.

dominance   A relationship between two or more dogs that's established by force and submission to gain power over others.

"down"   The command that means "Lie down, roll on one hip, and don't move." The hand signal is to sweep your flat hand, palm down, toward the ground.

fade   When teaching a new behavior, you reward with a treat every time your puppy complies. When he knows a skill, you can wean, or fade, him off treats by skipping an occasional treat reward while still using verbal praise. As you produce a treat even less often, he'll get one only once in a while for his best effort. If his response isn't reliable, you may be reducing the number of treats too quickly.

fear-imprint stage   A period lasts from approximately 8 to 12 weeks of age and usually starts soon after you bring home your puppy. Overwhelming or frightening incidents that occur during this time might stay with him for the rest of his life, and he'll always react to them with fear.

generalize   A puppy generalizes a lesson when he learns that a particular command means the same thing in many different places and situations.

"give"   The command that means "Put that item in my hand." The hand signal is to hold your hand open, palm upward, in front of his face.

glycemic index   A scale that measures the speed at which the body converts carbohydrates into sugars.

growth plate   Discs at the end of each long bone (of the leg, for example) made of soft cartilage. The cartilage is eventually replaced by bone.

heat   The period when a female dog is receptive to breeding and capable of getting pregnant. Also referred to as "in season," the cycle lasts 18 to 21 days.

"heel"   The command used in obedience competition that means "Come to this precise position at my left side" and applies whether the two of you are walking, sitting, or standing. Your Golden Retriever's ears line up with the seam of your pants, and he should be looking up at you.

holistic veterinarian or practitioner   A professional who addresses the whole dog, including mental and social factors, instead of limiting treatment to the symptoms of disease.

homeopathy   The practice of using herbs, minerals, and natural compounds to strengthen the body's natural defenses and cure disease.

intact   An unneutered male or unspayed female dog.

learning plateau   A phase when your puppy suddenly seems to have forgotten everything you've taught him. It's common in adolescent dogs and often happens around week 5 in obedience class. The phase might last 2 days or 2 weeks, but it does pass, and you'll see a surge in his progress once he's through it.

"leave it"   The command that means "Turn away from what you're looking at, and look at me."

"let's go" or "walk"   The command that means "Pay attention because we're going for a walk." The signal is to step off on your left foot when he is at your left side.

malabsorption   The body's inability to process and use the nutrients in food.

mark   In a hunting test, a bird is thrown or shot and the dog "marks" it by recognizing where it fell and remembering the location.

marking   When a mature dog deposits urine so other dogs can identify him and determine his age or readiness to breed. Marking also establishes territorial boundaries.

microflora   Microorganisms that live in the digestive tract and perform various functions, such as training the immune system, producing vitamins, and preventing growth of harmful bacteria.

neonatal period   The first 2 weeks of a puppy's life, when the puppy sleeps and eats and not much else.

"off"   The command that means "Put all four feet on the floor." The hand signal is to push your flat palm toward the dog, fingers spread.

"okay"   The command that releases your dog from whatever he's doing. Okay signifies "You're finished—relax," or "At ease." The hand signal is both hands palms up.

passive immunity   The protective antibodies a mother dog shares with her puppies via her milk that protect them from disease even though they haven't been vaccinated.

pheromone   A chemical secreted by an animal that another animal, usually of the same species, can interpret.

plaque   A buildup of bacteria on your dog's teeth that, if allowed to remain and harden, discolors and turns into tartar.

serotonin   A neurotransmitter involved in the transmission of impulses between nerve cells. It's found in the brain, blood platelets, and intestinal tract.

sire   The father of a litter of puppies.

"sit"   The command that means "Put your rear end on the floor and don't move." The hand signal is to scoop one hand upward, palm up.

socialization period   The period between 3 and 12 weeks of age when your puppy starts to explore his world. Positive or negative experiences during this time will impact his behavior for the rest of his life.

specialty show   A conformation dog show for a single breed of dog held by a breed club. In a Golden Retriever Specialty, the breed club often also conducts obedience, rally, hunting tests, and agility trials.

"stay"   The command that means "Do not move a muscle until I come back and touch you." The hand signal is your flat palm in front of the puppy's nose as you step off on your right foot.

"take it"   The command that means "Take this item" as you present it to him, like a toy.

titer   A test that measures the amount of antibodies to a particular disease your Golden Retriever is carrying in his body.

transition period   The time between 2 and 3 weeks of age when your puppy starts to be more aware of his environment.

weaning   The process of gradually changing a puppy's diet from mother's milk to solid food.

whelp   The process of a dog giving birth.

whelping box   A large nest where the mother gives birth to her puppies. There's often a ledge around the sides, so the mother won't accidentally crush a puppy against the wall.

withers   The highest point of a dog's shoulders, behind the neck.

zoonotic disease   A disease that's transmissible from one species to another—for example, from dogs to humans.

Body Condition Assessment

It's difficult to predict exactly what a Golden's size and weight should be at any given month during her first year. The most dramatic growth period your pup will experience is from birth to 6 months, when she grows to roughly 75 percent of her adult height. After that, growth slows dramatically until she reaches her full height at 10 to 12 months. Although the breed standard states that an adult male Golden should be 23 to 24 inches at the shoulders and females should be 21½ to 22½ inches, in reality, their size can vary greatly.

So when you read the following estimates, take your own Golden's build into consideration. There will be clear differences, even between two 12-week-old puppies. Even within a litter, puppies grow at different rates.

AGE, HEIGHT, AND WEIGHT ESTIMATES

The following numbers are estimates you can compare to, taken from the growth records of Golden puppies:

> **Birth:** 1 pound
>
> **8 weeks:** 10 to 12 pounds
>
> **12 weeks (3 months):** 20 to 25 pounds
>
> **16 weeks (4 months):** 25 to 35 pounds; 14 inches at the shoulder
>
> **20 weeks (5 months):** 28 to 40 pounds; 18 to 20 inches at the shoulder
>
> **6 to 12 months:** 50 to 65 pounds
>
> **Maturity (2 to 2½ years):** for males: 65 to 75 pounds and 23 or 24 inches at the shoulder; for females: 55 to 65 pounds and 21½ to 22½ inches at the shoulder.

All these heights and weights are approximate. It might be better to look at the percent of increase for a more accurate measure. For example, weight doubles between 4 months and 1 year.

IS MY PUPPY FAT?

Many Goldens today don't do the energy-intense work they were bred to do—a family pet, for example, doesn't need as many calories as a hunting dog. Even puppies can overeat, and this predisposes them to grow into heavy adults.

Being overweight puts extra stress on a dog's bones and joints. And because Goldens are prone to arthritis and other joint problems as they mature, a little light is better than a little heavy in this breed.

Don't feed your puppy according to the instructions on a food bag; feed her according to her current size, weight, condition, and overall health.

BODY CONDITION ASSESSMENT

Regardless of any charts and estimates, the best way to know whether your dog is obese, at an ideal weight, or too thin is to do a body condition assessment. You can use the following guidelines to check your dog at any age. If you have any doubts about your puppy's weight, consult with your veterinarian or your puppy's breeder for advice.

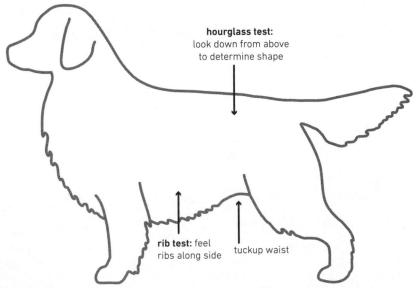

Use this illustration to help determine whether your puppy is ideal, too heavy, or too thin.

Have someone help you by holding your puppy in a standing position and keeping her relatively still. Look down on your puppy from above and look at where her rib cage ends. Also feel her body because her fluffy coat will hide her actual shape. See whether she is …

- **Ideal:** There's a slight narrowing behind her rib cage that continues to her rear. She's shaped like an hourglass.
- **Too heavy:** Your puppy is wider or rounder in the back half.
- **Too thin:** She appears dramatically narrower; you may also feel her ribs.

The size of your dog's rib cage won't change, but the padding on it will. Run your hands down each side of her rib cage to determine if she's …

- **Ideal:** You can find her ribs with little effort.
- **Too heavy:** There's a layer of fat, and that makes it hard to find her ribs.
- **Too thin:** You can feel her ribs without feeling for them. You may also easily feel her spine.

The bottom outline of your Golden puppy's body should start at her front elbows and tuck up slightly behind her rib cage. Check to see whether she is …

- **Ideal:** You can see or feel a slight rise after her rib cage. This varies between show and field Goldens, with field-bred dogs sometimes having a more prominent tuckup.
- **Too heavy:** There is no tuckup; her abdomen protrudes or sags.
- **Too thin:** There's a noticeable waist; you can probably feel her hipbones.

If you feel your pup is too heavy, cut back *slightly* on the amount you feed her—a drastic cut will leave her hungry. Supplement her meals with some vegetables (like beans or carrots) to help her feel full, and consider switching to a higher-fiber food.

If your puppy has a potbelly, have a stool sample checked for worms.

If your Golden is too thin, see your veterinarian. She might just need more food, or she might not be digesting her food properly.

Check your puppy's body condition regularly every 2 weeks during her first 18 months. As she grows, her calorie needs will vary. For the first 6 months of dramatic growth, you need to feed her increasing amounts of food. When she reaches full height, you can gradually reduce her daily amount to a normal adult quantity based on her size.

APPENDIX
C

Household and Yard Hazards

Puppies have no concept of what's good to eat or play with and what's dangerous. Never assume your puppy won't touch something. If it's different, out of the ordinary, has a smell, or is within reach, he'll probably investigate it.

PROBLEM FOODS

A number of foods can be a problem for your dog. Some may cause mild gastro-intestinal upset while others are poisonous and potentially toxic. If your puppy consumes any of the following, call your veterinarian or emergency veterinary clinic right away: alcoholic drinks (of any kind), caffeine, chocolate (milk chocolate is the least toxic; dark and baking chocolates are the most toxic), coffee, grapes and raisins, macadamia nuts, onions and onion powder, xylitol (including baked goods, gums, or candies that contain it), and yeast dough. As a general rule, don't allow your puppy to eat any spicy foods, fatty foods, leftover grease, or spoiled or moldy foods to avoid gastrointestinal upset.

HAZARDOUS MATERIALS

A wide variety of potentially hazardous materials are around your house: bug sprays, traps, and repellents; cigarettes, cigars, pipes, and tobaccos; cleaners and cleansers (floor, kitchen, bathroom, shower, countertop, toilet cleaners); craft supplies (beads, small pieces, paints and glues); holiday decorations (Christmas tree decorations, Halloween, electrical cords, ribbons, tinsel, batteries, plants); laundry products (detergents, bleach, fabric softener sheets); makeup, hair-care products, nail polish, and polish remover; mothballs; and houseplant fertilizers and insecticides.

MEDICINES

Almost all medications can have a detrimental effect on your puppy. Keep cold remedies, pain medications, prescription medications (especially antidepressants and anticancer drugs), and vitamins secure.

If you believe your puppy has ingested a medication, call your veterinarian or emergency veterinary clinic immediately. Do not wait for a reaction to begin.

IN THE GARAGE AND YARD

To keep up your home and yard, you often use a number of potentially dangerous substances. Keep these away from your pup: automobile care and maintenance products (gas, oil, antifreeze, cleaning products, waxes), paint, pest traps and poisons), and yard maintenance products (fertilizers, insecticides, herbicides, fungicides).

In the yard, be aware of frogs and toads, insects (ants, spiders, scorpions, and others), and snakes that will pique your puppy's curiosity.

POISONOUS PLANTS

Many common landscaping, decorative, and houseplants are potentially hazardous to your dog. Some may cause a contact allergy, such as poison sumac or ivy; others can be potentially fatal. For example, when ingested, castor bean, English ivy, and hemlock can kill a dog. If you have any of these plants in your house or yard, either remove them or be sure your dog doesn't have access to them:

Flowering plants: amaryllis, anemone, azalea, bird of paradise, buttercup, Christmas cactus, crocus, cyclamen, foxglove, impatiens, jasmine, larkspur, lilies, lily of the valley, morning glory, snapdragon, sweet pea, and verbena.

Bulbs, tubers, and fungi: amaryllis, calla lily, daffodil, gladiola, hyacinth, iris, jonquil, lantana, mushrooms and toadstools, and tulip.

Trees, decorative plants, and shrubs: asparagus fern, bottlebrush, boxwood, caladium, creeping charlie, croton, dieffenbachia, dogwood, dracaena, elephant ear, emerald feather fern, English ivy, heavenly bamboo, hemlock, holly, horse chestnut, hydrangea, ivy, mistletoe, nightshade, oleander, pennyroyal, philodendron, privet, rhododendron, sago palm, wisteria, and yew.

Vegetables, fruits, and nuts: avocado (leaves, stems, pit), eggplant, grapes (fruit), macadamia nut (nut), peach and other stone fruit (seeds/pits), potato (foliage), rhubarb, and tomato (foliage).

TIPS AND TAILS

The vegetables, fruits, and nuts list contains a variety of plants that contain different parts dangerous to dogs. If one specific part is dangerous, that's noted. If nothing is noted, the entire plant should be avoided.

Herbs, weeds, and miscellaneous plants: belladonna, castor bean, jimson weed, locoweed, marijuana, milkweed, pokeweed, poison ivy, poison oak, poison sumac, pokeweed, and sage.

WEATHER-RELATED HAZARDS

Some potential problems are only apparent during certain seasons. Because these products or hazards are around only occasionally, they can be more attractive to a curious puppy: antifreeze, blue-green algae in ponds (especially during hot weather), candles (lit or unlit), cocoa mulch, compost piles, ice-melting products, potpourri, and swimming-pool supplies.

Resources

When you need in-depth information or are searching for professionals to help you care for your Golden puppy, refer to the following list. It includes resources for registration information, dog clubs, health care, veterinarians, trainers, dog sports and activities, microchip registries, pet sitters, and more.

CLUBS

American Kennel Club (AKC): akc.org

Canadian Kennel Club (CKC): ckc.ca

Golden Retriever Club of America (AKC Parent Club for the Golden Retriever): grca.org

National Disaster Search Dog Foundation (SDF): searchdogfoundation.org

North American Hunting Retriever Association (NAHRA): nahra.org

United Kennel Club (UKC): ukcdogs.com

FOOD AND SUPPLEMENTS

Association of American Feed Control Officials: aafco.org

Food and Drug Administration (FDA) Pet Food Recalls: fda.gov/Safety/Recalls/default.htm

National Animal Supplement Council: nasc.cc

MICROCHIP REGISTRIES

American Animal Hospital Association (AAHA) Universal Pet Microchip Lookup: petmicrochiplookup.org

American Kennel Club (AKC) Reunite: akcreunite.org

AVID (American Veterinary Identification Devices): avidid.com

HomeAgain: public.homeagain.com

PERFORMANCE SPORTS AND ACTIVITIES

Barn Hunt Association: barnhunt.com

Canine Freestyle Federation: canine-freestyle.org

DockDogs: dockdogs.com

Dogs on Course in North America (DOCNA): docna.com

National Association for Search and Rescue (NASAR): nasar.org

National Association of Canine Scent Work (NACSW): nacsw.net

North American Dog Agility Council (NADAC): nadac.com

North American Flyball Association (NAFA): flyball.org

United States Dog Agility Association (USDAA): usdaa.com

World Canine Freestyle Organization (WCFO): worldcaninefreestyle.org

PET FIRST AID AND POISON CONTROL

American Red Cross Pet First Aid app: redcross.org/mobile-apps/pet-first-aid-app

American Society for the Prevention of Cruelty to Animals (ASPCA) Animal Poison Control: aspca.org/pet-care/animal-poison-control; 888-426-4435 (North America; fees apply)

Animal Poison Hotline (provided by North Shore Animal League and PROSAR International Animal Poison Center): 888-232-8870

Pet Poison Helpline: petpoisonhelpline.com
855-764-7661

Pet Tech PetSaver first-aid app: pettech.net/app/index.php

PET INSURANCE

American Kennel Club (AKC) Pet Insurance: akcpetinsurance.com

American Society for the Prevention of Cruelty to Animals (ASPCA) Pet Health Insurance: aspcapetinsurance.com

Embrace Pet Insurance: embracepetinsurance.com

Pets Best Insurance: petsbest.com

Nationwide Pet Insurance: petinsurance.com

PET SITTERS

National Association of Professional Pet Sitters (NAPPS): petsitters.org

Pet Sitters Associates, LLC: petsitllc.com

Pet Sitters International (PSI): petsit.com

THERAPY DOG TRAINING AND CERTIFICATION

Alliance of Therapy Dogs: therapydogs.com

Love on a Leash: loveonaleash.org

Pet Partners (formerly Delta Society): petpartners.org

Therapy Dogs International (TDI): tdi-dog.org

TRAINING AND BEHAVIOR ASSOCIATIONS

American College of Veterinary Behaviorists (ACVB): dacvb.org

Association of Companion Animal Behavior Counselors (ACABC): animalbehaviorcounselors.org/acabc_members

Association of Professional Dog Trainers (APDT): apdt.com

Certified Applied Animal Behaviorists (CAAB): certifiedanimalbehaviorist.com

International Association of Animal Behavior Consultants (IAABC): iaabc.org

International Association of Canine Professionals (IACP): canineprofessionals.com

National Association of Dog Obedience Instructors (NADOI): nadoi.org

Tellington TTouch: ttouch.com

TRAVEL INFORMATION

DogFriendly.com's Worldwide Pet Travel Guides: dogfriendly.com

PetFriendlyTravel.com's Pet Friendly Travel and Vacations: petfriendlytravel.com

PetsWelcome.com's Pet-Friendly Hotel Search: petswelcome.com

PetTravel.com's Airline Pet Policies: pettravel.com/airline_rules.cfm

VETERINARY AND RELATED ORGANIZATIONS

Academy of Veterinary Homeopathy (AVH): theavh.org

American Academy of Veterinary Acupuncture (AAVA): aava.org

American Animal Hospital Association (AAHA): healthypet.com

American College of Veterinary Ophthalmologists (ACVO): acvo.org

American Holistic Veterinary Medical Association (AHVMA): ahvma.org

American Kennel Club (AKC) Canine Health Foundation: akcchf.org

American Veterinary Chiropractic Association (AVCA): avcadoctors.com

American Veterinary Medical Association (AVMA): avma.org

Golden Retriever Foundation: goldenretrieverfoundation.org

Morris Animal Foundation: morrisanimalfoundation.org

National Animal Supplement Council (NASC): nasc.cc

Orthopedic Foundation for Animals (OFA): offa.org

PennHIP: info.antechimagingservices.com/pennhip

Veterinary Botanical Medicine Association (VBMA): vbma.org

INDEX

T-U